THE POWER AND INDEPENDENCE
OF THE FEDERAL RESERVE

THE POWER AND INDEPENDENCE OF THE FEDERAL RESERVE

PETER CONTI-BROWN

PRINCETON UNIVERSITY PRESS
PRINCETON AND OXFORD

Library of Congress Cataloging-in-Publication Data

Conti-Brown, Peter, 1981–
The power and independence of the
Federal Reserve / Peter Conti-Brown.
pages cm
Includes bibliographical references and index.
ISBN 978-0-691-16400-7 (hardback)
1. United States. Federal Reserve Board.   2. Federal Reserve
banks.   3. Banks and banking, Central—United
States.   4. Monetary policy—United States.   5. United States—
Economic policy.   I. Title.
HG2563.C596 2016
332.1′10973—dc23   2015019984

British Library Cataloging-in-Publication Data is available

This book has been composed in Sabon LT STD & Avenir.

Printed on acid-free paper. ∞

Printed in the United States of America

3 5 7 9 10 8 6 4 2

———

TO MY

CONTI-BROWNS,

AND TO

JULIAN ZELIZER

———

CONTENTS

PREFACE

Two hosts of eager disputants on this subject ask of every new
writer the one question—Are you with us or against us? And
they care for little else.

—*Walter Bagehot, 1873*

There is an old story, perhaps apocryphal, in which the Fed Chair
greets a newly appointed member of the Board of Governors of the
U.S. Federal Reserve System with an apologetic explanation of the
new governor's status. The chair predicted that when the man introduced himself back home to his friends and family as a "governor of the Federal Reserve," they were likely to think he was the
administrator of the U.S. government's unexplored western
forests.[1]

There was a time when that story was amusing. The Fed used to
be an obscure, backwater government agency. The general public
didn't really know what the Fed was about and probably didn't
much care. Even for those who paid attention to the economy, until
roughly the early 1960s the prevailing view was that the president
and his administration were the first and last stop for economic
policy. Central banking was in the hinterland; fiscal policy—the
stuff of taxes and budgets and spending and deficits—was at the
core. Bankers cared about the Fed's obscure activities. The rest of
the country wasn't paying attention.

That story used to work. It doesn't any more. Today, it's not just bankers who are paying attention. Over the last thirty years, and especially since the global financial crisis of 2008, the Fed has become the target of an extraordinary proliferation of scrutiny, praise, and condemnation. Today, it is not an exaggeration to say that in the popular imagination and in fact, the Federal Reserve sits atop the global financial system and, indeed, the global economy, in a way that no institution has ever done before. "We are going through a period with no precedent in American history," Alan Greenspan said in 2014 of the Fed's brave new world. And he's not the only one who has noticed.[2]

But where public knowledge of the Fed's existence has dramatically improved—people know the Federal Reserve deals with money, not forests—public knowledge of the Fed's structure and functions has not. The problem is not simply one of public ignorance, though there is plenty of that. The problem is that the Fed is one of the most organizationally complex entities in the federal government, with some of the most varied missions to accomplish tucked inside. The core questions about the Fed—how it is structured, who pulls its many levers of power, and to what end—are cloaked in opacity. Even the experts who study the Fed are left confused by the set of institutions that has survived the Fed's sweep through a century of history.

This book is an effort to cut through that morass of law and history. The focus, as the title indicates, is especially on how the Fed gained and uses its extraordinary power over the global economy and what is meant by the often invoked but rarely explained term "independence." "Power" here refers to the incontestable fact of the Fed's ability to influence every individual, institution, or government that interacts with the global financial system. If you have a mortgage, a car payment, or a credit card, the Fed had power over its terms. Every foreign government in financial crisis has felt its influence. Private banks are deeply connected to the Federal Reserve System. And as we all saw in the 2008 financial crisis, policy failures and triumphs within the Federal Reserve stirred financial havoc but likely spared us from financial cataclysm.

As we shall see, central bankers love metaphors, so let me begin this book with one of my own. My six-year-old son spends a lot of time writing and illustrating comic books whose quality long ago left me in their artistic dust. But when the heroes and villains fight, as they invariably do, the details defy even his artistic ability. He hasn't quite mastered the depiction of motion in two dimensions, and his protagonists inevitably disappear behind a mass of scribbles. Occasionally a head or a limb will sneak out from behind the bustle of color, but the fight itself is never for the viewer to glimpse in detail. We see only what goes in, who comes out, and that something dizzying happens in between.

Many discussions of the power and structure of the Federal Reserve occur behind a mass of scribbles. There is enough that we can see sticking out of the commotion to create common assumptions to support a debate—a reference to central bankers' long tenure shows up here, the Fed's budgetary autonomy sneaks out there, public opprobrium for politicians who attempt to dictate monetary policy makes an appearance, as does fear that central banks are wresting control of fiscal policy. But so much about these fundamental concepts of public governance occur behind an inscrutable mass.

This book steps behind the scribbles to depict the Federal Reserve, its internal structure, its external pressures, and the technical and nontechnical ways it makes its many policies, with more clarity than these questions usually receive. One of the barriers to this clarifying effort is, ironically, the very enthusiasm this subject creates in those likely to read a book titled *The Power and Independence of the Federal Reserve*. This is especially true in the years since the financial crisis of 2008. There is a strong temptation to become, as the epigraph suggests, "eager disputants" who demand an answer on where the author of such a book stands with respect to the Fed's virtues and vices, its independence and accountability, indeed its very existence. For such readers, these are yes-or-no questions. Anything more seems an equivocation.

This book is an effort to push back against the certainty of those absolutist narratives. To understand the unique place the Fed occupies at the intersection of financial markets and the U.S. government requires a dive into the very meaning of this curious intellectual and institutional construction, Federal Reserve independence. But trying to make sense of the Federal Reserve and its extraordinary power with yes-or-no questions about "independence"—is the Fed independent? Should it be independent?—is an impossible task: "independence," I argue, is a concept without much analytical content. This book argues instead that we must go deeper before we can draw the Fed out from behind this veil of mystery where it has so long remained. To put the point differently, before we can judge the Fed, we must first understand it.

Of course, this is not the first book to explain the Fed generally or even Fed independence specifically. The central bank has long been a subject of fascination for economists, journalists, historians, and others. This book relies on these extensive previous efforts. But it is also different. Using insights from law, history, politics, and economics, this book aims to give a deeper and more complete view of what the Fed is and how it became this way. The book's main comparative advantage is its grounding in law and history. Legal scholars, with important exceptions, have not paid much attention to the Federal Reserve; historians, too, have essentially ignored all but its creation in 1913. While this book is more a work of legal scholarship than history, I hope to persuade all readers—whether lawyers, historians, economists, political scientists, or members of the general public—of the value of looking at this old structure with new eyes. The ambition is to perform a scholarly exchange: by bringing insights and observations from multiple approaches, we can better understand what the Fed does, why, and whether we have the central bank that we want to have.[3]

These are, of course, controversial topics, and the final chapter includes reform proposals that might invite controversy (and hopefully productive discussion). The primary effort, though, is not to reform the Fed, but to explain it, and in the process to provide hard thinking about the Fed's governance, history, and authority in a way that, for example, would be useful to both former Fed chair Ben Bernanke and perennial Fed critic Ron Paul. Part of my optimism in the book's ability to guide between these poles is that I step back from the notion that Fed independence is either a fragile public good that needs protection or a nefarious dodge of public accountability. In this book, Fed independence isn't an object to be attacked or defended, but a set of relationships to explain. If I succeed, readers will not be able to take for granted invocations of "Fed independence," in attack or defense, as the final word on any question.

A few words about the book's methodological approach and its scope: While I draw extensively on published memoirs, annual reports, legislative history, and the historical record on the Fed generally, the book does not, after the first two chapters, tell a chronological story. Instead, I use scores of examples from Fed history in service of an analytical argument about the Fed's governance, its external relationships, and the ways it makes national and international policy. To keep this kind of analytical approach engaging to specialists and generalists alike, I leave the text as free of jargon and intramural academic debates as possible. For those interested in these details, I add them in the notes. To enhance readability, I leave those notes at the end of the book and restrict them to one note per paragraph.[4]

The book is also far from exhaustive. It raises countless avenues left to explore in understanding the Fed's place in government and the ways that insiders and outsiders alike influence its policies. The two main omissions are comparative: the framework developed here—a framework skeptical of "independence" as a valuable analytical tool for understanding policy making—touches only briefly on the details of central bank governance in other parts of the world, even less on similar questions for other kinds of governmental agencies in the United States or elsewhere. My hope is that the ideas here will generate useful insights for scholars who take on these other questions directly.

Finally, a word about the book's epigraphs, all taken from the great Walter Bagehot. Bagehot—pronounced BADGE-it in American English, BADGE-ot in Britain, a shibboleth of sorts in central banking circles—is widely viewed as the intellectual godfather of modern central banking. Whether his world has much to say to ours is an open question, but there are few wordsmiths in financial history quite as able as he. He is the author of magnificent sentences, very interesting paragraphs, and sometimes frustratingly indeterminate books. But because of the power of those sentences, I borrow liberally from his iconic 1873 book, *Lombard Street: A Description of the Money Market*, for the epigraphs that introduce each chapter (except for chapter 4, which comes from his other famous book, *The English Constitution*). Bagehot obviously had nothing to say about the Federal Reserve System, which was founded decades after his death. And he barely had more to say about the U.S. financial system (he wasn't very impressed with nineteenth-century U.S. finance). But his turns of phrases are too applicable and felicitous to pass by, even if the reader must change some of the proper nouns to make them relevant.

THE POWER AND INDEPENDENCE
OF THE FEDERAL RESERVE

INTRODUCTION

ULYSSES AND THE CHAPERONE

We must examine the system on which these great masses of
money are manipulated, and assure ourselves that it is safe and
right.

—Walter Bagehot, 1873

In the United States or any other country, one would be hard-
pressed to identify a governmental institution whose power is more
out of sync with the public's level of understanding of it than the
U.S. Federal Reserve System. Even as the Fed influences the economic decisions of individuals and institutions the world over, it
operates shrouded in mystery, cultivating a "peculiar mystique"
that even experts mischaracterize and miscomprehend. A central
part of that mystique is its curious location within government itself. Citizens do not interact with the Fed in the same way they do
with other political institutions, so it can be difficult to put the Fed,
its policies, and its power into our usual frames of discussion.

We are given a reason for this difference. The Fed is "above
politics," as President Obama has said, protected by statute from
the rough-and-tumble of our political process. It is, in a word,
"independent."[1]

That word: *independent*. It is everywhere in discussions of the
Federal Reserve. But what does it actually mean? Independent

how? To what end? From whom? And while we are asking questions, who or what do we even mean when we say "the Fed"?

Scholars and central bankers have answers to these questions. In economics and to a lesser extent political science, the concept of central bank independence has been so extensively studied as to earn its own acronym: CBI. In 2004, Alan Blinder, an academic and former central banker, called the study of central bank independence a "growth industry," and the growth has only accelerated in the years since. Although there are about as many precise definitions of central bank independence as there are authors who describe it, in reference to the Federal Reserve, we can gather from these studies a rough consensus of what central bank independence means. That consensus goes something like this. Fed independence is the separation, by statute, of the central bankers (specifically the Fed chair) and the politicians (specifically the president) for purposes of maintaining low inflation. The idea is that citizens in a democracy naturally prefer a prosperous economy. Politicians please us by giving us that prosperity, or at least trying to take credit for it. But when there is no prosperity to be had, politicians will resort to goosing the economy artificially by running the printing presses to provide enough money and credit for all. The short-term result is reelection for the politicians. The long-term result is worthless money that wreaks havoc on our economic, social, and political institutions.[2]

The widely invoked metaphors of central banking come tumbling forth from here. In the Homeric epic the *Odyssey*, when Odysseus—referred to in central banking circles by his Latin name Ulysses, for reasons that are unclear—ventured with his men close to the seductive and vexing sirens, he devised a scheme to allow his men to guide their ship past their seduction in safety, while he experienced the short-term joys of hearing their songs. Central bank independence is our Ulysses contract. We write central banking laws that lash us (and our politicians) to the mast and stuff beeswax in the ears of our central bankers. We enjoy the ride while the technocratic central bankers guide the ship of the economy to the land of prosperity and low inflation. (We are, by the way, the sirens

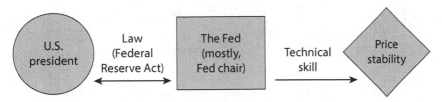

Figure 0.1. The Ulysses/punch-bowl account of Fed independence.

in this metaphor, too.) The other commonly invoked metaphor is even more colorful. In the oft-repeated words of William McChesney Martin, the longest serving Fed chair in history, the Federal Reserve is "in the position of the chaperone who has ordered the punch bowl removed just when the party was really warming up." The subjects of the metaphors differ by millennia, but the idea is the same: the partygoers and Ulysses alike want something in the near term that their best selves know is bad for them in the long term. Central bank independence is the solution.[3]

This view—which I will reference throughout the book as the Ulysses/punch-bowl view of Fed independence—suggests more or less five features. First, law does the work of separation—the lashes and beeswax are written into the Fed's charter, the Federal Reserve Act of 1913. Second, under this view, the Fed is a singular entity, even a single person: the Fed chair. In most discussions of Fed independence, little attention is paid to the internal governance of the rest of the Federal Reserve System. Third, the outside audience is a political one, usually the president, the only politician facing a national electorate. We seldom analyze which other actors attempt to shape Fed policy. Fourth, the reason for an independent central bank is to keep politicians away from the temptation to use the printing press to win reelection on the cheap. Fifth and finally, the reason the Fed can accomplish this task is that its work is technocratic: it requires special training but not the exercise of value judgments under uncertainty. Figure 0.1 presents the idea graphically.[4]

The Ulysses/punch-bowl model of Fed independence has taught us a lot about central banks and their institutional design. It has also motivated an extraordinary rise of a specific kind of central bank throughout the world. There is much insight to be gained by studying central banks and their legal relationships to politicians for purposes of combating inflation along the lines of this model.

The problem is that the standard account of Fed independence—the story of Ulysses and the sirens, of the dance hall and the spiked punch bowl—often doesn't work. Sometimes politicians whip up popular sentiment *in favor* of taking away the punch bowl—precisely the opposite of what we expect in a democracy. Sometimes the central bankers make headlines not for being boring chaperones but for bailing out the financial system. And in every case the creaky, hundred-year-old Federal Reserve Act leaves a governance structure that makes it so we barely know who the chaperone is even supposed to be.

This book takes a different approach. Instead, I argue that each of the five elements of that standard account—that it is law that creates Fed independence; that the Fed is a monolithic "it," or more often an all-powerful "he" or "she"; that only politicians attempt to influence Fed policy; that the Fed's only relevant mission is price stability; and that the Fed makes purely technocratic decisions, devoid of value judgments—is wrong.

To understand why, we must refocus our gaze not on one narrow feature of institutional design, but on the Federal Reserve as it actually is. We must understand the space within which the Fed operates. This space reflects a different orientation depending on the issue before it (inflation or not), the internal actor making the decision (Fed chair or not), the external actor interested in the outcome (the president or not), the tools Fed officials use to accomplish their goals (legal or not), and the values that inform their policy-making decisions (technocratic or not). This structural, geographic account allows the exercise of Fed power to tell its own story, even if and especially when that story has little to do with the Ulysses/punch-bowl narrative. Figure 0.2 illustrates the argument.[5]

More specifically, the geographic view of the Federal Reserve breaks down into five arguments.

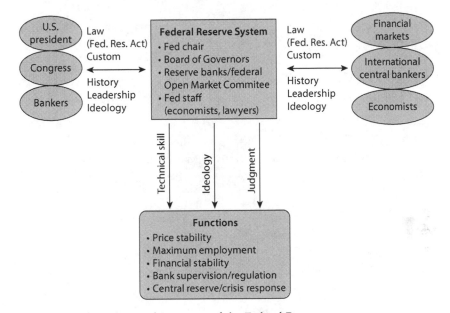

Figure 0.2. The policy-making space of the Federal Reserve.

First. The Fed is a "they," not an "it." While we fixate on the Fed chair—Alan Greenspan or Ben Bernanke or Janet Yellen—in fact the Fed is organized as a series of interlocking committees that all participate in various ways to make Fed policy. Putting these many and varied internal actors in their context is crucial to understanding how the Fed's policy-making process occurs.[6]

Second. We cannot understand the Federal Reserve System's structure without a close, historically sensitive reading of the Federal Reserve Act of 1913, as it has been amended over the last hundred years. Too few people who study the central bank take on this task. At the same time, the statute is also not enough. Law in practice differs in sometimes surprising, contradictory ways from law on the books. The argument is not that law is irrelevant; it is that the law is incomplete. As Rosa Lastra—a pioneer in the legal study of central banks—has written, "[c]entral banks inhabit a 'world of policy'. This does not mean there is no law. It means that the law has generally played a limited role in central banking operations."[7]

Third. Nearsighted presidents anxious to inflate away their electoral problems aren't the only outsiders interested in influencing the Fed's policies, even among politicians. Members of Congress, bankers, economists, international central bankers, and others all influence the shape of the space within which the system operates. How and to what effect they succeed are essential questions for understanding the Federal Reserve.

Fourth. The Fed's policy makers have, over the last hundred years, become much more than defenders against inflation. They are also, by statute and practice, recession fighters, bankers, financial regulators, bank supervisors, and protectors of financial stability. A theory of independence that accounts for but one function (price stability) among so many others is not a very good theory.

Fifth. These many missions are not the bailiwick of technocrats and mathematicians alone. The Fed's policy makers are people. They have values and ideologies, like the rest of us. And the policies they formulate and implement require the exercise of value judgments under uncertainty.

In this reconceptualization, "independence" fails to capture where the Fed fits within government, how it exercises its authority, and to what end. The Fed doesn't glow green with independence or red with political domination. Political scientist John Goodman got close to this proposition when he wrote that "[i]ndependence is a continuous, not dichotomous, variable. In other words, there are degrees of central bank independence."[8]

This book goes further still: independence is not really a quantifiable variable at all, but more of a sleight of hand that reveals only a narrow slice of Fed policy making at the expense of a broader, more explanatory context where Fed insiders and interested outsiders form relationships using law and other tools to implement a wide variety of specific policies. To understand more, we need to specify the insider, the outsider, the mechanism of influence, and the policy goal.

Looking at the power, governance, and purpose of the Federal Reserve in these terms, a new theme emerges. Rather than the site of a constant battle between populists and technocrats, the Fed's policy-making space becomes a balance between democratic accountability, technocratic expertise, and the influence of central bankers' own value judgments. Independence as an all-or-nothing proposition rings false. Instead, we see central bankers that are deeply embedded in their legal, historical, social, ideological, and political contexts. Pure separation from the political process was never a possibility, whatever the law said or says. And in the century since the Fed's founding, it has become only more embedded in a set of traditions all its own.

Once we have this view of Fed policy making, a view better informed by law, history, and practice, we will have an easier time finding a common frame for debating any question about the Fed's past and present, even when we disagree about what we would hope for the Fed's future. As Bagehot said of his own central bank, it is our duty to "examine the system on which these great masses of money are manipulated, and assure ourselves that it is safe and right." Settling on a more coherent and authentic frame for analyzing that system is the first step.[9]

PLAN OF THE BOOK

To reach the goal of providing that understanding, the book is structured around the following questions. What do we mean by the Fed, and how did it take the shape it has taken? What does the Fed do? Who influences the Fed's policies? And is the Fed we have the Fed we want?

In part I, we look at the first two questions: what is the Fed, and where did it come from? When people describe the Fed, they usually do so in one of two ways: as a single monolith ("the Fed announces a change in interest rates," or "the Federal Reserve bails out AIG") or as the institutional shadow of a single individual ("Yellen announces a change in interest rates" or "Bernanke bails out AIG.") The common assumption is that the Fed chair equals the Federal Reserve, and the Federal Reserve is an indivisible whole.

This assumption is false. The Fed is not a single individual, and the view that the Fed's power is concentrated into the hands of one is not correct. In fact, the Fed is one of the most organizationally complex entities in the federal government and has been from the very beginning. Part I tells the story of how the Fed took the curious shape that it took not only at the beginning in 1913 but through what chapter 1 calls the Fed's "three foundings": in 1913, 1935, and 1951.

My argument that the Fed is a "they," not an "it," can be exaggerated. Not all actors within the Fed are equal. The influence of Fed chairs, especially in the second half of its history, has been important, often decisive. Part of the Fed's institutional change occurs through the exercise of individual leadership by Fed chairs, even though the Federal Reserve Act gives them no particular legal claim for that authority.

But even when the Fed chair dominates, the Fed remains a complicated, multidimensional institution. Part I looks beyond the chair to these other features of Fed's governance. It analyzes the role of the Fed's two powerful committees: the seven-person Board of Governors, consisting of presidential appointments (confirmed by the Senate), and the Federal Open Market Committee, consisting of the Board of Governors plus the presidents of the twelve regional Federal Reserve Banks (only five of whom vote at a given time), who are appointed through a convoluted process almost completely outside the public eye. The president of the Federal Reserve Bank of New York is a permanent member of the committee; the other eleven Reserve Banks rotate as voting members in the other four seats. All twelve of the Reserve Bank presidents are in the room for FOMC meetings, though, and can make their views heard without restriction. By statute, the FOMC determines the Fed's monetary policies; the Board of Governors determines the rest. (As we will see, this oversimplification is part of the Fed's governance problem.) Figure 0.3 presents a graphical display of these committees.

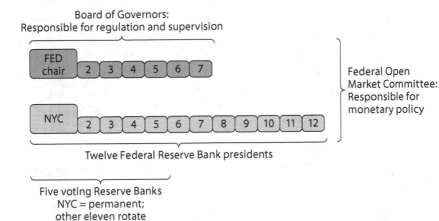

Figure 0.3. The structure of the U.S. Federal Reserve System.

Part I also confronts the expansive influence that two other actors have on the Fed's policy-making space: the Fed staff (especially economists and lawyers) and the twelve regional Federal Reserve Banks. The banks are perhaps the most controversial and least defensible aspect of the Fed's governance structure. They present a seat at the table for private bankers' representatives to make essential economic policy decisions. There are policy, constitutional, and governance problems with the Reserve Banks and not enough of value to justify the current structure given those serious costs.

Part II then turns to the question of the Fed's many missions. The logic of the Ulysses/punch-bowl view of the Federal Reserve depends on the idea that politicians will mismanage a nation's currency with an undesirable inflationary bias. The story of the development of that understanding is fascinating and important in its own right. But that account suffers from two weaknesses: the politics of money and inflation are not so straightforward, and the Fed is not now and never has been exclusively concerned with managing price stability. Part II explores the Fed's varied missions by asking and answering the surprisingly difficult question: What does the Federal Reserve do? The answer: many things beyond controlling inflation. The Ulysses/punch-bowl theory of Fed independence doesn't hold up for most of them.

In part III, we look at the outsiders who influence Fed policies. The Ulysses/punch-bowl view of Fed independence focuses on the president, and there we will begin. Part III then moves on to Congress, an essential audience for influencing Fed policy. It discusses the influence that individual members of Congress can have in defining the institution. Most of the focus, though, is on an especially curious quirk of the Fed's policy-making space: Congress does not use its traditional spending power to control the Fed. Instead, the Fed has that power on its own. It essentially creates the money with which it funds itself. What's more, this power is not directly authorized by statute. Part III explores the history and legal structure of the Fed's budgetary autonomy. Part III also continues to develop one of the primary themes of the book: law as written in the Federal Reserve Act matters, but not in the way that scholars, politicians, central bankers, and even lawyers have assumed.

The book concludes with part IV, a single chapter that discusses how the comprehensive approach to Fed power advanced here translates into a concrete program for Fed reform. That program focuses on preserving the best of the Ulysses/punch-bowl account of Fed independence: we really do want a central bank that will protect the currency from the winds of electoral politics, without losing the benefits democratic legitimacy and without indulging the myth that all central bank policy is purely technocratic. We can and should be comfortable with the reality that central bankers, like everyone else, are people whose life experiences—including their technical training—give them an ideological frame of reference through which they evaluate the world. The key to reforming the Fed is to know as much about the values of those central bankers as possible.

The watchword in this pragmatic approach is *governance*. Governance refers to the institutional decisions about who inside the Fed gets to establish which policies. As it stands today, the Fed's governance is, simply put, a mess. It can and should be clarified without sacrificing the essential tasks of regulating inflation and employment, free from the overwhelming influence of electoral politics. Consistent with these goals, chapter 11 highlights a few positive recent developments in reforming the Fed (including the creation of a separate Consumer Financial Protection Bureau) and recommend a few new changes to the Fed's structure and governance (including the reform of the twelve Federal Reserve Banks).

Two of the themes in this book permeate each chapter. First, any conversation about the Fed's power must recognize law's inability to remain what its authors intended it to be. That is not to say that we should abandon the enterprise of statutory central bank design. It means, instead, that we should tailor those efforts to minimize new legal rules that might well subject future generations to too many dead hands of the past. And second, an inescapable reality of central banking is that central bankers are people who bring with them ideologies and values that shape how they exercise their authority over the economy. Those values are also not fixed: interaction with others inside and outside the Federal Reserve System shape how central bankers think about the problems they confront. For both reasons, focus on understanding and simplifying Federal Reserve governance is an essential task to studying and reforming the Federal Reserve.

The U.S. Federal Reserve System has had an extraordinary century. In the words of one scholar, "the Fed's evolution into an economic power of first-rate importance is the most remarkable bureaucratic metamorphosis in American history." This book's challenges to the prevailing view of Federal Reserve power and independence is meant to invite greater understanding into that remarkable metamorphosis while grappling with the Fed's full, practical, historical context. The Fed's mystique is a function of both a lack of public knowledge of its inner workings, and a tangled governance structure that misleads even the experts. This book seeks both to increase public understanding of the Fed's many moving parts and to reconceive them in a way that allows for a better, more fruitful understanding of this essential institution.[10]

PART I

THE FEDERAL RESERVE IS A "THEY," NOT AN "IT"

Public and scholarly attention on the Fed usually focuses on a monolithic "it," or on the personal she or he. In fact, the standard grammatical practice—followed in this book, and, indeed, in the last sentence—is to refer to "the Federal Reserve" (or just "the Fed") as a proper noun. This is an institutional and grammatical error. The term "Federal Reserve" is not a noun, but a compound adjective. There are Federal Reserve Banks, Federal Reserve Notes, a Federal Reserve Board, and, taken together, a Federal Reserve System, all created by the Federal Reserve Act. But there is no "Federal Reserve" by itself. This vocabulary failure reveals a harder problem for thinking about the Federal Reserve System. Even though we rarely refer to it as such, to paraphrase Kenneth Shepsle, the Fed is a "they," not an "it."[1]

This is not a pedantic grammatical point. Understanding the Fed's complex internal governance structure—all those institutions and actors within the Federal Reserve System—is essential to understanding the Fed's power, the space within which it makes policy. It also represents a problem of governance. When the public is faced with a monolith, all debates about Fed actions—no matter where they occur within the system, no matter what those actions may be—easily spiral into confusion.

Part I is an effort to focus attention on the Fed's governance by tracing the history of the Fed's institutional development through what this book calls the Fed's three foundings (in 1913, 1935, and 1951). With that history in place, chapters 2 through 5 then consider the influence that, respectively, the Fed chairs, members of the Board of Governors, Fed staff, and the quasi-private Reserve Banks have on the way the Fed wields its authority within and beyond the government.

CHAPTER 1
THE THREE FOUNDINGS OF THE FEDERAL RESERVE

> In the last century, a favourite subject of literary ingenuity was
> 'conjectural history,' as it was then called. Upon grounds of
> probability a fictitious sketch was made of the possible origin
> of things existing. . . . The real history is very different.
>
> —*Walter Bagehot, 1873*

In the usual retelling of the Fed's history, the Fed came as Congress's answer to the problem of the mortality of J. Pierpont Morgan. The financial panic of 1907 was a dark one, but luckily for the U.S. financial system, Morgan, the legendary international banker, saved the day and stemmed the panic, and the system lived to fight another day. Congress recognized that it couldn't count on Morgan forever, so it got its central banking act together after two failed attempts and passed the Federal Reserve Act of 1913. The United States has had a central bank ever since.

As Bagehot says, "[t]he real history is very different." The problem with that story is that while the bare facts are true, the arc of the narrative is not. There was a financial panic in 1907, Morgan was involved, and the Federal Reserve Act of 1913 created something called "the Federal Reserve System." What the story misses is the epic fight to determine what kind of central banking system we would have in 1913, how the chosen system failed and had to be refounded, and how the modern sense of a central bank didn't come into being until nearly forty years into the Fed's history. This chapter tells the fuller narrative and looks at the three foundings of the Federal Reserve: in 1913, in 1935, and in an informal agreement in 1951 called the Fed-Treasury Accord.

At each founding, there were two ideas about who should wield power within the Federal Reserve System. First, as Paul Warburg, one of the architects of the 1913 Fed put it, the prevailing views at the time were "either complete governmental control, which meant politics in banking, or control by 'Wall Street,' which meant banking in politics." In other words, the question was private versus public control. And second, the successive generations of Fed founders worried about centralization and decentralization. The uneven resolution of these two debates guided the institutional development of the Fed toward the unique place in the government that it occupies today.[1]

It is unsurprising that these two questions would figure so prominently in the Fed's history. They have been with us since the beginning of the republic. Related questions pit Thomas Jefferson and Andrew Jackson against Alexander Hamilton and Nicholas Biddle in the early nineteenth century. In fact, it is not a stretch to say that partisan politics in the United States were birthed by a government-bank midwife. As the nineteenth-century financial historian Albert Bolles put it, "[w]hen the smoke of the contest [over government banks] had cleared away, two political parties might be seen, whose opposition, though varying much in conviction, power, and earnestness, has never ceased."[2]

How did these disputes—centralization versus decentralization, public versus private—manifest themselves in the internal governance structures of the Fed, as imagined by its congressional sponsors? This historical backdrop is worth exploring at length. It is at the core of the effort to map the geography of Fed power and independence.

THE FIRST FOUNDING: THE FEDERAL RESERVE ACT OF 1913

The conventional retelling of the Fed's founding starts in the right place: the financial panic of 1907, one of the most destructive in the nation's history. In that retelling, the panic was an accelerating financial bloodletting that the U.S. government could do nothing to staunch. It was only the intervention of that towering figure of Anglo-American finance in the late nineteenth and early twentieth centuries, J. Pierpont Morgan, that subdued the panic. Morgan, it was reported by his associates at the time, was "the man of the hour," whose pronouncements—bland and obvious in retrospect, such as "[i]f people will keep their money in the banks everything will be all right"—assumed talismanic significance. A sleepless night of Morgan's banking associates, locked by Morgan in his smoky library, led to the salvation of the U.S. financial system.[3]

As the story goes, after the financial panic, private bankers and government officials decided that an all-eyes-turn-to-Morgan approach to financial panics could not continue to be the basis of U.S. banking policy. After a secret meeting of bankers and their political sponsors in the U.S. Congress at the Jekyll Island Club, located on an island of the same name off the coast of Georgia, the Federal Reserve scheme was hatched. (Given that this secret Jekyll Island meeting came complete with disguises and codenames and Omertà-like oaths of secrecy, and only became public twenty years after the fact, it has been great grist for the conspiracists' mills in the years since.) President Woodrow Wilson signed the bill into law as the Federal Reserve Act of 1913.[4]

This is, again, the conventional retelling. And again, many elements are true: there really was an extraordinary global financial panic of 1907, J. P. Morgan did have a role (although that role has been grossly exaggerated) in arresting the spread of contagion, a secret meeting of bankers and politicians did take place in Jekyll Island, and the Federal Reserve Act of 1913 did eventually follow.[5]

But from the perspective of the *structure* the Federal Reserve System would take—including, especially, its governance—the story tells us almost nothing. The primary problem with this retelling is that it links, almost ineluctably, the panic of 1907 and the Federal Reserve Act of 1913 with a pit stop in this mysterious island meeting of a cabal of New York bankers. If we are to understand the Fed and where its unique governance came from, these uncritical links are a mistake. The six years in between the Panic of 1907 and the Federal Reserve Act of 1913 were decisive for the fate of the Federal Reserve System, including as they did two presidential and three congressional elections. When the electoral dust settled, power had shifted from Republicans—at the time, the bankers' primary supporters in Congress—to Democrats (the House changed in 1910, the Senate in 1912).

At the center of this political moment was the presidential election of 1912. Few presidential elections in U.S. history match it for its drama. Gone were the staid front-porch campaigns between two senior partisans. Instead, the election pitted two U.S. presidents, Theodore Roosevelt and William Howard Taft, against Woodrow Wilson, a college president who had entered politics just two years before. On the edge but not the fringe was the most popular socialist in American history, Eugene Debs, who captured 5 percent of the vote. Historians have debated how much policy daylight stood between the three main candidates—although there was little doubt that Debs represented something very different from the others— the perception at the time and continuing today was that the aspirations of each candidate represented distinct approaches to the role of government in society. In the words of one historian, the 1912 election "verged on political philosophy."[6]

That political philosophical moment in American history intervened between the 1907 panic and the Federal Reserve Act in ways that were essential in shaping the system's curious governance structure. Conspiracy theorists get close to their target in noting the existence and significance of the Jekyll Island meeting—the leading popular account of the conspiracists is called *The Creature from Jekyll Island*, an exposé that "set[s] off into the dark forest to do battle with the evil dragon." But they don't quite hit it. The reality is that the "creature" established in that meeting and sponsored by the Republicans in 1910 bore little relation, from a governance perspective, to the Federal Reserve System ultimately embraced by Woodrow Wilson as his greatest domestic accomplishment and signed into law on December 23, 1913.[7]

The difference was partisan politics. The first proposals following the Panic of 1907 were entirely Republican. Senator Nelson Aldrich was the Republican leading the monetary reform efforts. In 1908, Congress passed the Aldrich-Vreeland Act, which created the National Monetary Commission with Aldrich at the head. The commission imagined a structure very different from the system the Federal Reserve Act eventually created. That structure, the National Reserve Association (NRA), was to be a mix of public and private appointments, but dramatically weighted toward the private. For example, the board of the NRA was to have forty-six directors, forty-two of whom—including its three executive officers—were to be appointed directly and indirectly by the banks. The government did not figure into the scene at all.[8]

As the Republicans failed in successive elections, the NRA approach to Fed governance failed to carry the day. The emphasis here is on the Fed's governance. Much of the Republican bill survived in the final act as far as the new system's functions were concerned. But its governance was another matter.[9]

THE MONEY TRUST

At the same time that this shift from Republicans to Democrats was taking place, the country was rocked by hearings on the so-called money trust, led by Louisiana Democrat Arsène Pujo (himself a former member of Aldrich's National Monetary Commission). In these hearings, led by famed lawyer Samuel Untermyer, J. P. Morgan himself appeared to answer the charge that the nation's money and credit were subject to the same kind of monopolistic control as its sugar, steel, oil, or railroads had been. The charge was that these New York bankers were using "other people's money" to enrich themselves at the expense of the rest of society.[10]

Morgan was compelled to appear. In one of the most famous exchanges of the hearings, Untermyer asked Morgan to explain the basis on which someone can get a loan, on what security or collateral, on the theory that only the wealthy would qualify for loans through Morgan's banks. Morgan refused to concede the point. The provision of credit had "no relation . . . whatever" to do with the net worth of the man requesting it. An incredulous Untermyer pressed Morgan, "is not commercial credit based primarily upon money or property?" Came the improbable answer: "No, sir: the first thing is character. . . . A man I do not trust could not get money from me on all the bonds in Christendom."[11]

As quotable as Morgan was, he was humiliated by the hearings and angry that his character had been tarnished. He would die just weeks after the hearings, the victim (according to his family) of Untermyer's cross-examination. In a short time, he had gone from J. P. Morgan the savior of the financial system to J. P. Morgan, the money monopolist. The final governance structure of the Federal Reserve System owed itself to that transition.[12]

THE WILSONIAN COMPROMISE

As a result of the elections and the money trust hearings, the Democrats were ready to make the cause of currency reform (as the issue was known) their own. Recall the two poles that formed the basis for the governance controversy: centralization and public versus private control. On one end sat Paul Warburg, the German émigré banker whose ideas in the early 1900s set the stage for much of the debate preceding the enactment of the Federal Reserve Act. Warburg feared public influence over the new central bank, an institution that he, a private banker in the old-school European banking tradition, viewed as necessarily a private one. Carter Glass, the initial Democratic proponent of the bill, wasn't as interested in the governmental aspect of the decision: he was much more worried about the centralized versus decentralized aspect of the governance problem than the private versus public one. As much as the Republican bankers distrusted politicians in control of banks, Glass and the Democrats feared the bankers' control of politicians. The best solution from the Glass perspective wasn't to give the keys of the financial kingdom to the politicians; it was to take the keys away from the New York City bankers. Thus, Glass's answer to the governance problem was a private, decentralized sea of central banks spread throughout the country.

Wilson took a different view. This student of governmental structures saw the opportunity for constitution making in the tradition of one of his heroes, James Madison. Wilson wanted public control but recognized the need to compromise among the various factions. His proposal: a Washington-based, government-controlled supervisory board that he preferred on top of the essentially private, decentralized central banks flung by Carter Glass throughout the country. When the bankers and Glass both protested, Wilson imperiously asked, "Will one of you gentlemen tell me in what civilized country of the earth there are important government boards of control on which private interests are represented?" Hearing no objection, he followed up: "Which of you gentlemen thinks the railroads should select members of the Interstate Commerce Commission?" While the bankers continued to protest, Carter Glass was "converted to Wilson's position before they had even exited the office."[13]

Wilson carried the day in what might be called the Wilsonian Compromise of 1913. Before Wilson, this hybrid institution did not exist in paper or in thought. The result was the mostly supervisory, leanly staffed Federal Reserve Board, based in Washington. The board would include the secretary of the treasury as the ex officio chair of the system, with the comptroller of the currency—until then, the exclusive federal banking regulator—also serving on the board. In addition to these two automatic appointments, the board consisted of five presidential appointees, serving ten-year terms each. The rest of the system consisted of "eight to twelve" Reserve Banks—the initial legislation didn't set the definitive number. These Reserve Banks would each have a "Governor" and a nine-person board of directors. The Reserve Banks would be the private features of the system.[14]

The system would not, in theory at least, be dominated by either public board or private bank. The emphasis, at least to some of these early legislative framers, was on the *federal* in the Federal Reserve System. That emphasis meant that the balance of power was between local and national figures, much as the U.S. Constitution had done with states and national governments. That balance was at the core of Glass's conception of the new system. "In the United States, with its immense area, numerous natural divisions, still more numerous competing divisions, and abundant outlets to foreign countries," he said, "there is no argument, either of banking theory or of expediency, which dictates the creation of a single central banking institution, no matter how skillfully managed, how carefully controlled, or how patriotically conducted." To that end, the Federal Reserve System was "modeled upon our Federal political system. It establishes a group of independent but affiliated and sympathetic sovereignties, working on their own responsibility in local affairs, but united in National affairs by a superior body which is conducted from the National point of view." To drive the point home: "The regional banks are the states and the Federal Reserve Board is the Congress."[15]

Glass's view was of the Federal Reserve System as a series of central banks. He was, in fact, a steadfast defender of the Reserve Banks anytime the board sought to assert itself in the power struggles that arose. Glass wasn't alone in this emphasis. E. W. Kemmerer, an early observer of the creation of the Fed, called the arrangement of "twelve central banks with comparatively few branches instead of one central bank with many branches" the "most striking fact" about the system. Wilson also agreed: "We have purposely scattered the regional reserve banks and shall be intensely disappointed if they do not exercise a very large measure of independence."[16]

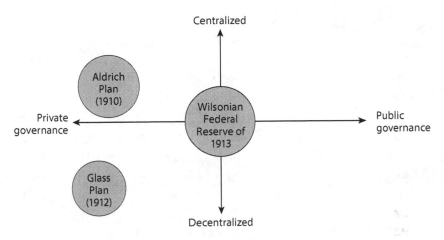

Figure 1.1. The Wilsonian Compromise of 1913.

The final result was the Wilsonian Compromise. Figure 1.1 illustrates the nature of the Wilsonian Compromise and its alternatives.

THE INSTITUTIONAL CHAOS OF THE FIRST FEDERAL RESERVE

The compromise, however, proved more brilliant in political design than institutional clarity. As Allan Meltzer has noted, tensions "between the Board and the reserve banks began before the System opened for business." Because the statute—in the tradition of many great political compromises—left room for divergent interpretation for competing factions, the legislative authors of the Federal Reserve Act never defined a number of key terms and largely did not specify the power relationship between and among the Federal Reserve Board and the Reserve Banks. In the two places where the Fed exercised the most power—the proactive purchase of securities in the open market and the reactive discounting of securities brought to the doors of the Reserve Banks—rivalries arose immediately, both between the board and the banks and among the banks themselves. Indeed, in one of the most interesting footnotes in Fed history, two Reserve Banks opened competing branches in Havana, Cuba, as a way to extend their international reach.[17]

Despite the federalist design of the system, the center formed in short order in New York City in the person of Benjamin Strong, the governor of the Federal Reserve of New York. According to his biographer, Strong was "one of the world's most influential leaders in the fields of money and finance," an assessment that subsequent commentary hasn't contradicted. From the founding of the Federal Reserve System until his death in 1928, "his was the greatest influence on American monetary and banking policies; he had no close competitor."[18]

Strong was ostensibly deeply committed to the public spirit of his work—in the top drawer of his desk, he always kept a note to himself (written "to the governor of this bank") to "never forget that it was created to serve the employer and the working man, the producer and the consumer, the importer and the exporter, the creditor and the debtor; all in the interest of the country as a whole." But not everyone agreed that his policies matched his aims: Herbert Hoover, for example, blamed the Fed generally (and the New York Fed in particular) for causing the Great Depression. "This orgy [of speculation] was not a consequence of my administrative policies," he wrote, but of the "mediocrities" at the Fed.[19]

"To understand the Great Depression is the Holy Grail of macroeconomics," wrote Ben Bernanke, then an academic economist. Because this isn't primarily a history of the Federal Reserve System, we will have to skip the important, almost endless quest to answer whether the Federal Reserve caused the Great Depression. For our purposes, though, it is important only to note that after Strong died and even before, the decision-making apparatus in this curiously governed institution was in disarray. Strong succeeded in guiding the Fed's policies during his life by dint of personality, not law. Outsiders to the system—including, ironically, Herbert Hoover himself—knew it wielded power but didn't know exactly how it did or by whom.[20]

Such was the state of things when Franklin Roosevelt's team of economic experimenters arrived on the economic scene. During the 1932 campaign, he argued that "[t]he country needs and, unless I mistake its temper, the country demands, bold persistent experimentation. It is common sense to take a method and try it: if it fails, admit it frankly and try another. But above all, try something." Roosevelt lacked a consistent theory of regulatory response; the pride of place following his 1932 election was for fast reaction, not necessarily legal or institutional coherence. As historian Richard Hofstadter put it, the New Deal was characterized as a "chaos of experimentation."[21]

Despite the Fed's centrality to the banking system, institutional reform of the Fed was not high on the initial list of priorities. There were nevertheless adjustments that came in the first round of economic legislation. In the Glass-Steagall Act of 1933—more famous for the creation of federal deposit insurance and the separation of commercial and banking institutions—Congress created the Federal Open Market Committee (FOMC) as the central body that would make proactive decisions about the purchase of market securities, including government securities. The failure of the pure model of governance by personality needed a legislative boost and received it in the creation of the FOMC. Importantly, though, the federalist system created under Wilson was reinforced in what scholars have called the "first New Deal," or the burst of legislative activity in FDR's first hundred days. The FOMC created in that initial burst consisted of the twelve Reserve Bank presidents and was meant to add a more formal structure on monetary coordination that excluded the "governmental" Federal Reserve Board.

Nibbling around the edges of the Wilsonian federalist central bank might have remained the order of the day had it not been for Marriner S. Eccles, perhaps the most intriguing figure in Federal Reserve history. Eccles's father was a Scottish immigrant, a Mormon convert, a bigamist (Marriner's mother was his father's second wife), and, in time, one of the wealthiest men in the state of Utah. Eccles thrived in his father's business and expanded it into mining, timber, and especially banking. He was a millionaire in his own right by the age of twenty-two.[22]

Eccles rose to national prominence in part because of his success as a banker during the height of the banking crises of the Great

Depression. With bank failure rates reaching unprecedented heights, Eccles's banks survived, largely owing to his own savvy ability to maintain credibility and confidence. While there were other successful bankers, what made Eccles noteworthy was that he was also something of a radical. For example, at the 1932 Utah State Bankers Convention, he laid out his theory of the Depression and its cure in plain language. "Our depression was not brought about as a result of extravagance," he said. "It was not brought about as a result of high taxation." It came, instead, because "[w]e did not consume as a nation more than we produced. We consumed far less than we produced. The difficulty is that we were not sufficiently extravagant as a nation." There was a simple reason for this:

> The theory of hard work and thrift as a means of pulling us out of the depression is unsound economically. True hard work means more production, but thrift and economy mean less consumption. Now reconcile those two forces, will you?

Eccles had a solution, too: "There is only one agency in my opinion that can turn the cycle upward and that is the government."[23]

In modern parlance, we'd call arguments like these Keynesian. But 1932 was four years before John Maynard Keynes had published his *General Theory of Employment, Interest, and Money*, the book that expounded the notion that government should be responsible for compensating for slack in consumer demand. Though they had never met, the millionaire Mormon from Utah had anticipated the dapper Cambridge don's worldview. In an amusing historical aside, the two did eventually meet during the Bretton Woods negotiations about the future of the world's postwar economic order. Despite their common diagnosis of depression and consumption, they didn't take well to each other. Eccles thought the British needed to make better assurances of repayment to the United States for prewar loans, a source of great consternation to the British. "No wonder that man is a Mormon," Keynes retorted to a colleague outside of Eccles's hearing. "No single woman could stand him."[24]

Eccles didn't make much more headway with the bankers and businessmen who heard him articulate these heretical views in Utah in 1932 than he did with Keynes in 1944. "Poor Eccles," a president of a western railroad is said to have remarked. "He must have had so terrible a time with his banks that he is losing his mind." No matter. Their opinions mattered much less than that of Rex Tugwell, already part of FDR's original "Brains Trust." In Eccles, Tugwell had discovered an indispensable resource: a western banker whose ideas were even more radical than the incoming administration's. Eccles came to work with the new Roosevelt administration as a special assistant to the secretary of the treasury.[25]

Eventually, Eccles was considered for the position of "Governor" of the Federal Reserve Board. To give a sense of how the board governor position was then perceived, the post became vacant when Eugene Black resigned—to take the position of governor of the Federal Reserve Bank of Atlanta.[26] Eccles refused the president's offer. In response to inquiries of his availability, he responded that he "would not touch the position of governor [of the Federal Reserve Board] with a ten-foot pole unless fundamental changes were made in the Federal Reserve System." Roosevelt invited him to propose his view of what those changes should be, and he and an assistant prepared a three-page blueprint of what amounted to a refounding of the Federal Reserve.

That refounding would eliminate the federalist compromise. He narrowed his sights on the Reserve Banks: "Although the Board is nominally the supreme monetary authority in this country," he wrote in a memo to Roosevelt, "it is generally conceded that in the past it has not played an effective role, and that the system has been generally dominated by the Governors of the Federal Reserve Banks." As an "unfortunate result," he continued, "banker interest, as represented by the individual Reserve Bank Governors, has prevailed over the public interest, as represented by the Board." Eccles's position was notable: Eccles was himself a banker whose views were represented by the Federal Reserve Bank of San Francisco, and yet he sought the banks' exclusion from national policy.

The problem wasn't only one of inappropriate banker influence on the system; it was also one of governance. "With such an organization" as the Federal Reserve System, wrote Eccles's assistant and partner in Fed reform, Lauchlin Currie, "it is almost impossible to place definite responsibility anywhere. The layman is completely bewildered by all the officers, banks and boards. Even the outside experts know only the legal forms." Eccles proposed a radical legislative overhaul to resolve both the problems of governance and banker influence.[27]

THE SECOND FOUNDING OF THE FEDERAL RESERVE: THE BANKING ACT OF 1935

Eccles sold Roosevelt on the proposal. He committed the presidency to the passage of Eccles's bill, and Eccles accepted the governorship so that he could more effectively lead the legislation through Congress from inside the Fed. The *New York Evening Post* summarized the point perfectly: "Marriner S. Eccles is a unique figure in American Finance—a banker whose views on monetary policy are even more liberal than those already embraced by the New Deal."[28]

Currie, a Canadian-born economist Eccles met when they both served at the Treasury, followed Eccles to the Federal Reserve Board. Currie was an economist whose academic work had been critical of the economic theory that supported Fed policy from its inception. Fortunately for us, he was also an active memo writer. The problem, as Currie saw it, was not just about eliminating private control as a formal matter: the original Federal Reserve Act had plainly stated that the Federal Reserve Board would "supervise" the Reserve Banks. The question was whether that supervision could be plausible.[29]

Currie described the situation in a 1934 memo to Eccles: "Decentralized control is almost a contradiction in terms. The more decentralization the less possibility there is of control." The problem was that "[e]ven though the Federal Reserve Act provided for a very limited degree of centralized control, the system itself by virtue of necessity was forced to develop a more centralized control of open market operations." The ad hoc institutional development consisted of "fourteen bodies composed of 128 men who either initiate policy or share in varying degrees in the responsibility for policy." (The fourteen were the twelve Federal Reserve Banks, the Federal Reserve Board, and the once powerful Federal Advisory Council, a group of bankers that advised the Federal Reserve Board.) These various bodies, and their governors and boards, made governance and public accountability a virtual impossibility. Currie glumly concluded that "[s]uch a system of checks and balances is calculated to encourage irresponsibility, conflict, friction, and political maneuvering" such that "anybody who secures a predominating influence must concentrate on handling men rather than thinking about policies."[30]

In light of these problems, in Eccles's (and Currie's) view, the structure had to change, and radically. Their timing was impeccable: the New Deal experimenters were embarking on a legislative frenzy known as the Second New Deal. In a single legislative session, Congress passed five major pieces of legislation, including the Social Security Act, the Wagner Act (which reshaped American labor law), the Public Utility Holding Company Act, the Banking Act, and the Revenue Act—a controversial tax bill known by critics and defenders alike as the "Soak the Rich" bill.[31]

Eccles's Banking Act of 1935 was the "least controversial" of the five. Least controversial, perhaps, but in some sense also one of the most consequential. The act created a system that represented a dramatic departure from every other experiment in central bank design in U.S. and indeed world history. It abolished the Federal Reserve Board created in 1913 and replaced it with the Board of Governors of the Federal Reserve System. (The term "Federal Reserve Board" remains in wide if anachronistic use to refer to the Board of Governors.) It also demoted the heads of the Federal Reserve Banks, who would no longer carry the name "governor." That title would be reserved for the members of the Board of Governors. At the Reserve Banks, the head would be the "president." This was an intentional demotion: unlike in politics, in banking lingo, a "governor" was an august title reserved to the central bank; a mere "president" could be any Joe from the corner savings and loan.[32]

There was one hitch to Eccles's sweeping reform: Carter Glass, that jealous guardian of the Federal Reserve System, its original sponsor in the House, Fed chair under Woodrow Wilson, and now Fed caretaker as the senior senator from Virginia. Eccles's proposals irked Glass greatly, who retaliated by holding up Eccles's confirmation hearings as the old Federal Reserve Board's governor. There may also have been a sense of longing for what might have been for Glass. The aging senator was very nearly Roosevelt's first secretary of the treasury and was in fact offered the position first. Had he accepted it, he would have been Eccles's boss when Eccles first floated the prospect of a demolition derby of Glass's beloved system. But Glass would have been a bad fit for FDR's administration, and not just because his health was fading. Glass was, in his core, deeply conservative and hated almost everything about the New Deal, despite lending his name to one of its signature achievements, the Glass-Steagall bill. In fact, "[h]is record of opposition to the New Deal, based on a study of thirty-one bills on which he voted, 1933–39, was 81 percent opposed—easily the highest of all Democratic senators of the period."[33]

Since the Reserve Banks were essential to Glass's view of what the Federal Reserve System must be, their continued participation within the system became a point of compromise in getting Glass to endorse Eccles's bill. As a result of that compromise, the Reserve Banks weren't removed entirely from federal policy-making, despite Eccles's preference for that removal. They became instead a presence on the newly reformed FOMC, which consisted of the seven-member Board of Governors, plus five Reserve Bank presidents on a rotating basis. As a result, while Glass's sponsorship allowed the Reserve Banks to continue to give the system hints of federalism, Eccles had undone the Wilsonian Compromise of the first Federal Reserve. Figure 1.2 illustrates the difference.[34]

The Reserve Banks weren't the only ones shown the door by the Banking Act of 1935. The treasury secretary was also out. For treasury secretaries like Andrew Mellon—the second longest serving

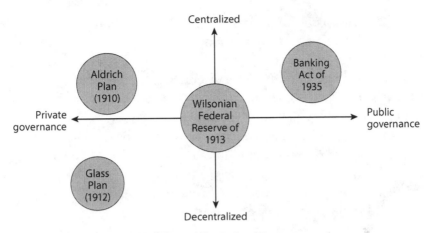

Figure 1.2. The second founding of the Federal Reserve.

secretary, second only to the early nineteenth-century secretary Albert Gallatin—the chairmanship of the Federal Reserve System was largely a ceremonial post. But others were different: Glass, Mellon's immediate predecessor as secretary of the treasury had, perhaps like the jealous father he was, essentially treated it as "a bureau of the Treasury instead of as a board independent of the Government." The removal of the secretary was Glass's idea, in fact. Apparently, if he couldn't control it, he wanted to make sure others in government couldn't either.[35]

As historian David Kennedy has written, after the 1935 act, "the Fed now had more of the trappings of a true central bank than any American institutions had wielded since the demise of the Bank of the United States in Andrew Jackson's day." It was more than that: The new Federal Reserve System looked not only like a "true central bank" but was a key step in what economic historian Charles Goodhart has called central banking's "evolution" from private banks running a private banking policy with public benefits to a public central bank in the modern sense of the word. The Fed didn't join the fold of central banks at last in 1935; Eccles and FDR had created a new central banking model altogether.[36]

Ironically, just as the secretary of the treasury (at the time, Henry Morgenthau) was removed from the Fed's Board of Governors,

Eccles sought to coordinate fiscal and monetary policy in the joint mission of lifting the economy out of Depression. "Coordinate" may even suggest more separation between the Fed and the Roosevelt administration than Eccles intended: he meant for monetary policy to be administration policy. In fact, Eccles's clear policy—expressed before Utah bankers or to FDR's Treasury—was to use all policy instruments at the government's disposal to do for the economy what consumers could not do: spend their way out of the depression.

It is no surprise, then, that the Eccles Fed in the 1930s saw less of a need to declare formal independence from government, as the Banking Act of 1935 had done in declaring independence from private bankers. Even during a brief and painful interlude of further recession in 1937–38, the Fed's policy during the 1930s was fully congenial to the administration's.[37]

And then came war. Eccles's views on fiscal-monetary coordination during economic depression were born of the fear of deflation: that is, he believed government was the only force capable of stopping the economic freefall. His views on fiscal-monetary coordination during war came to the same conclusion, via a different path: war on the nation's mortal enemies was no time for anything but full-throated support of everyone within the democracy, including and perhaps especially the central bank.

The day after the Japanese attack on Pearl Harbor, Eccles sprang into action to reassure the nation that the Fed would stand by the war effort. In its annual report in 1941, the Fed declared that it was "prepared to use its powers to assure that an ample supply of funds is available at all times for financing the war effort and to exert its influence toward maintaining conditions in the United States Government security market that are satisfactory from the standpoint of the Government's requirements." In practice, this meant that interest rates for government debt were "pegged": ninety-day bills at less than 0.5 percent, one-year bonds at less than 1 percent, and long-term debt at 2.5 percent. Despite the Fed's refounding in 1935 as an agency unto itself, the war brought it squarely under presidential control.[38]

THE THIRD FOUNDING: THE FED-TREASURY ACCORD OF 1951

After the war and with the new administration in place, the glory days of Fed-Treasury coordination against the common enemies of economic depression and fascism came to an end. The close relationship between the Fed chair and the president did, too. Eccles was Roosevelt's man, not Truman's. Whether because of differences in personality or policy perspectives, or no shared history, Eccles did not remember his time as Truman's Fed chair with warm regard. They were "years of frustration and failure, as I tried, in my limited capacity, to influence public thought and governmental policy."[39]

Part of the problem was not only that times had changed, but that Eccles had changed, too. From his early days as a proto-Keynesian in 1932, Eccles became what we would call today an inflation hawk. He saw risks of runaway inflation in continuing the "peg" he had established in 1942. Here, with others inside the Federal Reserve System (especially New York Fed president Allan Sproul), Eccles began an effort to subvert the subordination of monetary policy that Eccles's own policies had created. (A side note: central banking poets co-opted from war-making poets the metaphors of doves and hawks. Central banking doves are those more likely to prioritize a central bank's commitments to mitigating unemployment; hawks are more likely to prioritize the commitment to fighting inflation.)[40]

Truman was not impressed and had no patience for this kind of posturing. In 1948, in a unique instance in Fed history, Truman refused to reappoint Eccles to the chair he had held since 1935. Instead, Truman offered him the *vice* chair, presuming that such a public and obvious demotion would cause the proud millionaire to return to his business interests in Utah. Instead, Eccles expressed his interest in accepting the offer. Outfoxed, Truman ignored Eccles's acceptance and appointed industrialist Thomas McCabe as the new chair. The president pointedly never filled the vice chair, which stayed vacant until 1955.[41]

Truman may have hoped that leaving Eccles with neither chair nor vice chair would've finally pushed the Utahan out. It did not. For the first and last time in Fed history, the former chair stayed on as governor for longer than a perfunctory transition period. If Eccles made noises about removing monetary policy from the Treasury as Fed chair, he now made full speeches in something of a crusade to warn the country of the dangers of the inflationary pressures that were building. The peg had caused rampant inflation. The risks were dire. The Depression and wartime justifications no longer applied. Eccles advocated a policy that would end the Fed's domination by the administration.

Eccles's insubordination quickly and unsurprisingly reached the newspaper headlines. As the hostilities of what would come to be called the Korean War began, concerns about the conflict's inflationary consequences became a source of " 'open speculation' as to whether the Federal Reserve would continue to support the long-term government bonds" at the 1942 peg. Truman fought back and called the new Fed chair, Thomas McCabe, at his home and gave his subordinate the president's instructions. As McCabe presented to the board at their next meeting, "the Federal Reserve Board [sic] should make it perfectly plain . . . to the New York Bankers that the peg is stabilized." The alternative, the president warned, would be for the board to "allow the bottom to drop from under our securities." Truman concluded with an ominous warning: "If that happens that is exactly what Mr. Stalin wants."[42]

A war of public speeches followed. Treasury Secretary John Snyder implied that the Fed remained committed to the peg; New York Fed president Sproul countered days later. Eccles drew attention to the Fed's subtle but clear signal that the peg was not a guarantee. Finally, Truman had had enough and summoned—for the first and last time in Fed history—the Federal Open Market Committee to the Oval Office for a presidential lecture. Immediately thereafter, he issued a press release that presented the (false) view that the "Federal Reserve Board [sic] has pledged its support to President Truman," and "the market for government securities will be stabilized at present levels and . . . these levels will be maintained during the present emergency." (It is testament to the Federal Reserve System's confusing governance system that even the president referred to the Federal Reserve Board instead of the FOMC, the committee that would have had the authority to make the decisions the president hoped to see.)[43]

Eccles hit back hard. He leaked to two major newspapers the internal memorandum the board had prepared, on behalf of the FOMC, to summarize what had occurred at the Oval Office meeting, directly and publicly disputing the Truman administration's account. What became known as the "Treasury-Fed dispute" was now litigated in the public eye. As Eccles put it in his memoir, his press leak meant one thing: "the fat was in the fire."[44]

Cooler heads on the staffs of both the Treasury and the Fed intervened to come to grips with this internal dispute. They decided to resolve the issue once and for all by hammering out a durable compromise that would honor the Fed's desire to respond to inflationary pressures as they arose and the White House's fear that uncertainty in interest rates would make it impossible to fight Communism in Asia. From the Fed staff, Winfield Riefler led the way; from the Treasury, the assistant secretary of the treasury William McChesney Martin. The two of them constructed a single sentence that would allow both sides to declare victory, but committed no one to anything. It was a "truce," in the words of Fed historian Donald Kettl. After agreeing to the terms, both sides announced that they had accepted the compromise, which came to be known as the Fed-Treasury Accord. The problem? There was nothing more to the compromise than the awkwardly worded announcement itself. Here it is, in full:

> The Treasury and the Federal Reserve System have reached full accord with respect to debt management and monetary policies to be pursued in furthering their common purpose to assure the successful financing of the Government's requirements and, at the same time, to minimize monetization of the public debt.

Even a reasonably well informed citizen or lawyer of the day could not have recognized the extraordinary import of this dense sentence. In fact, some in Congress thought very little of so informal an arrangement. In congressional hearings after the announcement of the accord, Senator Paul Douglas (D-Illinois, 1949–67)—a prominent economist long critical of Treasury control of the FOMC—made clear that he thought the accord and Secretary Snyder's subsequent attempts to clarify its meaning were bogus. In Senator Douglas's words: "Talleyrand said that words were used to conceal thought. I have always thought that words should be used to express thought, and it is the lack of this quality which I find unsatisfactory in your testimony throughout."[45]

Senator Douglas's was a fair critique. In fact, there was more to the deal than this inscrutable announcement. Shortly after the release, Chair McCabe resigned from the board; Marriner Eccles followed in July. They were replaced with two Treasury insiders: William McChesney Martin as chair, and James Robertson, former first deputy of the comptroller of the currency. Senator Douglas saw the resignation of the two senior members of the Board of Governors, and their replacement by two Treasury insiders, as something of an unofficial deal that the "truce" declared in the accord meant business as usual for the Treasury-dominated Fed. Truman certainly hoped so: to enforce the uncertain terms, Truman was sending what he hoped would be his Trojan Horse.[46]

It didn't turn out that way. To the chagrin of his patrons in the Truman administration, William McChesney Martin, the former Truman insider, quickly established that the Fed-Treasury Accord did not mean what Truman thought it meant. After the accord, the Treasury continued to issue long-term debt at the peg rate, and Martin expressed willingness to support and coordinate those efforts. But he also pushed against the perception and reality of the peg and eventually made clear that he, too, would abandon it: markets, not the Fed, would set those rates. None of this sat well with President Truman. On Martin's report, at their next meeting at an event at a New York City hotel, Truman had but one word to say to the affable Martin: "Traitor!"[47]

With the Fed-Treasury Accord, the Truman administration's strategy seemed to be to speak inscrutably and appoint a big stick.

They succeeded on the first part, but not the second. As a result of Martin's appointment—on which more in the next chapter—the accord became seen as "the start of the modern Federal Reserve System," and a "major achievement for the country." It has become Fed's third founding, after the Federal Reserve Act of 1913 and the Banking Act of 1935. Unclear though it may be, written with the intent to conceal though it may have been, this sentence forms the basis in perception and in fact of the idea that the Fed's monetary policy is institutionally separate from the economic policies of the president. That idea is held sacred by most central bankers. It is at the core of the Ulysses/punch-bowl conception of Fed independence. And it comes from a sentence almost completely devoid of content.[48]

We'll see more in the next chapter how this empty sentence took on a life of its own. But the point to note now is not only that the words didn't have much content; the form didn't either. The Fed-Treasury Accord is purely informal. It is not a statute or regulation, nor binding law enforceable in any court. In fact, some within Congress in favor of separating monetary from fiscal policy thought the informality of the accord was extremely dangerous. Nonetheless, the accord stuck and has endured. In some ways, it performed even better than a statute might have done. Recall that in the Banking Act of 1935, the secretary of the treasury was struck from the Board of Governors. That statutory removal was essentially irrelevant to the question of the fiscal domination of monetary policy. The seemingly meaningless sentence published in the Federal Reserve Bulletin was not.[49]

CONCLUSION: THE THREE FOUNDINGS OF THE FEDERAL RESERVE

In 2013, the Board of Governors commissioned a mug as a gift to employees, to honor the Federal Reserve System's centennial. The mug is handsome, as far as mugs go. It's a striking cobalt blue with gold trim and carries on the front the seal of the Federal Reserve, a seal much like the seal of the U.S. president, an eagle over the semicircular stars and bars, but with both feet gripping olive branches instead of one foot with arrows. Circling the eagle are the words "Board of Governors of the Federal Reserve System." Underneath it all, the mug boldly declares its purpose in gold letters: "100 Years."

As readers of this chapter have learned and the mug's designers have either forgotten or chose not to disclose, the Board of Governors of the Federal Reserve System is not one hundred years old. The Board of Governors wasn't created until 1935, in the Eccles-written, Roosevelt-backed Banking Act of 1935. The parties celebrating the centennial announced on this mug shouldn't begin for another twenty plus years. The old Federal Reserve Board created by the Federal Reserve Act of 1913 no longer exists. The Board of Governors structure abolished it.

This chapter told the story of the Fed's three foundings. The narrative omits much about the Federal Reserve in its first half-century but is useful for setting the stage of understanding the Fed's unique governance and the geographic space within which it operates in two ways. First, it demonstrates just where this arcane, complicated, bureaucratic jumble that is the modern Federal Reserve System comes from. That jumble is the consequence of "institutional layering," or the reality that institutional design doesn't happen on a blank slate. The second founding of the Federal Reserve occurred not only against the backdrop of preexisting institutions, but also against preexisting people: Senator Glass in 1935 preserved part of what Representative Glass in 1913 had fought so hard to create, hence the continued presence of the curiously governed Reserve Banks even after the value of having these quasi-private and quasi-autonomous entities had been disproven. And the third founding, the Fed-Treasury Accord, came still on top of the others. New Federal Reserves grew on top of the old ones.[50]

Second, the Fed's three foundings demonstrate not only the importance of law but also the relationship between law and personality. Law is not irrelevant to the rise of the Federal Reserve System as a powerful and distinct actor within government, but it is insufficient to explain the full context of institutional change. The removal of the secretary of the treasury from the Fed's board coincided with a period of Treasury dominance of monetary policy. And in the third founding, the Fed-Treasury Accord, law was nowhere to be seen at all.

The message is simple: in the institutional evolution of the Federal Reserve, law matters, but not in the ways people always expect. And personalities matter, too. We'll see more of both in the chapters ahead.

CHAPTER 2

LEADERSHIP AND INSTITUTIONAL CHANGE

FROM PERIPHERY TO POWER

A cautious man, in a new office, does not like strong measures.

—*Walter Bagehot, 1873*

There is a tragicomic scene in the Fed's early history when the members of the D.C.-based Federal Reserve Board struggled with an awkward question of social protocol. The newspapers had dubbed the new board "the Supreme Court of Finance," and the board thought they were "entitled to a pretty high place in the social scale." How high wasn't exactly clear, but William McAdoo—the secretary of the treasury, first ex officio chair of the Federal Reserve Board, and the one who begrudgingly had to field these questions—understood sardonically that these bankers and bureaucrats did not want to be "pale and distant stars, lost in a Milky Way of obscure officialdom; they must swim in the luminous ether close to the sun!"[1]

The keepers of the official protocol at the State Department gave an apparently unsatisfying answer, at least to the new board members. The members of the Federal Reserve Board, said the State Department, would sit in line with the other independent commissions in chronological order of their legislative creation. That meant that the board would follow the Smithsonian Institution, the Pan-American Union, the Interstate Commerce Commission, and the Civil Service Commission. When this didn't satisfy the status-conscious members of the board, the question was taken to President Wilson. As Secretary McAdoo reported it, "the shadow of a frown pass[ed] over [Wilson's] face" as the nature of the question of the Fed's social standing dawned on him. "I can do nothing about it," the president remarked. "I am not a social arbiter." When McAdoo pressed him, the president retorted: "Well, they might come right after the fire department." McAdoo, evidently pleased by this recounted exchange decades later, explained that he "never told the members of the Board what the President had said. It would have caused them needless pain." The State Department's view of protocol carried the day.[2]

This chapter takes up the question of how an institutional backwater gasping for recognition behind the fire department and the Pan-American Union became an institutional juggernaut that occupies a singular space within government. To answer the question, we pick up the narrative where we left it in the last chapter: at the advent of the new dawn of Fed-Treasury relations. Again, the puzzle of the third founding is how a single confusing sentence could have such an outsized impact on the system's governance and power. The answer is that the work of institution building in 1951 was only the beginning. Had it ended, the Federal Reserve System would not be the central bank it has become.

This chapter will focus on that process of change. Here, again, the work did not occur through the legislative process in Congress, but through the exercise of slow, cautious, painstaking leadership within the Federal Reserve System. It was the caution, though, that made it most effective. As applied to the Federal Reserve, Bagehot's line that opens this chapter is not about a failure of leadership; it is the story of a careful and cautious reshaping of central banking institutions. Cautious measures made for strong results.[3]

The chapter's focus will be on three Fed chairs: William McChesney Martin, Paul Volcker, and Alan Greenspan. They were not the only Fed chairs during this period: I'm skipping three others.

Only historians and longtime Fed watchers remember the tenure of influential Fed chair Arthur Burns (chair, 1971–78), about whom we will have more to say in later chapters; fewer still recall the short tenure of G. William Miller (chair, 1978–79); and almost no one but alumni of Swarthmore College remember the name Thomas McCabe (chair, 1946–51, including, as we have seen, during the Fed-Treasury Accord), a prominent Swarthmore alum and donor for whom the school's library is named. These chairs certainly influenced the way that we think about the Federal Reserve System, but in terms of defining the Fed in the form it eventually took, these three (with Marriner Eccles)—Martin, Volcker, and Greenspan—are by far the most influential.[4]

Given how much influence these Fed chairs have had on the institutional development of the system, it is tempting to accept the Ulysses/punch-bowl account of independence and allow the chair to stand in for the entire system completely. But even this chapter's focus on the three chairmen doesn't support that view. First of all, we have already seen what Eccles did to influence the Fed when he was both a special assistant to the president and then after he was effectively removed from the Fed chair during the Fed-Treasury Accord. Second, the Fed chair's actions were and are constrained by various other actors within the system, as the next three chapters explain in detail. The point is to show how individuals matter in how and why the Fed became the institution it is today, even as the legal governance structure of the Federal Reserve System stayed mostly the same.

WILLIAM MCCHESNEY MARTIN: IMPLEMENTING THE ACCORD, CONSOLIDATING POWER

There is a good reason why the two main Federal Reserve buildings are named for Marriner Eccles and William McChesney Martin Jr. Eccles we already know. But Martin cemented the Eccles legacy and introduced changes of his own that have had consequences for the way that central banking is practiced throughout the world. Three changes in particular are worth attention. First, the *operations* of central banking. With Fed staff economist Winfield Riefler, Martin overhauled the practice of central banking so that it became focused on interventions in one narrow market: the market for short-term government securities. Second, the *language* of central banking. Martin loved metaphors and used them constantly. And his metaphors have become the standard explanations for central banking, especially in thinking about the Federal Reserve as more than the fighter of crises. And third, the *politics* of central banking. Martin launched a successful effort to give content to the ambiguous Fed-Treasury Accord, which included picking fights with U.S. presidents.

Martin was himself a child of the Federal Reserve System: his father was the first chair of the Federal Reserve Bank of St. Louis and in 1929 became its governor (and later, after the 1935 act, its president)—just in time for the Depression. Martin grew up in the company of his father's dinner guests, including Benjamin Strong and Carter Glass. In that presence, he was "provid[ed] a continuing seminar in central banking and public service." Although there is no record of exactly what Benjamin Strong and Carter Glass said in Martin's presence during those formative years, the elder Martin viewed the separation of central bankers "from the politician and the plutocrat" as central to his worldview.[5]

After Martin assumed the chair as part of the Fed-Treasury Accord, he set about a multiyear program for changing the modern practices of central banking. Working with Riefler, his chief economic adviser and one of the most influential economists in Fed history, he began to articulate an enduring framework for monetary policy that remained the standard practice for the next fifty years, until the beginning of the financial crisis in 2008. Martin described it as a "flexible monetary policy," by which he meant leeway to sometimes take "aggressive" actions inside the market and "give leadership" to market actors on where interest rates go, while at other times the Fed should cool its heels and let markets find their own way. Put differently, Martin wanted the Fed to nudge interest rates up when the economy looked a little overheated, then nudge them down when it looked a little cool. This outlook on monetary policy was different from the one he had inherited in 1951; today, it is so standard that economists and central bankers generally describe this approach as "conventional monetary policy."[6]

Martin's approach required major changes to the operations of the Fed as they existed at the time. Most importantly, it meant hacking away at the pride of place for the Federal Reserve Bank of New York. The consequence of Carter Glass's partial victory over Marriner Eccles in preserving the Reserve Banks in Fed policy making was that some bank presidents still sought to exercise more power than their statutory authority allowed. Because they had a seat at the table, exaggerating their stature was easy to do.

Allan Sproul, the president of the New York Fed, was one such president. His voice dominated three levels of monetary policy decision making. When the full FOMC met just four times a year, the New York Fed's president was the traditional vice chair and held a permanent seat on the FOMC (whereas the other eleven Reserve Banks had to rotate in the remaining four seats). Second, unlike today, the full FOMC was often not in session. In its place was an Executive Committee consisting of the Fed chair, the New York Fed president, two other governors and one other Reserve Bank president. This Executive Committee had roughly the same policy-making authority as the full FOMC. And finally, the New York Fed implemented decisions of the Executive Committee or FOMC on its own, from its trading desk in New York City. This included making decisions about which assets to purchase on what kinds of time horizons: that is, whether to buy short-term government bonds or long-term corporate bonds.

Martin sought, slowly and cautiously, to change all of this. To do so required confronting Sproul directly. Sproul was regarded as one of the preeminent central bankers of his era. Almost from the beginning, Sproul and Martin sparred for supremacy within the system. Their disputes were over the meaning of the Federal Reserve Act, and Sproul's contention that, even after the Banking Act of 1935, the Reserve Banks—and especially the New York Reserve Bank—

maintained some autonomy from the Board of Governors, even in open market operations.[7]

Sproul's approach to stand up for the New York Fed became clear almost immediately. In his capacity as vice chair of the FOMC and as member of the Executive Committee, Sproul would confront Martin relentlessly, conducting parallel statistical analysis to rebut the conclusions and recommendations that Martin would advance to the entire FOMC. And in the implementation of the decisions of either body, Sproul exercised autonomy by simply refusing to report: implementation was his part of the playground, not Martin's.[8]

Over the course of his first five years, Martin used suasion with his other colleagues on both the board and the FOMC to chip away at Sproul's—and New York's—authority. The FOMC voted to double their meetings from four to eight per year to get more participation from the other governors and Reserve Bank presidents. The committee then changed the rules to require, rather than allow, each member to speak his views, rather than letting a few voices—that is, Sproul's—dominate. The committee then disbanded the Executive Committee entirely. And, finally and most importantly, the committee changed the way that the Fed would implement its views on the economy by restricting the asset purchases largely to short-term public debt of the U.S. government (Treasury bills or "T-bills"). Even here, the movement would be in accordance with the Martin-Riefler approach to "flexible monetary policy" that required slow, slight movements rather than big, fixed interventions.[9]

All of this stuck in Sproul's craw. He viewed the economy as "a mixed Government-private economy" in which the central bank—by which he often meant the Federal Reserve Bank of New York—should play a decisive role in shaping credit conditions. He thought that limiting the FOMC and New York Fed to short-term government securities was a harmful development. The central bank should "not tie one arm behind our back by restricting transactions" to short-term Treasury bills. Instead, he and his colleagues "should be free to influence the supply, availability, and cost of credit in all

areas in the market . . . to promote economic stability and progress." Sproul also feared the political nature of the asset decision:
purchasing short-term government debt looked an awful lot like
the very kind of subordination that he, Eccles, and others had
fought to remove. The decision, then, on assets, should be made by
him and his staff in New York, not by politicians and their appointees in Washington.[10]

By dogged perseverance, cautious leadership, and the cultivation
of his colleagues on the FOMC, Martin won "a civil but relentless
debate" that absorbed Martin's first four years. Recognizing defeat,
Sproul gave up and resigned, although he was five years away from
the mandatory retirement age and less than a year into another
five-year term as New York Fed president. He was replaced by
Alfred Hayes, a banker who had had no previous Federal Reserve
experience. This resignation was widely seen as a victory for Martin, who wanted "more power centralized in Washington" and,
with the moves away from New York, succeeded "in cutting the
wings and humbling the pride of the New York Bank."[11]

The legacy of the Martin-Sproul fight was the unmistakable subordination of the New York Fed to the rest of the FOMC on issues
of monetary policy, including the key issue of asset purchases. The
Banking Act of 1935 had already accomplished as much as a matter
of law, but the New York Fed's continued presence on the FOMC
and its place of prominence in the heart of the U.S. financial system
meant that the legislative change was only partial. Personalities
matter, and Martin wrested from Sproul the control of monetary
policy, and with it a significant measure of the power of the Federal
Reserve System.

MARTIN AND THE POETRY OF CENTRAL BANKING

In addition to radically altering the balance of power within the
Federal Reserve System and changing the way that monetary policy
is practiced, he also changed the language used to describe the Fed's
function. It is hard to overstate Martin's love for metaphors: his
public speeches are full of them. Most famously, of course, is the

punch bowl, the idea that the Federal Reserve follows the Martin-Riefler flexible monetary policy approach of nudging interest rates up just as a "chaperone who has ordered the punch bowl removed just when the party was really warming up." But that wasn't his only enduring image. The Fed must also, he explained, "lean against the winds of deflation or inflation, whichever way they are blowing." Another he preferred, and used frequently, was that of the economy as a river: the Fed's aspiration was for money and credit to "flow . . . like a stream. This stream or river is flowing through the fields of business and commerce. We don't want the water to overflow the banks of the stream, flooding and drowning what is in the fields. Neither do we want the stream to dry up, and leave the fields parched."[12]

Martin changed the *language* of central banking to use terms we still use today, and as he did, he changed the public's perception of what the Fed did. This changed conception of Fed practice matched his view of "flexible monetary policy." By changing the practice and language of monetary policy, Martin offered a new theoretical justification for central bank independence, away from a bargain struck between bankers and politicians and toward the idea of technocrats managing the economy. In this way, his leadership not only pushed the operations of the Fed in a new direction but gave those operations a new, vivid basis in language. If the Fed operates in "an economy of words," as Douglas Holmes has put it, Martin's metaphors are the tools to explain and legitimize itself. The Ulysses/punch-bowl conception of Federal Reserve independence—the idea that the Fed is full of technocrats only doing the work in the long-term best interests of society and is better left alone so that it can perform it well—needs the metaphors of Ulysses and the punch bowl. Martin can't take credit for Homer's *Odyssey*, but he is the author of the punch bowl.[13]

MARTIN AND THE POLITICIANS

Martin's final legacy is more of a legacy of the Martin era. And that is the idea that the separation of monetary and fiscal policy is as much the bailiwick of the president as it is of the central banker. Martin showed a few acts of political courage during this time, but so much more depended on the president—for better and worse.

In Dwight Eisenhower, the country—and its central bank—had a strong hawk on inflation. In his first State of the Union speech, he noted that "[p]ast differences in policy between the Treasury and the Federal Reserve Board have helped to encourage inflation." His policy would be different: "Henceforth, I expect that their single purpose shall be to serve the whole Nation by policies designed to stabilize the economy and encourage the free play of our people's genius for individual initiative." Eisenhower would make his position clearer later. In 1956, the Board of Governors had just raised the discount rate, one way the central bank removes the punch bowl as the party is getting started. Politicians are rarely in a mood to stop dancing, including inflation hawks like Eisenhower.[14] But when asked at a press conference about his administration's opposition to Martin's move, President Eisenhower explained that "the only comment I can logically make is this: the Federal Reserve Board is set up as a separate agency of Government. It is not under the authority of the President, and I really personally believe it would be a mistake to make it definitely and directly responsible to the political head of the state." This is a fascinating endorsement of the Ulysses/punch-bowl view of Fed independence and certainly made Martin's political life more livable. If Martin was the poet of Fed independence, Eisenhower was the patron who let it be so.[15]

The Ulysses/punch-bowl conception of Fed independence had no such patron in the presidency of Lyndon Baines Johnson. For Truman, Martin just had to wait for the clock to wind down on an unpopular president. For Eisenhower, there was nothing for Martin to do but enjoy the autonomy (during the same time, of course, he had more intractable problems of internal governance with Sproul and the FOMC).

Lyndon Johnson was a different story. LBJ was, and remains, one of the most storied political operators in U.S. history. And he assumed the presidency with clear goals: he wanted to push forward with a large tax cut proposed by John F. Kennedy while simultaneously shepherding through Congress his metaphorical war on poverty and his literal war in Vietnam. He knew as a southern Democrat he faced a credibility problem with the Kennedy liberals whom he inherited upon Kennedy's assassination. He knew, too, that their loyalty and support would be crucial to his success as a national Democrat. With these thoughts in mind, Johnson launched his presidency with a liberal fiscal agenda. As he explained to Kennedy's chief economist soon after taking office, "Now I want to say something about all this talk that I'm a conservative who is likely to . . . give in to the economy bloc in Congress. It's not so . . . I'm no budget slasher. . . . I am a Roosevelt New Dealer. As a matter of fact, to tell the truth, John F. Kennedy was a little too conservative to suit my taste." The fiscally conservative William McChesney Martin and the New Dealer Lyndon Johnson were bound to conflict.[16]

The conflict came in two ways. First, on the relatively minor issue of the discount rate. Martin and his colleagues feared inflation and began to pull back on an overheating economy. They were also mindful of the international context and the Fed's obligations under the Bretton Woods system. True to the script, when the Bank of England hiked its interest rates from 5 to 7 percent, the Fed followed suit with an interest rate rise of its own. Johnson was livid and made clear that he expected the Fed to "guarantee that the higher rates will not hurt the economy."[17]

Here, Martin could have folded but did not. It was already significant that he was announcing Fed moves to the White House ahead of time, something that scholars have criticized. The most he would do beyond that heads up was to assure the public through an unprecedented press conference that this rise in rates would not restrict the availability of credit. As we will see in our discussion of the Fed and Congress in chapter 9, this spine of steel did not last during the Johnson administration. But it did illustrate, however weakly, Martin's push against presidential meddling.[18]

More significant was Martin's conflict with the President and Congress over the public debt. For a central banker, deficits are signs of trouble. As the government takes on more and more debt, the holders of its currency start to worry about the government's temptation to inflate away its sorrows and leave its creditors holding the bag. This is the very reason for the Ulysses/punch-bowl vision of Fed independence: the keeper of the currency is the one that has to enforce the commitment not to steal money through inflation. Martin saw the Johnson deficits as a signal of exactly this kind of pressure. What is fascinating about his reaction, though, is not that he recognized the potential costs of deficits to the credibility of the currency. That's basic macroeconomics. It is what Martin did in reaction to that fear—and, what he did not do—that is telling.

Rather than raising rates to aggressively force the government to adjust its fiscal policies, Martin tried to persuade the administration instead, in private and in public. To one group of business journalists, he said that he was "not at all sure that the present political climate of perpetual growth will be vindicated in terms of perpetual deficits and easy money." In another speech, after making a similarly hawkish statement, he self-deprecatingly admitted that he knew people's reaction: "There's old Martin again. He thinks the economy is overheating. He's always saying that." In a 1965 commencement speech that caused an uproar, Martin compared the Johnson years to 1929–33 and found "disquieting similarities" and concluded with a warning: "Then, as now, government officials, scholars, and businessmen are convinced that a new economic era has opened, an era in which business fluctuations have become a thing of the past." The implication of these speeches was clear: the politicians needed to right the fiscal ship.[19]

At times, there are those who complain bitterly when a central banker doesn't stick to her knitting of monetary policy and monetary policy alone.[20] To take a modern example, Fed Chair Janet Yellen spoke in 2015 about income inequality and the dangers it posed to the smooth growth of the economy. This caused some people to respond angrily that the Fed needed to butt out. What Martin's example here tells us isn't that this kind of nosing about in fiscal policy works. It actually didn't, in Martin's case. His warnings about incoming inflation were correct, but he did not or could not back them up with preemptive policy actions. Martin does tell us, though, that there is a venerable tradition of Fed chairs making comments designed to influence economic policy making far beyond the walls of the Federal Reserve building on Constitution Avenue.[21]

Martin's legacy, then, was threefold. First, he implemented the Fed-Treasury Accord, giving his Treasury sponsors an institutional surprise in the process. At the same time, he changed the operations of the Fed to create what we now call conventional monetary policy: the purchase of short-term government securities to influence interest rates in a reaction to inflationary or disinflationary pressures, one nudge at a time.

Second, he simultaneously created the language—especially the metaphors—of central bank "independence." It is a tribute to Martin that he was able to convey his technical approach of flexible monetary policy in words that are cited by journalists today. Generally, central bankers are not known for their felicitous phrasings. Martin was no Walter Bagehot, but he seemed to internalize another of Bagehot's many aphorisms: that money "is as concrete and real as anything else," and that "it is the writer's fault if what he says is not clear." Martin made himself clear.[22]

And third, the Martin era showed that, whatever the Fed-Treasury Accord meant, it did not mean that the Fed chair stayed out of politics. That can happen. It did with Eisenhower. It just doesn't have to happen, as in the case with Martin's public if sometimes oblique criticisms of the Johnson administration's fiscal policies, or with his standing up to Johnson's threats on the discount rate.[23]

VOLCKER THE MAVERICK

Few people tower—figuratively and literally, as Volcker stands at 6'7"—over late twentieth-century financial history like Paul Volcker. Volcker's contributions to central banking practice are many, but the most important is the view that the Fed was the only game in town when it came to combating inflation. As a result of the Fed's decisions during Volcker's tenure as chair, the conception

arose that the independence of the Federal Reserve exists to promote price stability. Although Martin coined the phrase, Volcker
became the quintessential Fed "chaperone."[24]

Volcker had had a personal connection to the Federal Reserve
System rivaling that of Martin. His first job out of graduate school—
Volcker began but abandoned doctoral studies in economics at the
London School of Economics—was at the Federal Reserve Bank
of New York. He stayed close to monetary affairs throughout his
public career, which included two stints at the U.S. Treasury, dur-
ing the Kennedy, Johnson, and Nixon administrations. During the
Nixon administration, for example, Volcker was one of the pri-
mary policy makers behind the policy to suspend gold convertibility—effectively, the end of the gold standard in the United
States and the advent of a currency fully managed by the Federal
Reserve. After brief stints in the private sector, Volcker had finally
been appointed in 1975 to the presidency of the Federal Reserve
Bank of New York.[25]

By the summer of 1979, Jimmy Carter was in the White House
amid a continuing economic slump and ever-increasing inflation, a
phenomenon dubbed "stagflation." In an effort to reboot his economic policies, Carter announced that he would engage in a dramatic reshuffling of his cabinet, including by announcing the resignations of his attorney general and secretaries of treasury;
transportation; energy; and health, education and welfare. To replace his retiring secretary of the treasury, Carter tapped the man
he had just installed as his own Fed chair, G. William Miller.

Miller was not regarded then or later as a competent central
banker. Miller was neither banker nor economist, but the former
CEO of the industrial conglomerate Textron Incorporated. His
only experience with central banking was one term on the board
of directors of the Federal Reserve Board of Boston. But this lack
of experience was part of his appeal. He was installed in the position with the surprising support of economists like Milton Friedman, who responded supportively to Miller's appointment: "We
have had enough of bankers," Friedman said. Within months,
though, it was clear that Miller's only institutional innovations

were an effort to make the meetings of the FOMC smoke-free (Volcker, then on the FOMC as president of the Federal Reserve Bank of New York, was inseparable from his cheap cigars, including in FOMC meetings) and to limit discussion with an egg timer he displayed during these meetings. It seemed his strategy for combating inflation from within the central bank was by making the FOMC meetings less tedious for him to endure.[26]

Whether Miller was removed from the Fed because of his failures there or brought to the Treasury because of Carter's confidence in him is the source of some controversy, but the recollections of Carter's staff suggest that the reshuffling at the Fed was one of history's great accidents. Volcker was not the Carter administration's first candidate, but he was the Wall Street favorite. As journalist William Greider wrote, Volcker's résumé "looked as if [he] had been training for this job for almost thirty years."[27]

Not everyone agreed, especially within the Carter administration. Many regarded him as too "rigidly conservative" and not enough of a team player. But his support among the members of the financial markets made him a leading candidate, and Carter interviewed him for the post. Volcker recalls—and contemporaneous reports confirm—that Volcker did most of the talking and pledged emphatically that he would be an "independent" central banker and would focus on using the Fed's authority to tackle inflation. Volcker thought his Oval Office performance disqualified him from the post, but Carter thought otherwise. Ignoring advice that the president's selection of Volcker would effectively "mortgag[e] his reelection to the Federal Reserve," Volcker was appointed to the post. The Dow Jones stock average rose at the news as the price of gold fell. Carter had apparently reassured the financial markets.[28]

At the time, the fiscal fight against inflation was entering at least its tenth year, but the political momentum behind it was much older. We already saw how much Eisenhower paid attention to inflation, including in his first State of the Union address. Richard Nixon had campaigned in 1968 on a promise of price stability and, in an effort to control inflation by executive fiat, had instituted a sixty-day price freeze in 1973. Soon after taking office, Gerald Ford had promised to make inflation America's "public enemy number one" and started distributing "Whip Inflation Now!" buttons to members in the public to encourage them to do everything they could (whatever that was) to control it. Carter continued the tradition by invoking inflation's specter as part of the reason the American people felt so dissatisfied with their government, economy, even society.[29]

TAMING THE DRAGON: THE BATTLE AGAINST INFLATION

Volcker's successful effort to stop inflation stemmed from an approach to monetary policy that had, until then, not been tried: rather than aiming its monetary policy at interest rate targets, as the Fed had done historically, Volcker began—cautiously, almost reluctantly—to target the amount of money in the system and letting the interest rates sort themselves out. Explaining the difference in approaches can get technical quickly, but the gist of the difference is that an interest-rate approach doesn't look too much at how much money is flowing through the system: it wants to keep interest rates relatively stable, and then move them one direction or another. In the interest rate climate at the time, however, the benchmark interest rate was already almost 11 percent, and tweaking interest rates in the traditional way meant playing a constant game of catch-up with the financial markets and the individuals, households, labor unions, and companies making decisions in the anticipation of what the dollar would be worth. Some of them played this game of catch-up using intuition, some using econometrics, and some with pure panic. By taking the Martin "flexible monetary policy" approach to raising nominal interest rates—the numbers actually quoted in the newspaper—in an environment where the inflation rate was galloping away, the Fed's central bankers were doing nothing to combat inflation and doing a great deal to help it. The result was an inflationary period that economists and historians have called the Great Inflation.[30]

The alternative favored by some influential economists was to engage in monetary targeting. With monetary targeting, the central bank lets interest rates float according to the quantity of money in the system, crudely measured. A central bank facing inflation could dramatically restrict the amount of money circulating in the economy, thereby allowing interest rates—the "price" that banks and soon everyone must pay to get money—to float where they would as a market-based reaction to the central bank's decisions. This scarcity of money would have dire consequences to the health of the economy. Millions would lose work as consumers stopped financing purchases, businesses closed, and the economy entered recession. But inflation would stop. This is what economist Milton Friedman meant by his famous dictum, "inflation is always and everywhere a monetary phenomenon." A central bank caught in an inflationary spiral has an easy exit, according to Friedman and his fellow monetarists: Starve the economy of money, and inflation will cease.[31]

Volcker himself took some convincing to make this regime change. He was opposed to monetary targets while on the FOMC as president of the New York Fed and expressed misgivings later. But under his leadership, monetarism became the official policy of the FOMC. Interest rates climbed above 22 percent in 1981 and came permanently below 10 percent only in 1984, causing a recession but ultimately slaying the inflation dragon. Doing so left a lasting legacy.

The Volcker FOMC's strategy—and it was the strategy of the entire FOMC, under Volcker's leadership—was dramatic, untested, damaging to the economy, and ultimately successful. Over the course of several years, and millions of jobs lost and skyrocketing interest rates, inflation came down to a manageable level, something the previous three Fed chairs could not accomplish. And with that success, costly though it was, came the conclusion that reinforced the vision of the Fed as a chaperone: despite constantly channeling anti-inflation rhetoric, the political branches were not up to the task of managing the value of the nation's currency. It not only took a central banker to perform the task; other central bankers of course knew about monetarism and its potential for combating inflation. It took Paul Volcker and his associates on the FOMC.[32]

Arguably, Volcker gets more credit than he deserves for this remarkable period in Fed history, for two reasons. First, here, as everywhere, the Fed was a deliberative body. The FOMC transcripts from this period show extraordinary deliberation, skepticism, and polarized views. Volcker was an able guide to these discussions, but his views were pushed and pulled from various directions. The decisions were made through committee, built on compromise.

And second, Ronald Reagan and his economic team also deserve credit for not using political tactics to subvert the Volcker FOMC. The short-term economic consequences of these actions were devastating. Volcker was not Reagan's man, and his team wanted him removed from his post even before Reagan was inaugurated in 1981. And yet, the administration gave the Fed's policy makers a free hand. This praise must be tempered by the fact that inflation was an overwhelming electoral concern, and the public was generally supportive of Volcker's efforts. But the pain caused to the unemployed was very real, and no politician likes facing an election in a recession. And true to expectations, the 1982 midterm election was a Republican drubbing in the House.[33]

Upon Volcker's resignation in 1987, well after his successes were clear, the paeans to his greatness came pouring in. Gerald Ford (whose "Whip Inflation Now!" program had ended without success) praised him for handling "domestic and international pressures and challenges with superb skill and unquestioned integrity." Margaret Thatcher, who had sought to follow a similar course acting as her own "independent" central bank, wrote that she "very much admired [Volcker's] resolute pursuit of sound monetary policies, and the great skill and understanding you have brought to the complex task of . . . reducing inflation in the world's largest economy." Even those affected by his policies wrote to extend their thanks. One man from Fredonia, Pennsylvania, wrote, "Though I was unemployed for an extended period, I always understood and agreed with your policy as chief of [the] Federal Reserve. You saved my life savings from becoming worthless. While a lesser person might have caved in to political pressure, you sir, served our nation and all its people with distinction."[34]

VOLCKER AND TOO-BIG-TO-FAIL BANKING

There is another side, however, to the Volcker legacy, this time more from the Board of Governors than from the FOMC. The 2008 financial crisis brought the term "too big to fail" into the public discussion in a profound and public way—there's even an HBO film by that name, based on the best-selling journalistic account with the same title by *New York Times* journalist Andrew Ross Sorkin. But there was nothing new about government-sponsored bailouts of large financial institutions. We've seen them throughout history, in this country and in others. Volcker, however, brought the doctrine into modern practice and provided the antecedent for its continued shelf life.

In 1982, in partial consequence of the Volcker FOMC's own interest rate policies but also owing to risk-management failures within financial institutions, the Fed became concerned about the level of risk in the financial system. "If it gets bad enough," he reported to the FOMC, "we can't stay on the side or we'd have a major liquidity crisis. It's a matter of judgment as to when and how strongly to react. We are not here to see the economy destroyed in the interest of not bailing somebody out."[35]

The FOMC followed his lead, and in 1984, in the largest bank loan to a single institution until that time, the Volcker Board of Governors, through the Federal Reserve Bank of Chicago, extended an unprecedented $3.6 billion loan to Continental Illinois. It wasn't enough; the bank failed anyway. But with the failure, the modern doctrine of "too-big-to-fail" banks was born. The Volcker Fed was the midwife.[36]

Volcker's contributions to the institutional development of the Fed are complicated. From a regulatory perspective, while he was more in favor of aggressive regulatory responses than some of his Reagan-era colleagues, the Volcker Fed adopted a posture to financial stability that would serve as a model, for good or ill, in the later crisis. From a monetary perspective, the priority of price stability over employment has caused some to wonder whether inflation might have been tamed with less costly measures.[37]

Even so, there is no dispute that Volcker's lasting contribution to the practice of central banking is in the personification of the modern central banker. After Volcker, people saw the Fed chair *must* be the chaperone to the populist Ulysses. Central bank "independence" is the mechanism that allowed Volcker to carry the day, the thinking now goes, even though the costs to the economy are exactly the kind of thing that democracies punish their politicians—including, as it happened, Jimmy Carter—for creating.

GREENSPAN THE ORACLE

If Paul Volcker was the embodiment of a central bank as inflation's master, Alan Greenspan came to be the icon of the central bank as the all-powerful deity of the economy.

Greenspan came to the Fed as Volcker's preferred successor. Very soon, Greenspan began putting his mark on the Fed by governing monetary policy under "the Greenspan standard," a style of central banking that meant, two economists quipped, "whatever Alan Greenspan thinks it should be." This extraordinary authority came because it seemed to work, and because it worked, Greenspan received adulatory attention from the public. Though it can be difficult to see it through the fog of the financial crisis of 2008, the image of the Federal Reserve during the Greenspan era was unlike anything in Fed history. Short of iconic presidents, few if any figures in U.S. history enjoyed the heights of fame and prestige that Greenspan enjoyed during his tenure.[38]

Consider two illustrations of this prestige: the journalistic scandal of Stephen Glass and the public discussions surrounding President Clinton's impeachment. One of the most notorious instances of sustained journalistic fraud occurred in the mid-1990s, at the hands of policy wunderkind Stephen Glass. Glass was just twenty-three years old, a recent graduate of the University of Pennsylvania, when he first started writing for the *New Republic*, then billed as the "inflight magazine for Air Force One." Glass wrote piece after piece depicting sensational plot lines. A convention that sold ribald Monica Lewinsky–themed paraphernalia. A cult devoted to the worship of George H. W. Bush (the "First Church of George Herbert Walker Christ"). And the one that led to his downfall, the story of a fifteen-year-old hacker who so impressed a large tech company with his defacement of the company's website that it sought to hire him at an absurd salary and a lifetime subscription to *Playboy* magazine.[39]

Among these fabrications was an article about the cult of personality that surrounded Fed Chair Alan Greenspan. "Praised Be Greenspan" outlined investment traders, Washington powerbrokers, and even everyday Americans who veritably worshipped the man. One arbitrageur kept a chair in which Greenspan had sat in the 1940s secured by blue velvet ropes: "Some nights when we've lost money," the trader said, "I come in here and sit in the chair and think. It gives me inspiration." One Washingtonian attending a large dinner party tried to shuffle seat assignments during cocktails, even at the expense of leaving his wife sitting with strangers. When confronted, he quipped: "I can have dinner with my wife any night of the week. In the course of human history, having dinner with Greenspan might be as important as the Last Supper."[40]

Many or all these quotes and quips were inventions of a creative fabulist. But they worked so well because they were so believable. The deification of the chair of the Federal Reserve System was, in the roaring 1990s, something of an undisputed fact. Glass could sell magazines with phony stories because his readers would nod their heads in amused agreement with what they took as an undisputed fact: Alan Greenspan really was that big of a deal.[41]

The second illustration comes from Gennifer Flowers, the Arkansan lounge singer and extramarital love interest of then Arkansas governor Bill Clinton. In an interview on *Larry King Live*, on the topic of the Lewinsky scandal, Flowers explained why people should welcome the resignation of the embattled president: "I think [most people] are concerned that if Bill Clinton were to resign to-morrow, that the bottom would drop out and we would all be devastated. But my research tells me that if he did resign tomorrow, we may have a little bit of a problem for a couple of days, but I would assure them that Alan Greenspan would step in there and make sure that our economy would become healthy right away."[42]

It may seem trivial to quote two people from 1990s history who many would like to forget. But the point is a profound one: Even in the midst of a potential constitutional crisis, the hope expressed on national television by a nonexpert reassured us all that Greenspan wouldn't let the economy collapse. Greenspan became a "capitalist hero and a political icon." Even Bob Woodward, the journalist famous for skepticism of power in high places, wrote a glowing short biography of Greenspan. By the book's title and contents, Greenspan was the Maestro. In our democratic society, he was the brilliant, omnipotent economic oracle. Greenspan was the Fed; and the Fed meant extraordinary, almost limitless power to keep the economic engine running.[43]

This popular faith in Greenspan—faith often missing in the rest of government—shows his profound influence on the mystique of an "independent" central bank. The Fed in the Greenspan years became, even in the public consciousness, an institution almost divorced from government. This view depended on the idea that the Fed had the ultimate authority over the economy and could guarantee stability, prosperity, and low inflation.

GREENSPAN'S SECRET: DISCRETION, FLEXIBILITY, AND THE GREENSPAN PUT

How did Greenspan achieve this extraordinary reputation? The short answer is, again, the record of low inflation and steady growth that coincided with his tenure. But the more comprehensive answer, and the key to the rise in the power of the Federal Reserve generally, is in two factors. First, maximal flexibility and discretion for Fed policy. And second, the reassurance to the financial markets that the Fed will provide whatever liquidity necessary to maintain stable market conditions. This second factor is sometimes called the "Greenspan Put."

The idea that the Fed should retain maximal flexibility was not Greenspan's, of course; it is the continuation of the Martin-Riefler approach. But it came at a time when economists began a systematic challenge to the desirability of discretionary central banking policy as a good way to organize economic policy. In a 1977 article that eventually contributed to its authors' Nobel Prize in Economics, economists argued that economic policy makers (including, principally, central bankers) who have complete discretion to determine future policy are going to do it badly. More specifically, according to this argument, a central banker sensitive to his appointment by politicians will have the same pro-inflationary bias as her political mentors. A politician's appointee wants to stay on the politicians' good side; no better way to do it than by assisting in inflationary support just in time for an election. The better approach, the authors argued, is to create a rule (through law) that establishes the central bank's credible commitment against inflation well ahead of time and limits the central banker from deviating from that rule. In that sense, the Fed ties itself to the mast, too.[44]

This approach to Fed "independence," of course, forms the backbone of the standard account this book criticizes. What is fascinating about the Ulysses/punch-bowl view of central bank independence in the Greenspan era is how much central banking in practice varied from that theoretical model. As two economists assessing the Greenspan Fed near the end of Greenspan's tenure put it, "the Fed brought inflation down dramatically under Paul Volcker and has controlled both inflation and real fluctuations well under Greenspan. In the process, it has built up an enormous reservoir of trust and credibility. And it has accomplished all this without rules or even any serious pre-commitments."

Even in his very words, Greenspan sought to retain full tactical control of the levers of central bank authority. As he famously said shortly after his appointment as Fed chair, "Since I've become a central banker, I've learned to mumble with great incoherence. If I seem unduly clear to you, you must have misunderstood what I said." Greenspan gathered power to himself and to the Fed through maintaining a freedom of movement. That freedom became one of his most important legacies.[45]

Policy discretion by itself isn't enough to send central bankers to the pantheon; it depends on what the policy maker does with that discretion that matters. With Greenspan, an important use of his discretion was the perception and fact that he was committed to giving financial markets a soft landing amid national and international turmoil. The idea here is that the Fed, embodied by Greenspan, would always be there to put the bottom to the market and to keep that bottom within investors' reach. This is the infamous "Greenspan Put," a name that comes from the world of options trading. A put option is a contract that allows its holder to sell an asset like a stock to someone else at a specific price. It's a kind of insurance, a guarantee that no matter how far the asset falls, the holder of the put option will always be able to recover at least something.

Alan Greenspan's leadership at the Fed during times of severe market disruption gave market participants the sense that they will always be able to land with their feet on the ground. As a report in the *Financial Times* put it in 2000, "when financial markets unravel, count on the Federal Reserve and its chairman Alan Greenspan (eventually) to come to the rescue." This perception—widely shared among market participants—was built on repeated assurances from the Greenspan Fed. This occurred when the stock market experienced the largest sell-off since the Great Depression, in October 1987; during the Mexican peso crisis in 1995, when markets grew skittish at the risk of a default on the peso; during the East Asian financial crisis of 1997–98, when attention shifted to currency crises on the other side of the globe; at the failure of the hedge fund Long-Term Capital Management; in response to the implosion of equity markets after the dot-com crash in March 2000; and, finally, in response to the attacks on the World Trade Center and the Pentagon on September 11, 2001. The precise policy response in each instance was different, and the idea that Greenspan was self-consciously "bailing out" market participants from bad decisions is too coarse a conclusion. But there was no question that the Greenspan Fed's monetary policy philosophy was consistent with this view. Because the Greenspan Put worked—because the economic boom continued without triggering inflation—it is not difficult to see why it was easy to believe that cults of Wall Street traders worshipped the central banker.[46]

GREENSPAN THE REGULATOR

The view of Greenspan as economic royalty, perhaps an economic deity, is not the only aspect of his legacy. In fact, in light of the financial crisis of 2008, it may not be the one most remembered by future generations. Instead, Greenspan's legacy as a regulator will continue to color the way he is remembered. It also demonstrates important aspects of the Fed's power and independence.

Greenspan was an obvious choice for Ronald Reagan from a monetary policy perspective, but he was a curious choice as a government regulator. The problem was that he came from an intellectual tradition that didn't believe in the legitimacy or efficacy of government regulation of private markets. In the 1950s, he became part of the ironically named "Collective," a group devoted to the person and teachings of libertarian novelist Ayn Rand (the irony was intentional: collective behavior was the polar opposite of their individualistic worldview). Greenspan was an active part of the Collective, writing its newsletter, attending its parties, engaging in its debates. Rand was, in his words, "a stabilizing force" in his life. His devotion to her was extraordinary. He subjected first dates to essays he had written for her and even credits her as having the vision to predict, almost alone, the internal collapse of the Soviet Union (Greenspan allows that Rand shares that distinction with Ronald Reagan). "It did not go without notice," he writes, "that Ayn Rand stood beside me as I took the oath of office [as chairman of the Council of Economic Advisors] in the presence of President Ford in the Oval Office."[47]

Even as Greenspan rose in government, first as an adviser to presidents and next as one of the leading officials in the late twentieth century, he maintained his Randian suspicion of governmental intervention in private life, especially private economic life. Under a Randian view of the world that Greenspan seemed to endorse at least early in his life, even taxation was immoral. If people valued essential government services like courts and national defense, they would volunteer to pay for them. In his memoir, Greenspan notes the irony of his government service and accepted it as a cost to fulfilling his public ambitions: "By the time I joined Richard Nixon's campaign for the presidency in 1968, I had long since decided to engage in efforts to advance free-market capitalism as an insider, rather than as a critical pamphleteer."[48]

After he assumed the Fed chair, it didn't take long for Greenspan's ideological hostility to regulation to make itself manifest. He made this clear himself: "Since I was an outlier in my libertarian opposition to most regulation, I planned to be largely passive in such matters and allow other Federal Reserve governors to take the lead." But "largely passive" isn't exactly correct, nor was he such an "outlier." Greenspan was a leader in a movement that asserted an intellectual basis for a conservative/libertarian worldview. Their influence in the Reagan administration was profound, and nowhere more powerful than in exactly the kinds of economic policies that Greenspan espoused.[49]

True to form, Greenspan actively sought to shape the Fed's regulatory agenda by limiting its overall commitment to several areas of banking regulation. As the consumer banking scholars Kathleen Engel and Patricia McCoy note, "[n]owhere was this more evident than in mortgage lending."[50]

Mortgage lending: in 2015, we know it as the potential source of catastrophic financial instability. What started in 2006–7 as the subprime mortgage crisis became the full-blown global financial crisis by 2008. While shelves groan under the weight of the books that diagnose the crisis and its origins, a common theme is that too many people borrowed too much money with too little ability to repay it. When housing prices stopped their vertiginous ascent and swiftly collapsed across the country, it became obvious that the extent of default on these mortgages far exceeded almost everyone's expectations, and the resulting sell-offs and uncertainty as to who held the remaining debt created the financial crisis. There are disputes about who is responsible for this chain of events—greedy banks? irresponsible homeowners? venal politicians? all the above? The basic connection between mortgage lending and financial instability, however, is clear.[51]

Among the parties not listed above is one of the most important. Following the crisis, the question was frequently asked: where were the regulators? The emphasis is on the plural. In the United States, unlike many other countries, financial regulatory authority is divided among roughly a dozen federal agencies and hundreds of state agencies. But the Board of Governors was uniquely situated to regulate almost all the mortgage market. This legal authority comes from, among other sources, the Truth in Lending Act, originally passed in 1968 but extended dramatically in 1994 to authorize the Fed to prohibit abusive practices in mortgage lending. As Engel and McCoy document, the Fed did not seek and did not want the authority in the first place. The Fed's vice chair at the time of the Truth in Lending Act's passage, J. L. Robertson, told Congress that the Fed lacked the expertise or staff to regulate mortgages and recommended that Congress place that authority within "an agency better suited to perform the function." Congress disagreed, and the Fed became the primary regulator of mortgage practices in the country.[52]

In law, but not in practice. Vice Chair Robertson's view of the Fed as a poor candidate for the job carried through, especially during the Greenspan era. Of course, crisis postmortems are notoriously prone to hindsight bias. It's very easy to see what went wrong after the fact and unfair to hold those in the past responsible for knowledge unavailable to them. Blaming the Fed for a failure to regulate mortgages, however, is more plausible, even after the fact. The question of the Fed's responsibility for mortgage practices was put to an active debate at the Board of Governors. One Clinton-era Fed governor, Edward Gramlich, was particularly struck by the mounting evidence that mortgage lending practices were violating the law and presenting significant risks to homeowners and to the broader financial system. While Gramlich was successful at forcing the Fed to expand some of its minor regulations, he was stymied by Greenspan from going any further. With respect to one key change—the publication of a voluntary code of conduct that would outline best practices for mortgage lenders—Greenspan wouldn't budge. "He never gave us a good reason, but he didn't want to do it," recalled one participant in the debates who, like Gramlich, pressed for greater regulation. "He just wasn't interested."[53]

After the mortgage markets exploded, but before full depths of the 2008 financial crisis, Greenspan was defensive about accusations that he had failed as a regulator. His defense sounds a lot like Robertson, the vice chair who thought Congress should look somewhere else for a mortgage regulator. To a reporter covering the collapse of the subprime mortgage market, Greenspan admitted that he knew "there were a lot of very questionable practices going on," but the problem was one of enforcement, and the Fed staff under Greenspan just wasn't up to the job: "the question is, who are the best enforcers? A large enough share of these cases are fraud, and those are areas that I don't think [the Fed's staff] are best able to handle."[54]

Greenspan's legacy as a regulator will continue to be assessed as historians gain greater distance from the crisis and the Greenspan era. And although Greenspan had the misfortune of publishing a clearly written memoir that outlined his ideological skepticism of government regulation on the eve of the greatest financial and regulatory crisis in three generations, he was far from alone in his ideological confidence in the successes of self-regulating markets. At the time, Democrats and Republicans alike embraced deregulation as a secret to unlocking the potential of the American economy, an ideology that comes up again throughout this book. But only the

Greenspan Fed held the keys to the regulatory authority. And under his watch, the regulatory apparatus that Congress had established and deposited into the Fed—sometimes against the central bankers' wishes—went largely unused.

Looking back on the Greenspan Federal Reserve, every aspect of the legacy has been called into question. The Fed's discretion is under assault, in large part because of deviations from predicted decision making in the early 2000s. The Greenspan Put became part of the entrenched mindset that the benefits of risk taking in the market were for the market participants, but the costs were for the public, through the central bank. And the Greenspan Fed's regulatory failures are widely documented and criticized as central to the cause of the 2008 financial crisis.

While Greenspan and the Fed generally haven't retained their luster since the financial crisis, each part of the Greenspan legacy is key to the story about what the Fed is and what it does. And in light of each aspect, the Ulysses/punch-bowl approach to Fed independence starts to fall apart. Rock stars are not usually quiet chaperones, and the Fed's inflationary successes—the focus of the Ulysses conception of Fed independence—aren't helpful in explaining its regulatory failures.

CONCLUSION: MAPPING THE INSTITUTIONAL GEOGRAPHY OF THE FEDERAL RESERVE

The story of the Federal Reserve as the chaperone of the U.S. and global economy, the enforcer of our Ulysses contract, is a story of bureaucratic change unrivaled in American history. Part of that change was the way that two pieces of legislation—the Federal Reserve Act of 1913 and the Banking Act of 1935—shaped its structure and defined its legal relationships to politicians. It also has to do with the power of leadership of the three chairmen highlighted above: Martin's defining role as a poet-politician of the new central bank and his solidification of power within the Federal Reserve System; Volcker's personification of the central banker chaperone through the taming of inflation in the early 1980s; and Greenspan's crisis- and inflation-defying oracular feats as the god of the boom-time economy. In the institutional developments that these chairmen wrought, key features of the oversimplified Ulysses/ punch-bowl vision of Fed independence came into sharp relief. In the chapters ahead, we will see that there is more to this story than that.

CHAPTER 3

CENTRAL BANKING
BY COMMITTEE

THE AUTHORITY OF THE FED'S
BOARD OF GOVERNORS

At present, the Board of Directors are a sort of *semi*-trustees
for the nation. I would have them real trustees, and with a
good trust deed.

—*Walter Bagehot, 1873*

In the mid-1990s, just before the true height of Greenspan-mania,
a "tremor shook the Federal Reserve Board's headquarters" as four
of the seven members of the board—including then governor Janet
L. Yellen—met with Chair Greenspan to demand better treatment.
As reported in the *Washington Post*, "[t]he four board members
were not complaining about policy. Rather, they were frustrated
that no one was keeping them adequately informed about the staff's
activities, including discussions with the Treasury Department and
research on international financial issues." They felt like figure-
heads, as though Chair Greenspan had used the staff to sideline
them despite their legal role in setting Fed policy. During the same

time, "a departing senior staff member [at the Fed] said he never had an interest in becoming a board member; it would have reduced his influence over the Fed's policies if he did." The complaining governors knew they were lower on Greenspan's totem pole than the senior staff; they wanted better.[1]

In congressional testimony following the *Post*'s reporting, members of Congress challenged Greenspan on his dominance of the Fed. He countered the charge by modestly invoking the Federal Reserve Act: "all of the authority of the Federal Reserve Board is within the board members themselves. I, as chief executive officer, have one statutory authority: I run the meetings." Legally, Greenspan was mostly right. The legal authority of the Federal Reserve System is not deposited in individuals, but two overlapping committees: the Board of Governors (for all regulatory authority) and the Federal Open Market Committee (for monetary authority).[2]

In practice, however, the authority of the Fed is quite different, as Greenspan well knew. He had, in fact, concentrated the authority of the central bank in the hands of a single individual arguably more than any of his predecessors. This extraordinary mismatch between the legal concentration of authority in the Board of Governors on the one hand and the practical authority in the person of a single individual is one of the most fascinating elements of the Fed's governance. As a result, the governors are, like Bagehot's Bank of England directors, almost "semi-trustees."

In this chapter, we will understand better how law and practice relate to each in creating this unusual trusteeship and how the governors participate, or not, in influencing the space within which the Fed makes policy. It is a more interesting—and more complete—story than the one that starts and ends with the Fed chair.[3]

THE LEGAL AUTHORITY OF
THE CHAIR AND THE BOARD

As noted in chapter 1, the exact character, even the very existence, of the original Federal Reserve Board was a source of controversy—the most controversial feature of the Federal Reserve Act of 1913. But the Banking Act of 1935 replaced the Federal Reserve Board with the more robust, if clumsily named, Board of Governors of the Federal Reserve System. The change to "Governors" (from "members") was especially noteworthy. The 1935 Act literally took away the prestige of the title from the heads of the Reserve Banks (called after 1935 "presidents") and deposited that prestige in the public appointees who would now govern the entire system. The idea in 1935 was to deposit in this seven-person committee—one of whom to be designated as chair—the authority of the Federal Reserve System.

There remains statutory and practical tension between the Reserve Banks and the Board of Governors, as we have already discussed and will discuss again. But there is another statutory tension between the governors and the Fed chair. The Federal Reserve Act is a much-amended and in some places quite technical statute. But the powers of the chair (or in the statutory parlance, the chairman) are very easy to summarize, if slightly more expansive than Greenspan's congressional testimony quoted above.

The total of the chair's legal authorities and requirements consist of appearing before Congress twice a year; serving a term of four years; being the "active executive officer" of the Board of Governors; presiding over the board's meetings; certifying in writing to the Federal Reserve Bank that a depository institution is "viable" for supervisory purposes; delegating nearly any board function to Fed employees; and authorizing the publication of certain kinds of sensitive information. There is also an old provision that governs how the Fed can redeem old notes under the gold standard. In other words, just eight duties. By contrast, the Board of Governors as a governing body is cited in the Federal Reserve Act over *four hundred times*.[4]

Even in these eight circumstances, the chair's authority isn't absolute. The vice chair—or even a chair pro tempore—can preside over board meetings in the chair's absence. More importantly, any single member of the board can effectively override the provision that allows the chair to delegate nearly any of the board's functions to nearly any employee within the system: "The Board shall, upon the vote of one member, review action taken at a delegated level within such time and in such manner as the Board shall by rule prescribe."[5]

One might argue that the key authority granted in the act to the chair is the whole ball game: the chair is the chair, after all, so surely that position means leadership, if not complete control. But even this authority is quite limited. The act suggests that, if anything, the chair reports to the board: "The chairman of the Board, *subject to its supervision*, shall be its active executive officer." That is, the governors are to supervise the chair, not the other way around. Of course, the chair is a member of the board, but that is the point. If the chair wants to promote a certain policy, he must convince a majority of colleagues first: three (for board matters) or six (for FOMC matters).[6]

To get a better sense of the legal story of the chair's primacy—or lack thereof—it's useful to compare it to another prominent committee of experts that presides over a significant portion of the American democracy: the U.S. Supreme Court. Like the Board of Governors, the Supreme Court is a committee that consists of one chief and several associates (in the court's case, eight associates, for nine justices total). All nine justices vote to choose the cases the court will decide; they all hear oral arguments and question the litigants' lawyers; they all vote on those cases' dispositions; and then they all write and sign majority, concurring, and dissenting opinions. Structurally, there's not much of a difference between the court and the board and FOMC. The justices each have one vote, just as the governors or members of the FOMC do.

Of course, the chief justice is not the same as the associate justices. He has specific duties not granted to the other justices. The chief justice appoints judges to the Foreign Intelligence Surveillance Court; oversees the Federal Judicial Conference (effectively, the chief justice is the chief executive of the judicial branch); and is on the governing board of the Smithsonian Institution. By practice, the chief justice is also the most senior justice, regardless of the timing of appointment. This means that he chooses who will write the opinion of any majority or dissent that will be joined by the chief justice.[7]

But that's about it. If the chief justice wants his view of a case to prevail, the votes of four colleagues must be gained through reason, not will. The same is true for any other justice. The votes of the chief and associate justices count the same. As a result of this formal and practical equality, associate justices are rightly viewed as important figures in our democracy with significant power over the lives of people in it. A rigorous and highly public vetting process surrounds their presidential nomination and Senate confirmation. They appear on *Sesame Street* and *60 Minutes*. Their views are heavily scrutinized in the media. The additional statutory responsibilities of the chief justice fall away as mostly immaterial. There is simply no denying the essential and distinct role that each associate justice plays.[8]

The Board of Governors is somehow different. Only the most avid of Fed watchers know the names of the other members of the board, and rarely does the public become excited about the appointment process that places its members there. In practice, there is also a tradition—emphatically unlike that at the Supreme Court—of near unanimity on board and FOMC decisions. Even with the most controversial of decisions, the board and FOMC usually speaks through the voice of the chair. While some members of the latter committee have issued dissenting statements from FOMC policy decisions, there are very few instances where the chair is in dissent. According to one former governor, "the Chairman is expected to resign if the [FOMC] rejects his policy recommendation." Exactly how that unanimity or near unanimity arose in practice is unclear. That it exists, however, is beyond dispute.[9]

The legal architecture exists for governors to influence Fed policy. But does it exist in practice? Historically, the answer is: sometimes. As the Kennedy and Johnson appointees began to reflect a very different economic orientation from William McChesney Martin, for example, the chair started adapting his views and even offered LBJ his resignation in desperation (it was rejected). And before there was palace intrigue about governor discontent at the Greenspan Fed, newspapers covered the same kind of intrigue at the Volcker Fed. Through the steady drip of appointments during the Reagan administration, Volcker started to lose control of his board and eventually lost a couple of close votes on the board when the Reagan appointees sought to support the administration in a way that Volcker found inappropriate. Although Volcker prevailed at reversing the first of these votes—largely through slamming doors and angrily threatening to resign—it was clear that the governors were more influential than the chair on determining board's policy outcomes. The president's strategic use of the appointment power to stack the board with his appointees, then, can allow a group of governors to act, together, as a counterweight to the Fed chair.[10]

INDIVIDUAL GOVERNOR INFLUENCE: THE CASE OF DAN TARULLO

Waiting for a likeminded majority is not the only way an individual governor can shape the Fed's policy-making space. The best illustration of individual influence is in the person of a current (as of this writing) Fed governor, Daniel K. Tarullo. Tarullo is arguably the most important non-chair governor in the history of the modern Federal Reserve System. His experience is worth considering in full.

Tarullo was not, early in his career, an obvious candidate for the title of "most influential non-chair governor in Fed history." Raised in the working-class suburbs of Boston, Tarullo excelled academically and eventually landed as an assistant professor at Harvard Law School during a time of bitter ideological clashes among the faculty and students. Tarullo came to be identified with the minority faction of legal theorists on the radical left and, as a consequence, was denied tenure out of "revenge by the right for the school's move in a liberal direction in recent years." Tarullo himself expressed the hope that he would "turn out to be a sacrificial victim rather than the first of purge victims."[11]

After leaving the academy to work on Senator Kennedy's staff and in the Clinton administration, Tarullo became a law professor at Georgetown. There, he wrote a significant book on the proposed framework for international banking regulation negotiated between 1999 and 2004 and colloquially known as "Basel II" ("Basel" after the city in Switzerland that hosts the Basel Committee on Banking Supervision, where the framework is negotiated and published; and "II" because it was the second such negotiated framework.) In it, he strongly criticized two of the essential components of the framework: the use of "internal ratings-based" models of risk management, or allowing banks rather than regulators to evaluate their own risk; and the definition of "capital" that Basel and the large financial institutions used in calculating and regulating that risk.[12]

Bank capital regulation is notoriously technical. Even so, Tarullo's criticisms are not difficult to grasp. The Basel Accords focuses on two aspects of banking: "capital" and "liquidity." "Capital" here is a tricky—and misleading—bit of banking jargon. It doesn't have anything to do with the bank's cash on hand, but with the way that it raises money from other people and institutions. "Capital" is the banks' "equity," that is, funding that comes through shareholders as opposed to creditors. The focus on capital is important because banks that carry too much debt become the centers of financial crises: in a crisis, debt is the mechanism that transfers risk. If investors lose their shirts in *equity* markets, they lose their own money. There can, of course, be significant and negative economic implications for equity crises, but we see financial crises only when people (and especially banks) are borrowing money throughout the economy. When questions arise about the banks' and individuals' abilities to repay that money, especially if those questions weren't widely foreseen, a panic can ensue.

From a banking regulatory perspective, virtually everyone agrees that banks that borrow too much create enormous instability for the rest of us. The Basel framework is designed to address the questions that arise after this relatively facile agreement on principle is reached, such as, How much debt is too much? How do you define "capital"? And whom do you trust to measure these things in the first place? Tarullo's book criticized Basel II's answers to the last two questions (among other criticisms of the process).

At the same time he engaged this rather technical debate of interest to few beyond the banking regulatory community, he had made friends with the junior senator from Illinois, Barack Obama. The two had almost overlapped at Harvard—Tarullo as the left-leaning junior law professor, Obama as a left-leaning law student. As leader among the students on the left closely following the faculty's tenure battles, Obama had almost certainly heard about Tarullo's lost tenure battle. By 2005, the two were once again in contact. Rather than join the presidential campaign of Hillary Clinton, as many of his associates from the Clinton years had done, Tarullo signed on with the Obama campaign in 2007 and began advising the senator on economic and financial policy.[13]

After the election, Tarullo was among the first announced appointments of the new administration: Tarullo would become a new governor at the Federal Reserve. This was an odd appointment. Fed governors are not typically the posts associated with presidential confidantes and leading economic advisers. For someone of Tarullo's proximity to Obama, previous experience in a Democratic administration, and broad base of expertise, a more appropriate appointment might have been deputy secretary of the treasury, director of the National Economic Council, or some other position of prominence. But Tarullo was not chosen for those posts and appears almost nowhere as a figure on the Obama administration's sometimes multiheaded economic policy team, that included director of the National Economic Council Lawrence Summers, Secretary of the Treasury Timothy Geithner, chair of the Council of Economic Advisers Christina Romers, and director of the Office of Management and Budget Peter Orszag.[14]

Where Tarullo stood on the pecking order of Obama's economic team is clear even in the president-elect's own press announcement.

Tarullo is an afterthought. After setting up the announcement as the president-elect's call for a "21st century regulatory framework to ensure that a crisis like this can never happen again," his press office announced "the nominations of two top regulatory officials: Mary Schapiro as chairwoman of the Securities and Exchange Commission (SEC) and Gary Gensler as the chair of the Commodity Futures Trading Commission." Only at the end of the press release did the public learn that "President-elect Obama also announced the appointment of Dan Tarullo to the Federal Reserve Board."[15]

No matter. Tarullo was part of Obama's intentional effort to change the way that banking regulation and supervision occurred at the Federal Reserve. In Obama's own words during the speech that accompanied the trio's appointment, "[t]he Federal Reserve's monetary policy function will continue to be critical in navigating us through these trying times. But, as many of you know, the Federal Reserve also serves a vital regulatory function." In reference to Tarullo's Basel book, Obama noted his "academic and policy work on financial regulation has anticipated some of the problems we have observed, and he has generated important ideas for how we should move forward."[16]

Tarullo wasted no time in acting on this mandate. Even in his confirmation hearing, he assured Senate Republicans that blame for the crisis lay not only with the financial industry, but with the regulators—including his new employees at the Fed—in Washington. His effort at increasing accountability for successful (and failed) bank supervision spread throughout the system. According to press reports, Tarullo wrote a "stinging internal review for bank supervision" at the Federal Reserve Bank of Atlanta. When the incumbent head of bank supervision at the Atlanta Fed retired shortly after Tarullo arrived, the Board of Governors "appointed three people from outside the area to temporarily run bank supervision" in Atlanta, a move that "several inside the central bank read as Washington tightening its scrutiny of regional offices."[17]

This wasn't just a problem with the Reserve Banks. Tarullo also is reported to have an "overbearing skepticism of banks and supervisors" generally, a skepticism so pronounced that some Fed supervisors "are so wary of being second-guessed [that] they ask him to approve even mundane bank applications." Not necessarily known for a gentle demeanor—some Fed staffers who work under him "trade tales about which Tarullo blowup was the most legendary"—Tarullo made clear from the very beginning that he thought the Fed supervisors had "made mistakes in supervision, and [that] he wouldn't justify their past actions."[18]

Tarullo has done more than reinvigorate banking supervision at the Fed—a process he called trying to get "supervisory stars" on the ground, working with the banks. He has also pursued the mandate Obama gave him at the start of his appointment. He has led the charge in banking regulation, giving major speeches—sometimes quite controversial speeches—on nearly every aspect of financial regulation. These efforts have included threats to break up the largest banks and otherwise make the cost of business for systemically important financial institutions greater to reflect the risks that such institutions bring to the system. It has included sometimes novel proposals, such as making banks' boards of directors more responsible for risk management through their fiduciary duties (a proposal that prompted swift and negative reactions from banking insiders).[19]

All told, Tarullo's efforts have appeared to some within industry as, to quote H. Rodgin Cohen, the dean of the banking law bar in New York City, "a true revolution in regulation." Revolution might be an overstatement, but there's no doubting that his influence has been felt on nearly every aspect of the way banking supervision occurs in the system, including through the deemphasis of the Federal Reserve Banks in the process.[20]

These efforts have come back to his old critiques of the international banking regulatory framework. He has shepherded the implementation of Basel III reforms, including increased capital requirements and the regulation of foreign banks operating in the United States, grounded in the critiques he made as an academic. He has even more recently signaled his continuing skepticism of internal ratings-based approaches to calculating capital. These reforms are part of the most important financial regulatory over-haul in three generations.

In each of these instances, they have been crafted and delivered not by the Congress or the president, and not the Fed chair or even a vice chairman: a Fed governor was the architect and spokesman for them all. In this sense, he was unprecedented. The conclusion of one profile sums it up nicely: "Unlike previous bank regulators and supervisors, he went further, pushed harder, and accumulated massive power, all while alienating some inside the cloistered, genteel Federal Reserve and those outside in the bank-ing industry as well with his combustible style."[21]

It is too early to assess Tarullo's legacy as a regulator, but it is not too early to conclude that he has been arguably the most influential governor in the history of the modern Federal Reserve System. Aside from Fed chairs, no other governor has left such an imprint on the space within which the Fed makes policy. It is possible, even likely, that there won't be another like him.

With all respect for the work that Tarullo has done as governor, this conclusion is not meant to be a compliment of his singular talents. In fact, there are four reasons for Tarullo's successes, three of which are essentially out of his control. First, Tarullo had the support of the president, and in fact was nominated as part of a team of regulators meant to change the way we think of financial regulation. Second—and perhaps more important—he had the full support of the Fed chair. Unlike other shifts in power within the Federal Reserve System over its history, Tarullo's influence was not wrested from an unwilling Fed chair but reflected a willing conces-sion. From the very beginning of Tarullo's tenure, Ben Bernanke deferred to him on banking regulatory matters, despite Bernanke's total of six years' experience as a banking regulator by the time Tarullo came aboard in January 2009. Third, at the time of his ap-pointment, the external political climate was highly favorable to Tarullo's reform orientation. Fourth and finally, Tarullo's own ex-pertise on the subject made him well suited to executing his agenda. Only the fourth factor was within Tarullo's control.

THE COUNTEREXAMPLE:
THE CASE OF ALAN BLINDER

To make sense of how important these other factors have been, it's worth comparing Tarullo's tenure to that of another distinguished— but far less influential—predecessor, Alan S. Blinder, the Fed's vice chair for eighteen months in the mid-1990s.[22]

Blinder was a star economist at Princeton, a well-regarded and influential macroeconomist. He came to Washington after Bill Clinton was elected and joined the administration as a member of the Council of Economic Advisers. When the vice chairmanship of the Board of Governors came open, Blinder was Clinton's pick, Clinton's first nomination to the Fed's Board. In fact, given that the previous three presidential terms had been Republican—two for Reagan, one for George H. W. Bush—Blinder was the first Democratic appointee in fourteen years.

Despite his stature—Blinder was certainly a more experienced economist than Greenspan, for example—he lacked the strong support of Greenspan. In fact, Greenspan may have viewed Blinder as a competitor: At the time of his appointment to the Fed, it was rumored that he was the logical choice as Alan Greenspan's successor when the latter's term as chairman ended in 1996.[23]

Perhaps as a result, Blinder's brief tenure was marked by discord between Blinder and the Fed staff, and Blinder and Greenspan, nearly from the beginning. Although this story may be apocryphal, it is said that when Fed insiders learned of Clinton's intention to nominate Blinder, one governor reviewed Blinder's record and reported that, while probably softer on inflation than the Republican central bankers he'd be joining, "it's not like he's a Communist." Greenspan allegedly replied: "I would have preferred if he were a Communist."[24]

The clash between Greenspan and Blinder didn't come through formal channels in differing votes on inflation. Blinder didn't dissent once during his time on the FOMC. They clashed instead on the internal politics of the Federal Reserve, by then completely in the thrall of the oracular Greenspan. One senior staffer's philosophical take on the dispute summarizes perfectly the tension between the legal form of the Fed's governing committees and the power of personality in abridging those forms. "You have an institution here where the Board of Governors is supposed, by design of legislation, to run the place," he said. Instead, it "is really run by the chairman and the senior staff, with the board having a certain rubber-stamp authority." Blinder didn't come to the Fed to be a rubber stamp. "He was looking for changes."[25]

Changes, however, weren't looking for Blinder. He clashed with the senior staff economists who expected he would accept the economic models they presented without challenge, as his colleagues on the FOMC had long done. Since those models and conclusions almost invariably supported the policy recommendations that Greenspan supported, Blinder sought more options from the staff, more interaction with junior staffers, and more opportunities for the other governors to participate in the hard work of making the nation's economic policy. Ultimately, it just didn't work; Blinder left the board after eighteen months and returned to academia. Greenspan was confirmed to this third term as chair a month later.[26]

Why would Blinder fail when Tarullo had succeeded? It is obviously not in the difference in their credentials, expertise, or respect they commanded in their fields: although law professors and economists don't compare perfectly, it is hard to imagine a better credentialed or regarded academic than Blinder. The difference was in the other three factors. Even though Blinder had been on Clinton's economic policy staff before his appointment to the Fed, he was not installed with a mandate to change the place. (As we will see in chapter 8, on presidential interactions with Fed chairs, Clinton made wooing Greenspan a central part of his political strategy.) In the announcement accompanying his appointment, Clinton did not identify the problem of chair-centrism at the Fed, nor the need for internal institutional reform. The economic climate of the time also did not suggest a public appetite for reform along the lines that Blinder proposed.

Perhaps most important of all, Greenspan did not support Blinder's efforts at reform. While Blinder denied any personal "feud" between the two, the changes Blinder sought were changes in the way that other governors participated in the Fed's policy-making process. In this way, whether Blinder was a competitor for the chair or not, he was certainly a threat to Greenspan's leadership: any enhancement of the governors that Blinder had in mind came at the expense of the chair and his close, dominating relationship with the senior staff.

The Fed is an institution of institutions. The chair has come to dominate it in the public attention, but such dominance is required neither by law nor by practice. As another former governor put it in his memoir, success on the Board of Governors is not a question of credentials or brilliance. "The fact is that it's also relationships—with the staff, your peers, and the Chairman—that influence your effectiveness as a governor." The individuals and their relationships within the Fed shape its institutional policy-making space in profound ways.[27]

CONCLUSION: CENTRAL BANKING BY COMMITTEE?

This chapter has argued that the law of the Fed governance and its practice are often at cross-purposes. The result is a curious dynamic: the Ulysses/punch-bowl theory of Fed independence emphasizes law but also emphasizes the idea that the central bank is a single, monolithic unit. In the case of the Federal Reserve, this conception is inconsistent with the Federal Reserve Act: any influence individual Fed chairs have on the system comes from the exercise of leadership, not the enforcement of statutory authority.

Committee structures in central banking became a norm around the world, part of a "quiet revolution" in central banking in the last twenty-five years. Even though the Federal Reserve System has consisted of a multitude of committees since its first founding in 1913, it does not offer a very clear example of a central bank led by a committee. The reality is a committee-based legal structure that can lie dormant, awaiting individual leadership and personality to give it practical effect. When, how, and whether that transition between legal structure and practical policy occurs can be difficult to predict.

CHAPTER 4

THE "DOUBLE GOVERNMENT" OF THE FEDERAL RESERVE

THE ECONOMISTS AND THE LAWYERS

But now the real power is not in the Sovereign, it is in the . . . hands of a committee appointed by Parliament, and of the chairman of that committee. . . . No other select committee has any comparable power; and considering how carefully we have fettered and limited the powers of all other subordinate authorities, our allowing so much discretionary power on matters peculiarly dangerous and peculiarly delicate to rest in the sole charge of one secret committee is exceedingly strange. No doubt it may be beneficial; many seeming anomalies are so, but at first sight it does not look right.

—*Walter Bagehot, 1867*

On September 15, 2008, Lehman Brothers filed for bankruptcy. It was the largest bankruptcy in U.S. history—at the time of the filing, Lehman had assets valued at $691 billion, roughly twice as big as the second-largest bankruptcy. Besides its size, the Lehman bankruptcy is unusual in another respect: it was not an unforeseen event, but a governmental decision. That decision was made by the Federal Reserve.

Much has been said about this fateful decision, about the economic consequences, about the political pressures surrounding the decision, about the changes to the world economic order that it has meant. But for purposes of understanding the Fed's internal governance, there's another important aspect to this decision: according to Fed Chair Ben Bernanke and others, the Lehman decision wasn't based on economics or politics and wasn't even a decision made by the Fed chair. It was, these insiders claim, a legal decision made by Fed lawyers. This chapter will have more to say about this explanation of events. But what it and other examples illustrate is that the Fed's policy-making space is influenced not only by its senior leadership, such as the chair or the governors. What these examples demonstrate is that there are many other hands on the Fed's tiller. To understand the Federal Reserve, we must understand the Fed's staff.[1]

As with so many other discussions of central banking, the focus in this chapter owes itself in some sense to the Victorian essayist Walter Bagehot. But whereas most discussions of central banking that invoke Bagehot look to his treatise *Lombard Street*, his other famous book, *The English Constitution*, tells us something about where to look for power within the Federal Reserve System. Bagehot argued that it is in the "double government," or the work behind the throne of the Crown where we can seek the real practice of English government and lawmaking: the Crown's ministers who performed their work as a kind of all-poweful parliamentary committee.

Bagehot diagnosed and described the fiction that the work of governing was located in the Crown but also sought to defend that fiction: "We must not let daylight upon magic," he wrote. Here, we will part ways with Bagehot. In this chapter, we will let the daylight into the Fed's inner governance and focus attention on the lawyers and economists who play such a significant role in shaping Fed policy. The effort is not an exposé, nor is it designed to discredit the work of the Fed staff. It is, instead, to note (as with the epigraph that opens the chapter, that the Fed staff has a uniquely important power: "considering how carefully we have fettered and limited the powers of all other subordinate authorities, our allowing so much discretionary power on matters peculiarly dangerous and peculiarly delicate to rest in the sole charge of one secret committee is exceedingly strange." This chapter is an effort to understand that power and how the decision to grant it to Fed staff has shaped the institution.[2]

More specifically, this chapter looks at the role of staff economists and staff lawyers within the Federal Reserve System generally, including the ways that each influence policy and shape discussions of the roles of the Fed in government and in the global economy. It also looks closely at two senior staffers who have exercised enormous influence over policy making at the Federal Reserve: Edwin Truman, an economist and head of the Division of International Finance at the Fed from 1977 to 1998, and Scott Alvarez, the Fed's general counsel from 2004 (still serving as of this writing). These examples are meant to be illustrative of the broader influence that senior economists and lawyers have on the space within which the Fed operates. The argument is not that these individuals exercised extraordinary power nefariously or inconsistently with public ends. It is only that they exercise extraordinary power, much more than many in the general public realize.

THE BARONS

At the Board of Governors in Washington, D.C., there is a select group of economists that profoundly influences the Fed's entire policy-making apparatus. They are the heads of the Fed's chief divisions: Monetary Affairs, Research and Statistics, and International Finance, together sometimes called the three "barons" of the Federal Reserve. These senior economists aren't mere adjuncts to the Fed. As one former governor recalled, "I often said when we were assembled together in a meeting that the governors work for the staff instead of the other way around." Even their salaries reflect this prominence. Their salaries are, with other senior staffers, higher than those of the governors, including the Fed chair. Recalled another former governor, "This agency is probably the closest thing in the United States government to a British ministry, where the permanent civil servants, who are highly skilled and deeply entrenched, dominate." The senior staff seemed to agree. According to one news account, a "departing senior staff member [at the Fed] said he never had an interest in becoming a board member; it would have reduced his influence over the Fed's policies if he did."[3]

To illustrate, consider the example of Edwin "Ted" Truman, the head of the Division of International Finance from 1977 to 1998, appointed to his position by the Board of Governors during the Burns Fed and in place through Miller, Volcker, and Greenspan. Truman began his career as an academic economist at Yale (where he was, interestingly, on a committee that conducted the oral examination of a graduate student named Janet Yellen). In 1972, he left academia and joined the Board of Governors. Within five years, he rose to the head of the Division of International Finance.[4]

At the board, Truman was regarded as a brilliant but temperamental figure who "thought he was guardian of the gate," one former governor recalled. "Governors were political types who came and went, and he was the protector of the institution, and he knew what was best." By the time Greenspan arrived in 1987, Truman's status as the keeper of the Fed's international portfolio was established, a position Greenspan defended through a number of challenges. According to contemporaneous accounts, for some international meetings that Greenspan could not attend, Truman would go in his place. Only the vice chair could be an exception to that rule: a presidentially appointed, Senate-confirmed Fed governor could not.[5]

Interestingly, it wasn't a question of economic expertise that prevented governors from taking a more robust role in these international affairs. For example, Bill Clinton considered appointing Peter Kenen, an internationally renowned monetary economist, to the Fed's board. Before Kenen would accept the position, he consulted with Greenspan and asked if he (Kenen) would be able to play a policy role in international affairs. Greenspan said no. "I was told that the representational role of the board in international matters were his and the vice chairman's and [Truman's]" Kenen recalled. "I could not expect to attend many international meetings on behalf of the board." Greenspan and Truman would also handle the more politically sensitive role of "close coordination" of international economic policy with the U.S. Treasury; the governors had no role to play there. Truman's work, then, was not merely the technocratic function of crunching numbers and shaping models where the staff economists exercised their influence: Kenen was qualified for that job, too. It was in the inherently political and diplomatic functions, as well. This was despite the fact that Kenen would have been the U.S. president's representative, usually the only qualification necessary to engage on the government's behalf on high-level policy issues.[6]

No period of international economic history demonstrates Truman's influence more than the financial crises in Mexico and Southeast Asia in the 1990s. During the Mexican crisis, called by some the "first crisis of the twenty-first century," many feared that Mexico's default on its public debt would not only wreak havoc on its own economy, but also affect its major trading partners—including the United States. The Clinton administration, led by Secretary of the Treasury Robert Rubin, wanted to avoid a Mexican default and sought authorization from Congress to extend a $40 billion loan: a "bailout" of the peso.[7]

Congress balked and refused to budge. Clinton's team at the Treasury—including then under secretary of the treasury Larry Summers, the assistant secretary Jeffrey Shafter, and deputy assistant secretary for international monetary and financial policy, Timothy Geithner—sought to figure out a way to use authority already granted them to stave off the crisis. The best they could do was use what is called the Exchange Stabilization Fund, a pot of money given to the Treasury to influence exchange rates without tapping directly into the central bank's money supply.

But even the Exchange Stabilization Fund (ESF) wasn't enough to provide what the Mexicans needed, and the Clinton administration's efforts to secure congressional support for more funds failed. Here is where Truman came in: he engineered a way for the Treasury and Fed to join forces to expand the reach of the ESF. Mexico could exchange pesos for dollars through an "international swap facility"—a structure the Fed had used before—between the Fed and the Bank of Mexico, an enduring policy move that had implications for the way the Fed would handle the financial crisis of 2008. Through the swap facility, Mexico could get access to dollars from the Federal Reserve that it could not secure in the private markets, or at least not at such favorable rates. Truman's policy innovation had allowed the Clinton Treasury and the Fed to overcome the lack of congressional authorization.[8]

The financial crises following soon thereafter in Southeast Asia saw Truman's similar participation in a policy and diplomatic role. As the currencies, financial systems, and economies of the developing Asian countries such as Indonesia and Thailand began to teeter, they threatened to bring down the rest of the region. The Clinton Treasury and the Federal Reserve sprang into action, with much of the work of selling their plans to the governments, including heads of state of the affected countries, falling to Timothy Geithner (at this time deputy assistant secretary for international monetary and financial policy) and, again, Truman. They met with foreign politicians, finance ministers, and central bankers to sell their plans for financial stability. It was high-stakes economic diplomacy and not an exaggeration to say that Truman acted on the country's behalf as one of its chief diplomats. His job titles during these talks stayed the same: staff economist for the FOMC and director of the Board of Governors' Division of International Finance.[9]

Their efforts paid off. First Mexico, then the Asian economies, were spared. *Time* magazine feted Rubin, Summers, and Greenspan as the "Committee to Save the World." While the *Time* article didn't go into detail about Truman's contributions, it should have: much of the policy making and diplomacy that went into those frenzied months and years came from him. By all accounts, although some protested his temper, Truman represented the best thinking on international financial crises within the United States.[10]

Truman's role at the Fed was certainly technocratic. His understanding of international monetary cooperation was considered unparalleled within the Fed, and he drew on that expertise throughout the crises. But it was also highly diplomatic. It is important that his counterparts elsewhere in the government were all political appointees, including future secretary of the treasury Geithner. Their task wasn't writing the policies or writing the rules to support them. It was an act of politics, diplomacy, and judgment, reflecting the value judgments about how U.S. interests should be represented to government officials throughout the world. And yet, Truman was, of course, a staff economist. The idea, then, that the work of the Federal Reserve is pure technocracy, the domain of mathematical economists solving proofs, is grossly inaccurate.

STAFF ECONOMISTS

Truman's globe-trotting adventures fighting international financial crises is an unusual example of staff economist influence on the political process. More often, but not less important, staff economists and their division heads also wield important policy authority inside the Federal Reserve building in Washington and at each of the twelve Federal Reserve Banks. The Federal Reserve System employs hundreds of such economists to play a core policy-making role.

Their roles are largely to serve three research functions: macroeconomic analysis (discerning what is happening in the economy), economic forecasting (discerning what will happen in the economy), and, relatedly, their own academic research. This work requires both technical expertise and also a feel for public policy. The work of monetary policy, financial stability, and everything else that goes on within the Fed is primarily the work of academic economists. For this reason, one Reserve Bank president concluded that, for economists, "university and [Fed] jobs are not all that different in terms of the role of independent research."[11]

Economists clearly dominate the scene at the Fed, at all levels of the bureaucracy. It wasn't always so. While economists have always played an important role in determining the scope of the Fed's power and institutional form, the Fed used to be more dominated by bankers and, to a lesser extent, lawyers. At the end of William McChesney Martin's tenure at the Fed, for example, the former banker let slip that he would "dispense with the kind of analysis" presented by the Fed's growing army of economic forecasters. Martin was swimming against the tide: economists have grown in importance at all levels of the Fed, including at the top. Indeed, being an economist seems to be something of a prerequisite for the Fed chair, not because the chair needs to be running regressions and modeling the economy herself. It's that the Fed chair has to be able to evaluate the work of the staff economists. Without a PhD in economics, according to one former governor, "the Fed's staff will run technical rings around you." And while bankers still dominate the boards of the regional Federal Reserve Banks, their influence as staffers and members of the Board of Governors has waned over time.[12]

The rise of the Fed's economists matters for another reason, beyond the control of the Fed's governors or even chair. The staff economists use their authority to make hiring decisions, plan economic conferences, publish scholarship, and much else that we associate with the production of knowledge in universities. And because the Fed hires so many economists, hosts many more in its conferences, and otherwise influences the nature and tenor of economic debate, what the Fed does in producing economic knowledge matters enormously.

Except the Fed isn't a university. The apparatus of knowledge production that occurs in universities—tenure review, outside publication requirements, public engagement, the airing of different conflicting ideas, and more—does not exist in the same way at the Federal Reserve. Of course, universities are far from perfect places, with compromises on some of these same principles. At the Fed, though, there's simply no way of knowing exactly how the knowledge-production function works with certainty. While Fed economists actively engage with others in the academy, how the Fed makes hiring decisions, plans conferences, or otherwise engages academic outsiders is too opaque to evaluate its objectivity.

From the Fed's perspective, there's a good reason for this opacity. The Fed has a horse in the race for producing economic ideas about its policy mission. Like members of any other institution, those within the Fed want both to perform their task well and, importantly, for others to think that they are performing their task well. In acting as a gatekeeper for the production of economic ideas, both inside and outside the Fed, there is a conflict of interest here: assessing the Fed's performance will sometimes necessarily mean that the assessment comes out the wrong way.

Some of those efforts might be intentional. For example, Paul Krugman—the Nobel Prize–winning economist and *New York Times* columnist famous for his liberal politics and criticisms of free-market economic ideology—spent a decade excluded from participating in the Fed's signature annual conference in Jackson Hole, Wyoming, because of his criticisms of Alan Greenspan. His exclusion became ironic in 2006 when the theme of the conference was, in fact, work that he had pioneered. The Fed's history of freezing out of critics within the economics profession is, unfortunately, a long one.[13]

More often, though, the Fed's failure to publicly engage critics occur not because staff economists or Fed leadership are acting petty or bitter. The problem is understanding the balance between producing knowledge and justifying policy action. And although that balance has profound consequences for public policy, it is not a balance that the public gets to strike.

There is a distinct problem to the rise of economics and economists within the Federal Reserve. Even if a diverse group of economists are consulted, if there is not greater methodological diversity in the approach to thinking about inflation, financial stability, employment, and the rest of the concerns that occupy the Fed, there is the broader risk of homogeneity of views that can lead to unproductive groupthink. As sociologist Neil Fligstein and his coauthors argued, this kind of macroeconomic approach may have played a role in the 2008 financial crisis as the "FOMC failed to see the depth of the problem because of its overreliance on macroeconomics as a framework for making sense of the economy."[14]

The takeover by the economists was gradual, not immediate. Historically, bankers and lawyers played a bigger policy-making role at the Fed than they do today. But there is no denying that the problems of Fed policy are seen as problems of economics. For understanding the Fed as a they, not an it, it is essential to consider not only the legal and political roles of Fed employees, but also their academic and intellectual roles, too.

ENTER THE LAWYERS

One of the fifteen divisions at the Board of Governors is the legal division, headed by the Fed's general counsel. This is unsurprising—every governmental agency has a chief lawyer, and the Fed exists in a world that requires determinations made about a staggering number of laws. And before the financial crisis of 2008, the Fed's lawyers weren't terribly different from their counterparts in other agencies. They served the political appointees in the agencies' main policy tasks: the work of economic analysis, forecasting, and building a monetary policy around both. Administrative law is a technical field, and while few if any area of law is completely divorced from value judgments and ideology, hiring specialists to tell the Fed's policy makers their duties under the statutes and Constitution was seen as a largely technical task.

After the crisis, though, we see something different: the Fed's lawyers were responsible not just for interpreting law, but also making policy. And they do so behind a veil of secrecy that makes it difficult, even impossible to evaluate their work.

Consider two examples. First, the Fed's enforcement proceedings, the administrative process by which banks under Fed oversight are held accountable for violations of federal law. Senior Fed staff members—namely, the director of the Division of Bank Supervision and the general counsel—have authority to supervise the Reserve Banks in reaching consent agreements in banks' enforcement proceedings. Of the over one thousand enforcement actions taken by the Fed over the last ten years, only eleven proceeded to an administrative hearing, and only seven of those eleven proceeded to the Board of Governors. The rest were resolved by the Fed staff.[15]

These enforcement actions are not always minor wrist slaps for failure to get administrative ducks in a row. For example, the Office of the Comptroller of the Currency (OCC) and Federal Reserve approved in April 2013 a multibillion-dollar settlement with major banks regarding their mortgage servicing practices. As Governor Tarullo stated in a letter to Senator Elizabeth Warren, that approval came without a board vote and without any governor requesting a review of the action. To be clear, Governor Tarullo stated that "Board staff frequently consulted with Board members before exercising delegated authority to approve the amendments to the foreclosure consent orders." But, he continues, "there was no vote."[16] These kinds of policy judgments were the staff's—especially the lawyers'—to make.

That lawyers influence an agency's enforcement strategy is not unusual in our administrative state. Nonpolitical appointees have that kind of influence everywhere in the bureaucracy. But the second example of the power of the Fed's lawyers is more unusual, and unique to the Fed. And that is the nature of the Fed's own authority in conducting monetary policy and in its functions as a lender of last resort. There's no mechanism provided by statute or judicial decision to review Fed actions in court.[17]

Section 13(3) of the Federal Reserve Act may be, after the 2008 financial crisis, the act's most famous provision. Before the crisis, only Fed aficionados and lawyers had ever heard of it. The provision was added to the Federal Reserve Act during the Great Depression, at the urging of the Hoover administration, and amended several times over the years. At the time of the 2008 crisis, it provided in part that "in unusual and exigent circumstances," five members of the Board of Governors can lend money through the relevant Federal Reserve Bank to any "individual, partnership, or corporation" so long as the loan is "secured to the satisfaction of the Federal reserve bank." Before making the loan, though, the relevant Reserve Bank has to "obtain evidence" that the individual, partnership, or corporation in question "is unable to secure adequate credit accommodations from other banking institutions."[18]

Note, then, that this authority had only four restrictions: circumstances must be "unusual and exigent," terms not defined by statute; at least five members of the board must vote in favor; the loan had to be secured "to the satisfaction of the Federal reserve bank"; and the "reserve bank had to obtain evidence" that there is no "adequate credit accommodations from other banking institutions." Even the five-vote requirement is honored in the breach: its invocation to authorize the J. P. Morgan acquisition of Bear Stearns was voted on with only four governors under a post-9/11 provision that relaxed the requirement in emergencies, a kind of emergency backdoor to the emergency backdoor.[19]

Under this authority, the Fed loaned money to Bear Stearns, AIG, and many others but refused to lend money to Lehman Brothers sufficient to prevent Lehman's bankruptcy. As mentioned at the beginning of the chapter, the justification for this uneven treatment was a legal one: Bernanke and Geithner have claimed that 13(3) barred them from acting on behalf of Lehman Brothers even as it authorized the bailout for AIG. But to justify this explanation, Geithner had to change its requirements. "Under 13(3)," he wrote, "the Fed could conceivably lend to a nonbank we deemed solvent, but only if it was in such deep trouble that no one else would lend to it, and even then only if we could secure collateral that could plausibly cover our exposure."[20]

This is not what the statute requires. There is no requirement that the institution be objectively solvent; the Reserve Bank only has to be satisfied with the collateral presented. And there is no requirement that "no one else would lend"; there only needed to be evidence—some evidence, any evidence—that the other alternatives weren't "adequate." It is as broad a discretion that Congress could've written short of announcing that the Fed was in the business of giving away free money.[21]

Geithner's defense of the Fed's use of 13(3), repeated by Bernanke—that is, that 13(3) allowed for bailouts at Bear Stearns and AIG (among many others), but not Lehman Brothers—is the product of one of two disconcerting explanations. First, it is purely an ex post rationalization, that in fact the Fed made a huge mistake in failing to bail out Lehman Brothers and was looking for a scapegoat in the Federal Reserve Act. There is some evidence for this explanation. The contemporaneous accounts suggest that the Fed's problem was a failure to complete the sale of Lehman Brothers to a willing buyer, despite near successes, and its mis-judgment of the markets' readiness for the collapse of such a large financial institution.[22]

The second explanation is more relevant to our understanding of the role of the Fed's lawyers. After the Lehman decision, Fed offi-cials like Ben Bernanke and Timothy Geithner did point to the Federal Reserve Act—and their lawyer's interpretations of it—to justify their decision to allow Lehman to fail. Perhaps the lawyers analyzed the statute and guided its enforcement in this inconsistent, even inaccurate way. Return again to the language of 13(3). The only requirements were that the board had to determine that the circumstances were "unusual and exigent," something they had al-ready done in the case of Bear Stearns in March 2008. And the loans to Lehman Brothers had to be secured "to the satisfaction of the Federal reserve bank," something that was left to the Reserve Banks to determine. If the Fed's lawyers approved the loan for Bear but not Lehman, it reflects an extraordinary amount of unreview-able power in the hands of those the public has no input in select-ing. The statute gives ample discretion to make those determina-tions, which means something other than law is dictating the decision-making authority. If the Federal Reserve Act is interpreted by the Fed's in-house lawyers, as Bernanke and Geithner have said, then this is a remarkable delegation of federal policy to the hands of central banking lawyers.

Perhaps there's no avoiding the importance of lawyers making quick and controversial policy judgments as they interpret the law during a crisis. Another aspect of the Fed lawyers' crisis practice is lamentable and impedes meaningful public accountability without any obvious benefit. And that is the so-called Doomsday Book, a secret compilation of legal authorities, precedents, and authorizations available to the Federal Reserve to use in a crisis, what former New York Fed president Tim Geithner called the Fed's "actual firefighting equipment." There are, it appears, three versions of this book: one in use during the financial crisis of 2008, but two others that have been updated to reflect the changes in law (in 2012 and 2014).[23]

What are these authorities? Are the legal interpretations defensible? Did the Board of Governors endorse them? Have the governors read them? The public doesn't know. And here, the influence of the authors of this book—almost certainly the Fed's lawyers—on the Fed's institutional geography is at its most powerful. A "double government," indeed.

IDEOLOGIES OF REGULATION: THE CASE OF SCOTT G. ALVAREZ

The crisis enhanced the status of Fed lawyers not only because of the questions about in-the-moment authority, but also because the legislative response to the crisis was so overwhelmingly detailed. As a result, there is an outsized role that lawyers play not only in enforcement and statutory interpretation, but in the formulation of regulatory policy generally. The Dodd-Frank Act of 2010 is a perfect example of the staggering scope of agency influence not in simply enforcing the law, but in writing it. The act is a huge piece of legislation, but also a dramatic delegation to the administrative agencies of defining the scope and applicability of the law. Because the Fed is the first among equals as a financial regulator, much of that authority falls to the Fed. And because the Fed's lawyers are the staff primarily in charge of overseeing that implementation, the ideologies and values of the Fed's chief lawyer is highly relevant to understanding how the Fed will define the space within which it makes its policies.

During and after the crisis, that chief lawyer—called by some the Fed's "eighth governor"—was Scott G. Alvarez. Alvarez has spent his entire career as a Fed lawyer, becoming the general counsel under Alan Greenspan in 2004.[24] Even with a governor like Daniel Tarullo taking over so much of the Fed's legal apparatus himself, Alvarez has had a major role to play in the implementation of Dodd-Frank's regulatory authorities. As one regulator put it, Alvarez "is a major player in everything. You can't overstate his role. Everything has to go to him for approval and to be passed on."[25] Given that authority and influence, it is important to get a sense of the "power behind the throne," as one profile termed it. Because of the secrecy within the Federal Reserve System generally and around its lawyers specifically, though, it's difficult to discern exactly what Alvarez's views are on regulatory matters. He goes on record with his views on theories of regulation very rarely, almost never.

An exception is his interview for the Financial Crisis Inquiry Commission, a fascinating tour through a Fed lawyer's take on banking history, theories of risk, and the 2008 financial crisis.[26]

The most important upshot from Alvarez's interview is that regulators aren't to blame for the financial crisis, nor is deregulation generally. For example, one key debate following the crisis was how much the political and regulatory climate in the 1980s and 1990s contributed to the financial crisis. During those decades, there was significant enthusiasm to remove New Deal–era restrictions on the kinds of activities that banks and bank holding companies could engage in. Under the New Deal model, banks had to choose between being commercial banks (accepting deposits, interacting with consumers) and being investment banks (advising clients and facilitating access to capital markets). In the Banking Act of 1933, known for its cosponsors Carter Glass and Henry Steagall, banks couldn't do both.[27]

In 1999, after decades of agency and judicial whittling down of the Glass-Steagall restrictions, the wall came down, as Congress passed the Financial Services Modernization Act—better known as

Gramm-Leach-Bliley, for its congressional sponsors. Gramm-Leach-Bliley essentially repealed the almost seventy-year-old Glass-Steagall. Afterward, banks could and did grow much more.

In the wake of the financial crisis of 2008, many criticized this deregulatory impulse, including the repeal of Glass-Steagall, for contributing to the crisis. Scott Alvarez is not among them. His argument, given in his testimony, is that the firms that presented the biggest threat to the system—Bear Stearns, Lehman Brothers, AIG, Freddie Mac, and Fannie Mae, for example—weren't the ones that benefitted from the repeal of Glass-Steagall's demise in the first place, so the problem was very different. But Alvarez went further: not only did Glass-Steagall's repeal not "cause the crisis"; Alvarez also rejected the idea that the repeal "exacerbated the crisis" at all.[28]

It's a defensible view that the financial crisis of 2008 owed itself to other factors beyond the Glass-Steagall's repeal. Here Alvarez's point is a good one. But to say that the deregulation and subsequent dramatic increase in the size of the banks' balance sheet had *nothing* to do with the crisis misses two key points. First, the crisis was extraordinary not only because the financial institutions on the first line of failure—not the ones affected by Glass-Steagall's repeal—imploded, but because their counterparties in the rest of the financial system were next in line. The case in point here was Citigroup, the entity whose very existence in present form owes itself to the fall of Glass-Steagall.[29]

Even if we accept that Alvarez is correct that Glass-Steagall wasn't the salvation of the financial system, the rest of his testimony defending the proposition is a steady march of arguments about why the Fed and its regulatory apparatus in the 1980s and 1990s had little if anything to do with the crisis. The two propositions are related: Glass-Steagall's demise didn't come at a stroke, but through decades of decisions within the Board of Governors and other banking agencies, supported by courts, to provide fewer restrictions on a number of different activities with direct relevance to the financial crisis. The role of the federal banking regulators in facilitating the breakdown of risk control is an essential part of the story of the financial crisis.

One wouldn't know this from Alvarez's retelling. The closest he comes to admitting regulatory failure is that the fractured nature of federal banking regulation, in which agencies share regulatory authority, meant that regulators had a hard time understanding where risk was concentrated in the system. Even Alan Greenspan could admit to greater regulatory failings than that.[30]

Indeed, at one point, the interviewer states what is objectively true: banking regulators in the 1980s and 1990s participated in the erosion of various regulatory standards through their interpretive and enforcement authority that was increasingly liberal in the interpretation of key statutory restrictions. Even this historically inescapable conclusion is too much for Alvarez: "these activities were found by the courts to be permissible," he corrected the interviewer. Bank regulators shouldn't be responsible for what courts decided. Of course, he concedes, "courts wouldn't have had to deal with the problem if the agencies didn't take actions. . . . But in the end, the courts were the deciders."[31]

Alvarez is correct to bring courts into the discussion of deregulation. A key but underdeveloped part of this book's story is the role that courts play in defining the Fed's policy-making space. This doesn't mean that courts don't matter. Especially in the context of administrative law and regulation, doctrines of agency deference have given the Fed and its lawyers the latitude to use their own ideas to give content to sometimes abstruse statutes. To oversimplify a vast set of legal doctrines and cases and scholarship interpreting them, under the canonical standards, when Congress writes an unclear statute, the agency tasked with clarifying the statutory content gets leeway from courts to chart their own path.[32]

Consider, though, what Alvarez's statement means here. A bank regulation from the Fed's Board of Governors and its lawyers authorizes the erosion of some relevant standard that has a direct implication on the financial crisis. Following long-established doctrines of deference to agency action, a court neither endorses nor condemns that interpretation, but lets it stand. And because it does, the court—not the regulator—is responsible for the outcome. That's a stunning theory of agency responsibility.

It is easy to run in the opposite direction and blame Alvarez for too much. He has always had a boss in the Fed chair and Board of Governors, and ultimately, responsibility for any failures or successes cannot lie squarely with him. But given how much power the Federal Reserve Act and the Dodd-Frank Act give to the Board of Governors and the lawyers who advise them in shaping federal policy, it is also important to know who these lawyers are and what they believe about the statutes, regulations, and policies they are assigned to interpret. Here, the Ulysses/punch-bowl theory of Fed independence, with its emphasis on technocracy and insulation from politics, is worse than useless. These judgments about the permissible scope of banking activities and the requirements of law are not exclusively, perhaps not even mainly, technocratic judgments. They reflect the values of the people making them. Because the Fed's board and its staff lie under a uniform, mystical blanket of Fed independence, it can be difficult to discern exactly what those personal values are.

CONCLUSION

That institutional insiders exercise extraordinary influence over policy is not news. Some of the earliest critics of the administrative state worried about bureaucrats shielded from democratic accountability. The defense of these kinds of technocratic, meritocratic positions was that the alternative—a political spoils system whereby an incoming administration could summarily fire his predecessors' appointments—was wasteful and corrupt.

What the discussion in this chapter suggests is that there is a line between the exercise of technocratic judgment and value judgment that gets crossed the higher within the Fed a technocrat rises. This chapter has focused especially on the general counsel, given the lack of reviewability for his decisions, and the experience of Edwin Truman, given the extraordinary position to influence national policy well beyond the Fed that he exercised during the crises of the late 1990s. The question we will leave to the book's final chapter is whether the current failure to subject these staff leaders to presidential appointment is appropriate given the authority they exercise. The Fed's chief economists approach that line; in light of the financial crisis, the Fed's chief lawyer crosses it.[33]

CHAPTER 5

THE VESTIGIAL AND UNCONSTITUTIONAL FEDERAL RESERVE BANKS

A many-reserve system, if some miracle should put it down in Lombard Street, would seem monstrous there. Nobody would understand it, or confide in it.

—*Walter Bagehot, 1873*

Throughout the history of the Federal Reserve System, the curious Federal Reserve Banks, sometimes called the "regional Feds," have been a source of controversy. They came into the world as part of the Wilsonian Compromise on the two structural debates discussed in chapter 1: whether the functions of central banking should be in public or private hands, and whether central banking functions should be centralized in a single entity or spread among many. To these questions, the Wilsonian Federal Reserve Act of 1913 sought a system that would balance interests off one another in hopes of pleasing all sides of the debate. As we have seen, in 1935, Marriner Eccles and FDR replaced that system with a mostly nonfederalized central bank located in Washington controlled by individuals appointed to their posts by the president, confirmed by the U.S. Senate.

Part of the problem of the original Federal Reserve System was—and is—the same one Bagehot described with a counter-factual Bank of England, or a "many-reserve system": "Nobody would understand it." Eccles deserves credit for his mostly successful attempt to simplify the Fed's governance structure, but he didn't succeed entirely. The twelve Reserve Banks—despite owing their existence to a historical compromise that few understand and fewer can explain—continue among us.

This chapter takes up the questions of how we can understand these institutions as a matter of governance, constitutional law, public policy, and congressional politics. A lack of public understanding of a confused governance structure is problematic enough. The structure may also be unconstitutional. While assessing that constitutional claim is the focus of most of this chapter, we will also explore whether the commonly proposed benefits of the hybrid governance structure bear up under examination, and why the present system has endured so long, despite its obvious defects.

WHAT ARE THE FEDERAL RESERVE BANKS?

What, exactly, are the Federal Reserve Banks? That question is easier to ask than to answer. The Federal Reserve Banks have always evaded easy definition, in large part because they began their lives as private corporations roughly dedicated to a public function and have become, over time, more and more like public regulatory institutions. In the process, they have retained elements of both public agencies and private corporations.

Legally, the Reserve Banks are private corporations chartered under federal law. They have stockholders: the private commercial banks—like Wells Fargo, Citigroup, and the like. The banks that join the Federal Reserve System must buy stock in the Reserve Banks and in turn receive a dividend set by statute at 6 percent.

Those private bank stockholders also elect two-thirds of the members of the Reserve Bank's board of directors. Each board is divided into three classes. Class A directors are stockholder bankers selected by the stockholder banks. Class B directors are nonbankers selected by the stockholder banks. And Class C directors are nonbankers selected by the Fed's Board of Governors in Washington.

Until 2010, the directors voted as a whole to select the Reserve Bank president. After the Dodd-Frank Act of 2010, only Class B and C directors take that vote, which is in turn reviewable by the Board of Governors. Even with the Dodd-Frank change in the voting process, it is unclear whether the Class A directors—that is, the private commercial bankers elected by other private commercial bankers—still participate in the vetting and selection discussions of the Fed's personnel. Also, under statute, all the directors from all classes vote together to fire the president of the local Federal Reserve Bank, for any reason they deem necessary.

The board of directors, under the Federal Reserve Act, is required to "perform the duties usually appertaining to the office of directors of banking associations and all such duties as are prescribed by law."[1] Beyond the election of the directors (and the directors' selection of the Reserve Bank president), though, the idea that commercial banks function as the Reserve Banks' private stockholders doesn't really fit. The banks can purchase only so many Reserve Bank shares and can't sell that stock to others. If the Reserve Banks are ever liquidated as federal bank corporations, the surplus goes to the U.S. government, not to the banks. In these senses, the Reserve Banks remain, much like the Federal Reserve System generally, creatures of statute, not of private contract.

The form of ownership is important, though: It is this corporate structure that leads to accusations that the Federal Reserve System is owned by the banks it regulates. But with the crucial exception of the appointment and removal of the Reserve Bank president—much more on that below—this critique is overstated.[2]

If they are not private corporations, neither are they purely government agencies. In 1952, when asked by Congressman Wright

Patman—a perennial scourge of the Federal Reserve System during his fifty years of service in the House of Representatives—about the legal status of the Federal Reserve Banks, the newly appointed Fed chair William McChesney Martin wouldn't give a straight answer. According to Martin, they were "corporate instrumentalities of the Federal Government created by Congress for the performance of governmental functions." The Reserve Bank presidents, in a joint statement in response to the same question, said that they were "government instrumentalities," not government "agencies," meaning that they were "partially part of the private economy and are part of the functioning of the Government (although not technically a part of the Government)." This ambiguity allowed the Banks to let the "public interest" be "dominant in their policies," even as they maintained their private "independence."[3]

In the confusingly legalistic language of "corporate instrumentality" or "government instrumentality" and "partially part" and "although not technically," we get a sense that nobody knew exactly how to define these strange quasi-private, quasi-public structures. This public-private ambiguity has been the source of extraordinary controversy over the course of the Fed's history.

THE RESERVE BANKS AND THE PRESIDENT: THE FED'S CONSTITUTIONAL PROBLEM

This definitional problem also has constitutional implications. As Patman, that congressional gadfly of the Federal Reserve, put it, a "slight acquaintance with American constitutional theory and practice demonstrates that, constitutionally, the Federal Reserve is a pretty queer duck." I'd go further: as far as the governance of the Federal Reserve Banks are concerned, the Fed is outside the constitutional framework entirely. If we cannot quite determine whether the Reserve Banks are public or private, political control over the functions they perform also becomes confused.[4]

To answer the constitutional question, we must begin with the somewhat curious approach that courts and lawyers take when analyzing the institutional design of governmental agencies. For almost a century, the Supreme Court has staked limits to congressional experimentation in the staffing of governmental agencies. Most of that judicial and scholarly focus has been on how "independent" from the president Congress can make the leadership of new agencies. A word of caution is appropriate here. As with the Ulysses/punch-bowl approach to central bank independence, "agency independence" means something very specific in the legal and constitutional context. It is a "legal term of art in public law, referring to agencies headed by officials that the President may not remove without cause. Such agencies are, by definition, independent agencies; all other agencies are not." Thus, "agency independence" in the standard sense is even narrower than the Ulysses/ punch-bowl approach: it refers only to whether the president can freely fire the person or persons in charge of the agency. Of course, one legal feature is not enough to tell us much about the operational independence of an agency, including and perhaps especially the Federal Reserve. Because of this narrowness, there is near scholarly unanimity that the removability focus is something of a fetish.[5]

One of the main arguments in this book is that "independence" as an analytical category isn't a very useful one largely because it is too narrow and legalistic. Even so, as the Supreme Court has explained it, the question of who has the constitutional authority to appoint senior governmental officials isn't simply a question of "etiquette or protocol": ensuring that the most important officials of the United States government—including members of the Federal Open Market Committee—conform to the requirements of the public accountability at the appointments level is "among the significant structural safeguards of the constitutional scheme." And when we make that constitutional inquiry about the Fed, we learn something important: as presently designed, the Reserve Banks are almost certainly unconstitutional.[6]

THE LEGAL DOCTRINE:
APPOINTMENTS AND REMOVABILITY

To understand why, we need to get a better sense of the legal doctrine as it starts in the U.S. Constitution and has been developed by
courts. Article II, section 2, clause 2, of the Constitution requires
"Officers of the United States" to be appointed by the president
with the Senate's advice and consent. If Congress wants to set up a
bureau or agency or department staffed by an officer of the United
States, presidential appointment and Senate confirmation is the required constitutional minimum. But there's an exception, written
in the Constitution itself, for "inferior Officers." In those cases,
Congress may vest "in the President alone, in the Courts of Law, or
in the Heads of Departments" the appointment of the inferior
officers.

The first question in determining the constitutionality of an appointment process is whether the officer in question—here, the heads
of the Reserve Banks—are "principal" or "inferior" officers. Because
the Constitution doesn't define the term, the Supreme Court has had
to assess different officers on a case-by-case basis. For example, in
Morrison v. Olson, a case we'll revisit in a moment, the court had to
decide whether an "independent prosecutor," one appointed by the
attorney general to investigate the U.S. president, was "principal" or
"inferior." This prosecutor wielded a staggering amount of authority
to investigate the president and his subordinates but was not appointed as a principal officer under the Appointments Clause. Despite the prosecutor's power to investigate even his own boss, the
court concluded that the prosecutor was still an inferior officer and
therefore could be appointed by the head of a department, in his case
the attorney general.[7]

The distinguishing factor in *Morrison* was that the appointment
was relatively short, limited in scope, and, importantly, could still
be ended by a superior who *was* a principal officer (again, the attorney general). As the court put it in a later case, "[w]hether one
is an 'inferior' officer depends on whether he has a superior." More-

over, " 'inferior officers' are officers whose work is directed and supervised at some level" by officers appointed by the president and confirmed by the Senate. If a federal officer has a boss who went through the presidential-appointment-and-Senate-confirmation process, that officer is by definition an inferior one.[8]

The first constitutional question we must tackle, then, is to determinine how the Reserve Bank presidents are appointed, and whether, in their roles on the FOMC, they have a boss subject to the Appointments Clause. There is a second question, which looks not at the Appointments Clause but the general principle of separation of powers that underlies the constitutional scheme everywhere.

And that question deals not with how officers are appointed, but how they are fired. This principle is familiar from grade school civics. We have three branches of government: executive (the president), legislative (Congress), and judicial (the courts). The president's executive function is defined in the Constitution—he must "take care that the laws be faithfully executed." He is one person, but his administration is legion. Hence the need to appoint officers, principal and inferior, to do the work of presidential administration. We've already discussed some legal restrictions on how these officials within the administration get their jobs; the separation of powers question concerns who gets to decide when and how they are held accountable if they pursue policies inconsistent with the public good. The main democratic mechanism for that kind of accountability is political pressure on the president to defend or fire an official in his government for his policies. If one of the president's appointees is running federal policy in a way that a citizen finds inappropriate, he can raise hell until the buck eventually stops at the president's desk and forces the president to confront his personnel strategy. And the decision he makes, either way, will have consequences for the president's reelection or legacy.[9]

Congress, however, has sometimes sought to control the appointment process more robustly than merely making a political stink about executive personnel decisions. This is where the separation of powers comes into play: At what point does congressional meddling with the appointment and removal power become an unconstitutional invasion of the executive function?

The Supreme Court encountered this very issue in 1926. Congress had passed a statute that subjected the appointment of postmasters—historically, a very important part of presidential patronage—to the usual advice and consent of the Senate but also subjected the removal of the postmaster to the same restriction. That is, if the president wanted to fire a postmaster, he needed the Senate's advice and consent.[10]

In *Myers v. United States*, Chief Justice William Howard Taft reviewed the statute and concluded it was a bridge too far. Chief Justice Taft's opinion—one he was uniquely qualified to give as the only former president to serve on the Supreme Court—concluded that the president must have more authority to determine who could or could not continue to represent him to the American people. The president must have some "power of removing those for whom he can not continue to be responsible." As a result, this particular form of congressional meddling in the officer-removal process was declared unconstitutional.[11]

It might have been thought, in fact, that *any* such restriction would run afoul of the same principle. Ten years later, however, the court retreated from this view. In *Humphrey's Executor v. United States*, the court confronted a situation where President Franklin Roosevelt fired the head of an independent agency for purely policy reasons, despite a statutory prohibition from doing so. The problem was William Humphrey, a commissioner of the Federal Trade Commission who was a notorious anti–New Dealer who loathed the newly elected Roosevelt. At first, FDR tried to persuade Humphrey to do the honorable thing: "You will, I know, realize that I do not feel that your mind and my mind go along together," the president wrote the commissioner, "and, frankly, I think it is best for the people of this country that I should have a full confidence." But Humphrey wouldn't budge: he wouldn't be talked down from his perch inside a government he plainly detested. And so FDR fired him, by letter: "Effective as of this date you are hereby removed from the office of Commissioner of the Federal Trade Commission."[12]

Humphrey sued, and after he died, his estate continued the litigation (hence the petitioner's name, "Humphrey's Executor"). Humphrey's argument was a winning one, from a statutory perspective. When Congress had set up the FTC, it specifically protected its commissioners from being arbitrarily dismissed. They could be fired only for "inefficiency, neglect of duty, or malfeasance." Humphrey had been guilty of disagreeing with the president on federal policy, not of any of these other derelictions.

From a constitutional perspective, though, Humphrey looked on much shakier ground. The court had already nixed this provision from an earlier statute, giving the president more control over his administration's personnel. And, of course, *Myers* suggested that the president could fire whom he pleased: Congress's role was not to dictate an administration's personnel policy.[13]

This time, however, the Supreme Court didn't agree with that constitutional analysis and unanimously ruled against the Roosevelt administration. Congress could limit the president's hand in removing federal officers, the Court reasoned, for *independent* agencies; only for *executive* agencies were such restrictions illegitimate. The difference was in the nature of these agencies. For the "independent" agencies, those tasks were different. An independent commission like the FTC was "to be nonpartisan; and it must, from the very nature of its duties, act with entire impartiality," the court reasoned. Such an agency's functions "are neither political nor executive, but predominantly quasi judicial and quasi legislative," with members "called upon to exercise the trained judgment of a body of experts appointed by law and informed by experience." As a result of *Humphrey's Executor*, these statutory restrictions on a president's ability to fire his appointees became the definitional hallmark of agency independence.[14]

For the rest of the twentieth century, the court kept this principle in place, expanding in some places, limiting in others. In *Morrison v. Olson*—as discussed above, the 1988 case about the independent counsel that explains the difference between "principal" and "inferior" officers—the court confronted a different kind of statutory restriction: removal protection not for the head of "quasi legislative" or "quasi judicial" commission, but inside the executive itself, in that case the Department of Justice. The court concluded that Congress gave the attorney general, an officer directly responsible to the president, "several means of supervising or controlling" the independent counsel, including the ability to "remove the counsel for good cause." There was thus no constitutional problem with the arrangement.[15]

In 2010, in *Free Enterprise Fund v. Public Company Accounting Oversight Board*, the Supreme Court confronted the combination of *Humphrey's Executor* and *Morrison*, what one judge called "*Humphrey's Executor* squared": agency heads that the president cannot fire except for good cause (in *Free Enterprise Fund*, the commissioners of the Securities Exchange Commission) who in turn cannot fire their subordinates except for good cause (here, members of the Public Company Accounting Oversight Board). The court held that "such multilevel protection from removal is contrary to Article II's vesting of the executive power in the President" and thus inconsistent with constitutional principles of separation of powers. Two levels of firing restrictions are one too many.[16]

To sum up the state of the law as of 2010: principal officers of the federal government need a presidential nomination and the Senate's advice and consent to be consistent with the Appointments Clause; inferior officers can be appointed by other governmental officials, including the heads of departments. Separate from the Appointments Clause, principles of separation of powers regulate Congress's ability to protect a federal officer from at-will employment termination: Congress can insulate an officer from getting fired by the President or the president's representative for any or no reason. But there is a limit: No nesting of such protections is allowed. Layers of bureaucrats cannot become entrenched from presidential supervision like so many Russian dolls.

THE RESERVE BANKS' UNCONSTITUTIONAL APPOINTMENTS PROCESS

How, then, do the Reserve Banks fit within that constitutional system? To answer that question, we must consider again the circuitously designed Federal Open Market Committee (FOMC). As we saw in chapter 1, Congress created the Federal Open Market Committee in 1933 as the Federal Reserve System's monetary policy committee. The institutional effort was to centralize what had been the quasi-autonomous monetary policies of the twelve Reserve Banks, themselves created under the original Federal Reserve Act of 1913. Two years later, in the Banking Act of 1935, Congress refashioned the FOMC to include all seven members of the newly created Board of Governors of the Federal Reserve System. Post-1935, the FOMC was made up of five of the twelve Reserve Bank presidents on a rotating basis. After 1942, the president of the Federal Reserve Bank of New York became a permanent member of the FOMC. By convention but not statute, he is also vice chair of the committee. The committee meets eight times per year to announce its outlook on the global and national economy and its decisions regarding various features of monetary policy.[17]

It is the presence of the Reserve Banks on the FOMC, and the fact that the president has nothing to do with their appointment or removal that creates constitutional problems, both with respect to the Appointments Clause on the one hand and separation of powers on the other.

First, on appointments, the Reserve Bank presidents are unconstitutionally appointed whether they are principal or inferior officers. In their rotating capacity as members of the FOMC, they certainly look like "principal officers," as the Supreme Court has interpreted that term. That's because they aren't supervised by anyone on the FOMC. As members of the committee, Reserve Bank presidents' votes count the same as those of their would-be superiors, the president-appointed, Senate-confirmed Board Governors. Indeed, again, it is the New York Fed president who sits in the second chair of the FOMC: if anything, he is "supervising" the Board of Governors, not the other way around.

But even if the Reserve Bank presidents were inferior officers, the Constitution doesn't give Congress free rein on those appointments. An inferior officer has to be appointed by "the President alone, . . . the Courts of Law, or . . . the Heads of Departments." The Reserve Banks' boards of directors—those in charge of the presidents' appointments—are neither courts of law nor heads of departments. And the president has nothing to do with the appointment of the banks' presidents. As discussed above, the Reserve Bank presidents are appointed by two-thirds of the bank's directors, subject to approval of the Board of Governors. The president never formally indicates any preference for their appointment to their posts at the Reserve Banks.[18]

Second, the Federal Reserve Banks also fail on the separation of powers "removability" question. Just as the president has no authority to appoint the Reserve Bank presidents, he has no authority to remove them. The Reserve Bank presidents are removable at the pleasure of the Reserve Bank directors, from all three classes. (Note that while the Dodd-Frank Act of 2010 took the bankers on the Reserve Bank boards out of the business of appointing the Reserve Bank presidents, the act did nothing about the bankers' ability to fire those presidents.) The Board of Governors can fire the Reserve Bank directors, but only after "the cause of such removal" is "forthwith communicated in writing by the Board of Governors of the Federal Reserve System to the removed officer or director and to said bank." That takes us to the Board of Governors. The president can also fire the Board members only "for cause," meaning, generally, the *Humphrey's Executor* limitation to "inefficiency, neglect of duty, or malfeasance."[19]

If this all seems very confusing, that confusion is part of the constitutional problem. Let's take an example: suppose the U.S. president does not like the way that the president of the New York Fed has been voting on the FOMC. To fire him the president must do the following:

1. Ask the Board of Governors to fire the New York Fed president, instructing them that he will deem their failure to comply with the request as "cause" for their own termination. The president must send this message not to the chair alone, but to all seven governors.

2. The governors must then turn to the New York Fed's directors and say that they themselves will be removed if they fail to fire the Reserve Bank president, as the U.S. president requested.

3. The New York Fed's directors—all three classes, including the two put there by the private bankers—would then have to fire the Reserve Bank president, who is removable at the pleasure of the board. The bankers' representatives would have to agree that the Reserve Bank president's failure to honor the U.S. president's policies—not their own—was sufficient for the Reserve Bank president's removal.[20]

It is precisely this kind of nesting of removal restrictions that the Supreme Court has held violates the Constitution. The president cannot remove bank president members of the FOMC without reaching through two explicit for-cause removal restrictions, on top of a third layer of at-will removability: from the U.S. president, to the Board of Governors (layer 1), to the Reserve Bank board of directors (layer 2), to the Reserve Bank president (layer 3). If the PCAOB (Public Company Accounting Oversight Board) was "*Humphrey's* squared," then the FOMC may be *Humphrey's* cubed.

Of course, the relationships between the three layers in the FOMC and the two in the SEC-PCAOB are different—the Reserve Bank presidents and the governors are colleagues on the FOMC, rather than separate, ostensibly hierarchical entities. To the extent that this difference matters, it only makes the Reserve Banks' constitutional difficulties worse. For these reasons, the Reserve Banks and FOMC, as currently governed, are unconstitutional. The separation between the U.S. president and the Reserve Bank presidents is simply too great.[21]

THE DECLINING SIGNIFICANCE OF THE BOARD OF GOVERNORS

Because the FOMC votes by a majority, and the Board of Governors have a statutory seven-to-five majority, it's tempting to think this doesn't matter. In fact, a high turnover rate and a presidential failure to reappoint governors means that the statutory majority for the governors isn't as ironclad as it seems. Figure 5.1 shows the

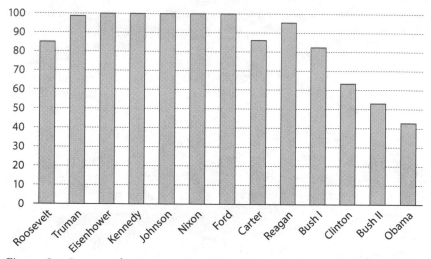

Figure 5.1. Percent of time governors enjoyed a majority on the Federal Open Market Committee, by president. *Source*: Board of Governors of the U.S. Federal Reserve System.

historical trend. After the newly created Board of Governors slowly displaced the abolished Federal Reserve Board during the last ten years of the Roosevelt administration, the governors enjoyed a majority nearly 100 percent of the time. From 1945 until 1977—the majority fell to parity, and never lower, for just sixteen days in thirty-two years. In the Carter administration, things started to slide. Carter's appointees (and their predecessors) on the board held an FOMC majority about 85 percent of the time, but that majority was back up above 90 percent during the eight years of the Reagan administration. The slow descent began after that, culminating in the Obama administration's abysmal record at 42 percent. That is, 58 percent of the time from 2009 until April 2015, private bankers' representatives have had at least equal representation on the FOMC.[22]

What's worse, the Obama administration holds another ignominious record touching on the constitutional debility of the FOMC: it is the first administration to take the governors to a four-to-five minority. Then it did it a second time. And then a third. In three different instances, the board has had three vacancies.[23]

The governors' majority is not stable on the FOMC. This reality represents a sea change over two generations. And in some cases, it's irrelevant anyway: the governors *never* had a majority of voices in the FOMC conference room. Even though only five of the Reserve Bank presidents vote at any time, all twelve of them speak and otherwise contribute to the FOMC's policy discussions. These two factors—that the governors' numerical dominance among voting members has been decreasing, and that the Reserve Bank presidents' numerical dominance among speaking members has been constant and overwhelming—mean that any defense of the seven-to-five public voting majority on the FOMC is no defense at all.[24]

JUDICIAL REVIEW OF THE FOMC

A common response to a claim that an existing governmental arrangement violates the U.S. Constitution is easy enough: someone should sue and get the courts to resolve the issue. That's what Humphrey's executor did, and the Free Enterprise Fund, and all the other plaintiffs whose cases built the doctrines of appointments and removability over a century. If the Reserve Banks are unconstitutional, why haven't the courts invalidated them as such?

The answer is, somewhat strangely, that courts refuse to hear these cases. There is a doctrine of "justiciability"—that is, the rules to determine when courts can properly hear a case—invented precisely to prevent this challenge to the FOMC from occurring. In the 1970s and 1980s, a series of petitioners—first a congressman, then a senator, then private citizens, and then again another senator—challenged the structure of the FOMC on roughly the basis described above. The litigation predated the holding in *Free Enterprise Fund* that makes the FOMC's constitutional problems even clearer, of course. But the litigants still challenged the structure as unconstitutional because the Reserve Bank presidents were making

federal policy without conforming to the constitutional requirements of presidential appointment and Senate confirmation. In
each case, the U.S. Court of Appeals for the D.C. Circuit refused to
resolve the issue.[25]

The problem was the court's conception of its own jurisdiction.
Article III of the U.S. Constitution limits the federal courts' jurisdiction; two centuries of judicial interpretations of these limitations
present a morass of rules that boil down to a requirement that a
party have an actual injury caused by the opposing party that the
court can correct. In the first case to challenge the FOMC, members
of Congress argued that the mostly private status of the Reserve
Bank presidents on the FOMC damaged the representatives' ability
to function as members of Congress, a curious theory of injury that
the court was quick to reject.[26]

Private citizens brought the next case, arguing that their investments in bonds whose price was unquestionably influenced by the
FOMC's decisions meant that they could challenge the Reserve
Bank's governance. The D.C. Circuit threw out the suit because the
citizens' complaints were merely "generalized grievances shared in
substantially equal measure by all or a large class of citizens"; subjecting those kinds of grievances to judicial resolution would "require the courts to decide abstract questions of wide public significance even though other governmental institutions may be more
competent to address the questions and even though judicial intervention may be unnecessary to protect individual rights." This
"generalized grievance" approach to limiting jurisdiction is a common one; the private citizens therefore had no case.[27]

In both cases, there is nothing surprising about these results. The
next two cases, though, were brought by U.S. senators—Senator
John Melcher, a Democrat from Montana, and Senator Donald
Riegle, a Democrat from Michigan—who claimed a very different,
very specific alleged injury. The senators' inability to advise and
consent on the appointment of a principal officer exercising federal
authority delegated by the U.S. Congress. In *Riegle*, the court found
that Senator Riegle's "inability to exercise his right under the Appointments Clause of the Constitution is an injury sufficiently per-

sonal to constitute an injury-in-fact." Senator Riegle had an injury, the Federal Reserve Act caused the injury (because it prevented him from weighing in on appointments to the FOMC), and the court could redress the injury by removing that obstacle. In *Riegle*, it seemed as though the courts could finally evaluate the Fed's structure for constitutional defects.[28]

Where the court gave with one hand, though, it took with the other. Expressly following the logic of a law review article written by a D.C. Circuit judge not on the panel, the court decided that "[t]he most satisfactory means of translating our separation-of-powers concerns into principled decisionmaking is through a doctrine of circumscribed equitable discretion." This new doctrine— "circumscribed equitable discretion"—meant that the court would refrain from evaluating the FOMC because it showed more respect for the other branches of government not to do so. As the court put it, "equitable discretion allows courts to dismiss a case that presents separation-of-powers concerns without making those concerns part of the standing test." Note the irony here. One of the Reserve Banks' unconstitutional defects is that Congress didn't show much respect to the president's separate powers. Now the courts refused to evaluate a related problem because it wanted to show respect for Congress's separate powers. No matter: federal courts have since applied this doctrine to preclude review of FOMC actions. As a result, the courts will take up the challenge to the constitutionality of the FOMC only if they reverse course on this curious doctrine of "circumscribed equitable discretion."[29]

This romp through the constitutional law of the Reserve Bank presidents' appointment and removal may seem like a side show to our inquiry into the meaning of the Fed's power, independence, and structure. In fact, the Fed's governance—who wields the power, and how they get to hold their positions—is central to these questions. There can be no dispute that, at the very least, "the optics of the [Reserve Banks'] governance," as former New York Fed president Timothy Geithner put it, "are awful." The Reserve Banks' proximity to the private institutions—by having their banks' CEOs on the Reserve Bank's board and having those CEOs and others participate in the selection and oversight of the Reserve Bank presidents—insulates them inappropriately from public oversight.

The mechanism in a representative democracy for controlling national policy is political. If someone in the government makes a decision that a citizen finds absurd, that citizen can raise the political costs for his representatives in keeping that official in place. If push comes to shove, the citizen can even make the appointments of certain kinds of politicians a campaign issue. But if the Reserve Banks' presidents, who wield significant power over the financial and monetary system, make decisions a citizen doesn't like, the usual political mechanisms break down. There is no such public recourse. And therein lies the constitutional problem.

POTENTIAL POLICY BENEFITS TO THE CURRENT STRUCTURE: ARE RESERVE BANKS A CHECK ON INFLATION?

As we saw in chapter 1, the existence of a federalist central banking system that deposited power across multiple committees in multiple jurisdictions was an invitation to struggle between Washington and the Reserve Banks. This structure served the purpose in 1913 of reassuring warring factions in a core dispute about American identity. Wilson's hope was that the hybrid system meant that neither the government nor the bankers would wield undue power to accomplish undue mischief. But as a federalist and institutional designer, Woodrow Wilson was no James Madison. Once the justification of ambiguous power sharing was removed, and the constitutionality of these kinds of arrangements more dubious, what defense of the quasi-private exercise of federal policy could there be?

A common defense raised by economists is that the existence of bankers' representatives on the FOMC is itself an enhancement of the Fed's "independence" in the Ulysses/punch-bowl sense of the word. These private citizens act as a brake on a politicians' (or politicians' appointees') inflationary biases. And in fact, a growing empirical literature suggests that the Reserve Bank presidents tend to be slightly more likely to dissent from a consensus than dovish political appointees.[30]

There are three problems with this hawkish defense of the Reserve Banks in their current form. First, the leading theoretical text that gives credit to the Fed's "founders" doesn't reflect the different monetary policy-making context that existed at the various legislative moments in 1913, 1933, and 1935 that set this structure in motion. It is clear we have inherited a hybrid system; it is also clear that the Wilson/Glass and Eccles/Glass foundings were motivated by different concerns than balancing hawks versus doves in the conduct of monetary policy. As political scientist Lawrence Broz thoroughly demonstrates, most of the attention in the pre-1913 political moment was on the international orientation that the Fed would take, facilitating the expansion of U.S. commerce in foreign markets. The structural decisions highlighted in chapter 1 came in a Wilsonian attempt to declare victory for all.[31]

To be fair, arguments about historical motivation are important for our exploration of the institutional evolution of the Federal Reserve, but still distinct from the question of whether a hybrid system makes for good public policy. But the empirical literature that suggests Reserve Bank presidents are more hawkish than the governors runs up against some hard practical realities that make it less able to bear the support that those who favor the hybrid system would put on it. Unlike other committees tasked with deciding central and contentious questions of federal policy—again, as we saw in chapter 3, the U.S. Supreme Court comes to mind—the FOMC functions almost exclusively by consensus. Most of these empirical studies use FOMC votes as a core part of their methodology, but there are simply too few dissenting votes to give us much confidence in the anti-inflation versus anti-unemployment, hawk versus dove tendencies of the Reserve Bank over the governors on the FOMC. For example, a 2014 study estimated on average one dissent per meeting between 1948 and 2014, with only six total in the period between 2005 and 2008. Former Fed governor Laurence Meyer put the point memorably: "think of the voting process as a game of musical chairs," he wrote. "There were two imaginary red chairs around the table—the 'dissent chairs.' The first two FOMC members who sat in those chairs were able to dissent. After that, no one else could follow the same course."[32]

Some scholars have begun to employ, profitably, content analysis on the FOMC transcripts to get a better sense of inflationary preferences that don't terminate in dissenting votes. But even here, the culture of consensus at the FOMC tells us less about how Reserve Banks shape the outcome of monetary policy decisions. In light of these conventional limitations, the argument seems barely more than an assertion that it should be obvious that banker-appointed representatives will favor tighter money than would political appointees. The logic here is often repeated but is fragile nonetheless.[33]

Finally, there is the availability of other alternatives for achieving the same goals. If the concern is that changes to the appointment structure of the Reserve Bank presidents, or even their removal from the FOMC, would make the central bank more inflationary in its monetary policy making, there are many other options available to anchor the Fed to a predefined inflationary path. Monetary policy rules, inflation targeting, consequences for failure to meet targets, forward guidance, and any number of other alternatives used in other jurisdictions would be superior to the wing-and-a-prayer method of hoping (most) of the Reserve Bank presidents will (always) be more hawkish on the FOMC in a way that will measurably influence policy outcomes.

THE POLITICAL POWER OF THE
FEDERAL RESERVE BANKS

The foregoing discussion leads to important questions: Why, if the Federal Reserve Banks are largely vestigial, unconstitutional, and unlikely to be much of a help even at their defined task, have they survived? Why hasn't there been a fourth founding, after the Fed-Treasury Accord of 1951, that removed them from our central bank entirely? The answer is simple enough: politics and federalism. Even though the Fed's popularity has plummeted since the 2008 financial crisis began, the Reserve Banks provide a protective buffer against the political forces that would reshape them.[34]

The political power of the Reserve Banks comes from the same source as their constitutional defects: the banks' problematic governance. Recall from the previous discussion: By statute, each bank is presided over by a nine-member board of directors. Class A directors are bankers selected by other bankers, Class B directors are nonbankers selected by bankers, and Class C directors are nonbankers selected by the Board of Governors (often after informal consultation with the regional bank and its leadership). A similar structure exists for the twenty-four branches of the twelve Reserve Banks: four board members are appointed by the Reserve Banks (through their own boards of directors), while three are appointed by the Board of Governors in Washington (again, often in informal consultation with the Reserve Bank and its leadership).[35]

This is where federalism—the concept of shared governance across multiple levels of sovereign jurisdiction—comes into play. In each case, the directors are leaders in their community. They are the presidents of banks and universities; the CEOs of major corporations and nonprofits; union leaders and museum presidents. In the event that the Federal Reserve Banks are threatened, there stands a ready-made, broadly distributed constituency of powerful and prominent Fed defenders ready to engage their senators in defense of the status quo. Some politicians can gather momentum behind policies that threaten the largest of financial institutions; few feel as comfortable challenging the directors of the community banks or labor unions. The Federal Reserve Banks, distributed through their districts and branches, have ready access to politicians who might balk at protecting Wall Street but have no qualms about protecting bankers, businessmen, and community leaders in their home districts. What politician would?[36]

Sometimes that political network is also useful in protecting the Federal Reserve System generally. Former Federal Reserve Bank of Dallas president Richard Fisher recounts a time when he flew on

Southwest Airlines in May 2012, just as the bruising Republican presidential primary had come to an end and when political criticism of the Fed from the right was at its height. Fisher and other Fed officials were flying on official Fed business, accompanied by Herb Kelleher, the CEO and founder of Southwest Airlines and chair of the Dallas Fed's board. As Fisher recounted it, "after reaching cruising altitude, Herb took the microphone" and said to the passengers, after introducing himself as the founder and CEO, that he wanted "to tell you about the Federal Reserve. Today, you have on board one of the most important people in the global financial system . . . me! Well, not really me, but I am chairman of the board of the Federal Reserve Bank of Dallas, and with me is the Bank's president, who sits on the committee that decides the amount and the cost of your money." Kelleher described how the FOMC worked in an accessible way. When he was done, "a big round of applause and attaboys" followed, including from the passenger seated behind Fisher. That passenger turned to his wife and asked, "Ethel, if Herb Kelleher is involved with the Federal Reserve, why did we vote for Ron Paul?" Having a band of bipartisan business and community leaders serving at the heart of the system certainly provides a useful source of institutional defense. [37]

This question of politics and federalism is not speculative or anecdotal: the Reserve Banks have used this political power to great effect. The case in point is in the recent lead-up to the passage of the Dodd-Frank Act. Senator Dodd sought to remove bank supervision from the purview of the Reserve Banks for the majority of banks and included that provision in the version of the bill reported out of his committee. Perhaps not coincidentally, there is no Reserve Bank in Dodd's home state of Connecticut.

The Fed insiders from the Board of Governors lobbying Congress on all the issues before it conceded to Dodd's staff that the Fed's continuing supervision of smaller banks wasn't a priority. The Reserve Banks disagreed and promptly made their presence felt. The final version of the bill left the supervisory bailiwicks of the Reserve Banks intact while it massively expanded the authority of the Board of Governors. The amendment that restored that supervision, sponsored by Texas Republican Kay Hutchinson and Minnesota Democrat Amy Klobuchar, passed ninety-one to eight, just barely less popular than an amendment that eliminated what Republicans had characterized as a permanent bailout fund (perhaps not coincidentally, there are Reserve Banks in both Minnesota and Texas).[38]

Reserve Banks, as a matter of politics, are thus almost certainly here to stay in their current form. As a matter of governance and accountability, this is lamentable. They make the separation of bank supervision and the enforcement of bank regulation—delegated as those are, in part, to the Reserve Banks by the Board of Governors—a process largely removed from the public eye. They are a layer of protection against public attempts to check the rise of a common outlook among Fed insiders and individuals and institutions in the financial industry. From a policy perspective, that proximity can be useful in some cases and destabilizing in others, as we will see more in chapter 10. But from a governance perspective, the consequences of the Reserve Banks' place in the Federal Reserve System scrambles the lines of accountability. The Reserve Banks' role in shaping the space within which the Fed makes policy makes the Fed increasingly incomprehensible to the outside public.

CONCLUSION: THE FALSE PROMISE OF A FEDERALIST RESERVE

We sometimes think of the Reserve Banks as the addition to the 1913 Federal Reserve Act created to thread the needle between governmental and private control. This isn't correct, chronologically. After the 1912 election, the Reserve Banks were always with us; it was the Federal Reserve Board that was added in the eleventh hour. At the time, the dominant conception of central banking was the private function. The Federal Reserve Board was the new creature, not the Reserve Banks.

But the Reserve Banks were intended to devolve control away from New York City and Washington. Their existence is what made the Reserve System *federal* (the leading legislative model that the Federal Reserve System replaced was called the *National* Reserve Association). But even from the beginning the "federal" aspect was misleading. The banks' very location reflected not a federal union between state and national governments, but political compromises concerning an America in 1913 that no longer exists in 2016. Leave to the side that fifty state governments are served by twelve Reserve Banks; the system the founders created included two Reserve Banks in the state of Missouri and only one west of Dallas. It is a curious theory of federalism that produces this kind of representative result.[39]

Whatever the federalist intentions of the first framers of the Federal Reserve System, time and experience have largely left behind the private model. Central banks evolved and became primarily public-facing institutions. The ambiguously public-private Reserve Banks have remained largely based on entrenched politics, not superior policy.[40]

We will question the Reserve Banks' status in the final chapter of the book. Their continued presence, in the form they are in, is one of the most important, least studied, and least defensible features of the governance of the Federal Reserve System.

PART II

THE FIVE HUNDRED HATS
OF THE FEDERAL RESERVE

The Ulysses/punch-bowl view of Fed independence tells us a story about a democracy's inability to manage its money. That story has a strong logic in theory and history. But over the course of the Fed's century, Congress, the president, and the public have placed within the Fed's walls many other functions that extend far beyond the maintenance of price stability. The chapters in this part explore those diverse missions, including price stability, and ask whether the Ulysses/punch-bowl theory of Fed independence is transferrable to these other functions.

No need to bury the lede: the answer is no. Part II explains why.

CHAPTER 6

PRACTICING
MONETARY POLICY

THE RISE AND FALL OF THE CHAPERONE

[A]ll our credit system depends on the Bank of England for its
security. On the wisdom of the directors of that one Joint Stock
Company, it depends whether England *shall be solvent or
insolvent*.

—*Walter Bagehot, 1873*

William McChesney Martin liked to tell stories. One he favored
was the story of an old economics professor who "always posed
the same questions" on his final exams. "When he was asked how
his students could possibly fail the test," given access to past exams,
the professor would reply with a smile. "Well, it's true that the
questions don't change, but the answers do."[1]

Before the 2008 financial crisis, there was a roughly universal
academic consensus on what the answers were to an old question:
What is a central bank designed to do? The answer was the Ulysses/
punch-bowl view: a central bank is an institution legally separate
from the head of state so that it can control inflation through the
exercise of technical expertise. How the central bank reached this

goal was also universally understood. Central bankers conduct monetary policy by raising or lowering interest rates with an aim toward price stability (and, eventually, toward maximum employment). This answer was applicable not only to the Fed. By the end of the twentieth century, independent central banks—in the Ulysses/punch-bowl sense of "independence"—were de rigueur. Stable economies needed independent central banks, which in turn would guide these economies toward stability by using a standard set of conventional tools.

As with so much else, the 2008 crisis changed everything. After 2008, monetary policy changed as these conventional tools were no longer equal to the task of guiding an economy through stable growth with low inflation. This realization has led to heated discussions among economists, central bankers, and the general public about the value of the tools in the Fed's (and other central bankers') toolkit. The problem was relatively simple. The economy was spiraling deeper into recession, unemployment rates were skyrocketing, and yet, the Fed's primary tool for combating this situation—lowering interest rates—was not available. Interest rates were already at zero, and the crisis was only beginning.

This macroeconomic reality, what most economists call a liquidity trap, raises important questions about the standard practice of central banking. It also calls into question the Ulysses/punch-bowl model of Fed independence. Under that model, the economists know what needs to be done. Take away the punch bowl before we all get too drunk and regret it in the morning. The politicians are supposed to prefer looser money; the chaperone is supposed to exercise the clear technocratic role of tempering those tippling enthusiasms.

Liquidity traps are different. After the crisis, the Fed was in the position of trying to get a bunch of wallflowers to take tequila shots. The politics around central banking had changed, and with that change, the theoretical explanation for the unique place of central banks in our government and economy. No longer was there a uniform clamor from the democracy for lower and lower interest rates that the wise central banking chaperone had to resist.

The experts, populace, and politicians were split on these important points.

This chapter explores these important changes. It argues that the Ulysses/punch-bowl tradition of Fed independence doesn't work in a crisis. The central bank here is not a chaperone trying to keep the party calmer than it should otherwise be. The better metaphor is a judicial one: the central banker must judge the best data against the best models of the economy informed by her own values and world views. As Bagehot said about the Bank of England, it is on the wisdom of these economic judges—at times technocratic, but always acting in a political context and making value-laden judgments—that the future of the economy depends.

HOW THE FED WORKS: UNDERSTANDING CONVENTIONAL MONETARY POLICY

Before we can understand how the 2008 crisis and unconventional monetary policy bring into question the Ulysses/punch-bowl vision of Fed independence, we need to understand more about the mechanics of conventional monetary policy from which post-2008 central banking is such a deviation. The Fed, through decisions made at the Federal Open Market Committee and the Board of Governors, controls monetary policy using a variety of basic tools. These tools are the federal funds rate, the discount rate, and reserve requirements. We will discuss each in turn.[2]

Since the Martin Fed in the 1950s and 1960s, control of the federal funds rate has been the most important and most commonly used of the Fed's tools. It's a confusing name: the "federal funds rate." Despite its name, it does not refer to the interest rate the federal government pays on its own debt. The federal funds rate refers instead to the rate at which banks lend money to each other, usually for short-term loans (overnight, or slightly longer).

The rate is connected to the federal government, though, through the mechanism used to change it. The FOMC, in its eight annual meetings, establishes the *target* federal funds rate, or the rate it wishes to see in the markets for these interbank, short-term loans. To reach this target, the Fed buys or sells securities on the open market, through the trading desk at the Federal Reserve Bank of New York. Here's the connection to the federal government: the New York Fed's primary conventional tool to accomplish the FOMC's objectives is the purchase and sale of short-term government securities. When the FOMC decides to raise interest rates, the New York Fed pulls cash out of the financial system by selling the short-term government debt securities the Fed keeps on its books; when the FOMC decides to lower interest rates, the New York Fed injects cash into the financial system by buying those securities back from market participants.

When the Fed buys a Treasury security on the open market, it provides the bank on the other side of the transaction with cash—an electronic modification to the bank's balance sheet. This purchase removes the security from a bank's balance sheet, and replaces it with greater reserves in the bank's account at its local Federal Reserve Bank. In this way, the Fed has expanded the money supply by removing from the banking system an asset that is harder to sell on the market—a government bond or, more recently, a mortgage-backed security—and replacing it with cash, literally Federal Reserve Notes (mostly electronic, of course). These notes are the easiest assets to use to exchange for other goods and services. Indeed, as the notes themselves report, they are "legal tender for all debts public and private." In the monetary metaphor, cash is the most "liquid" of assets. The Fed regulates how much cash banks must keep in their reserves, which are deposited at the bank's regional Fed. If the bank already has the requisite level of reserves required by the Fed, the cash that is added to its balance sheet through its sale of a Treasury security to the Fed is something extra.

Banks are generally in the business of taking the "something extra" and injecting it into the economy in the form of bank loans. Under normal conditions, the bank will lend the cash it has received from the Fed in exchange for its more illiquid security. Doing so expands the money supply in the economy as the bank borrower spends that money and multiplies the money's reach through a daisy chain of spending, investing, and saving. Because most consumers of bank credit—usually businesses, but also individuals—don't carry around much cash in their wallets or under their mattresses, the money the first bank receives through the Fed's initial market transaction goes to another bank or business, which goes to another bank or business, and on and on. The effect is a more or less predictable expansion of the money supply throughout the banking system.

When such a monetary expansion occurs, banks start to feel flush. Projects that otherwise would not get funded, get funded. People who would otherwise not get loans, get loans. The result, under the best conditions, is economic growth. As the lending expands, economically useful projects and expansions result in more jobs, more goods, and more economic activity to provide for a growing and striving population.

That's under the best conditions. Under other conditions, what looks like economic growth is, in fact, a monetary mirage. It's not more jobs, goods, and services that we see; it's just more money. And when more and more money chases the same (or shrinking) number of jobs, goods, and services, the prices of everything go up. These inflationary pressures threaten to undermine the economy's stability and consumer confidence in the level of prices and wages and have become the primary target of central bankers the world over. When the Fed fears that loss of confidence and senses that inflation, not growth, is driving expansion, the central bank intervenes. The chaperone has arrived at the party in time to take away the punch bowl.

More concretely, the Fed restricts the money supply by doing the reverse of the purchase of the Treasury securities described above—it sells them to its counterparties. When the Fed sells these securities on the open market, at the market price, it replaces cash on the bank's balance sheet with a less liquid asset, a short-term government security. In turn, the Fed's counterparty bank will either call in loans due—or, more frequently, initiate fewer subsequent loans—thus either diminishing or slowing the expansion of the money supply.

So far this explanation has skated over the significance of interest rates. After all, the Fed has done nothing explicitly with interest rates—it has merely injected or retracted liquidity to expand or shrink the money supply. The connection between open market operations and interest rates, however, is as basic as a supply-and-demand graph from introductory economics. Here, the supply and demand are supply *of* and demand *for* short-term bank loans, a commodity for which there is a market, just as there are markets for crude oil, pineapples, or squirrel traps. The price of money in these markets is the interest rate, here called "the federal funds rate." When there's less money available to banks to lend to each other, they will pay more for it—and the interest rates will rise. When there is more money, people will pay less for it, and interest rates drop. Thus, while the difference between the federal funds effective rate and the federal funds target rate is actually more complicated than this simple explanation suggests, the basic reality is that the Fed can and does affect interest rates through open market operations similar to the process described above: by affecting the availability of money, the Fed changes the price of money.

With this background in mind, loans through the figurative "discount window"—the other conventional approach to monetary policy—are more easily explained. The discount rate is the rate, set by the Reserve Banks with approval of the Board of Governors, at which the Fed itself lends directly to the banks. The discount rate used to be far more important to the maintenance of the banking system (the tussle described between William McChesney Martin and Lyndon Johnson in chapter 2 was about the discount rate). Before the crisis and the emergency lending that occurred through the window, it had long been in decline; as we saw in chapter 4 and will see again in the next chapter, the discount window for the implementation of the central bank's other functions is much more essential.[3]

Finally, there is the last instrument, the regulation of banks' reserve requirements. Reserve requirements are those regulations that tell banks how much cash they have to have in the vaults to satisfy the demands of their depositors. The smallest banks have lighter requirements; as banks get larger, these requirements increase, until they are eventually 10 percent of assets as defined by a relatively complicated set of factors.

In the decades before the financial crisis of 2008, reserve requirements were the least used of monetary tools. In that sense, in the precrisis popular perception, the Federal Reserve System was like the Holy Roman Empire: neither federal, nor reserve, nor really much of a system. It wasn't really federal, even from the beginning; these reserves weren't a very important part of its policy making; and by the time of the crisis, the Fed chair came to be seen (inaccurately) as the physical embodiment of all the central banking functions.[4]

After the crisis, though, questions arose about these much-neglected reserves, questions like these: What rate should the reserve requirements be? What is the connection between reserve requirements and financial crises? And perhaps especially, what kinds of assets will dictate the amount of cash the banks have to have on hand? Reserve requirements matter most, both before and after the crisis, as a kind of supporting actor in the conventional monetary policy story: it is deficiencies in the reserve requirements that primarily send banks into the federal funds market to borrow on a short-term basis until they can meet their standards.[5]

THE INTELLECTUAL AND INSTITUTIONAL HISTORY OF CONVENTIONAL MONETARY POLICY AND CENTRAL BANK INDEPENDENCE

These are the tools of conventional monetary policy. The Fed's and other central banks' successes at using these tools in response to economic overheating or cooling has come to define the Ulysses/punch-bowl approach to Fed independence. It's tempting to attribute the conceptual success of this approach to Fed independence to Marriner Eccles, William McChesney Martin, and the Fed-Treasury Accord of 1951. Many do. But the idea of placing the regulation of the currency outside of the main ministries of government was deeply unpopular in many corners. For example, liberal economists like John Kenneth Galbraith, Seymour Harris, and James Tobin, three of the most famous economists of the mid-twentieth century, thought the idea absurd. Galbraith called it "indefensible" to have the Fed "exercise arbitrary independent power to overthrow the decisions reached by" the president and his economic advisers. Tobin called it "a paranoiac mania" that would prevent the Treasury from working closely with the central bank on matters of mutual concern. And Harris, more expansively, thought Fed independence an "insane idea" insisting that it was "folly to allow the Federal Reserve to run in one direction and the Executive in another." The Fed could "push its views before Government decides on a policy," Harris argued, but once the president made a decision, "monetary policy must be an instrument of Government policy, not a barrier to its achievement." Liberals like Tobin, Galbraith, and Harris weren't the only ones who thought a policy separation problematic. Milton Friedman, the great monetary theorist on the right, thought central bank independence much less desirable than a straightforward monetary policy rule that increased the money supply at an agreed-on rate.[6]

And indeed, institutionally, any daylight between politicians and central bankers was the exception, rather than the rule. Through the 1980s, central banks throughout the world were largely dependent on the political branches, with only the United States, Germany, and Switzerland as the (partial) exceptions. The Bank of England, for example—the most storied of all central banks—was fully subordinated to the chancellor of the exchequer, an elected member of Parliament who formed part of the government, from 1946 until 1998. The chancellor could veto any decision made by the Bank of England and otherwise controlled the appointment and removal process for the bank's directors. In the words of Nigel Lawson, a former chancellor, the relationship between the government and the bank was simple: "I make the decisions, and the Bank carries them out."[7]

The real triumph for the Ulysses/punch-bowl conception of central bank independence came not during the 1950s, but in late 1970s, culminating in the mid-1990s, as a result of theoretical, empirical, and political support for the idea that politicians are uniquely bad at monetary policy in ways that predictably undermine public policy. On the intellectual end, two economists—Finn Kydland and Edward Prescott—formalized the view that economic policy, including monetary policy, faces what they called a "time consistency problem." That is, at one time period, society would rationally prefer one set of policies—loose monetary policy, for example—but those policies would lead to consequences down the line that society would rationally not prefer. The way to resolve this problem, Kydland and Prescott argued, was to write a monetary policy "rule" that would allow for the long-term best interests to carry the day.[8]

Almost as though on cue, Paul Volcker assumed the Fed chair a year after the Kydland and Prescott paper began changing people's views about the value of an institutional fix to the problem of time consistency. But Volcker's and the Fed's answer to the time inconsistency problem was not Kydland and Prescott's rules-based approach, but one based on personality and discretion. Volcker and his colleagues on the FOMC changed the practices of monetary policy in a way to resolve the time consistency problem by becoming more conservative than the average American in their approach to inflation. As a result, Volcker became the public face for an independent central bank, the view that the democracy's citizens could become both Ulysses and the sirens without fear that the ship of the economy would flounder in an inflationary muck. We had Paul Volcker and his team of sailors, beeswax in their ears, guiding the ship forward.[9]

Volcker's successes and the intellectual revolution in theoretical economics placed the central bank, as opposed to other parts of the government, as the protector of the value of the currency. In time, a corresponding empirical explosion followed that showed, time and again, that those central banks with strong legal independence—focusing on factors such as whether politicians sat on the banks' boards, whether the central bankers could be fired, the length of the central bankers' tenure, and much else—were the best at controlling inflation.

The empiricists looked at the legal aspects of central banks that made them "more or less independent of direct political control."

First is the control over monetary policy instruments, or "instrument independence." Instrument independence is separate from "goal independence," which is the statutory declaration that a central bank can choose its end goals—whether price stability, maximum employment, or something different; instrument independence means that the politicians choose the goals, but the central bank can choose how to get there.[10]

Second, the empiricists looked at the appointments procedure—one that "limits that [government's] ability to determine the composition of the bank's entire governing body increases the bank's independence." Third is the ability for the cabinet—or, alternatively, Congress—to "punish the central bank using ex-post sanctions, such as oversight, dismissal, policy veto, and budget cuts." These three questions, then, are the definition of central bank independence: if a bank has instrument independence, some limitation on appointments to the bank's governing board, and some safety from political harassment, it is said to be "independent." Of course, scholars in this field recognize that independence, so defined, is not a binary switch. As one scholar wrote, "[i]ndependence is a continuous, not dichotomous, variable. In other words, there are degrees of central bank independence."[11]

So it was that central bank independence caught intellectual and political fire in the 1980s: whether by a monetary policy rule or by the conservatism of the central bankers appointed, a (greater or lesser) legal separation from the politicians had allowed the chaperone to fulfill his technocratic functions. At the same time, a burgeoning empirical literature confirmed a strong correlation between certain legal features of a central bank's institutional design and its ability to control inflation (though not much else). As one scholar put it, "in monetary policy, macro political economy made the unthinkable thinkable, and more: it turned it into conventional wisdom."[12]

While institutional independence was not invented from nothing in the 1980s and 1990s—the chaperone metaphor, of course, dates from 1955, and there were good treatments of the concept even earlier—the theoretical, empirical, and even political focus of the time produced an outgrowing of institutional changes to central banks. In 1992, the Treaty of Maastricht that established the European Union required all member states to adopt an independent central bank, following the example of the German Bundesbank, with legal protections for an institution separate from the national government to control the quantity and value of the currency. That is, the Europeans put into their constitutional treaty a mandate for the Ulysses/punch-bowl conception of central bank independence. It was roughly around this time that the *Economist* declared that "[t]he only good central bank is one that can say no to politicians."[13]

Of course, untangling the political, theoretical, institutional, and empirical dynamics swirling around the design of central banks during the 1980s and 1990s is a difficult task. It's not easy, perhaps not possible, to determine with certainty whether the anti-inflationary successes of central bank design followed the institutional innovations, or if the causal chain works the other way, or if both are the product of other phenomena entirely. Economist Adam Posen argues, persuasively, that these correlations should not be mistaken for causation, as "there is no institutional fix for politics." That is, the same political impulse that pushes a country to adopt authentic legal protection for the protection of a currency pushes the country to make that commitment credible and deliver the policy results consistent with those policies. This much was clear, however: the era of central bank independence had arrived. Conventional monetary policy was the strategy; central bank independence was the institutional framework that made it possible.[14]

Until, that is, the global financial crisis of 2008.

UNCONVENTIONAL MONETARY POLICY

The 2008 financial crisis stretched the role of the central bank in a variety of ways, some of which we will explore in the next chapter. It also represented a change in the approach to the basic tools of monetary policy through the advent of "unconventional policies," especially what have come to be called "quantitative easing" and "forward guidance."

To understand quantitative easing, we have to understand the problem a central bank faces in a liquidity trap, described briefly earlier in the chapter. As explained above, a liquidity trap occurs when the central bank, facing a recession, has already dropped interest rates to zero (or close to it) and the economy is still sinking. The problem in a liquidity trap is how to convince individuals, households, firms, and banks to revive their confidence and their borrowing and spending so that the economy can stand up again.

Keynes first discussed these traps in his *General Theory of Employment, Interest, and Money.* "There is the possibility," Keynes wrote, "that, after the rate of interest has fallen to a certain level" such "that almost everyone prefers cash to holding a debt which yields so low a rate of interest. In this event the monetary authority would have lost effective control over the rate of interest." While Keynes didn't use the term "trap," the implication was clear: if there's no real advantage of holding interest-bearing assets, then individuals, firms, and banks will simply hoard cash.[15]

Most economists paid little attention to liquidity traps until the 1990s. The reconsideration came from the experience in Japan. There, Japanese central bankers had followed the handbook and dropped interest rates to just above zero, meaning that money was essentially free for the borrowing. And yet banks and borrowers weren't taking the invitation to spend. As a result, the economy fell in and out of recession throughout the decade (sometimes referred to as the "Lost Decade").

In response to the Japanese experience, and out of fear that it might be repeated in the United States in the early 2000s, economists and central bankers began developing the intellectual apparatus for dealing with liquidity traps. As a result, when the 2008 financial crisis came, there was already a great deal of theoretical and empirical discussion of what central banks could do in a liquidity trap. As Paul Krugman put it in an influential paper, the "point is important and bears repeating: under liquidity trap conditions,

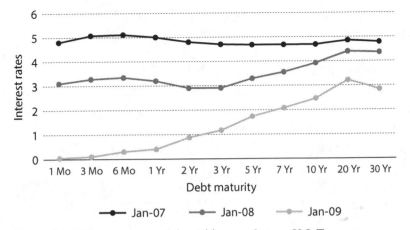

Figure 6.1: U.S. government debt yield curve. *Source*: U.S. Treasury.

the normal expectation is that an increase in [cash in the economy] will have little effect" on generating economic growth.[16]

The goal for the central banker in this context is to flatten the yield curve. This refers to the fact that interest rates on any kind of bond—government debt, mortgage debt, or really anything else—usually go up the longer the bond's maturity. The logic is simple: if you borrow money from your bank and promise to pay it back the next day, you'll get a lower interest rate than if you keep the same money tied up for thirty years. It's a less risky proposition to lend money on shorter time horizons than for longer ones. The "yield curve" refers to a graph of these interest rates like in figure 6.1, showing the yield curve for government debt in early 2014.

Because of the outcome of the great debate between William McChesney Martin and Allan Sproul in the 1950s, the Fed had largely been in the business of investing in short-term government debt for more than half a century when the financial crisis of 2008 hit. As a result, conventional monetary policy had already provided the answer it could give: the Fed had already dropped the near end of the yield curve as low as it can go. The new question was what to do with the rest. If the far end of the yield curve stays high, then individuals and firms are less likely to borrow money and expand their investments in themselves, their homes, their businesses: in a word, their economy.

The Fed then turned toward targeting the far end of the yield curve, to "flatten" it. Here is where unconventional monetary policy comes into play. Early in the 2008 financial crisis, the Fed targeted interest rates toward the right on the yield curve not just of government debt, but of all kinds of debt, including bank debt and mortgage-backed securities. In the recent history of the Federal Reserve—since roughly the 1920s—this represents a dramatic change in the practice of monetary policy. In March 2009, it held almost $2 trillion worth of such debt (this period of unconventional asset purchases became known, retrospectively, as "QE1," meaning the first round of quantitative easing).

When, in the Fed's view, this wasn't enough to revive the economy, it started buying up that long-term governmental debt to bring down those interest rates. Again, the Fed had significant experience with this kind of government debt purchasing back in the 1950s, but it had long lain dormant. The crisis brought back those kinds of purchases in what would come to be known as the second round of quantitative easing, or QE2. But those efforts, too, proved insufficient. While these actions succeeded in flattening the yield curve for governmental debt, the yields on longer-term securities outside the governmental debt context remained stubbornly high. This resilience meant, from the Fed's perspective, that not enough borrowing and lending was taking place to push the economy to employment and inflation levels that the Fed wanted to see. The idea is to get cash into the economy as fast as the central bank can. In one speech in 2002, Bernanke, then a member of the Fed's Board of Governors (but not the chair), alluded to a helicopter drop of cash on the general public as a way of getting growth and inflation back to desirable levels. (In light of subsequent events, and with that precedent in mind, his critics have sometimes called him "Helicopter Ben.")[17]

Ultimately, the Fed decided to focus not just on buying government debt, but on buying specific kinds of mortgage-backed securities, starting at $40 billion per month but eventually going up to $85 billion per month. This program ended in October 2014. By the end, the Fed had extended its balance sheet from roughly $800 billion in

2008 to almost $5 trillion at the end of QE3. Quantitative easing, in that peculiar jargon of central bankers, actually meant that the central bank had in fact sextupled the size of its balance sheet.[18]

The goal, again, of unconventional monetary policy is to flatten the yield curve. But even quantitative easing wasn't enough, from the Bernanke Fed's perspective. To do more, the Fed engaged in what it and others have called "forward guidance," or the clear announcements of the external indicators that will guide Fed policy. That is, the Fed announces that its unconventional approach to flattening the yield curve will continue indefinitely until, say, inflation ticks above 2 percent or unemployment falls below 6.5 percent. The idea here is that market participants will worry that the central bank's commitment to easy money won't last long enough to be relevant to their long-term borrowing considerations, and so they sit on their cash and await more certainty.

Forward guidance is a kind of Ulysses contract for the Ulysses contract: it binds the central bank to a mast of its own in an effort to convince participants in the economy that the Fed will honor its commitment to a certain policy for a certain period of time. As Krugman described it in his 1998 paper on liquidity traps originally, "a liquidity trap fundamentally involves a credibility problem—but it is the inverse of the usual one, in which central bankers have difficulty convincing private agents of their commitment to price stability." Instead, the problem in a liquidity trap is "that the markets believe that the central bank will target price stability, given the chance, and hence that any current monetary expansion is merely transitory." The solution is forward guidance: the central bank must commit that its monetary policy "will in fact be effective if the central bank can credibly promise to be irresponsible, to seek a higher future price level."[19]

These different approaches to staving off the devastation of expected deflation have been controversial, in public, politically and, to a lesser extent, among academic economists. Around the time the Fed announced its second round of quantitative easing, a Fed critic took to YouTube and created an animated short of little forest creatures of uncertain species to discuss the Fed and its bold chair:

Mammal 1: Who runs the Fed?

Mammal 2: The Fed is run by the Ben Bernank [*sic*, to great effect].

Mammal 1: Does the Ben Bernank have a lot of business experience?

Mammal 2: No, the Ben Bernank has no business experience.

Mammal 1: Does the Ben Bernank have a lot of policy experience?

Mammal 2: No, the Ben Bernank has no policy experience.

Mammal 1: Has the Ben Bernank ever run in an election?

Mammal 2: No, the Ben Bernank has never run in an election.

Mammal 1: So what qualifies him to run the Fed?

Mammal 2: I don't know. Maybe the fact that he has a nice beard.

Mammal 1: But my plumber also as a nice beard, and I would not trust him to play god with the economy.[20]

The dialogue—much better watched than read—is factually inaccurate: Bernanke had significant policy experience, as chair of George W. Bush's Council of Economic Advisers and as a former member of the Board of Governors, and was in fact elected to the school board of Montgomery Township, New Jersey. But the idea that the Fed chair "play[s] god with the economy" was a widely shared one.[21]

Politically, unconventional monetary policy, together with the emergency lending during the height of the crisis, put the Fed in the crosshairs of conservative politicians. Rick Perry, the Republican governor of Texas and a presidential candidate in 2012, made a point to hint at violence against Bernanke because of quantitative easing. "Printing more money to play politics at this particular time in American history is almost . . . treasonous," he said. "I don't know what y'all would do to him in Iowa, but we would treat him pretty ugly down in Texas." Other politicians had similar reactions expressed in less personally threatening terms. In fact, the Tea Party movement of the twenty-first century was born in reaction to the idea of further "bailouts," albeit from the Treasury to homeowners rather than from the Fed to the banks. And, of course, Occupy Wall Street was targeted directly at the accumulation of power in banking and the perception that that power controlled our public institutions as well.[22]

Some academics on the right have also criticized the Fed's experimentation with various unconventional policies. A group of mostly Republican economists and political strategists wrote a letter denouncing quantitative easing and the Fed's other experiments in 2010, arguing that the "planned asset purchases risk currency debasement and inflation, and we do not think they will achieve the Fed's objective of promoting employment." Allan Meltzer, an economist, Fed historian, and monetarist, has consistently criticized the program from the beginning, calling it "quantitative quicksand" and indicative of the fact that, "under Mr. Bernanke, the Fed has sacrificed its independence." Their common critique is that the experimentation is going to send inflation eventually skyrocketing.[23]

These critiques began in tandem with unconventional monetary policy. Inflation has not taken off in the six years following the critique, a point that the defenders of the Bernanke Fed have made repeatedly. The six years' evidence against their theory hasn't made critics rethink their views; they insist that the inflationary consequences of quantitative easing are yet to come. The Fed still has a $4.6 trillion balance sheet and will have to manage its return to conventional monetary policy. Whether they are correct, or the Bernanke Fed was correct, still awaits resolution.

ULYSSES AND THE UNCONVENTIONAL MONETARY POLICY

The kind of political backlash and academic disputes about the value of unconventional monetary policies cannot fit within the

Ulysses/punch-bowl view of Fed independence. Populists and politicians aren't supposed to prefer tighter money than the central banker; the sirens are not supposed to wreck the ship of the economy on the shoals of deflation.

Of course, the Ulysses/punch-bowl view of Fed independence has never been exactly correct. The presumption that there is a uniform preference for looser monetary policy on behalf of society isn't at all consistent with the historical record. To take one example, most historians associate the fight over the currency in the late nineteenth century as indicative of battle lines drawn precisely according to debtors in favor of soft money (or an expanded monetary base) and creditors in favor of hard money (or a narrower monetary base). These arguments usually include a citation to William Jennings Bryan, the Great Commoner and three-time Democratic Party presidential candidate, who famously insisted that he and his followers "shall answer [hard money enthusiasts'] demands for a gold standard by saying to them, you shall not press down upon the brow of labor this crown of thorns. You shall not crucify mankind upon a cross of gold."[24]

And yet, political scientist Jeffry Frieden discovered by analyzing congressional and census data around these debates that districts with larger debts *favored* the gold standard, rather than sought to rebuke it. Similarly, in Pennsylvania during the colonial period, "with surprisingly few exceptions," the issuance of paper money—that bugaboo of the creditor class—was "supported by both urban and rural dwellers; by merchants, artisans, shopkeepers, and farmers." In Pennsylvania, paper money "was virtually an 'apple pie and motherhood' issue throughout the colonial period." Or, as banking and political historian Bray Hammond described them, both "the Jeffersonian and Jacksonian agrarians were a rigidly hard-money lot."[25]

The point is that the scramble of monetary politics in the post-2008 crisis isn't particularly new. Indeed, it may be that the intellectual and political heirs to William Jennings Bryan's anti-bank, anti-deflation populists are Rick Perry and Ron Paul's anti-bank, anti-inflation populists and libertarians. This kind of popular opposition to Fed policies is often misinformed, perhaps reluctant to concede empirical counterarguments, and may ultimately be wrong. But these divisions demonstrate a different kind of political threat to the Federal Reserve than the Ulysses/punch-bowl conception of Fed independence would predict.

CONCLUSION: THE CENTRAL BANKER AS JUDGE

This breakdown of the Ulysses/punch-bowl function of the Federal Reserve doesn't mean that separating some of the Fed's functions from the day-to-day of electoral politics is unnecessary in the face of deflationary, rather than inflationary, pressures. In fact, the very opposite could be true: if there is a partisan movement in favor of economic policies that could result in a deflationary spiral, we would face the Great Depression redux. Keeping the power to trigger such a consequence away from partisan politics seems like a desirable goal for the institutional design of central banks.

But it also requires a different theoretical frame. It may be that the frame for independence is one that we already widely accept in society: judicial independence. The U.S. Constitution gives the federal judiciary life tenure and effective budgetary independence (that is, while they can't print their own money or raise it independent of congressional appropriations, the Congress cannot constitutionally lower judicial salaries). The reason is so that, to the fullest extent possible, any determinations that favor politicians occur either because the law compels it or because the judge and the politician share the same worldview. The idea that the judge is currying favor with the politician in hopes of further appointment or out of fear of getting her salary removed are taken off the table. It's not a perfect system, but it is one that most recognize as an important balance between democratic values (the politician gets to appoint the judges from the polity) and some degree technocratic, objective judgment (the judges decide the cases, not the politicians).[26]

The crisis and the reactions to unconventional monetary policy suggest that the Fed is often performing a delicate adjudicative function, not a simply technocratic one. The problem with the technocratic, Ulysses-contract view of central banking are the two fractured constituencies mentioned above. While most economists have endorsed the Fed's approach to postcrisis monetary policy, the "technocratic" view has been far from uniform. And, again, the populists aren't clearly clamoring for prosperity by way of inflation, contra that Ulysses/punch-bowl view. At least in a crisis, and arguably in other times as well, the central bank isn't resolving the "time inconsistency" that economists have placed as the center of the theoretical defense of central bank independence. They are evaluating conflicting views of uncertain empirical information analyzed within a model of the economy and refracted through the central bankers' own personal experiences and values.

If this summary of the central banking function is correct, then it is tempting to throw out the entire enterprise of central banking as politics by another name. That conclusion goes too far. Without question, central banking practice is plagued by uncertainty, model failures, imperfect data, and even central banker ideology. But central bankers at the Fed aren't throwing darts at a decision tree, nor is there any evidence of venality and corruption. Instead, they are adjudicating between conflicting views of that uncertainty, those failures, these ideologies. To judge against those competing concepts, central bankers at the Fed are using the technical apparatus of empirical and theoretical macroeconomics to reach a consensus that creates a policy conclusion. When these conclusions are contested, as they often are, we need an institutional framework for resolving those conclusions. The central banker as independent chaperone is not the correct model. The central banker as independent judge may be much better.

CHAPTER 7

THE ONCE AND FUTURE FEDERAL RESERVE

THE FED'S BANKING FUNCTIONS

> If we examine the manner in which the Bank of England has
> fulfilled these duties, we shall find, as we found before, that the
> true principle has never been grasped; that the policy has been
> inconsistent; that, though the policy has much improved, there
> still remain important particulars in which it might be better
> than it is."
>
> —*Walter Bagehot, 1873*

The framers of the Federal Reserve System would not have recognized the system right before the 2008 crisis. They may have had a slightly easier time recognizing it in the months and years since.

The reason for the change is that the Fed's original purpose, as its charter suggests, was "to furnish an elastic currency, to afford means of rediscounting commercial paper, to establish a more effective supervision of banking in the United States, and for other purposes." These are largely the *banking* functions of central banking and include three that became crucial to the conception of the Fed after the 2008 crisis. First, the Fed has acted as a *lender of last resort* in response to financial panic; second, it has *regulated* all banks' participation in the financial system, although the tenor and scope of those regulations have changed dramatically over a century; and third, it has *supervised* individual banking institutions to ensure that they comply with its regulations. Together, these functions provide a way for merchants and bankers to get access to an international financial system while providing, at the same time, a brake against crises both small and large. As a result of the financial crisis of 2008, scholars and central bankers have begun to discuss the "financial stability" function of central banks in a much more serious, comprehensive way. But this function isn't new: these functions defined the Federal Reserve System at its inception.[1]

Despite this banking-centric history, one reason these functions seem new is because of how uncomfortably they fit within the Ulysses/punch-bowl approach to Fed independence. It is a mistake, though, to think that the Fed's crisis response represents a deviation from the Fed's "traditional" functions. It is, in fact, the narrowness of the prevailing vision of central bank independence that is the modern innovation. The crisis dusted off old tomes about the Fed's banking functions and made them stylish again. It is telling that, when Walter Bagehot wrote *Lombard Street*, conventional monetary policy hadn't been invented yet. Today, Bagehot's advice on central banking has become a bible in these circles. The Fed has rediscovered its financial stability role and began an effort to understand how to reinvigorate it into an institution that had evolved differently.

This chapter discusses the four aspects of this once and future Federal Reserve System and looks at the ways that the Fed's disparate functions fit—or, as it turns out, do not fit—within the Ulysses/punch-bowl conception of Fed independence: the lender-of-last-resort function; bank regulation, the changing context of bank supervision within the Fed, and the advent of financial stability as a rival mandate to the Fed's statutory command to ensure price stability and maximum employment.

Besides failing to fit within the prevailing lens of Fed independence, there is another sense in which the Fed's banking functions present a problem for Fed governance and accountability: banking regulation and supervision in the United States are a jumble. It isn't a rational system. Political scientist Terry Moe may as well have been discussing the fractured and fragmented world of financial regulation when he wrote that "American public bureaucracy is not designed to be effective. The bureaucracy arises out of politics, and its design reflects the interests, strategies, and compromises of those who exercise political power."[2] As we shall see, the same is true for the banking regulatory state.

THE ORIGINAL FEDERAL *RESERVE*: THE LENDER OF LAST RESORT

We've already seen in chapter 5 that the "Federal" in "Federal Reserve" is something of a misnomer: there's nothing really federal about it. What about the "Reserve"? This refers to both the Fed's traditional function as a lender of last resort and to the member banks' reserves that are kept in the entire system. Some thought the advent of other banking regulatory functions (namely, deposit insurance) had cast the lender-of-last resort function into the archives of history. The 2008 crisis showed us how relevant the function remained.[3]

The idea of a lender of last resort is a simple one. In a banking panic, depositors show up en masse to withdraw their deposits. But as any fan of Frank Capra's *It's a Wonderful Life* can tell you, banking doesn't work that way. Banks operate on a "fractional reserve," meaning that savers deposit money in the vaults that then goes to work on loan to spenders in the field. To oversimplify, fractional reserve banking in its traditional form follows the 3-6-3 model: pay depositors 3 percent, lend out at 6 percent, and hit the golf course by 3 p.m. The business of turning short-term deposits, which savers can demand any time during banking hours, into long-term loans, like thirty-year mortgages or ten-year loans to a new business, is called "maturity transformation." This is the way that banks, historically, have made their money.[4]

Maturity transformation is what makes banks so vulnerable to failure. The system relies on an assumption that only a few short-term depositors will withdraw their money on a given day. When more depositors show up at a bank demanding even more in withdrawals than is on deposit in the vaults, the bank will fail unless new cash can be secured. The first priority of a bank facing a panic, then, is to publicly and ostentatiously demonstrate that it has secured new funds, usually from another bank. As soon as the panic is stabilized, a bank with a well-managed portfolio will pay back both its emergency debts to the other banks that have stepped into the breach and those that the bank owes to its regular depositors. (In the sometimes confusing vernacular of banking, the bank's "assets" include the loans it is owed by homeowners, business owners, and the like; its "liabilities" include the deposits that savers can demand at any time.)

If the panic spreads, however, the usual sources of short-term credit to the first scared banker—other banks—are themselves tied up trying to fend off bank runs of their own. At that point, a localized panic has become systemic. In that event, banks scramble in a dash to find liquidity in the system, wherever liquidity can be found. The central bank is the solution to this scramble for liquidity. The central bank is the "lender of last resort," the bank that exists to restore order to the financial system.

The concept of "lender of last resort" was first alluded to by a British banker, Francis Baring, in 1798, and then expanded on at great length by the lawyer and economist Henry Thornton. But the concept received its most famous articulation by Walter Bagehot in his treatise *Lombard Street: A Description of the Money Market*. In *Lombard Street*, Bagehot explained his view of the lender of last resort as one whose essential role is to keep the central reserve of cash and gold to be deployed richly and freely for the purpose of stemming panics. The advice is sometimes called Bagehot's dictum: in a crisis, a central bank should lend freely, at a high rate, against good collateral. When this occurs, if the theory holds, the banking panic should stop.[5]

Bagehot described what he had in mind most clearly in this famous passage:

A panic, in a word, is a species of neuralgia, and according to the rules of science you must not starve it. The holders of the cash reserve must be ready not only to keep it for their own liabilities, but to advance it most freely for the liabilities of others. They must lend to merchants, to minor bankers, to "this man and that man," whenever the security is good. In wild periods of alarm, one failure makes many, and the best way to prevent the derivative failures is to arrest the primary failure which causes them.

Of course, Bagehot was writing at a different time from our own. In 1873, the date of publication, the world was beginning what scholars have called the "classical gold standard" that lasted from roughly 1871 to 1914. And in this era for example, there was no such thing as government-sponsored deposit insurance, something that developed slowly during the late nineteenth century and only became more widespread after the Great Depression. In light of these developments, Bagehot remained little more than the subject of scholarly conversation, even there the assumption was that Bagehot's principles of the lender of last resort had been made irrelevant by the advent of deposit insurance.[6]

Once again, until 2008. Deposit insurance had largely, but not completely, eliminated the concern of runs on banks by individual depositors like the ones seen at the Bailey Savings and Loan. These local banks were far from the only participants in the financial system. Instead, the largest investment banks—some of which were not even under the regulatory purview of the Federal Reserve at all—were the ones exposed to risks and most likely to spread those risks to others.[7]

In the spring of 2008, staff and leadership within the Federal Reserve System faced what they feared to be a banking panic redux, but without the prospect of deposit insurance to mitigate it since it targeted uninsured investment banks, insurance companies, money market funds, and other uninsured financial institutions. Invoking emergency lending authority that had been unused for almost eighty years, the Fed picked up its "lender-of-last-resort" function and proceeded to deploy it throughout the economy. This is the (in)famous 13(3) authority discussed in chapter 4. The Fed's emergency lending-of-last-resort functions started with the investment banking giant Bear Stearns and in time extended to money market funds, traditional banks, and insurance companies. Bernanke self-consciously channeled the memory of Bagehot on multiple occasions.[8]

To say that some were uncomfortable with the Bernanke Fed's invocation of the lender-of-last-resort function is an understatement. Some of these criticisms even cut close to the central banking bone. In a rare instance of a former Fed chair criticizing current Fed policy, Paul Volcker, in a public speech immediately following the Bear Stearns bailout, viewed the move as "neither natural nor comfortable for a central bank." Articulating the Ulysses/punch-bowl view of Fed independence, he explained that the Fed is granted "a high degree of independence" to pursue its duty as "custodian of the nation's money." In that role, the Fed "should be removed from, and be seen to be removed from, decisions that seem biased to favor particular institutions or politically sensitive constituencies." The Volcker Fed, of course, was responsible for the modern revival of the too-big-to-fail doctrine in its response to Continental Illinois, in 1984. Volcker's view in 2008 demonstrates how completely he and others have come to accept the Ulysses/punch-bowl theory of Fed independence, despite how much Volcker's own banking policies in the 1980s do not conform to that account.[9]

Bernanke was motivated less by the lessons of the 1980s and much more by the specter of the 1930s. In the words of David Wessel, author of one of the definitive accounts of the crisis told largely from the perspective of Bernanke's Fed, Bernanke resolved to do "whatever it [took]" to prevent a repeat of the Great Depression from happening. Bernanke, both as an economic historian and as a central banker, changed the exercise of emergency lending and in the process changed the discussion of what, exactly, the Fed would do as a last resort.[10]

Volcker wasn't the only one to express dismay at the Bernanke Fed's actions. Public opinion of the Fed dropped from its historic highs, and Ben Bernanke became the least popular Fed chair to gain reappointment in the Fed's history (as measured by the breakdown in votes on his Senate confirmation). The Fed's emergency actions also changed the relationship between the Fed and the public: recognizing the Fed's loss in prestige, Bernanke launched in 2009 a full-court press of news conferences, televised interviews and town meetings, and other general public outreach. And everywhere he went, he was faced with hostility over the use of the Fed's lender-of-last-resort functions. "I'm as disgusted by [the bailouts] as you are," he told one town meeting. "Nothing made me more angry than having to intervene, particularly in a few cases where companies took wild bets."[11]

After these tumultuous decisions placed the Fed's central bank functions back in the public eye, the questions immediately followed. As Paul Tucker, a scholar and former central banker, put it, "[t]he underlying theme is legitimacy: how to ensure that the central banks' role [as lender of last resort] is legitimate in democratic societies where powers and responsibilities have in effect been delegated by the elected legislature."[12]

Critics have focused on this question of legitimacy, in two ways, both of which draw erroneously on the Ulysses/punch-bowl account of Fed independence. The first is that so much power to make these kinds of decisions should not be in the hands of a single individual. Representative Barney Frank, a staunch defender of the Federal Reserve during the 2008 financial crisis, is often associated with this view. When Bernanke and Secretary of the Treasury Henry Paulson approached Congress in the fall of 2008 about the need for new legislation to inject $85 billion into insurance giant AIG, Frank asked if the Fed had that kind money. Bernanke responded that he had $800 billion. Frank was stunned: "He can make any loan he wants under any terms to any entity or individual in America that he thinks is economically justified," Frank later said. "No one in a democracy unelected should have $800 billion to dispense as he sees fit."[13]

Frank wasn't exactly right, of course. As we saw in chapter 4, Ben Bernanke needed to convince at least four others on the Board of Governors and the relevant Reserve Bank each time the Fed invoked the emergency authority under section 13(3). But it was true that the Federal Reserve System had this extraordinary power, a power that Bagehot would have recognized and applauded.

Reflecting the discomfort with so much emergency power, the Dodd-Frank Act revised this emergency lending authority. After Dodd-Frank, the Federal Reserve Act now requires that the emergency lending not be targeted to a single individual company, but to "any participant in any program or facility with broad-based eligibility." That is, gone are the days when Bear Stearns can show up with illiquid collateral and receive an individual loan through the emergency discount window; such funds have to come through a broader program than that, aimed at more than a single institution.[14]

There is a second criticism against the Fed's emergency lending that is essentially inconsistent with the first: rather than make the emergency lending authority more subject to political control, a second set of critics argued that the Fed's crisis actions eroded the Fed's independence because it brought the Fed into such close decision making with the secretary of the treasury.

Superficially, this argument makes sense. During the crisis, it's unquestionably true that Bernanke and other central bankers at the Fed worked cheek by jowl with Paulson and others at Treasury. And Tim Geithner was the embodiment of that proximity, switching in 2009 from being the vice chair of the Federal Open Market Committee (as president of the New York Fed) to Obama's treasury secretary. There is no question that during the Obama adminstration Geithner and Bernanke were close. "We would talk constantly over the next few months," Geithner wrote about his time as a new Treasury Secretary, "basically a never-ending conference call, making sure we stayed on the same page, preventing nervous colleagues from pulling us back toward inertia." As he put it more directly elsewhere, "I doubt there's ever been a closer relationship between a Treasury secretary and a Fed chairman."[15]

This proximity wasn't only during the Obama Administration. Even at the beginning of the financial crisis—in spring of 2008, with the Fed sponsoring J. P. Morgan Chase's acquisition of Bear Stearns—the Fed's seemingly unilateral actions to be a lender of last resort occurred in tandem with administration policies. Bush treasury secretary Henry Paulson was apprised of developments as they occurred; Paulson was a principal negotiator of the terms of the ultimate transaction. When the rest of the financial system teetered over the edge, the Bernanke Fed and the Paulson Treasury paused their triage strategy and sought and received congressional participation. The Troubled Asset Relief Program (TARP) became one of the most controversial pieces of legislation in recent American history, spawned the resurgence of the right wing of the Republican Party, and has led, arguably, to the country's inability to govern its fiscal affairs credibly and consistently.[16]

Despite all of the above, the coordination-compromises-independence critique is Exhibit A in the damage that the Ulysses/punch-bowl view of Fed independence can wreak on understanding the Fed and its functions. There is simply no serious argument that the Fed and Treasury should have pursued distinct crisis policies, and a strong argument that working against each other would have been harmful. As one scholar and former central banker put it, "Think of waking up on the morning [after Lehman Brothers failed], for example. Should Ben Bernanke not have taken Hank Paulson's call?"[17]

Whatever the virtues in building institutional barriers between the Fed and the presidency to prevent coordination of monetary policy with fiscal policy, it cannot apply when the government is picking winners and losers in the financial market, precisely what the Bernanke Fed and the Bush and Obama Administrations did during the 2008 financial crisis. This fundamental reality is a truth that is not altered even if we accept that it was necessary to stave off a complete collapse of the global financial system. Nor is it feasible that these decisions be removed entirely from the Fed's orbit, in part because the Fed's ability to move quickly in a crisis is what makes the central bank a viable lender of last resort in the first place.

The best answer, then, is some kind of balance. It is exactly for this reason that Bernanke and Paulson sought *not* to use the Fed's emergency lending authority without congressional approval, even though the Federal Reserve Act would have allowed them to do so. And Congress seems to have appreciated, in its way, this kind of fiscal-monetary coordination: the invocation of emergency lending now requires approval by the secretary of the treasury.

That politicians and bankers coordinate policy in a crisis has a strong, if often forgotten, basis in history, including in the 1907 Panic that many presume led to the creation of the Federal Reserve in 1913. While many remember J. P. Morgan as the savior of the financial system, the reality is that Theodore Roosevelt's secretary of the treasury, George Courtelyou, was in constant contact with the New York bankers—and not just by telegraph. The Roosevelt Treasury ponied up tens of millions of dollars of public money, at no interest, to staunch the flow of funds out of New York. The incredibly delicate decisions about who succeeds and who fails in a financial crisis require exactly the kinds of judgments that are best made with some kind of political participation. The changes that occurred through Dodd-Frank reflect that sensitivity.[18]

These two critiques—that the Fed should not wield its lender-of-last-resort authority alone, and that the Fed worked too closely with the Treasury and thus compromised its independence—can't both be right. But they do illustrate how difficult it is to make sense of Fed independence through the Ulysses/punch-bowl lens. Under that standard account, the Fed is insulated by law to allow it to focus on price stability, an area where politicians will be predictably terrible if left to their own electoral devices. Ironically, that lens works poorly to explain the Fed in what is its eponymous role: as a central *bank*. The Fed is the central bank because it is the keeper of the central reserve, the lender of last resort, the one in the crisis to guide the rest of the financial system to safety. It is precisely here where solemn demands to respect Fed independence can be most confusing, misleading, and harmful.

THE FED AS A REGULATOR: A BRIEF HISTORY OF BANK REGULATION IN THE UNITED STATES

The Fed's roots as a central bank include its role as a lender of last resort. The same can be said about the role of the Fed as a regulator, but not without a few caveats. That is, the Fed was always a regulator of sorts; what has changed over its century, and accelerated after the crisis, is the expansive scope of its regulatory portfolio. This portfolio has expanded dramatically, even when the Fed has failed at significant portions of it.[19]

Bank regulation was a different animal in 1913 than it is in 2016. At the time, the regulation of banking was effectively the regulation of the Fed's reserve banking function: who could qualify for what kind of participation in the Federal Reserve System. The focus was on the resilience of the participants in the banking system, what we have come to call "microprudential regulation," or regulation that focuses on the safety and soundness of specific institutions.[20]

This rather isolated focus from within the Federal Reserve reflected the unusual, perhaps unique nature of bank regulation in the federal United States. In the United States, sovereign authority is deposited in both the states and the federal government, with vague overlapping authority between the two spheres. After the failure of the Second Bank of the United States in 1836, the country entered an era when banking developed almost entirely within the states. During and after the Civil War, the federal government entered the fray again through the creation of a national banking system consisting of "national banks" organized under federal law and regulated by the awkwardly named (and still open for business) Office of the Comptroller of the Currency.

Commercial banks after the passage of the two National Banking Acts could choose to be regulated by their home state (which gave them more liberty to transact a wider variety of businesses) or as a national bank. The national banking system was not particularly national; there were significant restrictions on interstate and intrastate banking during the entire period. Although these regional banks had correspondent networks that built a quasi-national system, the politics of banking regulation during much of American history depended on hard limits on these networks to prevent them from merging into single national institutions. Through significant political influence in state legislatures, the U.S. Congress, and the White House, state bankers were able to impose limits on the expansion of banking activities across state lines. These limits significantly influenced the development of the U.S. banking system, including in the ways that the Fed would eventually interact with that system.[21]

This was the regulatory context when the Fed was founded. The Federal Reserve Act introduced, through the Federal Reserve Banks, twelve new banking entities whose primary purpose was to regulate the ways that private banks—whether organized under state or federal law—could receive cash payment for the securities they presented to the Federal Reserve Bank (in banking lingo, what they would receive when they "brought their paper for discount").[22]

After the Great Depression, Congress made several significant changes to the regulatory landscape. By 1932, 25 percent of all banks had failed. Following the lead of some early state adopters, Congress introduced deposit insurance as a mechanism for preventing future panics. To regulate the federal insurance fund, the Fed created the Federal Deposit Insurance Company (FDIC), funded not by a congressional appropriation but from an exaction from the Federal Reserve Banks. The Banking Act of 1933 (better known as the Glass-Steagall Act, for its sponsors Carter Glass and Henry Steagall) also created a new institution within the Fed, the Federal Open Market Committee, consisting of the twelve presidents of the Federal Reserve, and, most famously, ordered the division of commercial and investment banks. It also defined a new entity, called "bank holding associations," or corporate conglomerates that included within them deposit-taking banks.[23]

For years thereafter, the Fed had only indirect regulatory authority over these holding companies. The companies had to receive board permission before voting their shares in member banks. Such permission carried with it some limited restrictions on the kinds of activities that such companies could pursue. But the Fed wanted more than Glass-Steagall provided, and Marriner Eccles especially sought but did not receive more regulatory authority over these bank holding associations.[24]

Eventually, in 1956, Congress passed the Bank Holding Company Act (BHCA) to define and regulate what had by then come to be known as "bank holding companies." While the Fed took no official position on whether it should regulate these new financial institutions, the Fed became their exclusive regulator regardless. Then chair William McChesney Martin was almost coy in the hearings that preceded the act's passage. When Senator Paul Douglas (D-Illinois) asked who the "single administering agency" overseeing the act's new expansive powers should be, Martin was cool: "We do not take a position on that." Senator Douglas pressed him: "Is the Federal Reserve Board a receptive candidate for this?" Martin, showing his skills at the hearing table and as a Washington insider, replied that the "Federal Reserve Board would accept it, but we are not trying to make a grab for power here." Another senator piped in: "You are not a candidate?" Martin then took a risk: "The Board is not a candidate." Martin knew his audience, though. The Congress put the Fed in place as the regulator of bank holding companies, something Eccles in all his enthusiasms for the role could never accomplish. Martin was always the better politician.[25]

Together with Glass-Steagall's prohibitions on commercial banks, the BHCA put the Fed in the business of defining "bank" and the "business of banking." This definitional authority would consume an extraordinary amount of regulatory and legislative effort over the fifty years following, and be the source of the Fed's ever expanding authority.[26]

As we have already seen in chapter 2 regarding the Greenspan Fed's lack of interest in mortgage regulation, during roughly the same time, Congress also questionably expanded consumer financial protection. Unlike the case of the BHCA, Congress did not give the Fed the exclusive regulatory authority over consumer financial protection—the Federal Trade Commission, for example, also took a prominent role. Nonetheless, the Fed saw, once again, a dramatic expansion in its regulatory function in a field that extended far beyond the business of discounting commercial paper and regulating bank reserves.

After decades of effort from the banks and their allies in court cases, regulatory proceedings, and, eventually, legislation, Glass-Steagall died in 1999, and the lines between financial institutions started to evaporate. Bank holding company regulation, however, remained and remains a significant part of the Fed's regulatory function.[27]

After the 2008 financial crisis, Congress passed the Dodd-Frank Act, a sweeping overhaul of the financial regulatory state. Among the many innovations, most relevant to our discussion of the Fed as a banking regulator was the introduction of essentially a new regulatory function for the Fed and others within the government: systemic risk regulation. While the Fed had already been in the business of "macroprudential" regulation—regulating the risks common to the system as a whole, and not focused on the idiosyncracies of individual firms—Dodd-Frank created a new institutional and regulatory framework. Dodd-Frank's primary institutional innovation was the creation of the Financial Stability Oversight Council (FSOC), a council of regulators that includes ten voting members and five nonvoting members. The voting members include the secretary of the treasury, who is the chair of the council; the Fed chair; and the other banking, securities, and financial regulators. The Fed is a first among equals on this council. Dodd-Frank puts the Fed, though not in the council's chair, directly in the business of systemic risk regulation. The FSOC can make any financial institution submit information to the Fed, register with the Fed, and, most importantly, submit to the Fed's supervisory authority. Those institutions with assets greater than $50 billion need not even be banks: if they are designated "systemically important," they, too, will fall under Fed supervision.[28]

Three aspects of this history are useful in thinking about Fed power and independence. First, Congress has given the Fed more and more regulatory responsibilities in broader and broader areas of the financial system. It has, to be sure, sometimes trimmed the Fed's sails, as in the near elimination of the Fed's role as a consumer banking regulator. But the creation of the Consumer Financial Protection Bureau is an almost unique exception in banking history: the trend from Congress has been the expansion of the Fed's regulatory bailiwick. Also, as in the case of the BHCA and, for example, the Truth in Lending Act, it is not true that the Fed has always sought that responsibility. Why regulators rely so heavily on the

Fed is not exactly clear, the fact of the reliance, however, is. The space within which the Fed operates, from a regulatory perspective, is constantly changing, almost always in one direction.[29]

The second takeaway is that the banking regulatory space has long been and still remains utterly fractured across both federal and state governments. The "dual banking system," which refers to the location of regulatory authority at both the state and federal level, is perhaps unsurprising given the nation's history with federalism and the political power that thousands of community banks have wielded throughout U.S. history. But there is more to it than that. The federal government has created new uniform laws in a number of regulatory spaces, from communications to civil rights to environmental regulation to nuclear regulation. In these areas, the states were essentially pushed out by virtue of the U.S. Constitution's Supremacy Clause ("preempted" is the technical legal term). And while there have been some rather extraordinary instances of federal preemption of banking laws, state banking regulation remains alive and well.[30]

The third implication of the regulatory history recited above is the way that it changes our view of the Ulysses/punch-bowl vision of Fed independence. Scholars and commentators have long said the Fed's "independence" is not as important in regulatory matters as it is in monetary policy matters. But it is the central argument of this book that the Fed's structure and governance sits atop *all* the Fed's policies, not just some. The formal and informal ways that politicians and other outsiders influence Fed policy do not stop simply because Congress has given the Fed more than one responsibility unrelated to its mission to chaperone our monetary party. As we will see in part III, these mechanisms vary, but they are also comprehensive in their application to all the Fed's authority. For example, the Fed's unique budgetary autonomy covers monetary policy and regulatory policy alike. The members of the Board of Governors serve the same terms in their capacity as members of the FOMC and as bank regulators. The point is simple: Institutionally, when you pick up one end of the Fed independence stick, you pick up the other.

BANK SUPERVISION

Some of these same issues are on display in another field of Fed endeavor: bank supervision. The words "supervision" and "regulation" are sometimes used synonymously, but they aren't the same thing. Bank regulation involves issuing specific rules that govern, to quote one Fed overview, "the operations, activities, and acquisitions" of banks and banking organizations generally, whereas bank supervision consists of "the monitoring, inspecting, and examining" of these banks "to assess their condition and their compliance with relevant laws and regulations," in other words, the difference between making system-wide policy and implementing (and enforcing) that policy.[31]

Policy implementation in bank supervision is not, however, a mechanical activity. It is a complicated process that involves two components linked, at least in concept, chronologically. First, a bank is "examined" on an individual basis to ensure that it complies with relevant law. And second, if the examination reveals a failure of compliance, enforcement proceedings are brought against the bank.

Both steps in that chronology have changed significantly over the years, but it is the role of the bank examiner that bears most directly on thinking about the ways that the Fed's policy-making space—its power and independence—is influenced by outsiders. When the Fed was founded in 1913, the practice of bank examination had been more or less stable for decades. O. Henry, the famous nineteenth-century short-story writer, described a stylized version of one bank examiner who cut an imposing figure in the story "Friends from San Rosario." "Indecision had no part in the movements" of this bank examiner, a Mr. J.F.C. Nettlewick, an unknown in the city where he came to conduct his business. The bankers were terrified of him. As the bank teller on duty prepared for Mr. Nettlewick's inspection, the teller "knew it was right to a cent, and he had nothing to fear." The teller was terrified anyway. "There was something so icy and swift, so impersonal and uncompromising about this man that his very presence seemed an accusation. He looked to be a man who would never make nor overlook an error." In O. Henry's retelling—based in part on his own experiences as a bank teller in the nineteenth century—the bank examiner was someone to be respected and, indeed, feared.[32]

The world of bank examination has changed dramatically since O. Henry's time. These shifts reflect not only a change in the sophistication of financial institutions, although those developments have clearly occurred. But it is also a change in the regulatory landscape described in the previous section. Whereas a Mr. Nettlewick could come to a distant city and open the books to ensure that the balance sheet added up and leave by the end of the day, bank examiners today have no such luxury. The sheer depth of complexity that afflicts bank balance sheets prevents even experts from discerning what banks own and owe, what they have sold and received, and whether they are compliant with the hundreds of banking statutes that form the architecture of modern bank supervision.[33]

There are a lot of problems with this level of new (and ever accelerating) complexity in the supervision of banks. But the principal problem is that bank examiners must, almost by definition, defer more and more to the banks examined. Instead of a Mr. Nettlewick striking fear into the hearts of bank tellers because of Nettlewick's comparative expertise, bank examiners in the twenty-first century must live with the reality that it is virtually impossible for them to know more about the bank than the bankers they supervise. Most bank examiners in that context will defer; even those who push back aren't necessarily rewarded for doing so.

In 2014, an example of this kind of problem in bank examination arose at the Federal Reserve Bank of New York. After the 2008 financial crisis, New York Fed president William Dudley worried that his institution had failed as a supervisor. To understand how the failure had occurred, he hired a former banker and professor at Columbia University, David Beim, to do an exhaustive, unlimited access review of the New York Fed and its operations. In return, the report would be secret.[34]

The Beim report disclosed a "culture that is too risk-averse to respond quickly and flexibly to new challenges," and bank supervisors who deferred to the banks they regulated in virtually every aspect of bank supervision, from developing and relying on internal risk management systems to deferring to banks' reactions to potential problem spots. The stated modus operandi of many bank supervisors was to avoid confrontation with the banks. This seemed a sure-fire way for the New York Fed to render itself complicit in fueling future crises.[35]

To Dudley's credit, the Beim report fueled efforts to change the New York Fed's approach to failed supervision. But institutional culture changes slowly, if it changes at all. Following its recommendation, the New York Fed hired a new crop of bank examiners, including one named Carmen Segarra. True to new expectations, Segarra was vocal when she spotted failures to comply with federal law at Goldman Sachs, the bank where she was stationed as an examiner. In particular, she concluded that Goldman Sachs had failed to have a firm-wide conflicts-of-interest policy to manage situations in which the firm's bankers would advise clients on decisions where those bankers had other interests—advising the purchase of a company where the banker owned stock, for example.

In some ways, the lack of a firm-wide conflicts-of-interest policy is astonishing: these conflicts have been at the heart of a series of Wall Street scandals throughout the twentieth century, from the Great Crash of 1929 to the accounting scandals in the early 2000s. And yet, this is what Segarra discovered and reported to her superiors at the New York Fed.[36]

But her superiors, with a few exceptions, didn't share Segarra's enthusiasm for pushing Goldman to change its practices. Because Segarra was worried about all that she saw, and in case she needed to support her version of events in the future, she started to secretly record her conversations at the Fed and at Goldman Sachs. She ended up with forty-six hours of recorded conversations, which ended when Segarra was fired. She worked at the New York Fed for a total of seven months.

As the news of Segarra's tapes, her accusations, and the New York Fed's banking culture leaked to the press—deeply researched reports appeared in *ProPublica*, and a major feature was aired on the public radio program *This American Life*—reactions divided roughly along two lines. Defenders of the Fed have said that Segarra's claims are inaccurate, overblown, and depend on cherry-picked quotes and are otherwise not reflective of the regulators' usual practices (and that her disclosures were themselves deeply unethical). Critics of the Fed have said that this is what the New York Fed does—it has always been captured by the banks it regulates, and this proximity is part of the Fed's DNA.[37]

There are at least two sides to this story, and the Federal Reserve Bank of New York has largely ceded the narrative to Segarra. It may be that there is more to her account than we know. The point is that we should not be surprised that bank examiners would defer to the banks in a way very unlike Mr. Nettlewick, even if Segarra's account is not representative in every respect. Given the complexity of modern banking and the proximity that puts the examiners into daily contact with the bankers, the examiners come to depend on the banks examined, both for information and for compliance. As one journalist who reported extensively on the Segarra story said of the examiners, "They see [bankers] every day, and they need to obtain the information from these banks, and it's easier to obtain the information if you're friendly and if you have a good relationship." That's not to say that bank examiners need to be "so icy and swift, so impersonal and uncompromising" that their "very presence seem[s] an accusation," as was the case with Mr. Nettlewick. But it does mean that such physical and ideological proximity can lead bank examiners to defer to bankers in ways that aren't consistent with the need to ensure the financial safety and regulatory compliance of the banks in question. In the geography of Fed power, the complexities and proximities of bank supervision give private banks greater control over Fed policy than the rest of the general public.[38]

CHANGES AFOOT IN BANK SUPERVISION?

There are signs that changes are afoot within the Federal Reserve System with respect to bank supervision. As discussed in chapter 3,

Fed governor Daniel Tarullo has radically changed the way that bank examiners are trained, recruited, and themselves supervised. While the Federal Reserve Act gives full legal authority to the Board of Governors for all matters regulatory and supervisory, the Fed has historically delegated much of that authority to board staff and, especially, the Reserve Banks. In light of the Reserve Banks' structural proximity to the commercial banks they supervise, the examiners' ability to keep a critical distance is arguably even more difficult.

In 2010, however, it appears that the Board of Governors has worked to move the Reserve Banks increasingly out of the business of supervising the largest banks in the financial system. In a secret document called the "Triangle Document" disclosed to select journalists in 2015 but written in 2010, the Fed revealed that Reserve Bank delegation had largely come to an end with respect to the largest banks, especially at the New York Fed.[39]

It is difficult to determine whether the changes outlined in the Triangle Document are good or bad for our efforts to make the Fed more comprehensible—and thus more accountable—to outsiders. The changes are good because there is simply no theoretical justification of bank examination as part of a central, sacred trust deposited in an "independent" central bank in the Ulysses/punchbowl sense of the word.

Consider again, though, how the Fed decided to disclose the new policy. Secret documents? Code names? Partial disclosures five years after the fact? It all seems so gratuitous. This kind of disclosure harms the banks supervised, since they may not have a clear sense of which institution within the Fed is calling the shots on a supervisory matter. And that same confusion makes it difficult for the public to supervise the Fed.

IS THERE HOPE FOR CONFLICT-FREE BANK SUPERVISION?

The foregoing discussion leaves an open question: how should we build a supervisory system within the Federal Reserve to ensure that bank examiners conduct their jobs rigorously and fairly? This question is one of the most vexing public policy issues in finance. Even the seemingly obvious solutions aren't clear. For example, some scholars and economists argue that pay is the problem. Bankers are paid too much, bank supervisors too little. The allocation of talent and attention with those kinds of wage signals is pretty clear: all else equal, more social resources (including talent and education) will go toward hiring bankers and lawyers who will help banks skirt the demands of supervision rather than hiring supervisors who work to ensure compliance. "Financial incentives tilt hugely in bankers' favor," wrote one economist after the 2008 crisis. "By outwitting regulations, bankers can become unimaginably rich."[40]

To remedy this imbalance, some scholars have proposed linking their compensation to regulatory successes, others that banks' shareholder liability should be altered to encourage more shareholder participation in supervision. But even as these scholars recognize, the causal link between supervisor pay and shareholder incentives on the one hand and supervisory excellence and financial crisis prevention on the other isn't as clean is it could be.[41]

Part of the problem afflicting bank supervision is also conceptual: we lack a clear theory of what bank supervisors are even supposed to do in a world with long lists of federal and state statutory compliance requirements. This theoretical confusion came to a head in 2014 Senate testimony. Senator Elizabeth Warren (D-Massachusetts) and New York Fed president William Dudley sparred about accusations that the New York Fed had failed as a bank supervisor, in direct response to the Segarra hearings. There, Dudley also articulated his conception of his role as a bank supervisor, disputing Senator Warren's view that the Fed needed to police bad behavior through bank supervision. Dudley disputed the idea that the Fed, as banking regulator, should be a heavy enforcer of the banking laws. "It is not like a cop on the beat," he said. "It is more like a fire warden."[42]

Of course every town needs both a fire warden and a cop on the beat. If the Fed's conception of bank supervision is dominated by the emergency-response mentality, it is likely to be bad at the necessarily uncomfortable policing behavior. There are strong signs from the Yellen Fed that it views both of its roles—lender-of-last-resort authority (more like a fire warden) and bank supervision (more like O. Henry's cop on the beat)—very seriously. But time will tell. There are no easy solutions to these difficult supervisory problems.

From the perspective of understanding the space within which the Fed operates, though, there is something deeply problematic about the governance structure of the supervisory system. There is simply no theory offered that justifies the legal insulation of the Fed from a variety of political pressures—for example, in the form of complete budgetary autonomy, the structure of the FOMC—for bank supervision. What's worse is that bank supervision is not only an inherently executive function we would want to place within inherently executive bureaus, such as the Treasury Department. It is also that the supervisory function is primarily lodged in the part of the Federal Reserve System with the greatest and most opaque political power: the Federal Reserve Banks. The decision to locate bank supervision in the Reserve Banks doesn't reflect a considered balance between political accountability and technocratic expertise; it reflects path dependency and historical inertia. The role of the Reserve Banks—either in their governance or in their functions—is nowhere more suspect than in their bank supervisory roles.

FINANCIAL STABILITY AND MONETARY POLICY

Related to but distinct from lender-of-last resort functions, bank regulation, and bank supervision is the idea that the Fed has a mandate to preserve financial stability. As mentioned earlier, there is nothing new about the idea that the Fed should concern itself with financial stability. The thinking behind the extensive market assurances during the Greenspan Fed—the so-called Greenspan Put—came from an impulse to provide the financial system with stability. Even before the crisis, scholars and central bankers have debated whether the Fed should (or already does) have a third mandate to provide financial stability. In that debate, some scholars thought that monetary policy should be used to ensure financial stability by raising interest rates when it looked as though bubbles were forming in certain sectors of the economy. In this view, monetary policy and financial stability could be accomplished by the same instrument: the target interest rate.[43]

Here, once again, Ben Bernanke the precrisis economist was contributing to the academic debate about issues that Ben Bernanke the postcrisis central banker would live with every day. From Bernanke's perspective, the use of monetary policy to promote financial stability was wrong. His argument: "Use the right tool for the job." The idea that it could be the "arbiter of security speculation or values" was impossible and, because impossible, potentially catastrophic.[44]

Bernanke's argument was that interest rates are a blunt instrument. A central bank that moves its target interest rate can't focus on specific asset classes while ignoring others. If there's a stock market bubble, and the rise of interest rates might help bring that bubble to soft landing, there's no way to use the broad interest rate tools to focus just on the stock market. Student loans, mortgages, business loans, and all other credit throughout the economy will be affected in the same way. For this reason, Bernanke argued that monetary policy as a tool for financial stability was like "trying to perform brain surgery with a sledgehammer." Instead, he thought, financial stability is best achieved through the Fed's banking toolkit—emergency lending, bank supervision, and bank regulation.[45]

This debate rages on. The important point is to understand the theory behind placing financial stability functions on an identical institutional footing as the conduct of monetary policy. There is an easy answer to this: we can't. There isn't a theory that would give us both.

Even if there were, it would fail because of a simple reality. The Fed is not the exclusive regulator charged with promoting financial stability in the U.S. government. The fractured nature of our system, both vertically between the state and federal governments and horizontally among various agencies at the federal level, is unrelenting.[46]

A perennial proposal would change this reality. To improve this horizontal division among federal regulators, though, presidents from both parties have long sought to consolidate all bank supervisory and regulatory functions into a single entity. Marriner Eccles and Franklin Roosevelt made the unification of banking supervision a priority in 1944. In a memo from Roosevelt to Eccles, the president expressed consternation at the "duplication or triplication of [bank] examinations" by the Fed, the FDIC, and the Comptroller of the Currency.

But nothing came of that effort, nor the many successive efforts by presidents of both parties to do the same. Most recently, Paul Volcker has made a similar proposal. "I think the financial crisis has exposed just how rickety and out of date our supervisory framework is," he said. "It's just a lousy system." Volcker has made a habit, he said, of asking various people if they think the system we have makes any sense. "I haven't found anybody yet who says yes."[47]

Be that as it may, not only has this idea gone nowhere, including because of the Greenspan Fed's efforts to block the Clinton administration's proposal along these lines. Instead, the federal regulatory system has gone in the other direction. Dodd-Frank introduced the Consumer Financial Protection Bureau and the Financial Stability Oversight Council, adding more players into the regulatory mix. The FSOC, especially, will now require greater regulatory coordination. The shape of the Fed's regulatory space—the way that it makes policy, for and by whom—is more circumscribed by the interests of other regulatory actors than ever before.[48]

Volcker's specific proposal would be to leave the Fed in charge of systemic risk and bank regulation, and lender-of-last-resort functions, but leave the examination and enforcement of bank supervision to a separate entity that would have all the authority of the scattered federal banking agencies currently in play. Whether dividing bank supervision from central banks is a good or bad idea is a perennial debate that empiricists have essentially been unable to answer. As one scholar recently described it, "[t]he nature of the involvement of a central bank in the supervision of financial firms and of infrastructure providers is a matter of endless controversy. It is probably incapable of an answer that is generally applicable at all times and in all places." And there are strong arguments that the central bank needs a hand in financial stability even on a more individualized level to ensure its ability to manage the financial system, especially in a financial crisis.[49]

Wherever one comes down on these important debates, the entire conversation—both about what the Fed should do for financial stability, including whether it should be involved at all—is an important one for understanding why the Ulysses/punch-bowl theory of Fed independence falls short. Because the financial stability mandate cannot be justified by the Ulysses/punch-bowl model of Fed independence, its inclusion under the same institutional umbrella confuses, rather than clarifies, the place of the Federal Reserve within government.

CONCLUSION: UBER-REGULATOR OF THE ECONOMY

The Fed's movement from its role as a banker's bank and lender of last resort to the god of the boom-time economy and back again is a stunning story of institutional change. The last two chapters have demonstrated that the Fed's authorities are many and varied, but also that our understanding of these authorities does not always match our view of what an "independent" central bank should be. More particularly, the Ulysses/punch-bowl view of Fed independence is at its strongest when describing the conventional role of a central bank making technocratic decisions about controlling inflation, decisions that politicians are likely to be bad at making because of their electoral pressures.

What the Ulysses/punch-bowl view cannot describe is the appropriate level of insulation when the pressures are coming not to inflate the currency during an expansion, but to deflate the currency during a contraction. The 2008 financial crisis demonstrated that deflation or disinflation can still subject the Fed to extraordinary pressures to reverse course on ideological, not empirical, bases. The sometimes inexplicable politics of monetary policy do not function as the Ulysses/punch-bowl view would predict.

This does not mean that political pressure on the Fed to *less* inflation is evidence that the Fed has become politicized, as some have suggested. To the contrary, if there is a lack of political will to battle deflationary pressures, and massive unemployment and the consequences of these phenomena would be devastating, then an institutional shield against those political headwinds would be desirable. After all, in terms of the damage to society and the economy, we should fear a Great Depression more than a Great Inflation.[51]

Note, though, the caveats. Fiscal politics in the United States suggest that it is desirable to look for aid from an institution beyond the floor of the House of Representatives to resolve vexing issues of macroeconomic policy. In these instances, the question is not purely technocratic but the evaluation of competing value propositions that will otherwise be resolved by partisan politics.

Here, again, we see that the role of the Fed is not to exercise technical expertise but to adjudicate between competing policy narratives. That is, the central banker looks less like a banker and more like a judge. The decision regarding the appropriate use of unconventional monetary policy instruments is the key decision, and that decision begins to look more like a judicial determination than a purely technocratic one.

The Fed's role as a banker, regulator, and supervisor requires even less insulation from politics than that. The political economy of these functions demonstrates this reality: as an emergency banker, the Fed worked hand in glove with the politicians during the crisis, and as a regulator, the Fed must coordinate its activities with still more governmental figures. Invoking the name of Fed independence to condemn or defend Fed actions in this space reveals how devoid of intellectual content the term "independence" has become.

This chapter and the previous chapter illustrate more than the difficulty that the standard account of Fed independence has in explaining the way the Fed actually works. They are also about how difficult it is for the interested public to comprehend the Federal Reserve at all. The Fed's many functions, its confused governance, the difficulty in attributing what to whom within the Fed—these factors all demonstrate the problem. The mass of functions within the Fed—as a fighter of inflation and deflation, the manager of the economic conditions of the labor force, a banker, a bank supervisor, a financial regulator, and the guarantor of financial stability—makes that task of democratic accountability in any practical sense exceedingly difficult. Much of the controversy surrounding Fed policy comes from this inability to parse these distinct functions.

PART III

THE SIRENS OF THE FEDERAL RESERVE

In the Ulysses/punch-bowl model of Fed independence, the influence to watch on the outside is presidential: the politician seeking reelection who will stop at nothing to win. History certainly supports this view, in part. Politicians do, in fact, care a lot about Fed policy. But this aspect of the Ulysses/punch-bowl version of Fed independence has two problems. It tells us little about *how* these outsiders succeed or not at influencing Fed policy. And second, it tells us still less about who else, besides the politicians, will try to do the same.

The reality is that there are many sirens trying to influence the Fed from the outside. Politicians are an important, but far from the only, voice in the mix. In the three chapters ahead, we will explore both the identities of the most important outsiders who influence Fed policy and the mechanisms by which they exercise that control. We begin with the president, the usual suspect for Fed influence, and move through Congress, international central bankers, private bankers and markets, and the community of academic economists. As with much else in this book, the emphasis will be on how law and personality, together and apart, limit and facilitate outside incursions on the Fed's many missions.

CHAPTER 8

THE PRESIDENT AND THE FEDERAL RESERVE

THE LIMITS OF LAW AND THE POWER OF RELATIONSHIPS

The Government is necessarily at times possessed of large sums in cash. It is by far the richest corporation in the country; its annual revenue payable in money far surpasses that of any other body or person. And if it begins to deposit this immense income as it accrues at any bank, at once it becomes interested in the welfare of that bank.

—*Walter Bagehot, 1873*

In the great political contests over the power of the economy, the president is the politician we would expect to care most about what goes on within the Fed. The president is the only politician who faces a national electorate. Any member of Congress can always plausibly blame the president or the other party or the Fed itself if the economy sours in a way that could affect the legislator's own electoral prospects. Avoiding blame is, after all, one of the primary motivators for electoral politicians.[1]

The president, like other politicians, has the same desire to take credit for the good and seek scapegoats for the bad. But unlike the others, the president has the hardest time avoiding that blame. And for all the Sturm und Drang one hears during electoral cycles about values, foreign affairs, and so much else, it is largely the economy that makes or breaks an incumbent president. Because electoral and legacy prospects depend in large part on economic performance, it's natural that the president is jealous of the powers shared with the Fed. Again, from Bagehot, given the awesome control over the nation's finances that the Fed exercises, it is little surprise that the president should "at once become . . . interested in the welfare of that bank."[2]

And yet, most presidents since Woodrow Wilson have treated the Fed with at least some degree of hesitant distance. Carter Glass, that great defender of the first Federal Reserve System (1913–35), once argued the president had no role whatever in determining Fed policies. In his florid way, Glass argued that Wilson (a personal hero of his) recommended as a "wise determination to refrain from executive interference with federal reserve administration and his refusal to permit politics to become a factor in any decisions taken. Unless the example thus set by President Wilson shall be religiously adhered to," Glass further intoned, "the system, which so far has proved a benediction to the nation, will be transformed into an utter curse. The political pack, regardless of party, whether barking in Congress or burrowing from high official station, shall be sedulously excluded." Despite this soaring rhetoric, Senator Glass frankly admitted that he himself, while serving as Wilson's secretary of the treasury and therefore chair of the Fed, indulged the temptation to treat the Fed "as a bureau of the Treasury."[3]

This tension between soaring respect for Fed independence and devilish temptation to interfere with its policies constitutes much of the interaction between the president and the Fed. Here is where the inquiry into the Fed's outside relationships begins. We cannot understand the Fed without understanding how presidents negotiate its policy-making space, including where law limits and extends that influence. In this chapter, we start with the Federal Reserve Act and the formal, legal influence that the act gives or withholds from the president. As with the rest of the book, the argument is not that the law is irrelevant, but that it is incomplete. The law matters here, but sometimes in counterintuitive ways.

Law is, of course, far from the only way that the president seeks influence. Presidents engage in personal, strategic behavior to shape that control constantly. Fed chairs do the same. From history, we can discern roughly four different modes of presidential influence over the Fed (primarily but not exclusively directed at the Fed chair): appointing Fed chairs and governors with identical policy outlooks who can be trusted to perform as expected, as seen in the relationship between Franklin Roosevelt and Marriner Eccles; the domination of a Fed chair through regular pressure, as seen in the relationship between Richard Nixon and Arthur Burns; a charm offensive whereby a president tailors his policy to suit the views of a politically popular Fed chair, as in the case of Bill Clinton and Alan Greenspan; and the coincidence of policy preferences that arise in reaction to specific problems, as in the case of Barack Obama and Ben Bernanke.[4]

THE LAWS OF PRESIDENTIAL CONTROL

Before we get to the power of these personalities, we have to confront the legal context of the president's relationship to the Fed. Appointments to the Fed are the president's primary mechanism for exercising control. "Despite the Fed's highly regarded independence," writes Kelly H. Chang, a political scientist who has studied Fed appointments in depth, "appointments remain an important avenue of political influence on monetary policy." What is fascinating, though, is how this influence occurs not just on the pages of the Federal Reserve Act, but in practice.[5]

Recall the discussion of the legal focus on agency independence we explored in chapter 4, with respect to the president's control (or lack thereof) over the Federal Reserve Banks. The logic for this focus on the president's ability to fire his subordinates is that the president is the executive; because she is going to be held responsible for failures of administration, including the administration of the monetary system, she should have a say in who gets to continue to represent her to the American republic.

How does the Fed fit within that president–as-CEO model of the executive branch? Can the president control the central bank by firing the central bankers? As with most any other aspect of the Fed's governance, there's no easy answer to these questions. This is true, in part, because the Fed chair serves two statutorily defined roles: she is the chair of the board, nominated by the president and confirmed by the Senate to a four-year term. She is also one of seven members of the Board of Governors, nominated by the president and confirmed by the Senate to a fourteen-year term. The Federal Reserve Act is clear that, in her capacity as governor, the Fed chair can be fired only for a good reason. The statute is silent, however, about whether the president can fire the Fed chair.[6]

This leaves the legal question: Can the president legally fire the Fed chair if she doesn't like the cut of the chair's jib, that is, for any or no reason at all? The answer should be yes, for both legal and policy reasons. The question of whether a president can fire a Fed chair should be one enforced by political legitimacy and fallout, not judicial intervention. The legal question is complicated, but the history and policy is not.[7]

First, history. It is true that the president has never written a letter to a Fed chair terminating her employment, as we saw with FDR and the right-wing holdover from the Hoover administration, William Humphrey. That said, one Fed chair was almost certainly fired: Thomas McCabe, who resigned as chair immediately as part of the Fed-Treasury Accord.[8]

As discussed in chapter 2, McCabe fell on his sword as part of the Fed-Treasury Accord, paving the way for William McChesney Martin, then an official in Truman's Treasury Department. In fact, McCabe made his resignation contingent on his participation in the vetting process that named his successor (McCabe favored Martin, even though the Truman administration did not). It's not exactly clear why Truman or his secretary insisted on a McCabe resignation. In fact, prior to the Accord, some on the Board of Governors—notably, former Fed chair Marriner Eccles, who remained a bur under President Truman's saddle by failing to resign after Eccles didn't get the chair reappointment—thought McCabe too close to Truman. That said, we do know that his departure, followed by a replacement from within the Truman administration, suggests some kind of pressure exerted on the Fed chair, by the president, to terminate his term before he was statutorily required to do so, for no other reason than the president's preference. Immediately after his early resignation and replacement by a Truman administration insider (Martin), at least one member of Congress called for hearings to see if this was, in fact, a firing of the Fed chair on the sly.[9]

Such a silent firing also fits Truman's view of other high-profile resignations, including that of Harry Dexter White from the IMF, who Truman insisted (probably incorrectly) was "fired by resignation" because of White's suspected Communist sympathies. Regardless, it became the common view that McCabe's resignation was part of a quid pro quo: "Chairman McCabe 'bled' for Fed independence," wrote one observer. It is likely that McCabe is the sole casualty in the president's appointment fight over the Fed's policies.[10]

Another example of a President injecting politics into the Fed's governance isn't as close to McCabe but also serves to illustrate the variety of ways a president might displace a sitting Fed official. And that is to fire by promotion. William Miller, President Jimmy Carter's first Fed chair, left the Fed after one year of what was widely viewed as incompetence at managing the growing inflation of the 1970s. Miller's removal was not to the ignominy of the nongovernment sector, however, but to his place as Carter's new secretary of the treasury.

To be sure, one can't quite call the appointment as the president's spokesman for the administration's economic policies a "removal," but there are historical precedents for such a phenomenon. Lyndon Johnson did this to Justice Arthur Goldberg by convincing him to leave the Supreme Court for the UN ambassadorship so that Johnson could give his consigliere Abe Fortas a seat on the court. And, although less well known, Richard Nixon fired CIA head Richard Helms by promoting him to become ambassador to Iran. Rather than letting him stay at the CIA until his sixtieth birthday, thereby allowing him to collect the CIA pension, Nixon made the transition too early and left him out to dry. Even years later, Helms recalled bitterly the "promotion" that ended his career and killed his pension.[11]

Given that the Fed chair is up for reappointment every four years, the more or less open question regarding the Fed chair's legal protection against arbitrary dismissal is an interesting, but relatively minor, question in assessing the chair's separation from the president (we dwell on it here only because of the issue's prominence in legal circles.) But it is relatively insignificant because the political costs associated with such a challenge will arise only at a time when a president deems the chair's actions sufficiently noxious to warrant removal. If that situation arises, the chair may recognize it and step aside, as did McCabe. The president may also provide the cover of appointment to another office, as may have been the case with Miller. Or the chair may fight back. The point is, the resolution will largely be political.

From a policy perspective, this question doesn't need a definitive legal answer, given the tools a president can use to push a Fed chair out. Politically, there would be costs for that kind of assault, but there are costs to every major decision a president makes, including on personnel. Given the statutory silence on the question, the fate of a president's decision to keep his (or his predecessor's) Fed chair should rise and fall on the political winds of the time, not the legal determinations of disputes long past.[12]

THE MYTH OF THE FOURTEEN-YEAR TERM AT THE BOARD OF GOVERNORS

The previous section dealt with the curious legal ambiguity about whether the president has the authority to fire a Fed chair. But, as we learned in chapter 3, most of the Fed's authority resides not with the chair but with the Fed's Board of Governors. We now turn to the president's equally counterintuitive legal relationship with those governors.

The institutional design of the Federal Reserve System is a self-conscious effort to balance democratic accountability and technocratic expertise. As the Fed's website explains, "[t]he Federal Reserve, like many other central banks, is an independent government agency but also one that is ultimately accountable to the public and the Congress." To this end, "members of the Board of Governors are appointed for staggered 14-year terms and the Chairman of the Board is appointed for a four-year term."[13]

The reality of the lived experience of Fed tenure is almost exactly the opposite. Governors' terms are a source of increased presidential control; chairs' terms are a source of increased Fed insulation.

First, the governors. When the Federal Reserve System was reorganized in 1935, Congress mapped out the transition from the old Federal Reserve Board system to the new Board of Governors that sought to protect the new board from presidential domination. The mechanism of protection was through a carefully calibrated appointment schedule. "Upon the expiration of the term of any appointive member of the Federal Reserve Board," the Act said, "the President shall fix the term of the successor to such member . . . in such manner as to provide for the expiration of the term of not more than one member in any two-year period."

The idea was to prevent the president from stacking the board. One appointment every two years meant that the president had to face the public in an election after only making two appointments to a seven-person board. Fourteen years is one of the longest terms of service in the federal government. Scholars have long discussed the Fed governors' lengthy tenure, usually uncritically for the propositions that, first, the fourteen-year term is "staggered" such that the president cannot immediately stack the board in his favor; or, second, that the term represents a "term of office for each member . . . made long enough . . . to prevent day-to-day political pressures from influencing the formulation of monetary policy."[14]

This legal guarantee is an empty one. The reason is a tradition of early resignations. Excluding the chairs, the median term of the governors since the board was constituted in 1935 is just over five years, well within the mainstream of independent agencies. It appears that only *one* nonchair governor in the history of the Federal Reserve—out of a total of sixty-two—served a full fourteen-year term (although two others served portions of two terms totaling fourteen years or more).[15]

As we saw, the fourteen-year term was not arbitrarily decided: it corresponds to the seven members of the Board of Governors, just as the previous ten-year term corresponded to the five-member Federal Reserve Board before the 1935 reorganization. The idea is that each president should get but two appointments to the board during a four-year administration. That's the law. Table 8.1 shows how it works in practice.

Under a staggered-term theory of the Board of Governors, the number in the column to the furthest right should be 0.5 (an appointment every two years). As Table 8.1 illustrates, only President Kennedy's appointment control over the board conformed to that statutory expectation. Although the legal mechanism was designed to prevent presidential control of governor appointments, the practice of frequent resignations has meant precisely the opposite.

The governors' decision not to serve a full term is all the more surprising in consideration of the statutory incentive to serve the full term: Governors are precluded "during the time they are in office and for two years thereafter to hold any office, position, or employment in any member bank." But there is a proviso: "except that this restriction shall not apply to a member who has served the full term for which he was appointed." The opportunities to translate the benefits of board service to personal rewards in the banking sector are significant. And yet, governors much more often than not end their terms early.[16]

This extraordinary instance of institutional design—a term of service that is more than double the norm for other independent commissions—illustrates perfectly the flaws in a model of Fed insulation from politics that depends on the language of the Federal

Table 8.1: Presidential Appointments to the Board of Governors, 1935–2015

President	Years in office	Number of governor appointments	Appointments per year
Roosevelt	9.7	10	1.0
Truman	7.8	9	1.2
Eisenhower	8	7	0.9
Kennedy	2.8	1	0.4
Johnson	5.2	6	1.2
Nixon	5.6	5	0.9
Ford	2.4	5	2.1
Carter	4	6	1.5
Reagan	8	8	1.0
G.H.W. Bush	4	5	1.3
Clinton	8	6	0.8
G. W. Bush	8	8	1.0
Obama	6.4	8	1.3
Average	6.1	6.5	1.1

Source: Board of Governors of the Federal Reserve System.

Reserve Act. Presidents can pick their boards because governors do not serve their full term. The statutory efforts to design, by law, the opposite structure haven't succeeded.[17]

THE MYTH OF THE FOUR-YEAR TERM

As the Federal Reserve's website quoted earlier explains, as the counterpoint to the insulation of a fourteen-year term for governors, the Federal Reserve Act gives the Fed chair a renewable four-year term. The idea, again, is to balance the independence of the governors with the accountability of the chair. In practice, here again the opposite has occurred. Because each Fed chair is also a sitting governor, she has two appointments: one a four-year renewable term as chair, the other a fourteen-year nonrenewable term as governor. Also, because the Federal Reserve Act allows each governor to serve the "unexpired term of his predecessor," a governor can extend well beyond the fourteen-year tour of duty. Because of the high turnover mentioned above, there is never a shortage of these "unexpired terms." Combine the two, and a Fed chair could serve for almost twenty-eight years, subject to presidential reappointment every fourth year.

In practice, the combination of these two features—doubling up the term for a governor and almost unlimited renewable terms for the chair gives the Fed chair the opportunity to engage in what some scholars have called "empire building." When a Fed chair seeks reappointment, that person is a leading candidate for that reappointment, even if the initial appointment was by the sitting president's political opponent. Because of the nature of past resignations and the interaction between the chair's four-year term and the fourteen-year term of the governor who occupies the chair, the current situation is that the president will nominate a chair roughly halfway through the president's term, usually when the chair is eligible for another four-year term as chair.[18]

The theoretical implications of this arrangements aren't obvious. One could imagine that a Fed chair might constantly play nice with successive administrations to curry favor in hopes of near perpetual reappointments. In this way, the four-year term accomplishes its goal: the Fed chair is more dependent on politicians. On the other hand, one could imagine an ambitious Fed chair currying favor with other factions inside and outside government to tie the incoming president's hands. In this way, the Fed chair becomes more independent of the president.

In the history of the Federal Reserve System, while there are examples of both dynamics, there are much more of the second. William McChesney Martin Jr. served through five presidential administrations, from Truman to Nixon. And at times, he conflicted intensely with the presidents who (re)appointed him. President Johnson found his intransigence in monetary policy vexing and sought to charm and then remove him as we saw in chapter 2. Martin himself nearly resigned but decided against it, lasting almost twenty years as Fed chair. While Martin has been criticized for the coziness of his monetary policies with those of the Johnson and Nixon administrations, his own diminishing base of support within the Board of Governors and his sense of powerlessness against the fiscal deluge brought on by the Vietnam War are better explanations for his late-term shift in more accommodation than even he thought wise. In reality, Martin was able to cultivate an independent base of support through most of his two decades at the Fed, a base that left even those presidents exasperated by his policies unwilling to absorb the political costs of failing to reappoint him.[19]

Paul Volcker represents another example of this kind of independent political base. Volcker presided over a debilitating recession before the 1982 midterm elections and was not President Reagan's preference for reappointment. Even before the 1981 inauguration, Reagan's chief domestic policy advisor warned the public that the president-elect would not commit to asking "Paul Volcker to remain" in his position as Fed chair. But because he was a candidate, Reagan and some of his advisors feared the consequences in the bond markets if Volcker was not reappointed. Volcker won that reappointment. Had he insisted on staying at the Fed in 1987, in fact, there is a real chance that President Reagan would have relented again. Volcker enjoyed extraordinary prestige at the end of his tenure, and the reappointment conversation occurred at the height of the Iran-Contra scandal, in many ways the nadir of Reagan's public image.[20]

Sometimes, too, the cost of failing to renominate a predecessor's Fed chair is financial, not political: President Obama reportedly renominated Chair Bernanke at some political cost out of fear that the financial markets would respond adversely at the suggestion of monetary and regulatory policies other than those pursued during Bernanke's management of the 2008 financial crisis during his four-year term as chair.[21]

The point is that because of the structure of the governor and chair appointments—the fact that the chair can serve almost indefinitely, and everyone knows this—the sitting chair is nearly always a candidate for presidential reappointment, whether the president likes it or not. As such, the Fed chair can and does cultivate relationships outside the presidency to build freedom of movement and to increase the political costs of the president's wish to exercise his legal discretion in making a new appointment. According to political scientist and historian Daniel Carpenter, this kind of cultivation of external contacts is the very definition of administrative autonomy. The Fed chairs have shown themselves adept at growing and deploying that autonomy.[22]

The four-year, renewable term for the Fed chair provides an opportunity for the president and public to reassess the accomplishments of the Fed chair. But no sitting chair with time left to serve as governor, who is interested in reappointment, can be dismissed as a candidate. The effective Fed chair builds a financial and political constituency for reappointment. The president must keep that constituency in mind when making the reappointment decision, whatever the statute says.

Indeed, it is telling that of the eight chairs of the Board of Governors since the position was created in 1935, five were reappointed by a successive administration. And four of the five were reappointed by a successor president of a different party—Martin, appointed by President Truman, reappointed by Presidents Eisenhower (twice), Kennedy, and Johnson; Volcker, appointed by President Carter and reappointed by President Reagan; Greenspan, appointed by President Reagan, reappointed by Presidents George H. W. Bush, Clinton (twice), and George W. Bush; and Bernanke, appointed by President George W. Bush, reappointed by President Obama.

PRESIDENTIAL CONTROL BEYOND LAW: THREE MODELS OF CONTROL

The law, then, isn't the predictable tool of independence or accountability that so many, inside and outside the Fed, have insisted. But this does not mean that the president is irrelevant. Far from it. It means instead that the president uses control outside of the statute to influence the Fed. We'll briefly consider three different examples: appointment, domination, and reverse control (where the Fed chair dictates policy to the president).

First, control by appointment. The idea here is one anticipated by the Fed's institutional designers from the beginning and is the central point of governance: the appointment power shapes policy. Give the appointment power to the private bankers, and they will usually pick candidates who favor their interests. Give the power to politicians, and their appointees will favor their electoral interests. There are exceptions, of course. Everyone can point to a Republican Supreme Court justice who becomes a stalwart liberal. And within the Fed, there is perhaps no better example than William McChesney Martin's betrayal of the Truman administration so soon after Truman made the unusual appointment.

More often, though, the appointment power functions as anticipated. Marriner Eccles is the paragon. Franklin Roosevelt knew his man when he made the appointment. They worked hand in glove in refounding the Fed during the second New Deal, a dynamic that did not change during the rest of the Roosevelt administration. This is ironic, in many ways: the Banking Act of 1935 that Eccles wrote and Roosevelt supported *removed* the president's representatives by removing the secretary of the treasury and the comptroller of the currency from the Federal Reserve Board. But with Eccles in place, Roosevelt didn't need to worry. Eccles was devoted to Roosevelt. They worked closely on monetary policy, appointments to the Board of Governors, legislative matters, war policy, and personal matters.

Although insulation from the president and Treasury became obsessions of future Fed chairs, Eccles felt no such qualms with his close relationship with Roosevelt. His memoir is filled with fond recollections of even minute policy discussions between himself and the president. He *was* Roosevelt's Federal Reserve; there was little daylight between them. As Eccles summarized it a few years after Roosevelt's death, "[t]hroughout his Presidency I usually found myself in agreement with Roosevelt's social objectives, although I often disagreed with his ideas as to the way they could be achieved. But whether I agreed or disagreed, whether I had moderate, slight, or no influence whatsoever on his particular decisions, I always felt we were working on the same team." There was no need for the president to control Eccles; the appointment had taken care of itself.[23]

CONTROL BY DOMINATION: RICHARD NIXON AND ARTHUR BURNS

The second example is control by domination, as seen in the relationship between President Richard Nixon and his Fed chair Arthur Burns. Burns was an eminent economist at the time; he was, for example, an early mentor to Milton Friedman and a longtime member of the economics faculty at Columbia University. But Nixon knew him better through his Republican loyalties and made no secret about his affection for Burns's partisan commitments over his intellectual ones. For example, in Nixon's famous book *Six Crises*, published in 1962 as a sort of political manifesto outlining Nixon's approach to politics and leadership, the former vice president and future president recalled that Burns reached out to him in the spring of 1960 with warnings that economic deterioration could interfere with Nixon's electoral prospects. To remedy this, Burns urged the Eisenhower administration, through Nixon, to do "everything possible . . . to avert this development." As Nixon recalled, Burns "urgently recommended that two steps be taken immediately: by loosening up on credit and, where justifiable, by increasing spending for national security." Ten years later, at Nixon's first opportunity, he knew who he would get for the Federal Reserve.[24]

Burns's tenure is widely regarded as a failure, in large part owing to his acquiescence to Nixon's domination. The recently published Burns diaries are filled with references to a close personal and emotional proximity between Burns and Nixon that raise modern eyebrows about the policy proprieties of that relationship. A few examples illustrate the point. Nixon told Burns about his appointment of prominent Democrat John Connolly as secretary of the treasury before announcing it publicly, and then told Burns that Connolly—a politician, not an economist or businessman—would learn the ropes of his new position from Burns. Burns attended cabinet meetings; had his speeches vetted by Nixon's staff; cleared his talking points with the president ahead of a meeting with other central bankers in Basel, Switzerland; advised Nixon on tax, wage, and other fiscal policy; and made pledges to remain the president's "true friend" on economic policies before the public.[25]

We could, of course, make a similar list concerning Eccles's proximity to Roosevelt. What made the Nixon-Burns relationship so unusual was Nixon's paranoid leadership style and the pressure that it brought to bear on Burns. One of the most confusing and intriguing parts of the Burns chapter in Fed history is that even while he was being bullied by the Nixon administration, he intoned regularly on the importance of the "independence" of the monetary authority. This declaration of independence was a thorn in the side of Wright Patman, a member of the House of Representative from Texas and constant scourge (as we will see in the next chapter) of the Federal Reserve. Burns's insistence that the Fed was and should be independent, even after he had coordinated monetary policy for Nixon's electoral ends, gave Patman even more fodder for his multidecade assault on the Fed. Burns's duplicitous assertions of Fed independence were an "arrogance we must not tolerate. No one man or institution should have this unbridled power. The people did not elect Dr. Burns, and he is not our king."[26]

In one unfortunate exchange, reported by Nixon's former chief of staff Bob Ehrlichman after the fact (and perhaps with an axe to grind), we see an eager participant in the bending of monetary policy toward Nixon's electoral prospects. "My relations with the Fed," Nixon allegedly told Burns, "will be different than they were with [former Fed chair William McChesney] Martin there. He was always six months too late doing anything. I'm counting on you, Arthur, to keep us out of a recession."

"Yes, Mr. President," Burns is said to have responded, pipe in his mouth. "I don't like to be late."[27]

We don't have to rely on others' perhaps skewed accounts of this dysfunctional relationship. Burns's attachment to Nixon, in spite of the abuse and cognitive dissonance, is perhaps most salient in his diary from the time. In one long passage, Burns records a conversation he had with Nixon late in the president's second term, as scandal and political crisis fell down on Nixon. Burns was there to reassure him; the passage is worth quoting at length (RN is Richard Nixon, WH is White House):

> I informed the President as follows: (1) that his friendship was one of the three that has counted most in my life and that I wanted to keep it if I possibly could; (2) that I took the present post to repay the debt of an immigrant boy to a nation that had given him the opportunity to develop and use his brains constructively; (3) that there was never the slightest conflict between doing what was right for the economy and my doing what served the political interests of RN; (4) that if a conflict ever arose between these objectives, I would not lose a minute in informing RN and seeking a solution together; (5) that the sniping in the press that the WH staff was engaged in had not the slightest influence on Fed policy, since I will be moved only by evidence that what the Fed is doing is not serving the nation's best interests; (6) that the WH staff had created an atmosphere of confrontation which led to the exaggeration of said differences about economy policy as may exist between the Fed and the Administration; that (7) squabbling or the appearance of squabbling among high government officers could lead to a weakening of confidence in government policy and thereby injure the prospects of economic improvement.[28]

Although some scholars argue that Burns's close proximity to Richard Nixon became clear only with hindsight, the Nixon tapes and other public contemporaneous accounts make clear that the personal connection between the two was strong and strongly influenced by Nixon's desire to control policy considerations.[29]

In terms of presidential control of the Fed, the Nixon era was a success for the president, a failure for the Fed and Arthur Burns.

But it does illustrate an important point of the reality of political influence on the Federal Reserve: a politician can control the Fed by sheer force of personality. It's the anti-example that Fed chairs should consider in their relationships with the executive.[30]

REVERSE CONTROL: BILL CLINTON AND THE GREENSPAN FED

The third model to consider is actually not of presidential control of the Fed, but Fed control of the president. The Clinton-Greenspan years were marked by one of the most noticeable periods of central bank and presidential cooperation in the nation's history. This is all the more remarkable because of the fact that there was no genuine domestic financial crisis that required close coordination that we would expect from central banks and the Treasury (as explained earlier in chapter 7). Instead, the Greenspan Fed and the Clinton administration worked hand in glove to battle international financial crises and, perhaps even more important, to determine domestic fiscal policy.

The truly noteworthy aspect of this cooperation, though, was not that it occurred. Fed chairs and presidents had conferred on fiscal matters before, as we have just seen. What was different is that the hand was Greenspan's, the glove Bill Clinton's. More than any other time in our history, during the Greenspan-Clinton years the Fed was in charge, and the president played catch-up. Although not an economist, Bill Clinton, one of the most astute national politicians in U.S. history, understood this viscerally. "You mean to tell me," he said to his advisers, that "my reelection hinges on the Federal Reserve and a bunch of [expletive] bond traders?" He didn't have to be told twice.[31]

The charm offensive from Clinton to Greenspan began almost as soon as Clinton was elected, before his inauguration. In December 1992, after Clinton had defeated Greenspan's friend and fellow Republican George H. W. Bush, Clinton invited Greenspan to visit the president-elect's Arkansas headquarters. When they met in Little Rock for the first time, Greenspan was impressed. "I could see why he was reputed to be a great retail politician," he wrote in his memoir. "He made me believe he really had been looking forward to seeing me."[32]

Clinton was there not just to charm the Fed chair, but to hear his advice on Clinton's domestic economic agenda. Their topic: the deficit. Greenspan saw that the key to Clinton's reelection prospects and the key to economic growth was getting the administration's fiscal house in order. This fiscal conservatism matched the recommendation from influential parts of Clinton's administration and was part of his political image as a centrist Democrat. Clinton was sold.

It is not terribly surprising that a libertarian central banker and a fiscally conservative Democrat would agree on the need to constrain governmental spending. It is more surprising that Clinton's political calculation included making use of that central banker's personal prestige. Clinton's very first address to a joint session of Congress in February 1993 was, unsurprisingly, on the economy. And deficit reduction featured prominently in that discussion. Perhaps unsurprisingly, too, Clinton didn't say a word about the Fed or monetary policy. But Alan Greenspan was central to that speech: in front of a televised audience, Clinton had invited Greenspan to hear this important address as the president's personal guest. He sat between Hillary Clinton and Tipper Gore, a symbol of the partnership between Greenspan and Clinton.[33]

Greenspan was more than a passive partner in this relationship. Just a week after Clinton's inauguration, Greenspan had testified before the Senate on behalf of the president's deficit reduction plan. Clinton had convinced Greenspan that he was serious about this issue, "by far the most pressing concern" that Greenspan had from his perch at the Federal Reserve. They had committed to a joint enterprise.[34]

The deficit wasn't the only front of common policy concern. Greenspan enjoyed a close personal relationship with Clinton's economic team, soon headed at the Treasury by Robert Rubin.

Rubin, an investment banker by profession, had been Clinton's first director of the newly created National Economic Council, a White House office designed to coordinate all the president's economic policy. At the NEC, Rubin had been a staunch advocate of what he described as the Fed's independence. He insisted that no administration official comment on Fed policy (although, he writes in his memoir, that Clinton "always adhered to the principle" of keeping presidents out of Fed policy). This wasn't just good economics; it was good politics: "evident respect for the Fed's independence can bolster the President's credibility."[35]

Soon, the respect for Greenspan became personal. Rubin, together with his deputy Larry Summers, forged a close bond with Greenspan on the tennis courts, at the breakfast table, and, importantly, on all questions of economic policy. While Rubin and Summers never told Greenspan his business, Greenspan felt comfortable telling them theirs. Their discussions ranged from preparations for meetings with foreign governments, responding to international crises, or just debates about economics generally. "These meetings were a cross between a graduate seminar in economics and a policy-planning meeting, with bits of gossip thrown in."[36] Over time, the three of them—Greenspan, Rubin, and Summers—"merged into a kind of brotherhood, with an easy rapport" oriented toward solving economic policy problems and creating a financial order that conformed to their common economic worldview. As a *Time* magazine essay put it in a famous cover story, they were the "Committee to Save the World," the "three marketeers." What they shared was a common ideology: "Their faith is in the markets and in their own ability to analyze them."[37]

As we've seen elsewhere in this book, unbridled faith in markets and economists' ability to analyze them proved fatal in the financial crisis. But for the 1990s, it meant that the Federal Reserve and the Clinton presidency had almost merged, with Greenspan as his own figurehead. As befitted his stature, when *Time* put the three on the cover of its magazine, Greenspan towered in the front, with the secretary and deputy secretary in the distance behind him.[38]

CONCLUSION: LAW AND PERSONALITY
WITH THE PRESIDENT

The law and practice of presidential attempts to control Fed policy demonstrate powerfully one of the book's main themes. Law matters, but not the way we would think from just reading the statute, and it is not enough to guarantee the balance between political control and technocratic expertise that congressional designers may have sought. This reality is most obvious in the way that Fed chair and Fed governor terms have reversed the attempt to balance democratic accountability and technocratic expertise: the increase of political accountability to the president that the four-year term is designed to bring has allowed for empire building among Fed chairs, whereas the apparent liberation of the fourteen-year term has become a mechanism for exerting presidential control on the Fed.

This chapter has also demonstrated how much personality and personnel matter in the determination of Fed policy, not just at the Federal Reserve but also at the White House. The exact identities of Ulysses (the president) and his chaperone (the Fed chair) matter enormously in determining the shape of the space within which the Fed exercises its extraordinary authority.

CHAPTER 9

CONGRESS AND THE FED

THE CURIOUS CASE OF THE FED'S BUDGETARY AUTONOMY

> He may make a theory that, since we admit and we know that
> the House of Commons is the real sovereign, any other
> sovereign is superfluous.
>
> —*Walter Bagehot, 1873*

When Ben Bernanke was asked in his final press conference as Fed
chair about words of advice for his successor Janet Yellen, Bernanke
responded clearly. "Congress is our boss" with "every right to set
up the terms on which the Fed operates." This is true from a constitutional perspective: Congress has the authority to pass all kinds of
legislation, including even abolishing the Federal Reserve, without
running afoul of the Constitution. Unlike, for example, the European Central Bank, the Fed enjoys no special constitutional protection. Although not exactly the same as the House of Commons,
Congress is, from the Fed's perspective, the "real sovereign."[1]

The history of the Fed makes clear that Congress has indeed been
a willing participant in changing the Fed's institutional design, in
ways both large and small. We have already discussed in detail the
Fed's second founding in 1935, a legislative act that redistributed

power within the system, created a new committee at the Fed (the Board of Governors), and redefined one that it had created just two years before (the Federal Open Market Committee). Even more often than that, the history of the Fed is a story of Congress passing a long string of new legislation giving the Fed more and more authority, some of which it did not seek. The Dodd-Frank Act of 2010 is but the latest example of this expansion.[2]

But as was the case with the president and the Fed, the relationship between Congress and the Fed is more complicated and much more interesting than that of the lawgiver creating new and different legal commands. In this chapter, we'll look at two ways Congress concedes or exercises influence over the Fed without actually passing laws: legislative threats and, curiously, an extraordinary acquiescence to the Fed's unique budgetary autonomy that Congress never granted by statute.

LEGISLATIVE THREATS

We have already seen how Congress influences the Fed through active legislation, such as the Banking Act of 1935, the Bank Holding Company Act of 1956, or the Truth-in-Lending Act of 1970. A different kind of influence from Congress comes through individual members' attempts to shape policy or win points with constituents with *threats* of legislation, whether through hearings, introduced legislation, or other mechanisms. Recent scholarship on this phenomenon shows that, while Republicans and Democrats differ on their specific policy proposals, legislative threats are countercyclical: that is, when things are going well, Congress tends to leave the Fed alone, but when the economy tanks, Congress starts paying attention. While it is difficult to determine whether these threats shape Fed behavior systematically, two episodes from Fed history demonstrate specific instances where congressional threats were, indeed, decisive on shaping the space within which the Fed operates.[3]

For decades, the name "Wright Patman" would fill Federal Reserve chairs with dread. Patman had, in the words of political historian Donald Kettl, made his career "as the populist scourge of the

Fed." Over the course of his five decades in the House of Representatives—he eventually became dean of the House, as its longest serving member—Patman was the Fed's perennial foe. He almost never succeeded in changing the Fed with the slew of formal legislative proposals, but his unflagging efforts demonstrate how legislative threats were sufficient to shape Fed behavior.[4]

A case in point is the Patman Hearings in 1964. Using the occasion of the fiftieth anniversary of the Federal Reserve Act to hold five months of hearings on Fed history, structure, and policies, Patman pushed Chair William McChesney Martin into the arms of a waiting Lyndon Johnson. The Patman hearings weren't the congressman's first foray into Fed heckling. Patman held significant hearings in 1952 on the questions of the separation of monetary and fiscal policy and the Fed's complicated governance (he was against both). During the Eisenhower years, too, Martin and Patman dueled at virtually every hearing where they both participated. The duels becoming "legendary," as Martin's biographer described them. But the 1964 hearings marked something different in character, not least because of their extended attention and, at times, their seeming popularity with Patman's colleagues. During the hearings, Patman also disclosed his suite of Fed reforms: eliminating the FOMC, increasing the Board of Governors to twelve members, and restoring the secretary of the treasury to the board. He also wanted to quash the Fed's budgetary autonomy by bringing the Fed under annual congressional appropriations.[5]

Normally, Martin could deflect these criticisms through his network of congressional and market contacts. He frequently used his political skills to take the wind out of criticisms of the Fed. But although the minority Republicans in the House did not share Patman's zeal, Patman's appeals were gaining traction with his fellow Democrats: after the 1962 election, Democrats held a 258–176 majority, and electoral prospects a few months ahead were looking increasingly rosy. Martin realized that the only source for his and the Fed's salvation was another Texan, the new president, Lyndon Johnson.

Patman and Johnson went back a long way. The older Patman had served in the Texas state legislature with Johnson's father and with Johnson himself for a decade in the U.S. House. But Johnson and Martin were then in the midst of their tussle over interest rates and economic policy described in chapter 2. Martin worried that appealing to the president would result in some "sense of obligation" for the Fed chair, especially when the president was Lyndon Johnson, "justly famed" for his preference and skill at political horse trading.[6]

These concerns notwithstanding, Martin made the appointment with Johnson to express his concerns about the 1964 Patman hearings and quickly received the "LBJ treatment": a long walk around White House grounds in full view of the press, with LBJ's heavy arm draped over the shorter man's shoulders. The conversation started on Johnson's terms with discussion of interest rates. Martin reiterated his inflationary fear and desire to push up interest rates in the short-term. Johnson's response was almost playful: "Now I have some pretty good people here and they don't agree with you . . . but we'll talk about it later."

The men then turned to the Patman hearings. Johnson listened to Martin's concerns without comment, but when they returned to the Oval Office, Johnson called the Speaker of the House John Mc-Cormak in Patman's presence to resolve the issue. Two weeks later—after five months of hearings that seemed headed for significant reform—the hearings ended without legislation.[7]

In the final years of the Johnson administration, Martin's resolute stand against inflation started to ebb. Although he remained committed to speaking out against the problems of deficit spending without limit, he was not successful at leading the Fed against the administration's desires to have an easier monetary policy to support its domestic (the Great Society) and international (the Vietnam War) agendas.[8]

Did Martin's failure come from his use of the president as a strategic partner against Patman? It's difficult to know with certainty. One would expect—as Johnson himself did—that a bureaucrat whose job was effectively spared by the president would owe LBJ some quo for the presidential quid. Martin was sensitive to those demands and continued to needle the Johnson administration at the margins, primarily through the discount rate. At one point, because of the obvious conflicts, Martin offered his resignation: if President Johnson wanted a different Fed chair who could support administration policies, he should have him. (Johnson rejected the offer but almost immediately regretted it after Martin compared the 1965 financial climate with that of precrash 1929).

But while Martin maintained his distance in the short term, there is also evidence that he began a conciliatory slide toward the president during the end of the Johnson administration, including by almost constant coordination of monetary policy with fiscal policy. This very proximity and coordination is, in Meltzer's view, one of the most significant errors in Martin's final years in office. That Martin felt compelled, at the very least, to coordinate these policies—with the harms that this kind of coordination brought—came from the same impulse that led him to seek and receive protection against the legislative threats of Wright Patman.[9]

Patman, of course, never succeeded at changing the Fed to the full extent that he had hoped, in part because of the sense that he was so extreme he couldn't build a strong consensus. But he succeeded at keeping Fed reform as a perennial topic of conversation, and likely succeeded in pushing the Fed into the arms of an eager president, precisely what Patman wanted to do. He is a strong example of congressional influence outside of pure lawmaking.[10]

HENRY GONZALEZ AND THE BIRTH OF FEDERAL RESERVE TRANSPARENCY

Henry Gonzalez was the member of Congress most active in Fed oversight during the 1990s. Gonzalez was in the tradition of Wright Patman—a Texas populist suspicious of the Fed's power, secrecy, and proximity to private bankers in New York. But his proposed changes to the Fed were more anchored around transparency in the form of pure sunlight: letting the public see how the FOMC made decisions by putting cameras inside the FOMC meetings and releasing the video on a sixty-day delay. Gonzalez introduced legislation to this end, which Greenspan adamantly opposed. He thought the idea of making the deliberations within the FOMC publicly available would turn these meetings into "a series of bland, written presentations." In that case, "[t]he advantages to policy formulation of unfettered debate would be lost."[11]

The Fed had a history with selective disclosure of what transpired in FOMC meetings. The Board of Governors had distributed summaries of FOMC decisions in the board's annual reports but also prepared much more detailed "memoranda of discussion" (MOD), which were something between detailed minutes and verbatim transcripts. The effort to control the production and distribution of those memoranda was a source of tension between the Fed and Congress before. Patman had demanded the full verbatim transcripts for the early 1960s at a time when Friedman and Schwartz's damning history of the Fed's role in exacerbating the Great Depression was published. Patman's committee received those transcripts, and shortly thereafter the Fed started releasing these MODs—but not the full transcripts—on a five-year lag.[12]

In 1974, Patman asked for more transcripts. Fed Chair Arthur Burns said there were none to give. There were transcripts once, but they were used only to create these MODs; once the FOMC's minutes were prepared, the transcripts were "routinely disposed of when they served their purpose." The Fed's retreat into secrecy went even further two years later. In response to the new Government in the Sunshine Act, the Fed became the target of lawsuits and pressure to disclose more about its internal deliberations. And so the Fed closed up shop on the distribution of the memoranda of discussions by a ten-to-one vote.[13]

Patman, as one would expect, was livid with these decisions. Here Burns showed himself adept at controlling the fallout. While refusing to restore the memoranda again, he proposed a compromise: the FOMC would publicly release what it called "Minutes of the Federal Open Market Committee" on a ninety-day lag. These "minutes" were hardly that. They contained a summary of the action taken, but no comments for attribution. The only time an individual FOMC member was singled out was if he dissented, and even then the minutes didn't explain the reason for the dissent. These minutes did the trick, though, and the dust-up over Fed transparency subsided.[14]

Burns, however, had a secret. What no one outside the Fed and almost no one inside the Fed knew was that Burns had kept the transcripts going, a practice continued by Greenspan. The FOMC meetings were recorded without members' knowledge, and transcripts were still being prepared for the chair's personal use.

During the course of what came to be called the Gonzalez Hearings, the truth about the still available transcripts came out. The Fed staff kept under lock and key the full transcripts of these meetings. When Gonzalez learned of the existence of these transcripts, he changed tacks away from trying to get these meetings televised and toward releasing the transcripts. He threatened to subpoena them if the Fed did not agree to their release. Greenspan permitted two lawyers from the House Banking Committee—one Republican, one Democrat—to listen to the most recent tapes. The Fed also decided, for the first time in its history, to announce publicly the specific policy intention that the FOMC had reached during each meeting, and to release transcripts of the meeting on a five-year lag.[15] Today, these lagged releases are a centerpiece of the Fed's public engagement.

One famous British central banker, Montagu Norman, once summed up his philosophy on central bank transparency: "Never explain, never apologize." This all changed in the 1990s. Some credit Alan Greenspan for those changes, but the full context of how the FOMC transcripts came into the public domain shows a different story. One of the most significant changes in the practice of central banking occurred not because of chair leadership, but legislative threats from a congressman whose legislative agenda never got close to enactment.[16]

BUDGETARY AUTONOMY: STATUTORY EVOLUTION AND CONGRESSIONAL ACQUIESCENCE

If legislative threats show members of Congress making efforts to hold the Fed to account, out next topic shows deep and long-standing congressional acquiescence. One of the primary means of congressional control over governmental agencies is the power of the purse, or the ability to fund or defund the relevant agency. This power represents a unique and often misconstrued aspect of Congress's relationship with the Fed. The Fed, unlike other agencies, is able to fund itself from the proceeds of open market operations that it controls with very limited interference from the political branches. Congress has conceded this most powerful tool completely.[17]

This budgetary autonomy is not misconstrued because it is secret. To the contrary, the Fed includes on its own website and in its detailed annual reports a frank admission that the system's "income comes primarily from the interest on government securities that it has acquired through open market operations." Instead, the Fed's budgetary autonomy is misunderstood because few know where this authority comes from. The bottom line is this: when Congress removed the Fed from the annual appropriations process, as it has done with several agencies through history, it also imposed strict, statutory limits on how the Fed could generate these nonappropriated funds. One by one, those limits have disappeared, but not through legislative annulment. Time and changing circumstances have intervened. The law of the Fed's limited budgetary autonomy remains on the books; the practice of the Fed's unlimited budgetary autonomy is very different.[18]

FUNDING THE GOVERNMENT

There are four forms of funding in government. First, the vast majority of governmental institutions—from the Congress to the courts to the White House, and most agencies, institutions, programs, and commissions in between—are funded through Congress's annual appropriations process. That is, the president proposes his budget to the Congress, based presumably on inputs from those agencies who require the funding, political machinations ensue, and a budget is passed funding the government. The process begins anew a year later.[19]

Second, the majority of actual government expenditures does not occur through this appropriation process but instead is part of the government's mandatory commitments. These commitments include entitlement programs such as Social Security, Medicare, Medicaid, and other forms of direct assistance; some kinds of disaster relief; and interest on the national debt.

And third, some governmental agencies, including some of the banking agencies, are "self-funded," meaning that they raise their money by assessing fees against the entities they regulate. For example, the Federal Deposit Insurance Corporation (FDIC), the agency in charge of insuring the nation's banking deposits, charges banks fees for that insurance. From those fees, the FDIC not only covers losses to the insurance fund but also covers its expenses. The new Office for Financial Research (OFR), an agency set up by the Dodd-Frank Act to provide the Treasury with research on financial stability, is funded by an assessment on members of the financial industry.[20]

And then there is the Fed. Like the FDIC or OFR, the Fed is "self-funded" in that it is not part of the annual appropriations process, nor is it a "mandatory commitment." But unlike the FDIC, most of its budget doesn't come from assessments against regulated entities. Instead, the Fed funds itself with a portion of the proceeds from its open market operations. As the Fed reported in its 2013 budget report, "[t]he major sources of income were interest earnings from the portfolio of U.S. government securities ($49.0 billion) and federal agency mortgage-backed securities (MBS) ($31.4 billion) in the System Open Market Account. Earnings in excess of expenses, dividends, and surplus are transferred to the U.S. Treasury—in 2012, a total of $88.4 billion."[21]

That the Fed funds itself largely from the proceeds of its substantial assets, taken together with the nature of the Fed's ability to create money in pursuit of its monetary policy objectives, means that the Fed's funding is unique in government. As we have seen, the Fed conducts monetary policy by, among other options, creating money with which it can buy government—and more recently, nongovernment—securities. These interest-bearing assets generate money that the agency can subsequently use to fund itself. The Fed thus has the ability to create from nothing the money it eventually uses to pay its employees, fund its conferences, and renovate its buildings.[22]

The Fed's budgetary autonomy is thus without equal in the federal government. But here is the striking reality: It is not expressly authorized by Congress. Instead, Congress created the Fed to look more like the FDIC. The Federal Reserve's funding mechanism is located in Section 10(3) of the Federal Reserve Act. That section grants the Board of Governors the "power to levy semiannually upon the Federal reserve banks . . . an assessment sufficient to pay its estimated expenses and the salaries of its members and employees for the half year succeeding the levying of such assessment." Unquestionably, this statutory authorization exempts the Fed from the congressional appropriations. On its face, however, it just looks like the Fed was given the same status as the FDIC: the ability to charge essentially private institutions for its own upkeep. The statute does not allow the Fed to create, and fund itself with, its own Federal Reserve Notes.[23]

THE RISE OF FED BUDGETARY AUTONOMY

How, then, did this relatively modest statutory authorization metamorphose into the Fed's complete budgetary autonomy? Three historical changes made the difference: the end of the budgetary autonomy of the Reserve Banks, terminated in 1935; the Fed's history with what was called the "real bills doctrine"; and the Fed's history with the gold standard.

Chapter 1 explained in detail the rise and fall of the autonomous Federal Reserve Banks. That autonomy was key to making sense of Congress's funding apparatus for the Federal Reserve system. With autonomous Federal Reserve Banks, the system had to battle for scarce resources just like any other participant in the market economy. And during the period of Reserve Bank autonomy, the banks were mindful of managing their earnings in ways that increased conflict between the Federal Reserve Board and the Reserve Banks. Even though the Federal Reserve Board participated to a limited extent in shaping the tenor of monetary policy, the reality is that the Reserve Banks could and did pursue their own monetary policy. As a result, there existed a separation between the assessment authority (which resided with the Federal Reserve Board) and the operations authority (which resided with the Federal Reserve Banks). The Federal Reserve Board in this early stage could not create the money with which it funded itself: it had to get that money from the Reserve Banks.[24]

This separation, of course, has disappeared. The statutory funding mechanism has not kept pace with U.S. central banking practice. The era of autonomy for the Reserve Banks ended with the passage of the Banking Act of 1935, which placed the authority for open market operations of the individual banks into the Washington-based Board. The assessment provision, however, was unchanged.[25]

By itself, the abolition of Reserve Bank autonomy isn't enough to show much distance between the Fed's budgetary autonomy today and its more limited budgetary autonomy in history. After all, if the Reserve Banks could create the money with which to fund themselves, then making the Federal Reserve Board beg them for money would only tell us that the location of this extraordinary authority shifted within the Federal Reserve System.

Two changes to the practice of monetary policy show how different the funding mechanism has become, no matter where within the system that authority is located. When the Federal Reserve Act was passed, the idea of a "fiat currency," or a currency not backed by gold or some other fixed exchange, was anathema to the system's legislative sponsors. To combat the temptation, two prevailing monetary doctrines kept the Reserve Banks from "printing money": the gold standard, and what would come to be called the "real bills doctrine."

In 1913, when Woodrow Wilson signed the Federal Reserve Act into law, the industrial world was at what would turn out to be the end of the classic gold standard. Under this standard, gold was the legal tender of international commerce. National money—the U.S. dollar, the British pound—was issued against gold, meaning that paper money could be redeemed for gold (although the regulatory requirements of that conversion varied from country to country). Governments that had committed themselves to the standard—did not have complete discretion in determining the value of their currency.

Bagehot referred to it not as the "gold standard" but the "cast iron system," because it locked the countries and their central banks into a commitment that would prevent them from printing money with reckless abandon. The gold standard prevented such monetary shenanigans because those engaged in international commerce based on that currency would start to demand gold convertibility, and if more paper IOUs were circulating than could be redeemed, the country's currency would plunge in value and its access to the international markets would collapse along with it.[26]

The carnage, disruption, and fiscal consequences of World War I brought the gold standard screeching to a halt. Postwar central banks fought mightily (and, at first, successfully) to restore a version of it, but that failed during the Great Depression. Post–World War II countries sought to restore it again, with less devastating consequences, but that effort ultimately and finally failed again in 1973. The U.S. dollar has been a fiat currency ever since. The result is that the Reserve Banks couldn't print money to fund themselves (or the Federal Reserve Board) in 1913, but the Board of Governors of the Federal Reserve System in 1973 could and did.[27]

The real bills doctrine is the final example of the limitations on the Fed's funding apparatus. To understand how it functioned, we need to know more about the practices of commercial banking at the time the Fed was founded.[28]

As Meltzer described it "the main business of a banker" during the late nineteenth century "consisted in issuing notes and discounting bills of exchange." Scholars trace the emergence of the bill of exchange to the thirteenth century, although there is evidence of an analogue in the Roman Empire.[29] This "discounting" function was a kind of loan. A standard loan involves two parties: the lender and the borrower, who agree on the amount of money loaned, the cost of that loan (that is, the interest rate), and the terms of that loan. The debtor and creditor become involved in each other's affairs during the life of that loan, until the borrowed money is repaid.[30]

Then as now, a two-way loan is limited by how much the lender knows about the borrower. It also requires geographic proximity. A bill of exchange is an answer for these limitations. A bill is a financing mechanism that involves four parties, not two, and is essential for the facilitation of "new ways of doing business and new types of commerce." At the time of the Fed's first founding, the primary businesses were across the vast stretches of the United States, to facilitate bringing agricultural products to market, and hopes of participating in a dollar-denominated international trading system. In either case, the four parties are the exporter and importer of specified goods, and the two corresponding banks at either end of that transaction.[31]

For example, if I want to sell some coffee in New York and know a coffee farmer in Brazil, we might finance the shipment with a bill of exchange: I would sign it, the Brazilian coffee farmer would sign it, and so would our two banks. With this bill of exchange, the farmer's bank is "lending" money to me, through my bank, by providing the farmer with the money up front that I promise to pay back after I receive the coffee and sell it to my customers. The bill of exchange itself is a letter from one merchant to another that requests funds on behalf of the importer to be paid to the exporter (in the exporter's currency) at a specified date.

The bill is then "discounted" by the banks, meaning that they will provide less than the full value of the transaction so that they can reap a profit. If I promise to pay my Brazilian business partner $1,000,000, the bank may provide $900,000, at a "discount" of 10 percent. The confusing terminology of the "discount rate" may be one consequence of the Catholic Church's prohibition on usury during the medieval era; the discount rate is just an interest rate by another name, but certain kinds of "interest" was prohibited by the church during this period. Instead, the bills of exchange were "discounted," meaning that the importer would pay the corresponding bank more than the face of the bill in order to compensate the bank for its provision of the short-term loan. A "discount" and an interest rate are economically identical, but the vocabulary difference was apparently sufficient to pass muster with theologians.[32]

A bill of exchange thus resolves the quintessential problem of international trade: who gets paid first, the provider of the goods transported or the one who will sell those goods at the other end of the transport? A bill of exchange makes that payment instantaneous to the exporter, but not payable by the importer until the funds are realized by the sale of the goods in question.

Again, as a four-way transaction, bills of exchange are relatively old. What is newer is their "negotiability." That is, the four transacting parties in a bill of exchange can quickly multiply, almost indefinitely, if the importer's promise to pay a fixed amount on a fixed date were transferrable—or negotiable—to another party. In that case, another party would pay the corresponding bank some amount less than the face value and then collect the amount of the bill from the importer when it became due.

When the Fed was founded in 1913, commercial banks actively engaged in the discounting of commercial paper. What was different about central banks' engagement in this business was the volume of discounting that could be done, on whose behalf, and with what relationship to the banking system generally. Private discounting of commercial paper, including bills of exchange, is a profit-generating exercise that can be necessarily laborious and costly. The cost of validating the credit of the importer—the one who has to ultimately pay off the bill at the due date—is high, perhaps insurmountably so, if the secondary discounter has to know about the importer's business, creditworthiness, and so on. If, on the other hand, the counterparty is a single institution, backed in part or in full by a trustworthy government, then the "transaction cost" of the secondary discount is reduced only to the cost of verifying the creditworthiness of the single institution. That was the benefit of a central bank at the turn of the twentieth century.

But a key part of the debate was exactly what kinds of bills could be discounted. Under the doctrine, not called the real bills doctrine until 1945, the only bills that could be discounted were those that represented an actual transaction that had already occurred and would be paid off in short order. The funding of speculative bills was the alternative, or those transactions that had not yet occurred and may never occur. My bill for $1,000,000 that pointed to the amount of coffee I had already bought and the boat that would bring it from Rio de Janeiro to New York City was "real"; some other coffee enthusiast's IOU for paying back a loan that I promised to use to find some coffee down in Brazil is "speculative."[33]

The real bills doctrine—endorsed by Bagehot as essential to the functioning of a proper central bank—meant that central banks would discount my bill, but not that of the other coffee enthusiast. This view of the world was placed directly into the Federal Reserve Act, which required that a "Federal reserve bank may discount notes, drafts, and bills of exchange arising out of actual commercial transactions," excluding "notes, drafts, or bills covering merely investments or issued or drawn for the purpose of carrying or trading in stocks, bonds, or other investment securities."[34]

Economically, the real bills doctrine didn't work very well. As Milton Friedman and Anna Schwartz wrote, "the real bills criterion . . . provided no effective limit to the amount of money." This is because of the inherent difficulty in determining what counts as a "real bill" that a Reserve Bank can permissibly discount. This uncertainty led to different interpretations and different economic consequences.[35]

The point is that even if the real bills doctrine didn't present an objective limitation in practice, at the time of the 1913 debates both it and the gold standard were seen as essential to the Federal Reserve Act's legitimacy. The claim that the new "Federal Reserve Notes" would represent "fiat money" were fighting words. The colorful Carter Glass's defense on the House floor against the charge is quotable at length:

> Fiat money! Why, sir, never since the world began was there such a perversion of terms; and a month ago I stood before a brilliant audience of 700 bankers and business men in New York City, and there challenged the president of the National City Bank to name a single lexicographer on the face of the earth to whom he might appeal to justify his characterization of these notes. I twitted him with the fact that not 1 per cent of the intelligent bankers of America could be induced to agree with his definition of these notes, and asked him to name a single financial writer of the metropolitan press of his

own town, to whom he might confidently appeal to justify his absurd charge. . . .

"Fiat money" is an irredeemable paper money with no specie basis, with no gold reserve, but the value of which depends solely upon the taxing power of the Government emitting it. This Federal reserve note has 40 per cent. gold reserve behind it, has 100 percent short-term, gilt edge commercial paper behind it, which must pass the scrutiny, first, of the individual bank, next of the regional reserve bank, and finally of the Federal Reserve Board.[36]

Note Glass's twin reliance on the 40 percent gold-reserve ratio, and the invocation of the "short-term, gilt-edge commercial paper" (although he exaggerated, perhaps intentionally, the role that the Federal Reserve Board would play in approving individual discounts). The gold standard and real bills doctrine were the selling points for the framers of the Fed. They represented a perceived limit on how money could be raised by the system. The point is not that the real bills doctrine actually provided no limit on which bills could theoretically be discounted. It is that some people within the system perceived such limitations, and acted accordingly, and that Congress thought that it was not granting to an institution unfettered access to money creation with which it could then, in turn, fund itself.

Glass was not alone; Woodrow Wilson felt the same way. "Let bankers explain the technical features of the new system," he said. "Suffice it here to say that it provides a currency . . . which comes into existence in response to the call of every man who can show a going business and a concrete basis for extending credit to him, however obscure or prominent he may be, however big or little his business transactions." Wilson's rhetoric, here as it so often was, was egalitarian in nature, but practical in implications: the "concrete basis" meant that the Fed couldn't just issue money out of nothing. It needed a "real bill" to cue the printing press.[37]

The recitation of these limitations is to make a single point: Congress's authorization to the Fed to go outside the appropriations process for its funding occurred in a system of Reserve Bank autonomy operating under the gold standard and real bills regime. That system is radically different from the same non-appropriations authorization without those central features. As one historian described it, the "automaticity" of the gold standard and the real bills doctrine meant there was much less discretion to exercise by the central bank. The modern Federal Reserve does not face these limits. The consequence is that the Fed can create its own budget using a statutory authorization from a different era, but with none of the restraints that existed at that time.[38]

In fact, this extrastatutory nature of the Fed's funding runs not only from the money that the Fed itself creates, but also to what the Fed does with the extra money left over. The proceeds of open market operations, after paying the system's expenses, are remitted to the Treasury for governmental consumption. Once again, the Fed is transparent about this practice. And once again, the practice is nowhere authorized by Congress. The remittance of the surplus of open market operations to the Treasury follows a similar trajectory of an original statutory basis (here expressly abrogated in 1933). The present practice occurred by public announcement by the Fed in 1947 and has continued ever since.[39]

Today's source of funding gives the Fed extraordinary latitude. It defines an important barrier between the Fed and the Congress by removing from Congress one of the most important tools of oversight. What, then, should be done? One recommendation, a favorite of Wright Patman's, although it has gained less salience in recent years, would subject the Fed to the annual congressional appropriations process.

This proposal may be well intentioned, but it would also be very harmful. Following that recommendation would end the Fed's ability to conduct monetary policy separately from the House of Representatives. If the Fed had to go to the Congress to receive its funding, the political concessions that Congress could exact would be tantamount to a declaration that monetary policy must be conducted by members of Congress. As Meltzer has written about the Fed in the 1960s, "[a]lthough the Constitution gives Congress power over money creation, few members found the details interesting enough to learn about the processes." When the Fed needs its separation from politics the most, the political interest in berating the Fed will be at the highest, from the left and the right. But there is no evidence that members of Congress will find "the details interesting enough to learn about the processes" at those critical points.[40]

For that reason, although the lack of clear statutory authorization for its extraordinary budgetary autonomy may be troubling, the removal of that autonomy would effectively be the end of monetary policy outside the halls of Congress. In an ideal world, the Fed would have the clear congressional authorization needed to justify its current practices. But the legislative politics of Fed reform don't operate in a perfect world. Opening the Federal Reserve Act on this technical question may only invite mayhem. Given the transparency of the Fed's budgetary process (and the frequency with which members of Congress like Wright Patman sought to change the practice), we can assume that Congress has essentially conceded the practice.

Arguments about how the Fed interacts with the money supply tend to provoke spirited arguments, to put it mildly. In light thereof, one final point should be emphasized: there is nothing secretive or nefarious about the Fed's use of open market operations to fund itself. The Fed includes its accounting of its open market operations in its annual reports and has done so, with varying degrees of transparency, for its entire one-hundred-year history. One of the reasons so many scholars and central bankers have misidentified the statutory basis for the Fed's funding is because the Fed is so transparent about how it funds itself.

Moreover, the Fed has, in a century under intense scrutiny from market participants and angry critics alike, had no major financial scandal. This is an impressive feat for any agency, let alone one that generates as much controversy as the Fed. For example, Ben Bernanke, even when he flew to far-off conferences in remote towns in South Korea or in the far-off Arctic, still flew commercial.[41]

Rather than an exposé, the point of this analysis is to explain the way that Congress created a specific set of fiscal relationships within the Federal Reserve System that no longer exists. Our understanding of the power and "independence" of the Federal Reserve requires an exploration of the basis for its exercise of this central authority. The point is one of the main arguments in the book: legal institutions, even when carefully lain, can shift dramatically over time.

CONCLUSION: CONGRESS AND THE FED

Remember Ben Bernanke's advice to Janet Yellen about Congress. Bernanke was legally correct: Congress made the Federal Reserve, and Congress can unmake the Federal Reserve. More broadly, of course, this book has argued that the Congress is not the only influence on Fed policy, even as it is the author of the missions placed before it. Even the narrow question of *how* the Congress influences Fed decisions is important to place in context. The most powerful authority Congress has is arguably the power of the purse. But in this respect, Congress has ceded authority to the Fed, giving the central bank the most important element of its separation from congressional control. The life of the Fed's budgetary autonomy demonstrates the ways that even relatively narrowly tailored legal institutional arrangements can be undercut through changes in political and financial arrangements. But because these changes happened in a transparent way, they only demonstrate how much nonlegal mechanisms can change institutions.

As we see in the examples of Wright Patman and Henry Gonzalez, members of Congress can also influence the Fed through the threat of legislative action. Fed history is filled with such examples. As we saw with the president, there are many ways that politicians can influence central banking policy outside of the use of their legal authority. Law may tie the political Ulysses to the mast, but only loosely; other ties come from other sources, where those ties exist at all.

CHAPTER 10
CLUB FED

THE COMMUNITIES OF THE FEDERAL RESERVE

> But, nevertheless, the objection which is urged against English
> bankers is at least equally applicable to these foreign bankers.
> They have, or may have, at certain periods an interest opposite
> to the policy of the Bank.
>
> —*Walter Bagehot, 1873*

The central assumption of the Ulysses/punch-bowl view of Fed independence is one of technocracy: there are objectively correct answers to problems of monetary policy that political interests in a democracy will get wrong. Remove monetary policy decision making from the political process and place it in the hands of the technocratic chaperone. The technocrat will reach that objectively correct answer.

But expertise has a political logic all its own. In this chapter, we will explore the source of some of that logic by looking at how members of three communities—markets, international central bankers, and academic economists—seek to influence how technocratic expertise is deployed. It is the interplay with these other outsiders that illustrates that the tension in the institutional design of the Fed is not only between political accountability and technocratic expertise. There is an important component at play in Fed policy making that reflects the experiences, values, and worldviews—in a word, the ideologies—of the central bankers inside the Fed.[1]

There is a Humpty-Dumpty danger in invoking the loaded term "ideology," a word that can mean whatever its speaker wants it to mean. But as the term is used here, arguing that Fed policy makers are ideological or influenced by ideology is not to impugn their motives or accuse them of dogmatic partisanship. Instead, following political theorist Herbert McClosky, ideologies are "systems of belief that are elaborate, integrated, and coherent, that justify the exercise of power, explain and judge historical events, identify political right and wrong, set forth the interconnections (causal and moral) between politics and other spheres of activity."[2] Everyone has ideologies. Fed policy makers are no different. In this chapter, the effort will be to understand how the ideologies of outsiders inform the Fed's policy-making space.

The way that each of the three groups addressed in this chapter—private bankers, international central bankers, and economists—influence Fed policy could receive their own chapters, even their own books. In this treatment, though, they are not equal actors. This chapter puts the most emphasis on the ideological influence that private market participants, especially regulated bankers, have on shaping Fed policy. The emphasis is justified because of one of the most problematic aspects of democratic governance. In designing the policies of the central bank, especially with respect to regulating and supervising the financial system, an advantage goes to those who are closest—legally, intellectually, culturally, and socially—to the central bankers. Private bankers aren't necessarily closer in this respect than international central bankers or economists. We care more about bankers because the regulation and supervision of international central banks and academic economists is necessarily less important from the perspective of democratic governance. For that reason, private bankers receive primary attention in the pages ahead.[3]

BANKER INFLUENCE: SUASION AND CAPTURE AND THE FEDERAL RESERVE BANK OF NEW YORK

How, then, do private bankers influence the space within which the Fed operates? We have already seen in chapter 5 one key aspect of the Fed's legal proximity: the governance of the Federal Reserve Banks. But that legal structure, important though it is, is only part of the proximity. The Fed's policy makers and private market participants are together in more ways than this, with important implications for the way the Fed exercises its power. Most people are relatively untroubled by private influences on, say, the Federal Reserve Banks in Cleveland or Minneapolis. This New York focus is appropriate: the New York Fed is the primary banking regulator of the nation's largest financial institutions. That bank's supervisory and regulatory work matters for not just the health of the institutions they oversee, but also the health of the entire financial system and indeed the entire economy.[4]

Focusing on the New York Fed, for example, reveals an important aspect of the Fed's proximity to the banks it regulates: there are social benefits to this proximity. The New York Fed's unique relationship to the banks and even market participants over whom the Fed has no legal claim whatever allows it to engage productively in what this chapter calls "regulatory suasion." Regulatory suasion refers to the regulator's ability to direct private activity without using coercive government authority. In this way, the Reserve Banks—and especially the Federal Reserve Bank of New York—act more as the coordinator of private actors rather than as a public regulator.[5]

It is this very ability to persuade that also exposes the New York Fed's primary weakness: in working so closely with the banks it regulates to find pockets of risk that harm them, the New York Fed adopts the ideologies of the commercial banks. They can become, in the academic parlance, "captured." Suasion and capture, then, are two sides of the same coin.

SUASION: HEDGE FUNDS AND DERIVATIVES

Two cases from recent history put these dynamics on full display. First, the resolution of what might have been an extraordinary U.S. financial crisis in the late 1990s, the collapse of the hedge fund Long Term Capital Management (LTCM).[6] Second, the 2007 intervention to improve the process by which financial firms cleared their trades on complex financial contracts—including some of the derivatives at the heart of the financial crisis of 2007–9. We'll address each in turn.

Long Term Capital Management was the king of hedge funds, a firm built on Nobel Prize–winning ideas by genius economists and traders who made a systematic bet that the markets are efficient in the medium term but roiling with inefficiencies in the short term. The basic idea of the firm was hedged arbitrage, a common Wall Street trading strategy whereby price discrepancies between two similar assets are identified and exploited for profit. An arbitrageur will buy the cheaper of the two assets, and sell or "short" the more expensive asset. If the prices converge, the arbitrageur makes a tidy profit. [7]

There are two tricks to making the profit something more than just picking up pennies and nickels. First, the trader has to have the correct theory of the mispriced assets. And second, the trader has to borrow as much money as possible to finance the trade on profitable terms. Borrowed money amplifies the return on exploiting price differences that would otherwise be much smaller.

The first prong is difficult in part because it is hard to come up with good, predictive theories of mispriced assets. But even with the right theory, it is difficult to be in sync with operations of markets such that others in the market come to the same conclusion early enough in the trade for the arbitrageur to make a profit. As the saying goes—often but probably falsely attributed to John Maynard Keynes—"the market can stay irrational longer than you can stay solvent." [8]

When the arbitrageur adds leverage to the mix, the trader's solvency can become even more fragile. A (very simplified) numerical example is helpful here. Suppose I have my eye on two stocks issued by companies that my arbitrage model tells me are essentially identical. For whatever reason, the markets aren't treating them the same: one is trading at $90 a share, the other for $100 a share. If my arbitrage model is right that these two companies are essentially identical, then all I need to do is buy the $90 share, sell the $100 share, and wait for the two prices to converge. If they converge at

$95, I've made a quick $10—$5 on the stock that went up, and $5 on the stock that went down (I'm ignoring the costs of actually making the trade for this explanation).

If I put up the full $90 (remember, I borrowed the $100 share), I've made an 11 percent return on my money. That's a pretty good trade. But suppose I only had $10 I was willing to devote to this trade, and so had to borrow the rest to pull it off. My first step would be to find someone to lend me another $80. Suppose I find someone willing to lend at 5 percent so that I have to pay back $84 when the trade is done. Then, after prices converge, I'm sitting on $5 from the shorted stock and $95 on the stock whose value just went up, for a total of $100. After I pay back my lender the $84, I have $16—the $10 I started with plus $6 more. In exactly the same trade, I nearly sextupled my return: 60 percent instead of 11 percent.

If we multiply these figures by a few billion dollars, then we enter the world of Long Term Capital Management. From stocks listed in two countries to similarly situated European debt to two kinds of mortgage-backed securities, the traders at the firm borrowed as much money from as many different banks as possible and laughed their way to their wealth as their returns exploded. In the first year, they returned 21 percent on their capital, the next year 43 percent, the year after 41 percent. Even in the heady days of the late 1990s, these were extraordinary returns.[9]

Then it all came crashing down. The reality about leveraged arbitrage is that when the trade goes your way, you are buried in riches; when the trade doesn't go your way, you are buried in debt. In the period of a few short months in 1998, the hedge fund that could do no wrong started hemorrhaging billions of dollars. Their models said that the assets they were trying to arbitrage were sure to merge in price. Those models might have been exactly right in general conditions. But the financial crises in Southeast Asia and Russia caused so much confusion in the financial markets that the hoped-for convergences stayed out of their reach.

The firm's managers knew they needed to resolve the problem. They tried. They called Warren Buffett and sought first a loan, then offered the entire firm to the Oracle of Omaha. But he balked at their terms, they balked at his. They called George Soros; same result. They called all their banker counterparties to seek relief from their debts. In proving the adage that the banker is the one who lends an umbrella on a sunny day but demands it back at the first sight of rain, these banker counterparties who were too eager to funnel money into the firm when it was profitable now demanded immediate repayment.

Here is where the New York Fed comes into the picture, for not altogether obvious reasons. The New York Fed is not the supervisor of hedge funds; it supervises banks that belong to the Federal Reserve System, bank holding companies, and a few others. It didn't have any regulatory relationship with hedge funds. But the New York Fed has never limited itself to the formal niceties of market actors. As Roger Lowenstein wrote, "in practice, [the New York Fed] routinely talked to traders at hedge funds, some of whom freely shared their opinions on the market and all of whom tacitly recognized the Fed's authority."

After sending the head of its trading desk to analyze LTCM's portfolio, the New York Fed's leaders sprang into action. The fear, in New York Fed president William McDonough's words, was that LTCM's exposures were so vast and so opaque that its failure could trigger a chain reaction that would bring the entire financial system to a grinding halt. "Markets would," he said, "possibly cease to function for a period of one or more days and maybe longer."[10]

The New York Fed's answer to this problem tells us a lot about its proximity to market actors, including how that proximity can give it credibility that other governmental actors don't have. The answer at the New York Fed was not to release Federal Reserve money into the financial system. The answer was to release Federal Reserve conference rooms.

Over several tense days, the New York Fed used its conference rooms and moral suasion to convince a great circle of rival banks and brokers (including many over whom the Fed had exactly zero regulatory authority) to lend money to a competitor. The failure to act would not result in any fine or jail sentence or other kind of government coercion, but the collapse of the financial system. It was a classic "collective action problem," where individual actors could not resolve a problem by acting independently, but could do so through coordinated action. And it took this action unilaterally. Then Fed chair Alan Greenspan was not on the front lines of this invocation of the New York Fed's soft power. In fact, just weeks before, he had already assured a congressional hearing that hedge funds were not his concern, nor the concern of any other regulator: "Hedge funds are strongly regulated by those who lend the money," Greenspan had said.[11]

The New York Fed was the coordinator. It provided the moral heft of a regulatory presence that had no basis in law. It solved the collective action problem and spared the financial markets what might have been an early cataclysm. The example shows the power of the Fed's unique regulatory suasion.

With so much ego and so much money involved, LTCM, while not exactly a household name, is a story that many know. There is a second example, though, that is much more obscure, but not less important. Just a few years after LTCM, then New York Fed president Timothy Geithner discovered that the process by which financial markets recorded their trades in derivatives was hopelessly outdated and completely opaque: traders would enter into these complex contracts over the phone, write their positions on scraps of paper, and then move on to the next kill. The "back office" was then in charge of sorting through those loose papers and trying to figure out who sold what to whom. The problem was, again, in the nature of these trades. Derivatives are contingent contracts: they are bets between people about the change in some future event, for example, the price of oil, the level of interest rates, or the default of a Fortune 500 company. If that event occurs, then the party that lost the bet has to pay up.

But what if the parties remember the terms of the trade differently? What if the details on one end were recorded according to one price point, but a different price point on the other? What if one or both of the counterparties pledges the value of the contract to another party altogether? These were the problems that faced the derivatives markets in 2005–2007. Alan Greenspan would later call it a "twenty-first century industry reliant on nineteenth-century practices." Because the trading system was all on paper routed through back offices with no clear way of knowing the terms of the contracts or even the identity of the ultimate counterparties, even a small financial crisis could become much bigger simply because there wasn't an organized way to handle these contracts. To give a sense of the scope of this problem, the total value of all the contracts in the global-derivatives market in June 2007 (around the time that Geithner discovered this problem), was $516 trillion. That's not a typo: trillion, not billion. By comparison, global GDP—meaning all the wealth in all the world generated in that year—in about the same time was $50 trillion. A failure to understand who owes whom what is a setup for a financial crisis. As one person close to the problem said, trying to figure it all out "would be like trying to untangle a vat of cooked spaghetti."[12]

Once again the New York Fed intervened. Once again, it did not regulate, legislate, or litigate; it threw neither money nor threats at the problem. Once again most of the participants were not under the New York Fed's regulatory purview. And once again, the problem was solved. By rounding everyone up in the New York Fed's conference rooms, Geithner and his associates were able to find a better resolution to the process by which derivatives are recorded. According to Geithner, this was a perfect problem for the New York Fed: "This was not a problem the market could solve on its own," he wrote. "It wouldn't make sense for one firm to upgrade its back-office operations, address its backlogs of unconfirmed trades, and invest in electronic trading unless all the major derivatives dealers did the same." The New York Fed had a solution: "We decided to try to induce all of them to do it together."[13]

This view of the New York Fed's role in the markets is not an argument about regulation, because regulation is not what accomplishes these goals. It is an argument about coordination. And when the solution is one that will benefit businesses "that are nevertheless unlikely to build it on their own," the New York Fed is at its best. And the Fed chair, again, wasn't really involved. When Geithner sought Greenspan's permission to begin this course, the chair was pleased to consent: "That's what you're supposed to do," he benevolently explained.[14]

THE PROBLEM OF CAPTURE

The very proximity and confidence that private market actors have in opening their books to the New York Fed and trusting it to resolve these thorny, systemic problems also exposes it to the process by which the worldviews of private bankers and central bankers begin to converge. Over time, the New York Fed and others within the Board of Governors and other Reserve Banks become, in a word, "captured."

That's a fighting word, almost an accusation that Federal Reserve's officials are corrupt. A standard definition of "capture," after all, describes it as "a process by which regulation . . . is consistently or repeatedly directed away from the public interest and toward the interests of the regulated industry by the intent and action of the industry itself." Making that accusation against policy makers at the Fed appears to be a claim that they are mere puppets of powerful market participants who want to bend the Fed to their own purposes.[15]

But this definition is too sure-footed: corruption and capture aren't the same concepts. As economist Luigi Zingales has written, "if regulatory capture was just due to illegal behavior, it would be easier to fight." The problem is that the ideology that animates many of the commercial bankers, traders, hedge fund managers, and other market participants is the same one at the New York Fed. Perhaps regulatory capture is the wrong term, because it focuses on the final actions that regulators like the New York Fed propose. Others propose "cognitive capture" or "cultural capture," which focus more on the upstream problem of insiders and outsiders at the Federal Reserve sharing a worldview that leads to significant blind spots. There is strong evidence that the New York Fed and other Reserve Banks share those blind spots, as they share those ideologies. It leads to a thorny question: are the New York Fed and other Federal Reserve Banks in fact pursuing supervisory policies at the expense of society and in favor of the private banks they regulate, because they share a common, particular world view?[16]

This is a difficult question to answer with empirical certainty, but there is strong evidence that many of the Fed's policy makers have grown increasingly close to the bankers they regulate. Most obviously is through their legally compelled physical proximity in the board rooms of the Reserve Banks. For example, during the run-up to the 2008 financial crisis, then New York Fed president Timothy Geithner's picks for his board were the CEOs of major banks that received not just direct financial lifelines, but constant insights about how the Fed's thinking about the nature of the crisis. During one memorable meeting March 2008, when the crisis was becoming very real for the Fed and bankers alike, Geithner recalls that "a team of the best economists at the New York Fed gave a presentation to our board on the potential losses ahead for banks, based in part on outcomes from recent recessions. Jamie Dimon [the CEO of banking juggernaut J. P. Morgan Chase] laughed at them. He told them to throw out their historically based estimates and triple their projected losses." What's fascinating about this exchange is not the exact observation that the private banker might know more than the Fed economist about projected losses; it's that the private banker was receiving this briefing as part of the formal governance of the Federal Reserve Banks in the first place.[17]

It's not just the governance of the Reserve Banks that compels this proximity. Recall the discussion of the Segarra case in chapter 7, about the problem of supervising the banks. One such example doesn't condemn an entire institution, of course, but the problem is that the New York Fed's uneasiness with bucking the banks is not unique to the Segarra case. The New York Fed has often ignored problematic behavior or affirmatively lobbied against proposals for change. When the Fed's Board of Governors and the Federal Deposit Insurance Corporation sought to finalize the rules limiting how much debt the world's largest banks could carry—arguably one of the most important regulatory changes to follow the 2008 financial crisis—New York Fed president William Dudley was, by his own admission, the courier of the banks' arguments that such regulation (almost uniformly praised by economists and politicians on the left and right) would somehow limit the Fed's ability to conduct monetary policy. While Dudley's argument—again, he has said that he merely meant to convey industry concerns, a curious point since industry insiders have been anything but silent on their opposition to these rules—failed to carry the day, it did succeed in delaying the implementation of the rule by several months.[18]

Geithner, too, admitted that as New York Fed president he didn't make regulatory change a priority, in part out of fear that banks would protest. For example, the New York Fed failed to police risky behavior in the mortgage-backed securities markets at the heart of the 2008 financial crisis, as described in chapter 2 (this is the same regulatory effort that Alan Greenspan thwarted). As Geithner wrote in his memoir, "Ned Gramlich, a Fed governor in Washington, was already leading a process to examine excesses and abuses in the mortgage business serving lower-income Americans." The problem wasn't that Geithner disputed Gramlich's conclusions. To the contrary, he "was impressed by Gramlich's work, and those issues seemed to be getting a fair amount of attention from the Fed in Washington. I didn't want us to be like kid soccer players, all swarming around the ball. I wanted us to focus on the systemic vulnerabilities that were getting less attention—starting with our own banks, but looking outside them as well." Geithner, like many New York Fed leaders before him, wasn't as interested in policing Wall Street's bad behavior; he was more interested in resolving its collective action problems.[19]

Another mechanism through which outside influences come from private market participants to the Fed is personnel. The list of private sector alums in senior leadership positions at the New York Fed is long and storied. Sometimes the connection starts in industry and ends in the New York Fed, as is the case with the current New York Fed president William Dudley. Dudley was a managing director at Goldman Sachs for more than twenty years before joining the New York Fed in 2007. Sometimes it moves in the other direction. Gerald Corrigan was an employee (and eventually president) of the New York Fed for twenty years and left in 1993 to join Goldman Sachs.

The New York Fed provides many useful examples of the location within the Fed where powerful market participants can shape Fed policy, but it is far from the only one, including on the question of common personnel. David Mullins, a former vice chair of the Fed's Board of Governors, left the board to join the hedge fund Long Term Capital Management, providing a personnel connection to this financial institution whose legal connection to the Fed was virtually nonexistent. And former Fed chair Ben Bernanke announced in April 2015 that he would join the massive hedge fund Citadel LLC, a fund with over $24 billion under management. Bernanke has a sizeable income from book royalties, speeches, and other sources. The motivation here isn't just money, but the access to power that central bankers have inside the Fed—access that they can get only from the financial markets. As James Kwak wrote after the Bernanke announcement, "when you've been at the helm of the global economy for eight years, where is there to go?"[20]

Whether the revolving door is a good or a bad thing is not the question. The point is that the links forged through common employment networks are a significant mechanism for bankers and other market participants to influence Fed policy. Just as bankers have a seat at the table in the board rooms of the Federal Reserve Banks, they have a business card and an alumni network when Reserve Banks and regulated banks are closely aligned.[21]

Again, it bears emphasis that a discussion of ideological and cultural capture at the New York Fed and elsewhere within the system does not mean the Fed is corrupt. The coordination function discussed earlier in this chapter yields impressive results. There is almost no doubt, for example, that Geithner's work simplifying the clearing of derivatives contracts in the years leading up to the 2008 financial crisis dampened the consequences of that crisis. But it is not clear that private actors are incapable of providing that function themselves. It may be that, after so much use of the New York Fed's conference room, they may have come to rely on it.[22]

These examples, in both the Fed's regulatory suasion and in its cultural and ideological capture, demonstrate the influence that private market participants have in shaping the space within which the Fed operates. This influence is unavoidable, and the line between paying attention and taking direction is hard to draw. The point is not that market participants' influence on the Fed is an unmitigated good or evil; it is only to recognize that that influence shapes the Fed's behavior in ways that we must acknowledge and analyze. There are many technical aspects to central banking. But there are many others that require the exercise of judgment, informed by ideology. In discerning the nature of Fed power, knowing the identity of the central banker—including the central banker's market ideologies and including the ways that the central banker will interact with markets in the moments that require that interaction—will be essential in evaluating the kind of central banker she will be.

The next chapter argues that the legislature made the wrong choice. The context of financial regulation and monetary policy in 2015 cannot justify that kind of proximity. The task for discerning the structure of the Fed's policy-making space in this chapter is to understand *that* market and banker ideology influences the Fed's decision makers. Whether it *should* do so is a separate question.

THE FED AND INTERNATIONAL CENTRAL BANKERS

By virtue of the size of the American economy, the Federal Reserve is, in the words of one former Fed insider, the "closest the world has to a global central bank." But this is not a job that the Fed does alone. International coordination is at the heart of modern central banking, particularly in the context of bank regulation and financial stability. Historically, it was international coordination that exacerbated the Great Depression. Liaquat Ahamed's Pulitzer Prize–winning book exaggerated only a little in calling the "Lords of Finance" the "Central Bankers Who Broke the World." Their breaking the world occurred through international coordination.[23]

International financial regulatory coordination is a fact of life; the reality is that the community of central bankers will influence each other in the actions that they take. Two examples are useful: the coordinated response to the 2008 crisis (through the use of international swap lines) and the coordinated regulatory response after the crisis.

Although the Federal Open Market Committee releases its minutes on a three-week delay, the full transcripts of its meetings aren't released until five years later. In late 2014, the Fed was in the process of releasing the transcripts of some of the most important meetings during the height of the 2008 financial crisis, giving a window for the first time into the most important decisions central bankers made during that tumultuous time.

It is perhaps surprising that so much of those meetings were focused not primarily on domestic considerations, but on international ones. Many of the FOMC's meetings at the height of the financial crisis were taken up with discussions of "international swap agreements," a tool the Fed had used during previous financial crises but had largely abandoned outside of crises. Under these swap agreements, the Fed would advance billions of dollars to foreign central banks at a specified exchange rate in return for foreign currency. The point of these swaps was to provide foreign central banks with dollars, an essential commodity at a time when U.S. investors were fleeing risky markets everywhere in their flight to the safety of U.S. government debt. Because the financial crisis was based so much on dollar-based assets, these foreign central banks desperately needed dollars to stay afloat.[24]

In that event, the Fed became something of a central bank to the world: it provided the currency that other countries needed to accomplish their own policies as lenders of last resort. This kind of coordination shaped the Fed's policies throughout the crisis. As the journalist Neil Irwin outlines, the main central bankers of the world were in close, sometimes daily contact as they coordinated policies to ensure maximal efficacy of their policies. While the Depression-era practice of subordinating domestic interests to international coordination was not apparent—in some instances, domestic interests clearly trumped (including the failure of UK regulators to approve the purchase of Lehman Brothers by the British bank Barclays)—there was no question that these central banks were performing on an international stage, working closely together.[25]

The struggles of international coordination are even more starkly demonstrated outside the context of crisis. Arguably the main event in domestic and international bank regulation is capital adequacy regulation, or the rules that govern the mix of equity and debt that a bank must maintain to fund itself. Bankers want to have access to as much debt as possible, but bank critics argue that this addiction to debt is precisely the cause of financial crises. In a crisis, debt is always the contagion. Limit the amount of debt a bank can carry on its balance sheet, and you limit the extent of a potential crisis.[26]

Largely for reasons of history, rules on capital adequacy are set by international agreement that falls well short of an international treaty but still sets the stage for domestic adoption. Meeting together at in Basel, Switzerland, central bankers join together within what was originally conceptualized as the central bank for central bankers,[27] the Bank of International Settlements. Today, one of the BIS's primary functions is to coordinate, through the Basel Committee on Bank Supervision, the so-called Basel Accords.[28]

The Basel Accords are political documents. While the BIS and the BCBS employ large technical staffs of economists to test the ideas that undergird the accords, the final documents are made through a political process that reflects the views of bankers, central bankers, and others with enough of a constituency to make their views heard. Some view the entire process as notorious and nefarious. But nothing so fully demonstrates the constraints that central bankers face not from politicians but from other central bankers as the Basel Accords. They set the parameters for domestic adoption. The Dodd-Frank Act, for example, did essentially nothing on capital adequacy. The domestic understanding was that these decisions would be made at Basel, and the regulators would then have the discretion to adopt and adjust those parameters as they arrived. But the starting point for negotiation would not be in Congress, nor even at the Fed: it would be in Basel, Switzerland.[29]

This kind of proximity, shared outlook, and common language for discussing problems inevitably shapes Fed policy making. That doesn't mean that the Fed is taking orders from the European Central Bank, Bank of Japan, or anyone else. It does mean that, together, international central bankers shape each other's worldviews. Because the work of central banking requires so much judgment under uncertainty, understanding where the Fed fits in the wider world helps explain how the Fed's policy judgments come to be.

THE FED AND THE ECONOMISTS

The Federal Reserve is the institution that economists built. We have discussed in detail the contributions of politicians like Carter Glass and Woodrow Wilson and bankers like Paul Warburg and Benjamin Strong. But the ideas that would come to be accepted by all warring factions originated not in the secret meeting on Jekyll Island, but in the journal articles of academic economists.[30]

The connection between the Fed and the economics profession has only grown stronger over the course of the century. Over the course of that period, the institution has become the de facto institutional home in government for leading economists. We saw in chapter 4 the ways that economists function within the Fed. Let us now consider the way that economists influence Fed policy from the outside.

Perhaps the most influential economist to shape the policies of the Federal Reserve System was Milton Friedman. Friedman was one of the founders of the view within economics of "monetarism," the doctrine that, among other tenets, held that inflation was "always and everywhere a monetary phenomenon." Put differently, the role of the central bank was not to second guess private markets, nor to support the government's fiscal policies, but to target the quantity of money in the economy. He and like-minded economists had preached his gospel of monetarism since the 1950s, largely to no avail.[31]

All of this changed with the rise of Paul Volcker. In a letter of congratulations for Volcker's appointment to the Fed chair, Friedman warned him that "there has [almost] never been both a greater need and greater opportunity for the [Federal Reserve System] to render service to the nation by courageous and steady policy of monetary restraint, experienced gradually and moderately." Friedman also made clear where he stood: "As you know, I do not believe that the system can rise to that challenge without major changes in its method of operation. My very best wishes to you for success in pushing those changes and those results." Friedman blamed Arthur Burns for the inflation, for failing to control the money supply.[32]

Friedman's solution—the "gospel" itself, as it was called—was this change in operating procedures, a change away from targeting interest rates and to targeting the quantity of money in the economy and letting the interest rates go where they would. This was considered heresy by most central bankers and was anathema to the Nixon, Ford, and Carter administrations.

Volcker was not a monetarist, but in his view, the psychology of the market favored a drastic change from what had come before. In a consequential meeting on October 6, 1979, the FOMC decided to make the "dramatic" change in techniques: the Federal Reserve had gone monetarist. It stayed there while interest rates soared to over 20 percent in nominal terms. The Fed would not return to targeting interest rates until 1993.

While Friedman's name was not mentioned in those early meetings, his influence was everywhere. Volcker kept Friedman in his thoughts and on his schedule. Friedman had powerful allies in Washington, especially after the election of Ronald Reagan in 1980. And while Friedman did not get everything he wanted out of the Fed—he wanted to replace the Fed with a monetary policy rule that would transparently hew to a fixed growth in money, whatever the economic climate—he was able to change, without any action in Congress, the way the Fed did business for a decade.

Friedman is hardly the only influential economist to shape Fed policy through blunt force of ideas. John B. Taylor, the Stanford economist whose simple monetary policy rule that relates interest rates, inflation, employment, and the "output gap" of GDP targets and economic performance, has dominated discussions of Fed policy inside and outside the Fed for the last twenty years, and especially since the crisis. And Michael Woodford, the Columbia economist who has contributed key papers on the principles of "forward guidance," or the public announcement of future monetary policy intentions, has shaped the debates of unconventional monetary policy.

Because of the nature of the Fed, economists shape the content of the Fed's policies by a combination of intellectual content and the central bankers' own ideological predilections. This is, once again, why the identity of central bankers matters so much. Just as senators spar with judicial appointees over the latter's views on, say, abortion or the death penalty, they should expect (and, hopefully, receive) insight into what the central bankers' views are on such ideas as the monetary policy rules, forward guidance, and the other theoretical and empirical components of influential topics in macroeconomics. These ideas did not hatch from the air; they were conceived and written by economists and shape the way that the Fed's central bankers think of themselves and their policy-making role.

CONCLUSION

The political scientist Peter Hall, in describing monetary policy making in Britain, called the process "social learning." In this view, policy making isn't just what happens inside the state or among state actors. It is a process embedded in society and its many influences, but "[n]owhere is the importance of such learning and alteration of perspective more clearly demonstrated than in the economic doctrines prevalent in any given period."[33]

The Fed learns socially. It is influenced from within; so much we know from part I of this book. It is influenced by the president and Congress, through both law and leadership. And it is influenced through the shared values, experiences, and legal and nonlegal interactions with society, including those of economists, bankers, market participants, and international central bankers. These values, or ideologies, are the confounding factor in the usual retelling of Fed independence. That story focuses on the balancing act between democratic accountability and technocratic expertise. But there is more to that story. Outside ideology informs policies in ways that don't promote either goal of accountability or technocracy. To map the space within which the Fed operates, the task is to identify those ideologies and understand them.[34]

PART IV

THE DEMOCRATIC DEMANDS OF FED GOVERNANCE

REFORMING THE FED BY CHOOSING THE CHAPERONE

CHAPTER 11
PROPOSALS

I shall be at once asked—Do you propose a revolution? Do you
propose to abandon a one-reserve system and create anew a
many-reserve system? My plain answer is that I do not propose
it. I know it would be childish. Credit in business is like loyalty
in Government. You must take what you can find, and work
with it if possible."

—*Walter Bagehot, 1873*

In the summer of 2013, the uncertainty around Barack Obama's
appointment of a new Fed chair generated a large amount of political chatter. This attention was, to great extent, personality driven:
forces organized in opposition to the appointment of Lawrence H.
Summers, former treasury secretary and president of Harvard,
highly regarded scholar, and close economic adviser to President
Obama. There was no question as to Summers's qualifications as
an economist, but Summers had made personal enemies and alien-
ated constituencies that then rallied to defeat his candidacy. The
alternative was Janet Yellen, herself an eminently qualified candidate who had served three times on the Federal Open Market Committee, including as the vice chair of the Board of Governors at the
time her candidacy was debated.

Some found this press frenzy anathema. George Will, the *Washington Post* columnist, wrote that "the *campaigning* by several *constituencies* for and against what supposedly were the two leading *candidates*—Larry Summers and Janet Yellen—to replace Bernanke as chairman of the Federal Reserve" meant that the Federal Reserve "can no longer be considered separated from politics." And R. Glenn Hubbard, a former economic adviser to President George W. Bush and himself once a leading candidate for the Fed chair, thought the political attention to Obama's decision something of a disgrace: "In place of this serious discussion, the White House has allowed, if not orchestrated, a circus campaign of personality."[1]

Will and Hubbard are wrong. Whether one was part of Team Summers or Team Yellen, the attention to the Fed chair brought a tremendous amount of insight and political accountability to how much personalities matter in shaping the power and policies of the Federal Reserve System. Because the legal rules written in the Federal Reserve Act that dictate this or that policy are so slippery—even where those rules are highly specific—the attention to the selection of personnel is an essential aspect of the current system.

For those who despise political gridlock and mock the uselessness of U.S. democratic institutions, attention to these personnel decisions may seem a bug, not a feature. For those who accept the arguments of this book—about law's limited role in defining the boundaries between the Fed and the politicians, about the influence of individual values on technocracy, about the efforts of insiders and outsiders to influence Fed policy—the implications are clear: public vetting is the best opportunity for allowing democratic participation without subverting the benefits of separating monetary policy from the floor of the House of Representatives.

Those who doubt the importance of focusing on personnel within the Federal Reserve are also wrong for another reason. Once we accept that there is a role to play for government in implementing policies that redound to the social good—a sometimes contested proposition, but one that enjoys widespread support—we face an unavoidable decision: Who gets to implement those policies?

While this book has not presented a formal theory of political appointments, the arguments presented here support a view that focuses on answering the "who?"question in institutional design. Not only are personnel considerations essential in their own right, they are in some ways more important than striking detailed political bargains that dictate specific policy outcomes, whatever those policy outcomes may be. As we have seen, the laws of central banking quickly take on a life of their own. It is better, then, to focus the institutional reform efforts on ensuring that we know who is pulling which levers of Fed power, and when. In other words, the focus should be on governance, not micromanagement—people, not policies.

This kind of attention to institutional governance may be important as a general matter, but it is essential to effective public oversight at the Federal Reserve. As we have seen, the jumble of different functions that Congress has given the Federal Reserve over the course of a century has undermined the efficacy of the appointments process. It is hard to know much about an appointee when we do not understand the function of the appointment. Perhaps one of the reasons we see Occupy Wall Street and the Tea Party joined in opposition to the Fed is because partisans from each side are looking at two different aspects of an almost incomprehensible system.

This final chapter outlines some ways that the Fed has been and can be reformed so that its governance structure provides a more realistic opportunity for the public to provide meaningful oversight without injecting the day-to-day of electoral politics into the day-to-day monetary policy.

The chapter moves through three sets of reforms. First, it looks at two reforms in the Dodd-Frank Act that are useful in promoting the goal of creating a more comprehensible governance structure. Second, the chapter looks at reforms that move even further in this direction, including by changing the terms of the Board of Governors and the Fed's general counsel, as well as reforming the governance of the Federal Reserve Banks and removing them from the Federal Open Market Committee. Third and last, the chapter critically evaluates and rejects two proposals for Fed reform: the comprehensive public audit of the Fed's monetary policy actions and the addition to the Federal Reserve Act of the so-called Taylor Rule. These proposals misfire for the same reason: they inject political processes not at the appointments level, where politics belong, but at the level of policy execution, exactly where it is likely to be least predictable and most damaging.

As with the proposals Bagehot made about the Bank of England, it may seem that changing the board's and Reserve Banks' governance structure appears "a revolution," something akin to another founding of the Federal Reserve, perhaps even, an abolition of the independence of monetary policy from politics generally. This book makes no such proposal. Simplifying the Fed's governance merely allows the public to provide more accountability without compromising that crucial insulation of monetary policy from partisan politics. The point is more fundamental about the false basis of the Ulysses/punch-bowl approach to Fed independence generally: democratic accountability and political insulation are not in some equilibrium where more of one necessarily means less of the other. Values and personality matter, too. The Fed can have more accountability in the ways described below so that the public can understand better who wields the Fed's extraordinary authority by understanding whether the Fed's policy makers' backgrounds and experiences are consistent with one's own policy goals. We can have more accountability and more insulation.

DODD-FRANK'S REORGANIZATION
OF THE FEDERAL RESERVE

In the history of law reviews, it is probably safe to say that there has never been an article more influential in institution building than the one by Elizabeth Warren and a coauthor proposing what would come to be the Consumer Financial Protection Bureau. Warren began an earlier version of the argument with a compelling logic: "It is impossible to buy a toaster that has a one-in-five chance of bursting into flames and burning down your house," she wrote. "But it is possible to refinance an existing home with a mortgage that has the same one-in-five chance of putting the family out on the street—and the mortgage won't even carry a disclosure of that fact to the homeowner."[2]

Why the discrepancy between our regulation of consumer products and our regulation of consumer finance? It was not a problem of insufficient laws protecting these abuses, Warren and her coauthor argued, but a problem of institutional design. The quantity of law wasn't the distinguishing factor between consumer product safety and consumer financial safety. The quality of the institutions enforcing those laws was.

Few issues were as fraught with political peril as the design and implementation of Warren's idea as part of the Dodd-Frank Act. Those within the Obama administration who saw the 2008 financial crisis through the lens of systemic risk and financial stability (led by Treasury Secretary Timothy Geithner) viewed the proposal—and Warren herself—as at best a distraction and at worst a threat to their own reform efforts. Before the passage of the Dodd-Frank Act, Geithner and his senior aides developed an "Elizabeth Warren strategy," which was "a plan to engage with the firebrand reformer that would render her politically inert." But the bureau was popular with Democrats and even some Republican critics of the other parts of the Dodd-Frank Act and eventually received the critical backing of Larry Summers, President Obama's primary economic adviser. In making the case for the CFPB as part of the financial regulatory overhaul, Summers explained by analogy to the president that "the airline safety board shouldn't be in charge of protecting the financial viability of the airlines." Neither should the regulators responsible for the health of the financial system be in charge of policing abuses in the ways these firms lent money to consumers.[3]

Most Republicans, though, hated the proposal and fought hard to prevent it from becoming law. Legislative politics were not on their side, however, and the CFPB became a signature component of the Wall Street Reform and Consumer Protection Act, better known as Dodd-Frank for its sponsors Senator Chris Dodd and Representative Barney Frank. In fact, the CFPB *was* the consumer protection piece of the legislation. Selling the Dodd-Frank Act to the electorate meant making Warren's CFPB a centerpiece of the reform.

Republicans were not deterred by the passage of the legislation and publicly threatened to block Elizabeth Warren—most Democrats' favored candidate—or even anyone else to lead the new bureau. Interestingly, their most common public critiques were not about the wisdom of consumer protection laws generally, although some conservative and libertarian scholars have certainly made that case. Republicans refused to confirm a director because they opposed the bureau's institutional design, specifically objecting both to the bureau's funding outside of congressional appropriations and to its supervision by a single director rather than a multimember commission. This impasse even led to something of a constitutional crisis resolved only by the Supreme Court and the invocation of the so-called nuclear option that eliminated the Senate's filibuster for most presidential appointments.[4]

What does this debate have to do with the Federal Reserve and the need to simplify its governance? This book has nothing to say about the benefits or costs of our consumer financial protection laws, either as they existed before Dodd-Frank or as they were expanded thereafter. From the perspective of institutional design, however, this kind of governance reform is exactly what we should hope to see. Previously, most of the consumer protection laws came under the bailiwick of the Federal Reserve. As a result, there was no clean way for public oversight of the consumer protection function. The Fed had become a jumble of activity, with monetary policy receiving the most attention in the political process. Consumer financial protection was largely ignored.

This reality is why, whatever the virtues or vices of substantive consumer protection laws, hiving off those functions into a separate, politically accountable bureau is exactly the right approach to resolving the thorny problem of Fed governance. Before Dodd-Frank, any citizen or politician with a problem with the Fed's regulation of, say, mortgage lending practices under the Truth in Lending Act had to take that fight to the Federal Reserve and its chair. We saw that story earlier in the book, when people—including a member of the Federal Reserve Board itself—tried and failed to reform the way the Fed approached subprime mortgage regulation. There was too much else going on at the Fed that was seen as much higher priority. In the edifice of Federal Reserve policy, as one politician put it in support of the CFPB, monetary policy was the penthouse, bank supervision something of an afterthought in the middle, and "way down in the basement is consumer protection."[5]

The relationship between the Fed's jumbled governance and public policy accountability is not theoretical. In the mid-1990s, the Clinton administration approached Laurence Meyer, a well-regarded economic forecaster and professor of economics at Washington University in St. Louis, about filling a vacancy on the Fed's Board of Governors. According to Meyer, when Clinton's chairman of the Council of Economic Advisers, Joseph Stiglitz, called to tell him of the nomination, Stiglitz said "he didn't want to pressure me on any issues on behalf of the Clinton administration, but he did want me to know that the administration was strongly in favor of CRA," an acronym that Stiglitz did not define.

Meyer reacted with silence: he had never heard of "CRA." Immediately after hanging up, Stiglitz sent Meyer a sixty-five- page history of the Community Reinvestment Act for Meyer's educational benefit. Meyer proudly noted that "not much more than a year later, I was named head of the Board's oversight committee on consumer and community affairs. I became the member of the Board to testify before Congress on issues related to CRA. I went around the country and supported work that community groups in banks were doing in providing affordable housing for low and moderate income groups. In other words, I was CRA all the way. I guess I'm a fast learner."[6]

Meyer's anecdote demonstrates the problem of locating too many functions within a single institution: When there is no clear focus among the many (sometimes conflicting) missions, some of these functions will fade into obscurity. A candidate to lead the Consumer Financial Protection Bureau will have opinions on the Community Reinvestment Act, one of the most important and controversial pieces of consumer financial legislation in U.S. history. But Meyer wasn't a candidate for the Fed because of his expertise on consumer affairs; he was a candidate because of his prowess as an economic forecaster and reputation as an economist. Despite his plainly acknowledged ignorance, obvious even to the administration that had appointed him, Meyer became the U.S. government's leading consumer financial protection regulator.[7]

The creation of a separate Consumer Financial Protection Bureau, headed by a Senate-confirmed presidential appointee, makes a result like Meyer's essentially impossible. No one could survive the presidential vetting and Senate confirmation process as the government's enforcer of consumer financial protection laws without knowing what those laws require. The creation of the CFPB, then, is precisely the kind of institutional change that this book's arguments about law, personality, and changes over time would support. Every five years, the president and Senate must convene to discuss publicly the kind of person we want to execute the government's consumer financial protection laws. This kind of public vetting allows those people interested in those laws—either because they find all such laws morally repugnant, they believe consumer financial protection laws should be stricter, or something in between—to make their voices heard. The appointment can become a campaign issue. The democracy can weigh in. This was theoretically possible but much less likely under the Fed's previous organization, given that Fed appointments implicated such a broad range of policy issues.[8]

THE VICE CHAIR FOR BANK SUPERVISION

The Dodd-Frank Act innovated in another way that is, to a lesser extent, also a step in a similar direction of simplifying the Fed's governance. The act creates the position of a "Vice Chairman for Bank Supervision" who, according to the statute, "shall develop policy recommendations for the Board regarding supervision and regulation of depository institution holding companies and other financial firms supervised by the Board, and shall oversee the supervision and regulation of such firms." This is the broadest grant of authority to an individual in the Federal Reserve Act—greater than even the explicit authority given to the Fed chair.[9]

The creation of the vice chair for supervision signals a potential shift of regulatory duties away from the rest of the Fed to a single individual. The identity of that vice chair will presumably set the tone for the Fed's entire regulatory apparatus, which is significantly expanded under Dodd-Frank. Whether this occurs in practice has yet to be determined. Because so many of the Fed's practices are determined by precedent and convention, the identity and practices of the first vice chair for supervision will matter—everything that official does will have ramifications for the way the office is held thereafter.

Despite its importance, however, as of this writing five years after the passage of the legislation the position remains unfilled. Daniel Tarullo, the Fed governor profiled in chapter 3, has assumed the de facto role of vice chair for supervision by virtue of his public and private focus on the subject, his role representing the Federal Reserve in interagency and international meetings dealing with these issues, and his congressional testimonies. But because he has not been nominated and confirmed for the position, the public has not had a chance to weigh in on this singular position in financial regulation, nor do Governor Tarullo's actions carry the same institutional weight that the actions of a presidentially appointed, Senate-confirmed vice chair would have. A formal nomination is long overdue. The statutory purpose will not be fulfilled until the position is formally occupied. In the many areas of appointment failure during the Obama administration, this failure is among the most vexing.

PROPOSALS FOR REFORM: PEOPLE, NOT POLICIES

The work started by the Dodd-Frank Act is incomplete. There are still too many diverse functions and policy makers located within the Federal Reserve whose complex relationships make it difficult to provide appropriate, intermittent democratic accountability through the appointments process. Three proposals would further clarify the Fed's governance structure in ways that would allow more meaningful accountability without compromising the need to keep monetary policy outside the day-to-day of partisan politics. They are, first, changing the governance structure at the board to eliminate the problems of chair empire building and governor irrelevance. Second, increasing the accountability of members of the Fed's senior staff, especially the general counsel, through presidential appointment. And third, reforming the governance of the Federal Reserve Banks.

REFORMING THE BOARD OF GOVERNORS

Reforming the Board of Governors does not require changing the statutory vision of a politically accountable Fed chair and a legally powerful and politically insulated Board of Governors. That vision is already in place. The task is to improve the institutional design to realize those goals. As discussed in chapter 8, the problem of the fourteen-year term for the governors is not that it is too long for purposes of democratic oversight; it is that the governors resign too frequently to make them fulfill the statutory intention. At the same time, the chair's ability to serve renewable four-year terms, together with the option of adding one fourteen-year term to the unfilled term of a predecessor, gives the chair the opportunity to build a political empire independent of the president, as we saw with Chairmen Martin and Greenspan. In both cases, the decisions made toward the end of their tenure have been the flashpoints for the most controversy. Just as we recognize the need to change leadership at the presidential level more often than every twenty years, we should seek the same for changes of leadership at the Fed.

One way to improve the power and importance of the Board of Governors is for the president and Senate to fill those vacancies. Over the last fifty years, recent trends accelerated during the Obama

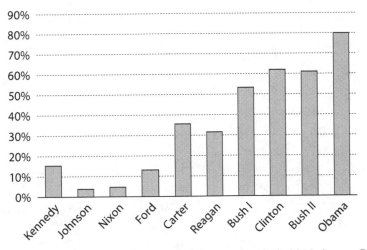

Figure 11.1: Vacancy rates on the Board of Governors, 1960–2015. *Source*: Board of Governors of the Federal Reserve System.

administration. Figure 11.1 shows the trend. As we see, between the Kennedy and Reagan administrations, presidents from both parties kept vacancy rates on the seven-person board below 40 percent. But under the Obama administration, that rate has climbed to an astounding 80 percent.

The blame for the neglect of these appointments lies in part with the Republicans in the Senate. Republicans rejected the nomination of MIT economist Peter Diamond in 2011, arguing that he was unqualified for the job. Diamond is a Nobel laureate and one of the most distinguished economists of his generation. His rejection is inexcusable and may be the most egregious example of politics over substance in the history of Fed appointments.[10]

But Diamond's rejection is unusual. The main problem during the Obama Administration is that the president has failed to advance nominees in the first place. More than any other president in history, President Obama has not made appointments to the Fed a priority. If the Board of Governors is to function as a full committee of presidential representatives overseeing the Fed's many functions—including supervising the Reserve Banks—future presidents should focus on those vacancies. The appointment process is one of the only ways the general public, through their representatives, can influence the Fed and its policies. There is no such restriction on that influence from large market participants. Presidents should not deprive the Senate and the public of that essential element of public accountability.[11]

Filling the board vacancies doesn't do much to stem the high turnover of those who serve on the board, nor does it influence the chair-centric regime that so easily arises within the Fed. A more important approach may be to reconsider the governance structure of the board entirely. Both problems that afflict board governance—high turnover and chair domination—could change by increasing the de facto tenure of governors by, perhaps counterintuitively, decreasing the length of their legal term.

Along these lines, one reform would be to give a governor a single, nonrenewable ten-year term. A governor could also no longer serve the balance of a predecessor's term left vacant owing to death or resignation: each ten-year term would begin anew when the president appointed and the Senate confirmed a new governor, much like the vacancy-filling process on the federal judiciary. To fulfill the Federal Reserve Act's intent to limit vacancies during a presidential term, the board could also be shrunk to five governors, a change that would bring the Fed into line with other federal agencies.

The new result: five governors serving ten-year terms with vacancies arising either organically, because sitting governors resign early, or at a predictable two-year interval. At the appointment process, the public could evaluate the appointments as they come due, mostly one at a time, in a public vetting process that is, as the Supreme Court said, "among the significant structural safeguards of the constitutional scheme."[12]

To limit the chair's undue influence in sustaining a multidecade appointment, under this proposal the chair's term would be for five years, renewable exactly once (if the president chooses as chair a sitting governor, the term would be limited). When it is time to renew or not the appointment of the Fed chair, the president must determine whether the continued service on the board of a governor demoted from chair would be consistent with the president's political and policy goals (we saw what happened with President Truman in a similar dynamic with Marriner Eccles). No matter how popular the chair, though, once the ten-year term ends, so ends the chair's service. And the chair would continue to serve at the pleasure of the president (as argued above); his dismissal, like the dismissal of others appointed to their posts to exercise technocratic judgments, would be under political considerations, not legal ones. Whether a tradition would arise that every chair gets a full ten years would be for future resolution.

The result of a five-person Board of Governors led by a public-facing, term-limited chair would go further to make the promise of the Federal Reserve Act a reality. As it currently exists, the potential for and reality of governor irrelevance and chair domination gets the necessary balance between insulation and accountability exactly backward.

FED STAFF: PRESIDENTIAL APPOINTMENTS?

Chapter 4 explored the influence that Fed staff, especially senior economists and the general counsel, can have on Fed policy. The question for a governance-based approach to Fed reform is whether the staff is exercising the kind of values-oriented judgment that should demand greater democratic accountability, or whether those roles are strictly technocratic and therefore better placed at a remove from partisan politics.[13]

There is no single answer for all the heads of the Fed's fifteen divisions. Before Dodd-Frank, there was a much stronger case that the head of the Division of Bank Supervision and Regulation should be given a public vetting through the presidential appointment process. The presidential appointment of the vice chair of supervision makes that question mostly moot.

The question for the three economists sometimes called the three "barons"—the heads of Research and Statistics, Monetary Affairs, and International Finance—is different, and harder. The heads of Research and Statistics and Monetary Affairs have the best claim that theirs is a more strictly technocratic role and that public input on their selection is unlikely to help and indeed likely to hurt the chances of the most skilled economists reaching those positions. But as this book has argued at length, even these technical questions require the exercise extraordinary value judgments. The wisdom of, say, quantitative easing and maintaining a policy of zero interest rates cannot be resolved by resort to objective standards of economic science.

Having a say in the selection of those who supervise the production of the Fed's economic models and empirical data may be an appropriate and limited way for the public to participate in the identification of those values. As Alan Blinder has put it in an interview about the role of the Fed's senior economists, "I don't know of any interesting question in economic or social policy to which there is only one clear answer." Perhaps it's appropriate to reevaluate the appointment process for those policy makers within the Fed to assure that the "interesting questions" on economic and social policy are debated. At the very least, it would be a valuable debate to have.[14]

Moving further along the spectrum is the role of the director of the International Finance division. There is much in the position that is technical. But, as seen in the case of Edwin Truman, there is much, too, that is highly diplomatic. If the head of International Finance is essentially the Fed's chief diplomat, presidential appointment is much more desirable. The Fed's role in the international economy has increased substantially in the last thirty years, as Truman himself has documented in detail. The argument for presidential appointment for this key position is stronger than the other two division heads. Representing the United States government in delicate diplomatic affairs is a quintessentially executive function usually subject to presidential appointment and Senate confirmation. Again, at the very least, this is a debate worth having.[15]

The strongest argument for presidential appointment among Fed staff is in the position of general counsel. The Fed's chief lawyer, as discussed in chapter 4, exercises extraordinary authority both in times of crisis—to justify and legitimate the Fed's crisis policies—but also in shaping the Fed's entire regulatory and supervisory apparatus. Again, one of the book's central themes is that the laws governing the Federal Reserve are complex and require not just the technical skills of lawyers to interpret, but also invite value judgments. The position of the Fed's general counsel (and the lawyers he supervises) requires value judgments informed by technical expertise. These functions should not be made by politicians in campaign commercials, but the case for allowing the public to vet the appointment of the chief lawyer is very strong.

Two points of comparison are useful in a discussion on the appointment status of the Fed's chief lawyer. First, unlike the case with the other "barons" of the Fed staff, the Fed's Board of Governors is not in a position to exercise significant oversight over the Fed's chief lawyer. As discussed above, the Fed—including the board—has become increasingly dominated by economists, a transition away from a tradition of bankers and lawyers. There are good reasons for this transition. One consequence, however, is that the Fed is not well equipped to push back against or even understand the value judgments that a lawyer must make with regularity, couched as they are in the arcane apparatus of legal analysis. This failure of supervision is not the board's fault, but it is a consequence of their different comparative expertise. As of this writing, there are two lawyers on the Fed's board, but only one who has spent a significant portion of his career dealing with the legal issues relevant to the Fed's regulatory work.[16]

Second, while most other general counsels at administrative agencies are not presidential appointments, the Fed's chief lawyer makes judgments of extraordinary importance that are unlikely ever to be reviewed by a court. Courts have made clear for eighty years that they will not review the Fed's decisions about monetary policy, including when those decisions require novel interpretations of law. And in the crisis, the Fed made emergency decisions that have been effectively removed from judicial review, despite potential violations of state corporate law and even the Constitution.

While courts do review many of the Fed's regulatory determinations, in places where value judgments are of the most consequence, the Fed's lawyer is the first and last word on what the law allows or forbids.

Avoiding judicial review may be a feature, not a bug. The idea of protracted litigation tying up emergency lending or monetary policy changes is not a good one. But that only shifts the need to be more transparent with respect to the appointments of those lawyers who will fulfill this monitoring role. For this reason, the Fed's chief lawyer should be a presidential appointment: without democratic oversight at the appointment level, many of the most important value judgments the Fed's lawyers make will never receive that review.[17]

The section title above ends in a question mark. There are, perhaps, arguments that the extension of presidential appointment and Senate confirmation into the organization would be destabilizing to the Fed's internal operations. Very likely, those opposed to these ideas would say that the Fed's "independence" would be compromised by increased political oversight. If they have read this far, hopefully they see how little weight the concept of "Fed independence" can bear on asking these kinds of questions about internal governance. But there may be arguments in favor of insulating the "barons"—including the general counsel—from more public scrutiny. At the very least, this is a debate that Fed reformers should engage.

REFORMING THE FEDERAL RESERVE BANKS

That leaves the Reserve Banks. As argued throughout this book, the Reserve Banks—and, given its location, perhaps especially the Federal Reserve Bank of New York—have the potential to make policy and constitutional trouble for the rest of the system. Reforming the Reserve Banks by revisiting the question of the appointment of their leaders should be the top priority of anyone who wants the system to conform to constitutional requirements and to allow meaningful democratic accountability without compromising the benefits of an institutionally distinct central bank.

There are four alternatives for addressing the problem of the Reserve Banks' problematic and arguably unconstitutional governance. First, give the Board of Governors the authority to fire at will the heads of the Reserve Banks, satisfying the constitutional requirement as articulated by the U.S. Supreme Court, but still appoint them largely by their private boards. Second, make the U.S. president and Senate responsible for appointing and confirming the Reserve Bank presidents under the Constitution's Appointments Clause. Third, single out the president of the Federal Reserve Bank of New York for a Senate-confirmed appointment. Fourth and last, make the Board of Governors responsible for *both* appointing *and* firing the Reserve Bank presidents, taking private bankers out of the business of Federal Reserve governance, but without extending unnecessary and duplicative political appointments throughout the system.

Let's take each proposal in turn. First, leave the appointment system in place, but change the way that a Reserve Bank president is removed. This appears to be the institutional fix favored by the Supreme Court. As discussed in chapter 5, the court, in the 2010 case *Free Enterprise Fund v. PCAOB*, held that the Constitution permits restrictions on the president's ability to fire his subordinates only one level into the bureaucracy. Applying the court's reasoning to the Fed, this would mean that restricting the president's ability to fire the members of the Board of Governors is permissible, but limiting the governors' ability to remove at will the Reserve Banks' presidents is not. The court's solution in *Free Enterprise Fund* wasn't to invalidate the entire structure of the subordinate agency, but to eliminate from the statute the offending removal procedure. In *Free Enterprise Fund*, that meant that the members of the Securities and Exchange Commission could remove at will the members of the subordinate Public Company Accounting Oversight Board (PCAOB), but the PCAOB still continued to perform its statutory functions. In the Fed's case, that would mean the Reserve Banks would continue to exist in their current role; it would just mean that the Board of Governors would be able to fire any officer for any or no reason.

If the FOMC removability issue were ever litigated to conclusion, we might expect a similar treatment. The members of the FOMC not appointed by the president would be rendered removable at will by the Board of Governors, just as the governors supervise the Reserve Banks in every other aspect of the Fed's wide regulatory berth.[18]

While this judicial fix might satisfy the Supreme Court's requirements, it is not a satisfying result in terms of the theory of democratic governance that this book has advanced. Courts may worry only about firing policy makers, but the theory advanced in this book—a theory about the importance of transparent, comprehensible governance—looks not at who fires the central bankers, but who appoints them. And the basic problem of appointment at the Reserve Banks is the dramatically disproportionate influence that regulated banks have on the people who become their overseers. From the perspective of democratic accountability, banker influence at the appointment threshold is the real issue.

The second alternative, a perennial proposal, is an improvement in this regard. That proposal is to vest the appointment of the Reserve Bank presidents in the U.S. president, with the Senate confirming those appointments. It resolves the constitutional issues entirely and would also allow the Reserve Banks to remain on the FOMC as equals to the governors. Given the diversity of their views, this seems a promising reform.

The recent trend toward failing to fill the appointments on the Board of Governors may suggest that the fate would be the same for the newly installed presidential appointments at the Reserve Banks. It is unlikely, however, that we would see the same vacancy rates at the Reserve Banks as we have at the Board of Governors, for two reasons. First, filibuster reform made it much harder for the minority party to block presidential nominees. And second, the vastly expanded Senate franchise at the Federal Reserve might make Reserve Bank presidents look more like ambassadors or U.S.

attorneys, positions that don't usually attract the same kinds of partisan political attention we associate with Senate gridlock.[19]

There are, however, two major problems with this proposal. First, it would almost be sentimental, eliminating the differences between the Reserve Bank presidents and the Board Governors in all but name. If all members of the FOMC become presidential appointments, what, then, would be the difference between the governors and the Reserve Banks? The value of a nineteen-person committee must come from something other than the process of their appointment (the strongest justification, however weak, for the current arrangement). If there are no differences, then we have created an unwieldy monetary policy committee.

Second, making the Reserve Bank presidents subject to the Appointments Clause only illustrates how arbitrarily distributed they are across the country. Does Ohio really need a seat at the table? Does Missouri need two? And should there really only be one seat west of Dallas, Texas? These decisions, of course, were the product not only of their economic times, but of their political times. That the Reserve Banks live in the governance shadows only demonstrates how much we are still subject to political compromises of eras long past.[20]

The third proposal is a variation on this theme. Senator Jack Reed (D-Rhode Island) has proposed making the president of the Federal Reserve Bank of New York a Senate-confirmed presidential appointment, but leaving the other Reserve Banks alone. The idea here is that, given its location and the private banks under its supervision, the Federal Reserve Bank of New York and its president are by far the most important players in the system from both banking and monetary policy perspectives. The public, the thinking goes, should have more of a role in determining who pulls the levers at this important institution.[21]

We have certainly seen, especially in chapter 10, how much influence the New York Fed has over the financial system. That said, there are three reasons to be skeptical of this New York Fed only approach. First, it does nothing to the larger constitutional defect.

It's probably useful to have the vice chair of the FOMC (by tradition, the New York Fed president) under presidential appointment, but what of the others? Despite its centrality, New York isn't the only banking center interest in the United States. Wells Fargo and Bank of America are each banking juggernauts. Is it really reasonable to say that their regulators don't need to be presidential appointments? Second, there are worrisome implications for strategic behavior by banks seeking more sympathetic regulatory treatment by changing their seat of incorporation out of New York and into another district. This wouldn't mean many jobs would leave New York, or that New York would cease to become a global capital. It would just mean that banks would comply with the legal requirements to move their identity to a more sympathetic Federal Reserve District where they could have a say in selecting their regulatory overseer.

Finally, this proposal could backfire. Making the New York Fed president a political appointment would focus the attention of industry representatives on that selection. Regardless of the party in power, the subject of that appointment would become the targets of intense industry lobbying and could create an even more redoubtable base within the Federal Reserve System for private banks.

There is a better way than these three approaches. We should reform the Reserve Banks by vesting the appointment and dismissal of the Reserve Bank presidents in the Board of Governors. Here, the constitutional problem is resolved since there would no longer be multiple layers of removal protection. And the governance problem is resolved since there would never be a question of whether the Board of Governors should be responsible for the failures of the Reserve Banks. The responsibility for any of the Reserve Banks' actions would rest squarely at the governors' feet.[22]

A natural extension of this governance change would also be to remove the Reserve Banks from the Federal Open Market Committee. They could participate in deliberations, of course, but the proposal above would essentially turn them into branch offices of the Federal Reserve in the twelve cities where they are located. There's not much point in their maintaining an equivalent policy role with their clear superiors on the Board of Governors. Further, consistent with Carter Glass's original conception, the board could then expand its presence even more evenly to other cities, even removing regional banks from places where they no longer serve a useful purpose. That way, we could revisit some of the decisions about the design of the system that were curious even in 1914 when they were decided.

The elimination of the Reserve Banks from the FOMC would have another desirable outcome: it would change the identity of the vice chair of the FOMC, currently the president of the Federal Reserve Bank of New York (although, again, this is a tradition only). Indeed, even if this proposal were to render the Reserve Banks subordinate to the Board of Governors, revisiting the status of the vice chair of the FOMC would be desirable. The better candidate is the vice chair the Fed already has: the vice chair of the Board of Governors. In 2015, the vice chair is Stanley Fischer, one of the most eminent scholars of macroeconomics of the last forty years. His students have become important figures in macroeconomics in their own right, including former Fed chair Ben Bernanke, president of the European Central Bank Mario Draghi, and economist and former chair of the Council of Economic Advisers Greg Mankiw, among others. Fischer was also governor of the Bank of Israel, where he won high marks for leading the bank and the Israeli economy through the thick of the 2008 financial crisis.[23]

As impressive as these qualifications are, they are not Stanley Fischer's most important qualification. His most impressive credential is that the U.S. president nominated him and, after a not uncontested nomination process, the U.S. Senate confirmed him. Nothing like the same can be said of the president of the New York Fed. Replacing the representative of some of New York City's leading financiers and citizens with the candidate considered by the president and the Senate for the post would improve the Fed's accountability without compromising the quality of its candidates.[24]

Some protest that the Reserve Banks, including with their obscure and conflicted governance structure, are necessary because they preserve the legitimacy and "independence" of the Federal Reserve System. Obviously, this book has tried to make not-so-quick work of "independence" as an analytically coherent concept. The claim is that the Reserve Banks' proximity to private bankers enhances their technocratic role in fighting inflation against the efforts of an election-hungry president—that is, the Ulysses/punch-bowl conception of independence.

For all the reasons this book has discussed, this conception just doesn't work: it suffers from too narrow a view of technocracy, separation, the nature of influence, and the policies that Reserve Banks participate in making. Besides, even from the perspective of the appointment power, if the Reserve Banks were fully subordinate to the Board of Governors, there would no greater role for presidential participation in the formulation of monetary policy. There would be only less of a role for bankers and their representatives in that governance system. Flawed though it is, even the Ulysses/punch-bowl conception of Fed independence is not that *bankers* should provide ballast against politicians in the formulation of monetary policy; it is that *technocrats* should. The argument that banker-dominated governance is necessary to insulate the Fed from politics conforms to an outdated (by many decades) mode of thinking of central banking.

Perhaps more to the point, this book has argued at length that the mechanisms of separating the Fed from politicians are many and varied, not least the Fed's unique separation from the congressional appropriations process. This view is supported by the empirical literature on central bank independence. That literature looks at any number of legal mechanisms for establishing independence from politics; *banker* control of some seats isn't prominent among them. Fed independence, then, isn't about increasing banker influence on the Fed's decisions, but neutralizing political influence. If anything, subjecting the Federal Reserve Banks to Board of Governors appointment would further insulate the Fed from political interference, from the regulated banks rather than the politicians. Politics, of course, is practiced not only by politicians. Bankers have proven themselves adept at the trade for centuries.[25]

Another argument, from one commentator, is that "having the Federal Reserve Bank presidents on the FOMC increases the diversity of opinion and economic methodology on the committee." This defense of the Reserve Bank's governance structure is even more confusing than the idea that banker-dominated boards enhance Fed independence. Recently, *nine* of the twelve were PhD economists. Economists obviously are not a homogeneous group, but the idea that the current governance structure produces a valuable range of intellectual diversity that a more transparent structure would not isn't at all obvious. A centrally administered appointment system at the Board could be much more sensitive to intellectual diversity than the decentralized process that currently exists.[26]

Perhaps most important of all, the problem of Fed governance is a threshold problem. Having the right institutional design at central banks—and institutional design that insulates the day-to-day of monetary policy from the day-to-day of electoral politics without compromising the democratic and constitutional requirements of accountability—isn't a side show to the real questions of monetary policy and financial regulation. Governance may in fact be the whole show. We can argue to the point of exhaustion about any number of aspects of Fed behavior and policy, in the past and the present. But until we get a better ability to comprehend the Fed's governance structure—who wields which powers, and to what end—we will not make much progress.

QUESTIONABLE REFORMS: AUDITS AND RULE-BASED MONETARY POLICY

There are two proposals for reform that have circulated historically that should be carefully considered but ultimately rejected. First, a proposal to subject the FOMC's monetary policy operations to a public audit, or the "audit the Fed" bill; and second, a proposal to write into the Federal Reserve Act a default monetary policy rule that the Fed must either follow or face an immediate congressional hearing to explain its departure. For similar reasons, these proposals should be rejected. In each case, they engage in precisely the kind of micromanagement that is unlikely to be helpful in the ways their proponents support and are inferior to a governance-based reform system.

AUDIT THE FED

The first proposal is to subject the Fed to an annual, transparent audit performed by the Government Accountability Office. Many within the Fed view the "audit the Fed" bills and their proponents with fear and loathing and equate the practice with an end of Fed independence. This characterization is misguided, at least in part. That is, the public audit part of the proposal is consistent with an essential component of this book's argument, that we cannot understand what the Fed is, what it does, and who on the outside influences Fed behavior, without knowing more about how the Fed operates. And historically, Congress has put the Fed to public audit, extending the Government Accountability Office's reach in various parts of the Fed's activities. In each instance, the Fed was opposed. For example, in the latest iteration—an audit of the Fed's emergency lending activities that passed as part of the Dodd-Frank Act of 2010—the Fed fought hard, making claims that such an audit would, predictably, compromise the Fed's "independence." The Fed was wrong to oppose these audits. What we learn about Fed practices, especially from its lending behavior during the crisis, is essential to our comprehension of this opaque institution.[27]

Even, so a permanent, comprehensive, public audit of the Fed is still a bad idea. The problem is the audits' regularity. There is no claim that the Fed is hiding scandals that need to be brought to light. As noted in chapter 9, it is true if astonishing that the Fed, its robust budgetary autonomy notwithstanding, has never had a scandal involving the misappropriation of Fed funds by an employee of the kind such as those that have plagued other agencies.

Instead, "audit the Fed" is motivated by a desire to punish specific Fed actions (most recently, its emergency lending and unconventional monetary policy programs). But there are better ways to make these changes: simplify the Fed's governance structure and then put inside the Fed those who are more likely to make alternative policies. If not, the risk is that members of Congress will use cherry-picked quotes and facts about the Fed's policies from the annual GAO audit to score political points and seek to influence the Fed by confusing the public and making the Fed appear more sinister or partisan than it is. For example, Senator Rand Paul—the leading congressional sponsor of this legislation in 2014 and 2015—defended the proposal by claiming that the Federal Reserve itself was approaching bankruptcy. There are serious discussions to have about the way that the Fed manages its own balance sheet; this is not one of them.[28]

We saw in chapter 9 that Congress has many tools at its disposal to influence Fed policy, including legislative threats in committee hearings, individual efforts by members of Congress who take an active interest in the Fed, and proposed legislation that threatens to limit the Fed's authority. A permanent, public audit of the Fed's monetary policies adds little to that toolkit. It does, however, represent a threat for more political control without corresponding benefits of accountability.

MONETARY POLICY RULES

The second of these proposals is similar. That proposal would require the Fed to adopt a monetary policy rule and then explain why and how it deviates from it. The rule selected and written into the Federal Reserve Act is the so-called Taylor Rule, a model of monetary policy conceived by Stanford economist John B. Taylor.

If adopted, the legislation would require the Fed to conform its monetary policies to an arithmetic formula that relates a number of variables, including the level of current inflation, unemployment, and targets for economic growth and inflation. The Fed would input a standard set of coefficients to its empirical determination of the economic indicators (inflation, unemployment, the output gap, and so forth). The equation would then produce an interest rate that the Fed would subsequently target. The Fed could also deviate from this rule, but only if it explained why or how. Within forty-eight hours of each FOMC meeting, the committee would submit to the GAO its determination of the Taylor Rule and be audited thereafter by the GAO. If the Fed deviated from the Taylor Rule, the Fed chair would have to appear before a congressional committee to explain itself.[29]

This is a controversial bill, for good reason. Part of the problem goes to great, decades-long debates on the virtues of rules-based monetary policy versus a more flexible, discretionary policy. This is a significant and unresolved debate about the superiority of one regime over another. The question has divided experts; there is not now and may never be a consensus on whether a rules-based or discretionary-based policy is superior for all times and all places.

Indeed, the papers that first proposed the Taylor Rule point to this reality. The first paper did not purport to prescribe a policy rule, but to describe one, and did so on the basis of just a few years of data (specifically, 1987–92) as a useful heuristic for guiding monetary policy. During those years, the United States did not face a liquidity trap, a financial crisis, an inflationary spiral, or many other external shocks that can complicate the monetary picture.

The bills' sponsors argue that the proposal has an escape hatch: the Fed can explain why it has departed from the rule by referring to these very external conditions. But doing so requires both a full audit by the Government Accountability Office to determine whether in fact the FOMC is being honest in its announcement that it is or is not following the Taylor Rule, and the Fed's chair must then face a congressional hearing to explain his her view of the economy. A congressional hearing in the midst of a crisis to explain inherently controversial decisions would cripple the Fed's ability to make policy in anything other than a full-blown legislative process. In this respect, the policy rule bill is worse for insulating monetary policy from partisan politics than is usually assumed about monetary policy rules generally.[30]

This concern about monetary policy by congressional politics would come up only if the Fed deviated from the rule. This raises another problem with equating monetary policy rules with legislative rules. Writing the Taylor Rule into the Federal Reserve Act could be devastating if, in fact, it's just the wrong rule. There are many rules we might select to dictate monetary policy. The gold standard was a monetary rule. So was the rice-based currency in medieval Korea. The point is that before settling on a rule, in statute, it would be better to have more certainty about its lasting viability.[31]

The debate among economists about the superiority of rules-based versus discretion-based monetary policy will continue; this book does not attempt to contribute to that economic debate. But the policy rule proposal illustrates the problem with committing to statute the detailed policy wisdom of the day. Intricate rules like the one proposed in the Taylor Rule are likely to have a life of their own in ways that its authors cannot predict. By writing the Taylor Rule into the Federal Reserve Act, inserting the GAO into the monetary policy equation, and allowing congressional hearings immediately after the release of FOMC decisions, there will be institutional consequences in the way that monetary policy is made and received in ways that no one can predict. Law can be sticky; changes in social and practical contexts will interact with current law in unpredictable ways. If a consensus among economists and experts comes that the Taylor Rule, in fact, is not a useful basis for forming monetary policy, for reasons that the present generation cannot conceive, the statutory endorsement would remain. It is not enough to say that lawmakers would enact the next economic consensus. That's not the way that lawmaking works, as the continued structure and location of the Federal Reserve Banks surely indicate.

The better approach would be to focus on the more flexible appointment process. Perhaps the Taylor Rule is exactly the right approach to monetary policy. If that's the case, the governance-based approach to the Fed reform this book endorses would still not support writing the rule into law. If the Taylor Rule is the best policy, don't amend the Federal Reserve Act; appoint John Taylor to the FOMC.

CONCLUSION

There are good ways and bad ways to reform the Fed. This book has argued throughout that the Fed's governance is complicated, confused, and opaque. This confusion is in part a problem of "institutional layering," or the reality that we never start from scratch in institution building. But this does not mean we are always stuck with the institutions we inherit from previous generations. This chapter has focused on three kinds of reforms: those that have succeeded at simplifying the Fed's governance (as with the CFPB), proposals that would go further in this direction (such as simplifying the Board of Governors and subjecting the Reserve Banks to Board appointment), and proposals that should be avoided (such as enhancing the role of the Reserve Banks, "audit the Fed," and the Taylor Rule).

The point in each example is the same. Ideological influences on the Fed are inevitable. Policy mistakes are, too. The best hope we have of understanding this curious institution and balancing the demands of technocratic expertise and democratic accountability is to simplify its governance. These proposals are efforts at that simplification. Given the extraordinary power inside the Fed, it may be true that we live in a "republic of central bankers." But if so, it is a democratic republic. The people are still sovereign.[32]

CONCLUSION

THE FREEMASONS AND THE FEDERAL RESERVE

There has been so much fierce controversy as to this Act of
Parliament—and there is still so much animosity—that a single
sentence respecting it is far more interesting to very many than
a whole book on any other part of the subject.

—*Walter Bagehot, 1873*

In the fall of 2013, I presented an early version of this book in the
beautiful Cash Room of the U.S. Treasury, as part of the U.S. Treasury Historical Society Speaker Series. I told some of the stories and
made some of the arguments that I present here—about Marriner
Eccles, the Fed's proto-Keynesian second founder and son of the
Mormon West; about the undeniably iconic, yet ambiguous and
legally impotent Fed-Treasury Accord; and about the incoherence
of debating Federal Reserve "independence" when we have not
resolved what, exactly, the term "Federal Reserve" even means.

At the end of the talk, a young man in a nice suit approached me.
He was enthusiastic, more than you would expect of someone who
had just heard rather academic arguments on a rather technical
topic. He pumped my hand and thanked me profusely for the presentation, explaining that he was himself a student of the Federal
Reserve System and its history. Then, in a hushed tone, he asked:

"What do you think about the influence of the Masons on how the Fed controls the economy?"

I realized then, and I still fear now, that my hope to make nuanced and accessible arguments about a technical and complex institution could shade too easily, in the minds of some readers, from critical to conspiratorial. (At the time, I wanted to call this book *Ulysses and the Punch Bowl: The Independence, Accountability, and Governance of the Federal Reserve*, if for no other reason than to throw the conspiracists off the scent with a more obscure, academic title; probably for the best, others with more sense of how to market these things pushed a different course.) Although I very much want to reach people like my young interlocutor, such readers may be more interested, as Bagehot warned in the epigraph above, in the hard-hitting single sentences about the Federal Reserve and thus have little patience for a comprehensive book on the same topic.

Regrettably, losing those readers may be unavoidable. The Fed attracts conspiracists better than most governmental agencies. Anyone who has perused the HG 2500 section of the library will know that the shelves groan under the weight of Fed conspiracy theories. These range from the absurd to the detestable, but also show that in at least one slice of the public's imagination, the Fed is a dark and brooding omnipresence that can be accounted for only with nefarious explanations.

I'm comfortable losing the fringe conspiracists. Who I don't want to lose are the Fed's clear-eyed defenders or critics. My aim is to engage those audiences, to push back against both defenders and critics alike who are certain they have the Fed figured out, whether they love it (not uncommon during an economic boom, and not uncommon ever for central bankers) or hate it (much more the zeitgeist among sectors of the public as this book goes to print). Most of all, the book is for those readers who are eager not for single sentences, but for the quieter and necessarily lengthier discussion.

That lengthier discussion has been an effort to break down the Fed's structure and functions, laws and traditions, to challenge the prevailing ideas about independence, governance, and accountability that even the most knowledgeable of Fed watchers may misunderstand or take for granted.

To put the point differently, recall my son's scribbles, discussed in the preface: he just couldn't draw superhero motion in two dimensions. To make my argument, challenging the prevailing ideas of Fed independence has required illustrating in three and four and five dimensions the contested spaces where the Federal Reserve makes its policies, separate and together with other actors inside and outside the government, by using technical skill and making value judgments, under legal and practical authority. The prevailing conception of Fed independence, I have argued, is just too narrow to tell us much of anything about the Fed, its structure, and its functions. This book's more comprehensive account aims to replace those narrower views.

For experts who study central banks, this reconception may provoke a collective yawn. Scholars who view independence according to the Ulysses/punch-bowl account—that Fed independence is the legal separation between the Fed (especially the Fed chair) and the politicians (especially the president) for purposes of price stability, performed by technocratic central bankers—may plead "no contest" to my accusation that they are missing the whole picture. Their questions and my questions are simply different, they might say, substantively and methodologically.

To them, I say that I have no quarrel with simplifying assumptions that allow scholars to focus on one part of a complex phenomenon. The problem here is that these simplifying assumptions don't work. When you pick up one end of the Federal Reserve stick, you pick up the other. And the whole Fed stick consists of the individuals and institutions inside it, beyond the Fed chair; the welter of outsiders who influence Fed policy, beyond the politicians; the large and multiplying number of missions within the Fed's bailiwick, beyond inflation prevention; values beyond technical economics; and the variety of laws, traditions, and other tools available to all to turn their wishes into policy, beyond the provisions of the Federal Reserve Act. My hope is that scholars working on the

Fed and other governmental institutions who think hard about independence as an analytical tool will thus find something of value in the more comprehensive approach I have outlined here.

But this isn't a book only for scholars. People in the general public, including those like the young man in the Treasury's Cash Room, are eager but often confused about an institution that influences decisions they make about their families, their jobs, their futures. It's tempting to blame the public for not working harder to understand the Federal Reserve based on information already widely available. But the problem is not just a lack of understanding. It is also failure of institutional design. When we place a mishmash of separate, sometimes competing committees and individuals within a single institutional framework, under a single misleading name ("the Fed"), and then give that ill-defined framework the task of deciding questions as varied as bank supervision, check clearing, systemic risk regulation, price stability, and employment regulation, we will inevitably see a failure of public governance. Rather than just bringing the public to the Fed, we must also bring the Fed to the public.

Charles Goodhart, a leading scholar of central banking, has described it best: "It is one of the proper functions of academics regularly to reassess and to challenge the legitimacy and value of existing institutional arrangements." In this book, I have taken up that cause, to explain why some features of these institutional arrangements are conducive to, while others are confounding of, public engagement and oversight. In the process, it allows those interested in this understanding to focus their critiques less on first principles and existential challenges and more on the questions of whether we are best served by the institutional arrangements we have inherited.

Perhaps it will also allow those who wonder about the Federal Reserve and the Freemasons to turn their attention to more profitable enterprises. For those readers, I apologize for burying the lede: the Freemasons just aren't a part of this story.[1]

ACKNOWLEDGMENTS

During the last six years, I have worked with questions of Fed independence at least weekly and often daily. To bring Bagehot in one last time, "a slowly written book on a living and changing subject is apt a little to want unity." This book doesn't pretend to reach the heights of *Lombard Street*, but I have had the same problem of my slow pace and the subject's fast change. I have also discovered that a book isn't written as much as it is decided, thousands of times over, sometimes in gut-wrenching ways. Fortunately, I have been far from independent myself in making these decisions. Along the way I have had the lively support of many scholars, mentors, and friends who have helped substantially improve this book and related projects. While no one but me bears the blame for errors of fact, interpretation, or style, it's a delight to thank and acknowledge those who are responsible for seeing me through.[1]

My first thanks to my partners and colleagues at the Stanford Law School Library for their enduring commitment to this project. This book is a testament to the importance of libraries and librarians even and especially in this digital age. They helped me track down sources near and far, primary and secondary, always with speed and good humor. To Paul Lomio, Sonia Moss, Rich Porter, Rachael Samberg, Sergio Stone, Erika Wayne, George Wilson, and George Vizvary, and the other research librarians at SLS: my warmest thanks and affection. Paul, a great mentor, friend, and supporter of this project, tragically died too soon. I miss him dearly and thank his family on his behalf for all his work to support this book.

To Dan Siciliano and Evan Epstein at Stanford's Rock Center for Corporate Governance, my thanks for giving me a home in 2010–11, and for allowing me to continue the fellowship out of residence through more years than they anticipated. In addition to access to my librarians, the continued affiliation has also allowed me to have an academic home in the law while I have traveled far from Stanford as a law clerk, lawyer, historian, and finally a business school professor. My thanks, too, to Rob Daines, Joe Grundfest, Larry Kramer, and Liz Magill for that same continued support.

I enjoyed a productive writing summer in 2014 at Harvard Law School, courtesy of Jonathan Zittrain and the Harvard Law School Library and Lucian Bebchuk and HLS's Program on Corporate Governance, for which I am very grateful.

I presented versions of the book and assorted chapters at various places over the years and thank: George Washington University Law School (Art Wilmarth and Lisa Fairfax), the Social Science History Association and the Fiscal Sociology Workshop (Isaac Martin, Ajay Mehrotra, and Monica Prasad), Stanford's Graduate School of Business Finance Faculty Workshop (Anat Admati), Stanford's Constitutional Law Center (Michael McConnell), Columbia Law School (Jeff Gordon and Kate Judge), Max Planck Institute for Collective Goods (Martin Hellwig), MIT's Sloan School of Business (Simon Johnson), Ohio State University Law School (Steven Davidoff Solomon and Christopher Walker), the U.S. Treasury (Frank Noll), the American Enterprise Institute (Michael Greve and Alex Pollock), the Brookings Institution (David Wessel and Kerry Grannis), Princeton University's Conference on Central Banking and Monetary Policy (Raymond Hicks, Christina Bodea, Helen Milner, and Harold James), Princeton University's Legally Engaged Graduate Students Workshop (Kim Lane Sheppele), George Washington University's conference on the Fed's centennial (Paul Berman and Michael Whitehouse), the Bank of England (Rosa Lastra and Graham Nicholson), and George Mason University Law School (Michael Greve). My thanks to my hosts and the participants for their excellent feedback.

My academic and professional mentors in law and beyond read drafts, heard ideas, and gave me encouragement as I grew into this subject first as a student and then as a scholar, not to mention the unseemly amount of professional and career advice and support. My thanks to Anat Admati, Dick Craswell, Rob Daines, Ron Gilson, Simon Johnson, Michael McConnell, David Skeel, Ezra Suleiman, Mary Waters, and Jonathan Zittrain for that mentorship. To my mentors in the practice of law, Judge Stephen Williams, Judge Gerard Lynch, and Deepak Gupta, my thanks for the hours of time you helped me honing my craft as a lawyer and writer.

I've drawn on several previous publications, including "The Institutions of Federal Reserve Independence," published by the *Yale Journal on Regulation* (parts of which show up in chapters 8 and 9); "The Twelve Federal Reserve Banks: Accountability and Governance in the 21st Century," published by the Brookings Institution (part of chapters 5 and 11); "Governing the Federal Reserve System after the Dodd-Frank Act," published by the Peterson Institute for International Economics (co-authored with Simon Johnson, here as part of chapter 3); "The Constitutional Crisis at the Fed," published by *Politico Magazine* (part of chapter 5); "Is the Federal Reserve Constitutional?," published by the Library of Law and Liberty (also part of chapter 5); testimony before the Senate Banking Committee (part of chapter 11); and various blog posts at *Notice and Comment*, an administrative law and regulation blog hosted by the *Yale Journal on Regulation*. I'm grateful to editors and staff of each institution for their support and help.

As with sausage and legislation, the book-writing process can produce some ugly byproducts along the way. Fortunately for me, generous colleagues didn't mind watching the whole thing unfold and read part or all of various versions of the manuscript and gave me terrific and challenging comments. To Anat Admati, Sarah Binder, Alan Blinder, Michael Bordo, Sarah Carroll, Nikki Conti-Brown, Andrew Edwards, Jeff Garland, Charles Goodhart, Harold James, Simon Johnson, Rosa Lastra, Roger Lowenstein, Paul Mahoney, John Morley, Alex Pollock, Eric Posner, Meg Tahyar, Ted Truman, Sean Vanatta, Philip Wallach, Steve Williams, Art Wilmarth, Andrew Yaphe, David Zaring, and Julian Zelizer—my sincere thanks for imposing rigor and clarity on sometimes scattered ideas.

To my new colleagues at the Wharton School of the University of Pennsylvania, I have already enjoyed and benefitted from our conversations on this and many other topics. I look forward to many years ahead and promise that I will not always bring everything back to the Federal Reserve. I'm also grateful to my Wharton Research Assistants, Tanner Bowen and Sean Egan, who carefully proofread the final manuscript.

Thanks, too, to the staff and editors at the Princeton University Press, especially Kathleen Cioffi, Richard Comfort, Eric Crahan, Seth Ditchik, Kathleen Kageff, Theresa Liu, and Samantha Nader for their superb editorial help at every step of the process.

A few more personal notes of thanks. When I think of all the time and energy Sarah Carroll has devoted to this book and related projects, I feel grateful and embarrassed. Not only did she read every word of the manuscript, but she has read most every word about the Fed I have written, including tens of thousands that were not good enough to see the light of day. Sarah has one of the sharpest minds for legal writing and style I have ever known, and her generosity in sharing those talents—and her friendship generally—have meant the world to me.

My thanks to Meg Tahyar for the detailed, sometimes line-by-line care she gave to the full manuscript, including the end notes and bibliography. She spared me from many errors of fact and interpretation (though we disagree on much, too; she, like the others, is not responsible for my bullheadedness). That a partner at a leading global law firm would take this time, despite other demands, speaks to Meg's collegiality and intellectual range in law, banking history, and English grammar.

Thanks to Sean Vanatta, my fellow political and financial historian and brilliant friend. In addition to his trenchant comments on the manuscript, including at last minutes and random hours, Sean's insights—ranging widely in subjects from banking history in pre-statehood Oklahoma to the economics of credit cards to muscular fitness—kept me sane and in good health during the final year of writing and revisions.

I mentioned Judge Williams earlier, but his role in this project requires more credit. My boss at the U.S. Court of Appeals for the D.C. Circuit, he has been a splendid mentor and reader on these topics since the beginning, always with extraordinary—and sometimes, frankly, quite challenging—comments and critiques. I loved working as a clerk for Judge Williams, but continuing the intellectual association has made the relationship even more rewarding.

Andrew Yaphe has held my feet to the fire to great effect for years. I'm not sure he has enjoyed anything I have written—there is no accounting for his nonmonetary tastes—but his sharp eye for style and clarity substantially improved (by negative displacement) a previous version of the introduction. His willingness to enforce Ulysses contracts of a different sort have made him an indispensable scold and a deeply valued friend.

I went to Princeton to do a PhD in financial history so that I could work with a trio of scholars—Alan Blinder, Harold James, and Julian Zelizer—who have shaped my thinking on all aspects of this project. They have provided me, I humbly submit, with the best graduate education one could imagine for the study of the political, financial, and institutional development of central banking. Alan—a towering figure in central banking policy, practice, and scholarship—prepared me for my general examination in the economics of central banking, a process that paid dividends in thinking through the intellectual history of central bank independence that shows up here. His course on the macroeconomics of central banking also provided significant fodder for my discussions in many other parts of the book.

My two courses and countless conversations with Harold were critical to placing my work in a deeper international context. I can still picture Harold's far-off gaze as he contemplates a question I've asked or argument I've made, and then the rich deluge of insight that invariably followed. I am grateful for his mentoring and friendship.

I have never known anyone like Julian Zelizer, my primary advisor at Princeton. I frankly don't know how he functions within the constraints of time and space: he is a first-rate, prolific, publicly engaged historian and yet is always ready to carve out time for his students. His enthusiasm and encouragement for me to pursue this project as a book are responsible for its existence. If I am breaking a rule of authorial etiquette by double dipping on the dedication page, I'm okay with that. Without Julian, there would be no book to dedicate.

I also am grateful for my friends and family away from this project. To my siblings, especially Samuel Brown, who taught me the painful lesson that a book is never finished, only abandoned (something my editors probably wish I had heeded earlier in the revising process); my beloved mother, Diann Brown, whose legacy to me of careful reflection and scrappy resilience have guided me throughout my life; and to the memory of the gentle goodness of my grandfather Charles Brown, who died just as this project was getting started. He would have loved to see the final product. Also to Dana Boehm, Paul Boehm, Nicholas Hall, and Britton Olson: I love how much you have become my family, too.

A special thank you to Addie Purnell, a dear friend who reminded me at a key moment in the end stages of this project how much more there is to life than the independence of the Federal Reserve.

Mostly, I am grateful to my best friend, partner, editor, and counselor, Nikki Conti-Brown. My secret weapon as an academic is that my life partner is literally a genius with a more finely tuned sense of style and clarity than anyone I have ever known. Nikki heard every argument, weighed in on every editorial decision, and has allowed the Federal Reserve to invade our lives far longer than is probably good for a marriage. I still have a reflexive pit in my stomach when I hear her say "Now, there is probably something obvious that I am not getting, but . . ." Because there was nothing obvious that she was not getting; I just either explained myself poorly or didn't have a clear sense of what I was trying to say in the first place. I am going to confidently assert the untested claim that Nikki knows more about the Federal Reserve System than any other landscape architect in history. Thank you, my love, for being my partner in this project, as in all our many others.

And then there is the support of the Conti-Browns generally. As we have bounced around the country, I have been in daily awe of Gabriel, Caleb, and especially Nikki. Being your father and husband are the greatest honors of my life. There's no close second. I dedicate this book to you.

NOTES

PREFACE

1. I have searched high and low for a citation to this story, which circulates among former central bankers, but I haven't found one.
2. Lemann (2014).
3. There are exceptions, of course. The most important is the work of European legal scholar Rosa Lastra, who has focused on international central banking coordination generally for twenty years. See Lastra (1996, 2006). Gerding (2013) puts central banks in the context of political economic cycles of regulation and deregulation. Baker (2012, 2013) analyzes the Fed's legal responses to various aspects of the 2008 financial crisis, including their use of international swap lines and in new approaches to the classic lender of last resort function. Hockett and Omarova (2014) discuss of government as market actors, which includes engagement with the Federal Reserve System. Most recently, see Wallach (2015) for the most comprehensive assessment of the Fed's and Treasury's legal response to the crisis. See Canova (2011a, 2011b) for a sustained critique of central bank independence from a partially legal perspective. For an excellent though by now dated overview of the Federal Open Market Committee, see M. Bernstein (1989).

   As one of the most important pieces of legislation to come out of the Progressive Era, it is unsurprising that the Fed's founding has attracted attention from the era's historians. For arguments that the Federal Reserve Act represents basically a business-oriented conservatism, see Wiebe (1962), Kolko (1963). For a similar argument from a Marxian lens of class consciousness among bankers and capitalists, see Livingston (1989). Sanders (1999) makes the counter argument, that the farmers and populists had more to say about the Fed than the previous consensus had allowed. A historically grounded work in political science that challenges the almost obdurately domestic focus of the previous work is Broz (1997). Broz argues that the Fed's primary purpose was not simply the alleviation of domestic monetary concerns, but the opening up of international markets to American finance (and, therefore, business).

Appropriately to their methodological considerations, the histories of the Fed by economists reflect their concerns about theoretical debates important to economists. The classic history of the Fed's first fifty years, Friedman and Schwartz (1963), makes sophisticated use of vast primary resources, but the focus is on developing a theory of monetarism that explains the macroeconomic consequences of Fed action and inaction. Meltzer's sprawling three-volume history of the Fed follows a similar vein. Meltzer's history (2003, 2010a, 2010b) is a seminal reference work for scholars. As the notes will indicate, I am indebted to him. But Meltzer's is not a useful narrative history for nonspecialists given its long excursions into monetarism and explaining why the Fed's failures to adhere to the doctrine's dictates have had harmful policy consequences. This is not to criticize Meltzer's magisterial work—the erudition and care taken to produce this 2,100-page history make it a defining achievement in Federal Reserve historiography. It is to say that the style and viewpoint will prevent it from a wide readership, even among scholars specializing in the field. An accessible, single-volume narrative history of the Federal Reserve has yet to be written.

4. A note on the notes: references to statutes and court cases are cited in full and not listed in the bibliography. The same for primary sources not otherwise in the public record. Other citations are listed by author's last name and year of publication, with full citation in the bibliography.

INTRODUCTION: ULYSSES AND THE CHAPERONE

1. Lee (2013) (quoting President Obama).
2. Blinder (2004, 1). A recent search among economics journals yielded 2,116 articles discussing central bank independence. I'll be engaging the standard account—which I refer to as the Ulysses/punch-bowl account—throughout this book.

   It is important to note, though, that this standard account is my own reduction of several strands of scholarship and public commentary. The argument is not that everyone who thinks about the Fed focuses only on these elements, but that each element taken in turn forms the usual basis for discussion. For example, economists and political scientists studying central bank independence are largely concerned with inflation, law, and political influence but have a more nuanced appreciation for the Fed's internal structure; popular commentary is often concerned with nonlegal interactions between the president or secretary of the treasury and the Fed chair, but with no clear sense of the Fed's internal structure. And so on. There are few if any experts on the Fed who would endorse the Ulysses/punch-bowl account in its entirety. It is instead to provide a reductive composite that allows engagement with each component.

3. Martin (1955a). For more recent examples of the punch bowl metaphor, see Brennan and Lo (2014). Interestingly, nearly every scholar to reference the

metaphor does not source it. This includes Meltzer (2010a, 474) and Bremner (2004, 276), neither of whom provide the source for the quote. Martin himself purports to cite someone else (although he, too, does not source his quote). The full quote is this: "The Federal Reserve, as one writer put it, after the recent increase in the discount rate, is in the position of the chaperone who has ordered the punch bowl removed just when the party was really warming up." Martin (1955a, 12).

Kydland and Prescott's (1977) paper established the field, though they do not refer to the Ulysses contract as such. Elster (1977, 2000) provides the theoretical link between the Ulysses contract conception and central bank independence, one followed by, among others, Clark (2002) and Tabellini (2005). Martin's quip and especially the Ulysses-contract view of Fed independence provide the theoretical and empirical underpinnings of central bank independence.

4. Rogoff (1985) formalized the anti-inflationary benefits of the conservative central banker model, building on Kydland and Prescott (1977) and Barro and Gordon (1983).

5. By "structural," I mean to bring my conception of Fed independence into dialogue with two academic literatures: the "structure and process" theory in political science and the "state-structural" accounts of state power. In the structure-and-process approach, as Gersen (2010, 339) summarizes it, "[a]lthough the structure and process thesis now has many variants, its simplest form asserts that legislatures can control agency discretion (policy outcomes) by carefully delineating the process by which agency policy is formulated." Here, I am interested in the relationship between the political actors and the Fed, but also the influence of nonpolitical external actors and the internal institutional variety of the central bank. For representative work, in structure and process, see McCubbins, Noll, and Weingast (1987, 1989).

In this sense, it is similar to Hall's state-structural accounts, or those that "emphasize the impact on policy of the state's structure and its actions, but [that] are less inclined to insist on the autonomy of the state vis-à-vis societal pressure. Instead, they accord interest groups, political parties, and other actors outside the state an important role in the policy process. Their main point is that the structure and past activities of the state often affect the nature or force of the demands that these actors articulate." Hall (1993, 276).

6. I paraphrase Kenneth Shepsle's original and influential description of Congress. Shepsle (1992).

7. Rosa M. Lastra orients her discussion of CBI around mechanisms of independence—she refers to them as "safeguards"—that come in three varieties: "organic, functional, and professional." Lastra (1996). Organic and functional safeguards echo the legal separations that form the basis of economists' empirical models of CBI; organic safeguards refer to "the legal safeguards directed towards the organization of the central bank and to its institutional relationships with the government" and include mechanisms such as appointment, terms of office, dismissal, salary, prohibitions on central bankers while

in office, prohibitions on central bankers after they leave office, and liaisons with the Treasury. Lastra (1996, 12, 27–36). Functional safeguards refer to legislative restrictions on "the functions of the central bank and the scope of the powers entrusted to it." Lastra (1996, 12). "Professional" safeguards are part of what Lastra calls "de facto" independence and are "determined by: the personalities of the governor and the minister of finance (and in some countries of other high officials), the political and economic circumstances (e.g., economic expansion or recession); the history and national priorities of the country concerned; the depth and quality of monetary analysis; the rate of turnover of central bank governors and other factors." Lastra (1996). Similarly, Cukierman, a leader among the empiricists in studying central bank independence, distinguishes between "legal independence" and "actual independence," sometimes referred to between de facto and de jure independence. See Cukierman (1992, 371–72). See also Fernández-Albertos (2015) for a more recent discussion of these and related issues. For the Lastra quote, see Lastra (2015, 30).

8. Goodman (1991, 330).
9. Bagehot (1873/1999, 19).
10. Kettl (1986, 9).

PART I

1. There used to be a Federal Reserve Board. As will be discussed in much more detail throughout the book, the Federal Reserve Board created in 1913 was replaced by the "Board of Governors of the Federal Reserve System." It is conventional to refer to the Board of Governors as the Federal Reserve Board, even though the two entities have little in common organizationally.

   To highlight this grammatical point, in the original debates during and for many years following the passage of the Federal Reserve Act of 1913, the only word capitalized was frequently "Federal": it was the "Federal reserve board" and the "Federal reserve banks." See C. Glass (1927). For others following Shepsle, see Vermeule (2005) and Rao (2011).

CHAPTER 1. THE THREE FOUNDINGS OF THE FEDERAL RESERVE

1. Warburg (1930, 12).
2. I choose the term "government-sponsored bank" carefully. Although frequently indulged, the temptation to refer to the first and second Banks of the United States as "central banks" is to engage in a kind of prochronism that is without defensible intellectual basis.

   Henry Clay is an interesting character in these debates—like James Madison and many other Jeffersonian Democrats politically active long enough to debate both the First and Second Banks of the United States, Clay was initially opposed to these banks, but eventually in favor. For overviews of the shifting alliances, see Howe (2007, 80–86) and Wilentz (2005, 391–425). Historians such as Howe have not been kind to Jackson's economic worldview; for a stout defense, see Temin (1969). For a discussion of the political philosophies at play in both episodes, see Hoffmann (2001). For the quote on government banks and politics, see Bolles (1883, 32).

3. Herbert Satterlee—Morgan's son-in-law, business associate, and attendant to the events of that fateful fall—was the chronicler of the Morgan mythos. Satterlee (1939).

4. The Jekyll Island meeting gets a lot of attention, far more than it should. It is mysterious, intriguing, and hints at a secret cabal of politicians and bankers. But the details of getting to the island are more interesting than the influence that their plan—as distinct from the many plans that existed before the meeting—had on the Federal Reserve Act. For more on Jekyll Island and its place in the Fed's history, see Wiebe (1962), White (1983), Kolko (1963). For entertainment but not information, see Griffin (2010).

5. Examples of this conventional retelling are legion. For an example, see Bruner and Carr (2009).

6. For a modern example of attention to the 1912 election, see Goodwin (2014). On the variety (or not) of the candidates' political ideologies, see Smith (1999, 410–11), who views the candidates on a right-center-left progressive spectrum, with Taft on the right, Roosevelt in the center, and Wilson on the left (Smith isn't as interested in Debs but still locates him within this spectrum). Smith is disputing Kolko's (1963) conception that clumped the candidates rather narrowly as so many conservatives. See also Milkis (2009, ix), who sees in the election "the central political events of the 20th century: the rise of direct democracy and the expansion of federal administrative power." For the "political philosophy," see Cooper (1983, 141).

7. Berg (2014, 298–315).

8. The vote in the House of Representatives was 298 to 60; only two Democrats voted against the bill, whereas 35 Republicans voted in favor. In the Senate, the vote was 43 to 25 (with 27 not voting). The Democrats were unanimous in favor, and all but three Republicans voted against. Clifford (1965, 40) has the details. For more on the NMC, see Meltzer (2003, 65–68), Friedman and Schwartz (1963, 18–24) and Kemmerer (1922, 64).

9. A spirited, if somewhat intramural, debate about who could claim paternity of the Federal Reserve System broke out in the two decades following the act's passage. The candidates were Paul Warburg, one of the Jekyll Island participants and author of early position papers laying out the Republicans' plan for "currency reform," as it was often called; Carter Glass, the House sponsor of the Federal Reserve Act and a conservative Democratic congressman from Virginia; James Laurence Laughlin, an economist who had written extensively before and during the debates on currency reform; and H. Parker Willis, Laughlin's student and Glass's assistant who did much of the grunt work of writing the technical statute. This is not to mention Woodrow Wilson, Nelson Aldrich, or even J. P. Morgan and the others at the infamous Je-

kyll Island meeting. In a nearly two-thousand-page compendium of his speeches and other primary records, Warburg defended his view that the Federal Reserve Act passed by the Democrats represented only minor differences from the Aldrich bill that he essentially wrote. Glass—who is quoted as saying that "next to [his] family, the Federal Reserve System is nearest to my heart"—took extraordinary umbrage to this suggestion and saw the Aldrich bill as essentially unrelated to the Glass-Owens bill, the version ultimately adopted into law. As cited in Schlesinger (1960, 296). See Willis (1923), C. Glass (1927), and Warburg (1930).

The historians of the Fed's founding—from Sanders to Livingston to Wiebe to White—essentially ignore the main functional contributions of the Federal Reserve Act: its facilitation of the rise of the United States as a financial center. Lawrence Broz (1997) offers a more thorough and compelling account. He carefully reviews each section of the act, engaging in an important scholarly effort that Kolko somewhat dismissively called "the exegetical problem" that must be taken up in any description of the Federal Reserve in history. See Kolko (1963, 222).

Broz's argument is essentially that the banking system, as it existed before the passage of the Federal Reserve Act, created serious domestic barriers to the internationalization of the U.S. financial system. The arguments in favor of farmers, or the class consciousness of bankers, or the domestic longing for order, or the triumph of conservatism, miss what the statute was actually about. The Federal Reserve Act, according to Broz, responded directly to those concerns by (1) reiterating the nation's commitment to the gold standard, a commitment that was controversial less than a generation before the act's passage; (2) adding liquidity to the secondary markets for financing international trade; and (3) creating a mechanism whereby reserves could be shifted within the system to those institutions most in need of those reserves in a panic. We mentioned how the Federal Reserve Act created a market for international bankers' acceptances; the act also made it possible for other parties to buy those acceptances after they have already been drawn. Doing so not only made the rancher in South Dakota more likely to accept the order from the tanner in Manchester but also made the banker who would finance the entire deal more likely to be in Chicago than in London. If there were a thriving secondary market in the United States for such acceptances, then there would be no need for the financing of a dollar-denominated transaction to occur anywhere other than a dollar-denominated economy.

10. The term "other people's money" comes from Louis Brandeis's book *Other People's Money and How the Bankers Use It*, which summarized the Pujo hearings. See Brandeis (1913).

11. For more on the Pujo hearings and the Money Trust hearings, see Geisst (2012). For the quote, see Morgan (1912, 49–50).

12. See Chernow (1990, 149–59).

13. Berg (2013, 300). Wilson, interestingly enough, was a devoted fan of Walter Bagehot, but of *The English Constitution*, not *Lombard Street*. Had he read

the latter, he would have recognized that his certainty about institutional design was well wide the mark in the context of central banking. Bagehot took a dim view of government meddling in central bank appointments. See Bagehot (1873/1999, 70). For Wilson's intellectual debts to Bagehot, see Wilson (1885/2006).

14. The term Wilsonian Compromise comes from Wiebe (1966, 221) and refers to Wilson's general legislative program, one where he forced—through will and reason and the exercise of political power—otherwise hostile groups to bargain one with another to reach conclusion. In this, Wiebe concludes, "[n]either Wilson, his advisers, nor the leaders in Congress could pretend that this remarkable balance followed a master plan." It was in the "dextrous management" of the initial legislative projects that Wilson's skills were on display. The dysfunction of the institutional design, in the case of the Federal Reserve at least, didn't manifest itself until after Wilson was out of office. For the statutory details, see House Report on Glass Bill (reprinted in C. Glass 1927). Note that in the Glass bill that passed the House of Representatives, the secretary of agriculture would also be an ex officio member, with each member of the board serving six years. The House version would have set the floor at twelve and put no limit on the final number. C. Glass (1927). See chapter 5, below, on how complicated a question the status of the Reserve Banks actually is.

15. Glass House Report, H.R. 7837, reported H. Rpt. 63–69 at 12 (1913); C. Glass (1927).

16. Glass House Report, H.R. 7837, reported H. Rpt. 63–69 at 12 (1913). Kettl (1986, 32). After the Federal Reserve Board took a stronger hand in setting discount rates in 1927, Glass sought to clamp down on the board's authority. For more about how these kinds of disputes between the Reserve Banks and the original Federal Reserve Board came about, see Meltzer (2003, 62–75); Clifford (1965, 66–67); Kemmerer (1922, 64).

17. Meltzer (2003, 75). For discussions of how, for example, the U.S. Constitution created similar power vacuums, see Rakove (1996). For more on the indeterminacy of the Federal Reserve Act, see Clifford (1965, 103–9). On competing Cuban branches, see Warburg (1930).

18. For more on this tumultuous period and Strong's role in it, see Ahamed (2009), Eichengreen (1992), and Meltzer (2003, 110–21). For the quote, see Chandler (1958, 3).

19. For the desk note, see Chandler (1958, 1). For Hoover, see Hoover (1952, vi). Hoover further complained that the Fed (under Benjamin Strong) turned American optimism into "the stock-exchange Mississippi Bubble" (1952, 5). Hoover also makes this connection explicit. (1952, 7). History has agreed with Hoover's conclusion, but not his reasoning.

20. See Bernanke (2000). For continued modern relevance in public and scholarly debates, compare Shlaes (2008) with Eichengreen (2015).

21. The presidential address is Address at Oglethorpe University in Atlanta, Ga., May 22, 1932. Hofstadter (1960, 304). For more on New Deal experimentation, see Katznelson (2013), Brinkley (1995).

22. Eccles's biographical details can be found in his memoir, Eccles (1951) and biography, Hyman (1976).

23. Eccles (1951, 83–84).

24. As recounted in Skidelsky (2003, 813).

25. Keynes had circulated these ideas before the *General Theory*, as early as 1929, but Eccles claims never to have heard them. And regardless, Keynes was not the first to espouse these views. See Laidler (1999). The point is that Eccles was something of an original article. For the quote from the condescending banker, see Eccles (1951, 84).

26. Eccles (1951, 84).

27. "Ten-foot pole," see Hyman (1976, 155); on Reserve Bank dominance, Eccles and Currie (1934/2004). Hoffmann (2001, 139–45) sees Eccles in a classic Benthamite utilitarian position of justifying "state action" to insert itself "where nature ends, to ensure optimal outcomes." I see Eccles as more of an interest-group theorist, skeptical of banker domination of the financial system and eager to apply a proto-Keynesian worldview to the special case of a deflationary spiral. He would have seen himself as a practical businessman.

28. Hyman (1976, 161).

29. There is reason to suspect that Eccles shared Currie's views on these issues: Currie and Eccles were, in fact, the authors of the memorandum that first proposed the Fed's overhaul, and they engaged in a flurry of correspondence during the months before the bill's enactment. These memos are included in the Eccles Papers, housed in hard copy at the University of Utah, but almost fully digitized by the Federal Reserve Bank of St. Louis, through their Federal Reserve Archival System for Economic Research (FRASER). This extraordinary and comprehensive collection of documents is a national treasure and essential resource for monetary and financial historians.

30. Currie memo to Eccles, April 1, 1935.

31. For more on the Second New Deal, see Kennedy (2001).

32. For the lack of controversy on the Banking Act of 1935, see Kennedy (2001, 265).

33. For more on the near miss, see Brands (2008, 292). For Glass's conservatism, see Patterson (1967, 20).

34. The permanent presence of the president of the Federal Reserve Bank of New York didn't get added until 1942.

35. For Mellon's role at the Fed, see Cannadine (2006, 321–22). Glass is quoted in Hackley (1972, 71–72). An explanatory note is appropriate on the provenance of Hackley's extraordinary book. Hackley, then general counsel for the Fed's Board of Governors, prepared this two-hundred-page manuscript for internal purposes. It is an invaluable scholarly source that contains both references to other useful primary documents (such as early opinion letters from the comptroller general) and is a useful reflection of the board's view of several important legal issues at the time. Upon learning of the document's existence from William Greider's journalistic history of the Fed—see Greider (1989, 49, 736)—I asked the reference librarians at Stanford Law School if

they could secure it. For more details on Erika Wayne's impressive success, see Conti-Brown (2011b).

Besides the secretary of the treasury, another institution within the Federal Reserve System was demoted to the point of irrelevance: The Federal Advisory Council. Prior to 1935, the FAC (which consisted exclusively of bankers and their representatives) had presented itself as an authoritative voice on monetary and financial policy, often failing to identify itself as anything other than "the Fed." This sleight of hand earned Eccles's ire; the FAC never recovered. It still exists today but is a largely ceremonial committee far from the contributing role it enjoyed during the first Federal Reserve. For more on the FAC in the early Fed, see Warburg (1930, 376) and Eccles (1951, 188).

36. Kennedy (2001, 274). On Mellon, as Benjamin Strong put it, "At no time has the Reserve System been so free from anything approaching control by the Treasury as it has since Mr. Mellon took office." As quoted in Cannadine (2006, 292). But he wasn't completely absent. Cannadine (2006, 389). For the evolution of central banking, see Goodhart (1988).

37. Friedman and Schwartz (1963, 446–50); Meltzer (2003, 415–20).

38. Chandler (1958, 408) provides an excellent overview of the Fed's wartime policies. See also Meltzer (2003, chapter 7). For the 1942 announcement, see Board of Governors of the Federal Reserve System (1942, 1).

39. Eccles (1951, 397).

40. On the nineteenth-century martial origin of hawks, see Howe (2007, 85). For skepticism on these reductionist metaphors that I share, see Irwin (2013b).

41. For more on the vice chair battle, see Eccles (1951, 437–42); Meltzer (2003, 655–56), Clifford (1965, 208–11), and Kettl (1986, 63–64).

42. The "open speculation" quote is from Kirshner (2007, 144), quoting press accounts. For more on the chronology to the Fed-Treasury Accord, see Eccles (1951), Clifford (1965), Kettl (1986), Hyman (1976), Meltzer (2010a). For briefer treatments, see Hetzel and Leach (2001) and T. G. Moe (2013). The quote about Stalin is from Kirshner (2007, 144) (quoting Federal Reserve Board, Minutes, January 31, 1951, pp. 9–12).

43. See Kirshner (2007, 144).

44. Eccles (1951, 496).

45. 37 Fed. Res. Bull. 267 (1951). For a slightly fuller contemporaneous discussion of the accord, see the Board of Governors (1952, 98–101).

46. Kettl (1986, 74). Clifford (1965, 267–68).

47. Bremner (2004, 91).

48. "The start" is from Hetzel and Leach (2001, 53); "major achievement," Meltzer (2003, 712).

49. Clifford (1965, 253–55).

50. Mahoney and Thelen (2009). Chang (2003, 135–37) takes a different view on the 1935 restructuring and argues that the Republicans and Democrats in fact were bartering between appointment power and centralization. This view is insufficiently attuned to the historically contingent nature of these final structures, in both 1913 and in 1935.

CHAPTER 2. LEADERSHIP AND INSTITUTIONAL CHANGE: FROM PERIPHERY TO POWER

1. McAdoo (1931, 286).
2. McAdoo (1931, 287–88).
3. Kettl (1986) provides a first-rate, but often overlooked, development of the argument that personal leadership at the Fed is responsible for its independence and position within government. I don't endorse the thesis completely: this book's argument is not that law is irrelevant, but that it is an incomplete. But I have benefitted tremendously from Kettl's account and the sources to which he points.
4. McCabe was a patron of his alma mater, where the library and much else is named in his honor. See http://www.swarthmore.edu/mccabe-scholars/about-thomas-mccabe-15.
5. Bremner (2004, 13). William McChesney Martin Sr. offered an impassioned speech in favor of the National Reserve Association, the Fed's predecessor, precisely along these lines. See Bremner (2004, 9).
6. Riefler deserves the title of most influential Fed economist for three reasons: first, he revolutionized monetary policy in his first tour of duty as a Fed staffer in the 1920s, by helping the Fed move away from the real-bills doctrine. Second, because he was the coauthor of the Fed-Treasury Accord. And third, because he helped revolutionize the practice of monetary policy again when working on flexible monetary policy with Martin. See Meltzer (2003, 161–65).
7. Bremner (2004, 4). For more on Sproul versus Martin, see Clifford (1965, 272–74). Sproul had long sought to undo some of the damage to the Reserve Banks wrought by the Banking Act of 1935. For example, he thought *any* credit policy—including the discount function—should be given fully to the FOMC, not to the board. Clifford (1965, 216–22).
8. Bremner (2004, 111).
9. Reining in the New York Fed was a slow process that required the participation of other members of the FOMC beyond Martin. For more on Martin's mastery of internal Fed politics, see Meltzer (2010a, 55–57), Bremner (2004).
10. Bremner (2004, 101).
11. Clifford (1965, 291) (quoting *Economist*, June 2, 1956).
12. For "punch bowl," see Martin (1955a, 12). For wind and stream, see Bremner (2004) and sources cited therein.
13. Bremner (2004, 189). For "economy of words," see Holmes (2013). On Martin's authorship of the "punch bowl," even that is questionable. In the speech he gave, he is actually quoting an unnamed and unsourced "writer."
14. Eisenhower (1953).
15. Eisenhower (1956).
16. Johnson is quoted in Caro (2013, 397). For more on Johnson's political skills and ambitions, see Zelizer (2015). For more on LBJ and Vietnam, see Logevall (2001).

17. As quoted in Bremner (2004, 195).
18. Bremner (2004, 195). Meltzer took a dim view of Martin's coordination with the Johnson administration. Meltzer (2010a, 527).
19. Sources collected in Bremner (2004, 200–202). For more about the implications of these debates for Johnson's domestic political strategy, see Zelizer (2015, 269).
20. For readability, I have used generic gendered pronouns in the singular to avoid the somewhat clumsy "he or she." In odd chapters, the pronouns are masculine; in even, feminine.
21. For the Yellen speech that caused the commotion, see Yellen (2014). For an example of the criticism, see Pethokoukis (2014).
22. For an example taken essentially at random (it was the most recent one in the Washington Post), see Mui (2014). Bagehot (1873/1999, 1).
23. Martin was not perfectly insulated from political influence, though; economists have viewed his later tenure (the late Johnson, early Nixon years) as evidence of an inability to continue to stand firm against these administrations. See Romer and Romer (2003).
24. Silber (2012, 202–16).
25. The biographical details are from Silber (2012) and Treaster (2005). For a less sympathetic but well-researched account of the Volcker Fed in a broader political context, see Greider (1987).
26. Silber (2012).
27. Meltzer (2010a). Greider (1987, 20–21, 34). A note is in order on Greider's very impressive volume. Greider is a journalist, not a historian, but treats the political history of the Fed with more breadth and depth than other major histories of the Fed. And he has received something of a bad rap among subsequent commentators: Geithner, for example, mistakenly viewed Greider's as a book that "savaged the Greenspan Fed" with a "populist critique." Greider's is certainly a critique from the left, but it was published in 1987, the same year Greenspan was installed as Fed chair. The book barely mentions Greenspan. Meltzer's three-volume history mentions Greider a handful of times but misspells his name throughout.
28. Greider (1987, 35).
29. Meltzer (2010b). For more on how inflation altered the American political landscape, see Samuelson (2008). Carter's take on inflation came through clearly in his infamous "Crisis of Confidence" speech—sometimes mocked as his "malaise" speech, though he never used the term—is a fascinating piece of moral and political theater. See Carter (1979). Reflecting the views of many at the time, Carter viewed inflation as a function of the importation of foreign oil and the price shocks imposed by artificial scarcity. For more on inflation in the political consciousness, see Jacobs (2007).
30. For more on the interest rate climate of the time, the Fed's mistakes, and the consequences of the Great Inflation, see Bordo and Orphanides (2013), especially Orphanides and Williams (2013). For some skepticism of the centrality of Volcker to this narrative, see Blinder and Rudd (2013).
31. For more on monetarism and the Great Inflation, see Meltzer (2010b). The

Fed formally abandoned monetary targets in 1993. See Blinder and Reis (2005).

32. In one ironic moment that reflected the difference between the new Fed chair and one of his predecessors, Arthur Burns, Nixon's Fed chair, seemed to endorse a quantity theory of money in a public speech but said that it was impossible to do so in a modern economy because of the difficulty in convincing various parts of the democratic state to participate. Volcker attended the speech but had to leave early largely so that he could commence the first of his changes at the FOMC that would do just this. "The difference between Burns and Volcker," monetarist and Fed historian Allan Meltzer has written, "is that Volcker left [the speech] early to do what Burns said could not be done—control money growth." Meltzer (2010b, note 18).

33. For more on Reagan's support of Volcker, see Meltzer (2010b, 1012, citing interview with former Fed staffers).

34. Silber (2012, 264–65) collects these and many others. Not everyone praised Volcker, though. James Wright, the Democratic Speaker of the House who had sparred with Volcker over the high interest rates, was not a Volcker fan. As Silber recounts: "When asked to describe Volcker's term as chair, Wright replied, "Long." Silber (2012, 263). Hall (1993) provides an excellent overview of the politics and social learning of Thatcherite monetary policy.

35. Sorkin (2009). For more on bailouts throughout banking history, see Grossman (2010, 86–98). Volcker's quoted statement is cited in Meltzer (2010b, 1105).

36. For more on Continental Illinois, see Silber (2012, 242–47); McCollom (1987). For its implications for the future, see Johnson and Kwak (2010, 200–202).

37. Greider (1987), Blinder and Reis (2005).

38. Blinder and Reis (2005, 14).

39. This line comes from the film *Shattered Glass* (2003) and may have been a tweak at the magazine's self-importance, as the only characters who use the term are *New Republic* staff writers. For the George H. W. Bush article, "Peddling Poppy," see S. Glass (1997). For the Monica Lewinsky article, "Monica Sells," see S. Glass (1998b). For the hacker article, "Hack Heaven," see S. Glass (1998a). *Slate*, the online news magazine, wrote several contemporaneous and retrospective accounts of the Glass saga. Especially interesting are Shafer (1998) and Plotz (2003). For the article that first exposed the scandal, see Penenberg (1998).

40. Chait and Glass (1998).

41. For a look back at why Glass was so effective, see Bradley (2014).

42. For evenhanded treatments of Gennifer Flowers, including her background as a lounge singer, see Gormley (2010). For the transcript of the *Larry King Live* interview, see King and Greenfield (1998).

43. Brands (2007, 205); Woodward (2001).

44. As we will see, Kydland and Prescott play an important role in the development of the Ulysses/punch-bowl narrative. The foundational rules-based ideas

in economics come from Friedman and Schwartz (1963), Kydland and Prescott (1977), Fisher (1995), and Taylor (1993). But this is a growing literature. For a more recent review, see Bilbiie and Straub (2013).

45. Blinder and Reis (2005, 16). For a first-rate overview of the power of words, and especially the change in central banking practice in their use, see Holmes (2013). Although the tone and references from cultural anthropology will be foreign to most scholars of central banking, Holmes's account of the power of words as an instrument of monetary policy provides a richer account of the sweep of options available to central banks than those that focus exclusively on the technical details of influencing reserve balances, asset prices, and interest rates through open market operations. I will have more to say about the rules versus discretion debate in chapters 6 and 11.

46. *Financial Times* (2000). For a survey of market participants on the Greenspan Put, see Miller et al. (2002).

47. Greenspan (2007, 52, 97, 138). The last point demonstrates Greenspan's devotion to Rand more than his knowledge of diplomatic history: the dean of American Sovietology, George Kennan, had made this prediction in the late 1946 in perhaps the most famous of diplomatic cables in American history. It became the basis for much of American policy during the Cold War. See Gaddis (2011).

48. Greenspan (2007, 52).

49. Greenspan (2007, 373). For more on the conservative revolution in policy and economics, see Rodgers (2011, chapter 2).

50. Engel and McCoy (2011, 189).

51. The best chronological accounts of the crisis are Wessel (2009) and Sorkin (2009); for the "second draft of history," see Blinder (2013). For a useful but somewhat dated guide for historians, see Neal (2011). For an unequivocal account of housing markets and the crisis, see Wallison (2015); for a journalistic investigation, see Morgenson and Rosner (2011). For a focus on the legal development of the housing crisis, see Engel and McCoy (2011).

52. For example, see Financial Crisis Inquiry Commission (2011). For more on Robertson and the Truth in Lending Act, see Engel and McCoy (2011, 194).

53. Andrews (2007).

54. Andrews (2007).

CHAPTER 3. CENTRAL BANKING BY COMMITTEE: THE LEGAL AND PRACTICAL AUTHORITY OF THE BOARD OF GOVERNORS OF THE FEDERAL RESERVE SYSTEM

1. J. Berry (1996). The other three governors were Edward W. Kelley Jr., Lawrence B. Lindsey, and Susan M. Phillips.

2. As cited in Berry (1996).

3. In this section I draw on the policy brief I wrote with Simon Johnson, published by the Peterson Institute for International Economics. I'm grateful to

Simon, the Peterson Institute, and the excellent editorial staff and peer reviewers for their help. See Conti-Brown and Johnson (2013).

4. Appearing before House and Senate committees for testimony every six months (alternating between House and Senate Financial Services and Banking Committees), or when requested by one of these committees. The provisions of the Federal Reserve Act cited are, respectively, 12 U.S.C. §§ 242, 244, 247b, 248(s), 248(k), 467, 244.

5. 12 U.S.C. § 244; 12 U.S.C. § 248(k). To be sure, unlike in the corporate governance context, the supervisory board cannot remove the chair from his position. Chapters 5 and 8 will have more to say about the peculiar removal restrictions in the Federal Reserve Act.

6. 12 U.S.C. §§ 242, 248i.

7. For Foreign Intelligence Surveillance Act court, see 50 U.S.C. § 1803; Federal Judicial Conference, 28 U.S.C. § 331; Smithsonian, 20 U.S.C. §§ 41–70 (2006).

8. See Maya (2014) on *Sesame Street*; Kroft (2007) for *60 Minutes*; Dworkin (2010) on Kagan.

9. I discuss the practices and academic study of dissents on the FOMC in chapter 5.

While there are few instances of the chair in dissent, they are not unheard of. For example, William Miller reportedly lost the support of his board. On nonmonetary policy, for example, Paul Volcker voted in the minority in approving a merger shortly before his resignation in 1987. See Wallach (2014).

10. Silber (2012, 256–58); Greider (1987, 698–703).

11. Common to the tenure standards at law schools in the 1980s, Tarullo didn't write much as a junior scholar: his first published piece was a short, coauthored review of an edited book called *Managing Trade Relations in the 1980s: Issues Involved in the GATT Ministerial Meeting of 1982* (S. Rubin 1984; Gross and Tarullo 1985). His second piece was a more substantive (but still largely ignored) symposium essay on U.S.-Japan trade relations. Tarullo (1986a). His major pieces were thorough explorations of ideas that challenged conventional articulations of law in international trade. Tarullo (1986b, 1987).

Interestingly, in the first of these articles, he dealt with the problem of democratic legitimacy and the transfer of tariff regulation from the political sphere to "an administrative law scheme that implemented binding standards of general application." Tarullo (1986b, 287). He describes in the article the history behind how "this intensely contested issue [tariff regulation] was consigned completely to an executive administrative process that was both insulated from representative democratic politics and exempted from the administrative lawmaking procedures and constraints that define most other forms of economic regulation." Tarullo (1986b, 287). The parallel to monetary policy jumps off the page. Tarullo caught it too. After describing court treatment of the Federal Reserve Board, he noted: " Ironically, then, the solution eventually fashioned for the legitimacy and efficiency problems of tariff-making (and maybe monetary control as well) was to remove these highly politicized issues from any significant control by Congress, either through direct action or through judicial supervision to ensure that congressional policies not be subverted." Tarullo (1986b, 343). There's not much to discern here about his future actions, but enough to recognize that he had thought hard about the problem of technocratic expertise and democratic accountability.

For more on the details of Tarullo's tenure battle, see the *Harvard Crimson* (1986). He didn't turn out to be what he'd hoped he'd be; the faculty denied tenure to two other critical legal theorists in the two subsequent years. Kingson (1987).

12. Tarullo (2008).
13. Capital regulation is probably the most important area of banking regulation in the aftermath of the crisis. For the best general account of the issue, see Admati and Hellwig (2013). For some historical background on capital regulation in the United States, see E. Posner (2014).
14. In Ron Suskind's account of the Obama economic policy team, Tarullo appears to be mentioned exactly once, in a single sentence (reassuring a frustrated candidate whose views on Iran were misconstrued by cable news). Suskind (2011, 15).
15. Office of President-Elect Barack Obama (2008).
16. Office of President-Elect Barack Obama (2008).
17. Hilsenrath and Paletta (2009).
18. For "overbearing skepticism" and "wary of being second-guessed," see Hilsenrath and Paletta (2009); for legendary blowups, see Cook (2013); for not justifying past mistakes, see Torres and Hopkins (2012a).
19. Torres and Hopkins (2012a). For example, see Tarullo's speech on intermediate holding companies, Tarullo (2012) or his speech on fiduciary duties in bank holding companies, Tarullo (2014). For press on breaking up big banks, see Tracy and McGrane (2014). See American Bankers Association (2014) for controversy on the fiduciary duty speech.
20. Torres and Hopkins (2012b).
21. As quoted in Cook (2013). See also Torres and Hopkins (2012b).
22. This is a difficult section to write objectively, as Blinder is a mentor, graduate school advisor, and someone I admire enormously as a scholar and person. I include it because the comparison is useful for the reasons stated in the text. I note only that I did not ask permission to include the section, did not interview Blinder for his recollections, and took care only to include material from the public record.
23. Cassidy (1996). Woodward (2000, 127).
24. Cassidy (1996).
25. Cassidy (1996).
26. Grim (2009) summarizes and sources the factual details.
27. Meyer (2004, 9).

CHAPTER 4. THE "DOUBLE GOVERNMENT" OF THE FEDERAL RESERVE: THE ECONOMISTS AND THE LAWYERS

1. For two different critiques of the Lehman decision, see Skeel (2010) and Blinder (2013).
2. Bagehot (1867, 211). For a review of Bagehot, see Magliocca (2012). For a more recent extension of Bagehot's argument to the national security context, see Glennon (2014). Political scientist Daniel Carpenter has expanded our historical understanding of the influence of what he calls "mezzo-level" employees within the bureaucracy. In thinking through the impact of Fed economists and lawyers, I have relied on the paradigm he built for the Department of Interior and FDA especially. See Carpenter (2001) and Carpenter (2010).
3. For the quote on governors working for staff and the British ministry, see Cassidy (1996). For the salaries, see Flaherty (2014), available at http://www.huffingtonpost.com/2014/10/17/federal-reserve-pay-janet-yellen_n_6001202.html. For the staff's self-regard, J. Berry (1996).
4. J. Berry (1996).
5. As quoted in Blustein (2001, 187); J. Berry (1996).
6. J. Berry (1996).
7. For discussion of the "first financial crisis of the twenty-first century," see Boughton (2012, 456); see also Geithner (2014, 46–48).
8. Geithner (2014, 46–59), Truman (2014), Blustein (2001, 187–93).
9. Appropriately, in December 1998—after the events described here—Bill Clinton appointed Truman to the political position of assistant secretary of the U.S. Treasury for international affairs. See Geithner (2014).
10. Ramo (1999).
11. Kocherlakota (2014).
12. For more on the influence of economics on the founding of the Fed, see Mehrling (2002). For the influence of Winfield Riefler, an early Fed economist, see Meltzer (2003, 161–65). For Martin's distaste for forecasting, see Bremner (2004, 271). For the growth of economists at the Fed, including the quote, see Fox (2014).
13. See Ip (2006). For more on this topic, see Zingales (2013). For more on this history, see Auerbach (2008, chapter 5) and Friedman and Schwartz (1993).
14. Fligstein et al. (2014, 3).
15. Alvarez (2010).
16. Tarullo (2013).
17. As of this writing, there is an unprecedented case before the Court of Claims regarding the 13(3) decisions about AIG. That this case is proceeding in such an unusual forum, seven years after the fact, tells us something about the kind of judicial review available for 13(3) decisions. See Scism (2014) for more details.
18. Federal Reserve Act § 13(3), 12 U.S.C. § 343 (2006).
19. 12 U.S.C. § 248(r).

20. Geithner (2014, 83).
21. For more on how Congress writes broad or restrictive language as a way of agency control, see Huber and Shipan (2002).
22. See Wessel (2009), Sorkin (2009).
23. Geithner discusses the Doomsday Book in Geithner (2014, 83, 151).
24. Eisinger (2013). For biographical details, see Alvarez (2010).
25. Eisinger (2013).
26. Eisinger (2013).
27. For more on Glass-Steagall, see Wallach (2014) and Rahman (2012).
28. For more on Gramm-Leach-Bliley, see Omarova (2013). For Alvarez's testimony, see Alvarez (2010).
29. For more on Glass-Steagall's role in the financial crisis, especially with respect to Citigroup, see Wilmarth (2014). For skepticism at a more conceptual level, see Blinder (2013, 266–67).
30. See Alvarez (2010, 9). For Greenspan's partial mea culpa, see Andrews (2008a).
31. Alvarez (2010, 34–35).
32. The canonical cases are *United States v. Mead Corp.*, 533 U.S. 218 (2001), *Chevron v. NRDC*, 467 U.S. 837 (1984), and *Skidmore v. Swift*, 323 U.S. 134 (1944). The scholarly literature is vast, but a useful place to start is a retrospective symposium in volume 83 of the *Fordham Law Review*, especially Hickman (2014), Gluck (2014), Shane (2014), and Walker (2014). For more on Congress's acquiescence to agency deference in Dodd-Frank specifically, see Barnett (2015). For a thorough investigation of the Fed's lawyers' interpretations of their statutory authority in the bank holding company context, see Omarova (2011). For a useful but dated overview of judicial review of banking regulation, see Friedberg and Gordon (1988).
33. Blinder (1997) develops this theme of values and technocracy at more length. We will return to and challenge these ideas in chapter 11.

CHAPTER 5. THE VESTIGIAL AND UNCONSTITUTIONAL FEDERAL RESERVE BANKS

1. 12 U.S.C. §§ 341, 301.
2. 12 U.S.C. §§ 287, 290. For typical discussion of the Reserve Bank ownership of the Fed, see Griffin (2010).
3. As quoted in Hackley (1972, 34).
4. It can be a tricky needle to thread, making constitutional claims about the Federal Reserve. The claim that the "Federal Reserve" is "unconstitutional" entails a broad family of arguments, two of which I do not engage. First, the Fed is unconstitutional because it pursues bad policy. That is, "unconstitutional" and "pursues bad policy" are treated as synonyms: when the Fed pursues good policy, it is constitutional; when it pursues bad policy, it is unconstitutional. Second, the Fed is unconstitutional because our federal government

is one of enumerated powers, and nowhere does the Constitution identify the creation of the central bank. This is an existential challenge: accepting this argument necessarily means the abolition of the Federal Reserve. And third, central banking fits within the constitutional framework, but specific *features* of the Federal Reserve violate specific constitutional principles or provisions as the Supreme Court has construed them. In that sense, the Fed itself is not unconstitutional so much as the participation of private citizens on the Federal Open Market Committee is constitutionally impermissible. I'm much more interested in the last question. For alternatives on the existential constitutional debates, see Rakove (1996, 347–62) (on the First Bank of the United States), Howe (2007, 373–86) (on the Second Bank of the United States), and Timberlake (2012) (on the unconstitutionality of the Federal Reserve as a central bank on a fiat-currency standard).

Much of this section on the Reserve Banks' constitutionality comes from Conti-Brown (2015). I'm grateful to the *Yale Journal on Regulation* for allowing me to reprint some of these arguments here. For "duck," see Patman (1966).

5. Gersen (2010, 347–48). For example, scholars contend that the paradigm: focuses on the wrong mechanisms of independence, see Vermeule (2013), Barkow (2010), and Bressman and Thompson (2010); ignores the ways in which executive agencies (i.e., those whose heads are removable at will and, separately, whose actions are subject to presidential regulatory review) use presidential review to increase "self-insulation," Nou (2013); creates meaningless distinctions between executive and independent agencies, Datla and Revesz, (2013); is focused on the wrong problems, Barkow (2010); identifies the wrong parties, Magill and Vermeule (2011); reflects a misunderstanding of how the administrative state actually functions, Freeman and Rossi (2012); elides ways in which the president controls independent agencies beyond removability, Bressman and Thompson (2010); and gives to courts review of decisions that are fundamentally incompatible with judicial review, Huq (2013). For an alternative view and a stout defense of the judicial doctrine, see Rao (2014).

Vermeule summarizes the problem with the legal focus well. Identifying a "mismatch" between "the doctrinal law as embodied in judicial decisions and the revealed behavior of political actors," he notes that "the legal test that courts deem central to agency independence is neither necessary nor sufficient for operative independence in the world outside the courtroom. The legal test . . . does not capture the observable facts of agency independence in the administrative state." Vermeule (2013, 1168).

For another account of "the fetishization of independence," this time in the corporate governance context, see Rodrigues (2008).

6. *Edmond v. United States*, 520 U.S. 651, 659 (1997) (citing in part *Buckley v. Valeo*, 424 U.S. 1, 125 [1976]).

7. *Morrison v. Olson*, 487 U.S. 654 (1988).

8. *Edmond v. United States*, 520 U.S. 651, 662–63 (1997).

9. U.S. Const. Art. II, § 3.

10. *Myers v. United States*, 272 U.S. 52, 116, 164 (1926). For more on the importance of the postal system to the development of the American state, including through the appointment process, see chapter 3 of John (1998, especially 72–80). To move briskly through the constitutional issues, I am skipping a mountain of detail. For more analysis of this case law, see Vermeule (2013), Huq (2013), and Barkow (2010).

11. *Myers v. United States*, 272 U.S. 52, 116, 117 (1926).

12. *Humphrey's Executor v. United States*, 295 U.S. 602, 619 (1935).

13. *Humphrey's Executor v. United States*, 295 U.S. 602, 619 (1935).

14. *Humphrey's Executor v. United States*, 295 U.S. 602, 624 (1935).

15. *Morrison v. Olson*, 487 U.S. 654, 695–96 (1988).

16. For "squared," see *Free Enter. Fund v. Pub. Co. Accounting Oversight Bd.*, 537 F.3d 667, 686 (D.C. Cir. 2008) (Kavanaugh, J., dissenting). For the Supreme Court case, see *Free Enter. Fund v. Pub. Co. Accounting Oversight Bd.*, 561 U.S. 477, 484 (2010). For more discussion about some of the strangely nonlegal aspects of the court's analysis, see Vermeule (2013, 1167).

17. Pub. L. 73–66, 48 Stat. 162, enacted June 16, 1933.

18. E.g., 12 U.S.C. § 301. There does remain the question of whether monetary policy is, in fact, federal policy of the kind that will trigger Appointments Clause concerns. I think the answer is unquestionably yes: indeed, the very foundation of the Federal Reserve System presupposed the inability of private systems—like, for example, the clearing house model in place before the Federal Reserve System—that some governmental structure was necessary. If that was true in the monetary conditions of the early twentieth century, I think it beyond dispute in the vastly more complicated—and vastly larger—monetary context of the early twenty-first. On Reserve Bank representation at the FOMC, see 12 U.S.C. § 263(a). (Note that while the statute does not require that the Reserve Bank representative be the president, the president is in practice almost always the bank's representative on the FOMC.)

19. 12 U.S.C. § 242.

20. There is some statutory ambiguity whether the Board of Governors and the Reserve Bank boards share this authority; there is no ambiguity that the Reserve Bank boards have it. Compare 12 U.S.C. § 248f with 12 U.S.C. § 614. Whether the Board has this authority or not is constitutionally irrelevant.

21. I made similar arguments in Conti-Brown (2013).

22. I first introduced these ideas in Conti-Brown (2014c).

23. Source: Members of the Board of Governors of the Federal Reserve System, available at http://www.federalreserve.gov/aboutthefed/bios/board/boardmem bership.htm.

24. For a thorough exploration of vacancies in administrative agencies, see O'Connell (2009).

25. See *Melcher v. FOMC*, 836 F.2d 561 (D.C. Cir. 1989); *Committee for Monetary Reform v. Board of Governors*, 766 F.2d 538 (D.C. Cir. 1985); *Riegle v. FOMC*, 656 F.2d 873 (D.C. Cir.) (1981); *Reuss v. Balles*, 584 F.2d 461 (D.C. Cir.) (1978). As Mark Bernstein explains in his excellent (if dated) treatment of the FOMC's constitutionality, the first challenge to open market activities

was actually in the Second Circuit under the Federal Reserve Board system that antedates the FOMC structure. See M. Bernstein (1989, 132 n. 90).

26. Standing doctrine is, in a word, a mess and essentially always has been. See Fletcher (1988). For a very good recent overview of the doctrine, see Redish and Joshi (2014). For the quote, *Reuss*, 584 F.2d at 467.

27. *Committee for Monetary Reform*, 766 F.2d at 543 (citing *Warth v. Seldin*, 422 U.S. 490, 499 [1975]).

28. *Riegle*, 656 F.2d at 873.

29. McGowan (1981). McGowan wrote his theory in a law review article, but was chief judge of the D.C. Circuit at the time. For "circumscribed equitable discretion," *Riegle* 656 F.2d at 881. The Supreme Court, in its subsequent treatment of legislative standing in *Raines v. Byrd*, 521 U.S. 811 (1997), has mostly embraced a similar conclusion regarding legislators' ability to challenge statutes' constitutionality. While the facts in *Raines* didn't address the question of a senator being denied the ability to give advice and consent to a principal officer's appointment to a federal position, the decision is animated by a similar theory. See *Raines*, 521 U.S. at 816–17 (citing *Moore v. U.S. House of Representatives*, 733 F. 2d 946, 950–952 (D.C. Cir. 1984). *Moore* relies substantially on *Riegle*. The doctrine of equitable discretion has been severely criticized, including from the bench. Judge Bork refused to acknowledge the authority of *Riegle*. In his words, "I do not consider myself bound by the panel decision . . . in *Riegle* . . . . *Riegle* . . . purported to change the law of legislator standing in this circuit without submitting the issue to the full court. Under the established practice of this court, that may not be done." *Crockett v. Reagan*, 720 F.2d 1355 (D.C. Cir. 1983) (Bork, J. dissenting).

30. The anchor theoretical paper here is Faust (1996). For the empirical treatment, see Thornton and Wheelock (2014).

31. See Broz (1997). This is not to fault the theoretical effort: Faust (1996) can hardly be faulted for failing to take into account historical arguments that were published after him.

32. Meyer (2004, 53).

33. For the low estimate of dissents, see Thornton and Wheelock (2014). For the content analysis, see Schonhardt-Bailey (2013).

34. Compare Jones and Saad (2013), where the Fed's net positive approval rating was only 15 percent, the second worst of federal agencies measured (the IRS took the cake). In 2005, the net positive rate was 44 percent. Carroll (2006).

35. 12 U.S.C. § 306.

36. One can peruse the biographies at the Reserve Banks' websites.

37. As recounted in Fisher (2015).

38. See Irwin (2013a, 192–97) for the full account of the Reserve Banks' lobbying effort, including via the deployment of the member banks. See also Kaiser (2013, 304–6).

39. Binder and Spindel (2013b) has an excellent overview of the politics of the Reserve Bank Organization Committee's decisions.

40. Goodhart (1988).

CHAPTER 6. PRACTICING MONETARY POLICY: THE RISE AND FALL OF THE CHAPERONE

1. Martin (1955a).
2. See Axilrod (2013); Mankiw (2014, 614–22). For the Fed's own dated overview, see Board of Governors (2005).
3. The rates given at the discount window actually refer to three different kinds of loans: primary credit, secondary credit, and seasonal credit. For ease of explanation, I collapse all three into the generic "discount rate." For more explanation on the discount window and alternatives to it, see Judge (2014).
4. I am skipping an important and politically fraught discussion about the Fed's decision to pay interest on those excess reserves, a counterintuitive move that encourages banks to keep reserves beyond those required by regulation in their accounts at the Federal Reserve Banks. For more on the economics of this discussion, see Cochrane (2014).
5. For more on the controversy involved in the related "liquidity coverage ratio," see Conti-Brown (2014b) and Bank of International Settlements (2013).
6. See Galbraith (1965, 331); Tobin (1965); Harris (1965, 356–57). For Friedman on central bank independence, see Friedman (1962).
7. For more on the structure of the Bank of England, see Fay (1988) and Blair (2010, 21–27, 115–18). For more on the institutional context of the 1980s and 1990s, see Bernhard (2002). For the Lawson quote, see Bernhard (2002, 2).
8. Kydland and Prescott (1977). They were far from the first to propose a central banking rule. The gold standard is a rule; so is a medium of exchange based on rice. See Seong Ho (2014) for a fascinating account of commodity monies in medieval Korea. More relevant to the discussion of central banking, Friedman proposed a monetary rule that pegged monetary growth to a fixed rate. See, for example, Friedman (1973). Nelson (2008) provides an excellent overview of Friedman's evolution on monetary rules. A true intellectual history of central bank independence would also have to include Vera Smith's *The Rationale of Central Banking and the Free Banking Alternative* (1936).
9. Economist Kenneth Rogoff formalized that kind of personnel-based approach to central bank institution building shortly before Volcker resigned. Rogoff (1985). We will return to the question of monetary policy "rules" versus "discretion," in chapter 10, but for now, the important point is that there was a growing recognition among scholars that the design of central banks could resolve this problem in a way that leaving rational optimal economic policy making in the hands of elected representatives could not, even if the politicians were acting in exactly everyone's best interests.
10. For the quote on political control, see Bernhard (2002, 42). For more discussion of "instrument" and "goal" independence, see Fischer (1995).
11. For punishment by sanctions, see McCubbins and Schwartz (1984); for dis-

missal, see Lohmann (1992); for policy veto, see Ferejohn and Shipan (1990). For budget cuts, see Bernhard (2002). For the quote about appointments and sanctions, see Bernhard (2002, 21). See also Eijffinger and de Haan (1996) for an overview of these issues from the perspective of the mid-1990s. For the quote about degrees of independence, see Goodman (1991, 330).

12. The quote on conventional wisdom is from Lohmann (2006, 536). For the first treatment of central bank independence as such, see Grove (1952). My thanks to Sonia Moss at Stanford Law School for tracking this volume down. Of course, going by another name, the idea of governmental versus private control of the currency is much older, including a discussion by Bagehot (1873/1999, 70–72). For the classic studies in the empirical literature, see Bade and Parkin (1982) (looking at three variables within central bank statutes across twelve countries), Grilli et al. (1991) (looking at sixteen variables within statutes across eighteen countries), Alesina and Summers (1993) (combining the insights of Bade and Parkin and Grilli et al. to construct a new index), Cukierman (1992) (adding surveys to supplement statutory analyses), and Fry et al. (2000) (using surveys by the Bank of England). For a three-decade overview of this literature, see Parkin (2012). For an excellent review of these literatures that discusses the politicization of central banks, see Fernández-Albertos (2015).

13. For the European Central Bank and Germany, see H. James (2012, 269–77). For the economist quote, see "Liberating Central Bankers," *Economist*, February 10, 1990 (as quoted as the epigraph in Eijffinger and de Haan [1996]).

14. Quoting Posen's title (1993). See also Posen (1998).

15. For Keynes's discussion, see Keynes (1936, chapter 15).

16. For its redevelopment in the 1990s and beyond, see Krugman (1998, and p. 158 for the quote), Bernanke, Reinhart, and Sack (2004). For more on the Japanese problem in the context of the 2008 financial crisis, see Krugman (2009, 56–77).

17. See Bernanke (2002a). Bernanke (1999) developed the theme earlier. In Bernanke's defense, in the paper he was referring to a "hoary thought experiment," almost certainly in reference to Friedman (1969, 4). For useful empirical summaries of unconventional monetary policies, see Chodorow-Reich (2014) and especially Krishnamurthy and Vissing-Jorgensen (2011). The latter article provides a schematic for understanding how unconventional monetary policy proceeds through the financial system through various channels. For a fascinating take on the history of differences in government maturities, see Vanatta (2012). For more on why monetary policy by helicopter is in fact *superior* to the current regime, see Mian & Sufi (2014)

18. I'm eliding a subtle but important difference between two different kinds of unconventional policies that sometimes go under the same label of "quantitative easing": first changing the mix of securities a central bank owns, and second, dramatically expanding the size of the balance sheet. In the first case, a central bank like the Fed historically in the business of purchasing short-term governmental securities can change borrowing expectations by exiting the traditional market and entering another, like the market for mortgage-

backed securities. This isn't a quantitative easing per se, as the central bank's balance sheet has stayed roughly the same size. The second is an expansion of the balance sheet by purchasing more assets than the central bank has historically done. These assets can be untraditional ones, but they don't have to be. The Fed pursued both courses by purchasing long-term government debt and mortgage-backed securities (thus changing the mix on its own balance sheet) and by dramatically expanding the size of that balance sheet. For more on these discussions, see Blinder (2010) and Bernanke and Reinhart (2004). For reasons why the Fed didn't engage in more changes to the composition of its balance sheet by purchasing, for example, equities, municipal bonds, and the like, see the legal restrictions in the Federal Reserve Act, 12 U.S.C. § 355. For a skeptical account of those legal restrictions, see Shill (2015).

19. Krugman (1998, 139). See also Eggertsson and Woodford (2003) and Woodford (2007).
20. For the video, see Malekan (2010).
21. For an example, Karabell (2014).
22. Zeleny and Calmes (2011). For more on the rise of the Tea Party and its connections to bailouts, see Skocpol and Williamson (2012).
23. Asness et al. (2010) for the letter, Meltzer (2013) for quicksand, Meltzer (2009) for the sacrifice of independence.
24. Bryan (1896).
25. Frieden (2014, chapter 2), Schweitzer (1989, 314), Hammond (1957, 13–14 n. 8). Hammond's is the most significant blow to the idea of clear, unanimous cleavages among Democrats as a monolith in favor of cheaper and more inflated debt.
26. Scholars have long analyzed the politics of judging. For a historical discussion of politics around judicial appointments, see Shugerman (2012). For a conceptual overview, see R. Posner (2010). For an example and review of the empirical literature, see Choi et al (2007). For an essay that draws the comparison between central bankers and judges differently than I do here, see Goodhart and Meade (2003).

CHAPTER 7. THE ONCE AND FUTURE FEDERAL RESERVE: LENDER OF LAST RESORT, SUPERVISION, REGULATION, AND FINANCIAL STABILITY

1. See Acharya (2015) for an example and summary of the relevant literature.
2. T. M. Moe (1989, 267).
3. Bordo (1989).
4. For a critique of fractional reserve banking, see Levitin (2015).
5. See Thornton (1802).
6. Bagehot (1873, 36). For more on Bagehot's conception of the lender-of-last-resort function, see Tucker (2014), and Bordo (1989) and Grossman (2010). For skepticism of Bagehot's dictum as a viable strategy in 2015, see Conti-Brown (2014a) and (2014d).

7. For a discussion of the "runs" on nondeposit institutions, see Gorton (2010).

8. See Mehrling (2010) for a reconceptualization of Bagehot after the 2008 crisis. Bernanke (2013,7, 77). Bernanke (2008).

9. Volcker (2008, 8).

10. Wessel (2009, 1–8).

11. Andrews (2009).

12. Tucker (2014).

13. Andrews (2008b). For the events surrounding this exchange, see Sorkin (2009, 402–10).

14. 12 U.S.C. § 343. I'm skeptical that these reforms will have much teeth in a crisis. The Fed's lawyers have shown themselves to be very able at defining structures and entities in a way that is consistent with the law's letter but still aimed at unfettered deployment of emergency funds.

15. Geithner (2014, 180, 359).

16. For Paulson's perspective on that spring, see Paulson (2010, 93–121). For more on the dire state of fiscal politics, see Wessel (2013) for a journalistic view, and Johnson and Kwak (2012) for a more conceptual and historical one.

17. Blinder (2013, 484).

18. For more on the post–Dodd-Frank lender-of-last-resort function, see Wallach (2015), especially 274–79. For more on Courtelyon, see Goodhart (1969).

19. What follows is a sketch. There is a small but sophisticated historiography of bank regulation. The best although not exactly compatible recent histories are Gerding (2013) and Calomiris and Haber (2014). Although precrisis, Shull (2005) is remarkable in its prescience for the Fed's ever-expanding bailiwick.

20. For more on prudential regulation, see Gerding (2013, 228).

21. Calomiris and Haber call this political context in favor of unit banking the "Game of Bank Bargains." See Calomiris and Haber (2014, 27–60). For more on the quasi-national nature of networked regional banks, see J. James (1978, 95).

22. For more on the development of U.S. banking in the nineteenth century, see Hammond (1957, 1970), Bodenhorn (2000, 2002), J. James (1978), and Wicker (2000).

23. Wicker (1996). For more on banking in the Great Depression, see Meltzer (2003, chapter 5), Friedman and Schwartz (1963), and Bernanke (2000). For an entertaining though dated narrative, see Galbraith (2009).

24. Chapman and Westerfield (1942, 319–36). I am grateful to Meg Tahyar for bringing this excellent book on pre-BHCA holding company regulation to my attention (and to my possession).

25. Martin (1955b, 47). I'm grateful to Sean Vanatta for bringing this exchange to my attention. For an excellent overview of the BHCA's history, see Omarova and Tahyar (2011).

26. See Omarova and Tahyar (2011) and Omarova (2009).

27. See Omarova (2010). For more on the demise of Glass-Steagall, see Wallach (2014).

28. Skeel (2010) provides an excellent overview of Dodd-Frank; Blinder (2013) goes into even more detail. See also Schwarcz and Schwarcz (2014).
29. For a full elaboration of this history, see Shull (2005).
30. For a full articulation of preemption, see Nelson (2000). Legal scholar Arthur Wilmarth has explored these issues at length. See Wilmarth (2004). See also the Supreme Court's decision in *Watters v. Wachovia*, 127 S. Ct. 1559 (2007). New York's state banking regulator has been particularly active since the crisis. See, for example, Protess and Silver-Greenberg (2014).
31. Board of Governors (2005, 59–60).
32. Henry (2014, 217).
33. Financial journalist Jesse Eisinger and law professor (and former derivatives trader) Frank Partnoy took a deep dive into the annual reports of Wells Fargo and found them opaque and obscure, including in the disclosure of hundred-million-dollar losses. Eisinger and Partnoy (2013).
34. This account is taken from the exhaustive reporting at *ProPublica*. See J. Bernstein (2013a, 2013b, 2013c, 2014).
35. Beim (2009, 2).
36. For a description of these conflicts preceding the Great Crash, see Perino (2010, 136), especially for particularly moving examples of what happens when these kinds of interests conflict. For conflicts on Enron, see McLean and Elkind (2003, 189–210).
37. For example, the New York Fed's own statement, Federal Reserve Bank of New York (2014); for the critics, see Cohan (2014).
38. "Icy and swift" from Henry (2014, 217); quote from journalist from interview on *Morning Edition* (2014).
39. Hilsenrath (2015).
40. Berk (2011).
41. Henderson and Tung (2011) propose a change to bank regulatory pay systems; Conti-Brown (2011a) and Admati, Conti-Brown, and Pfleiderer (2012) discuss different versions of changes to shareholder incentives.
42. McGrane (2014). For an academic account of the difference between this approach to congressional oversight, see McCubbins and Schwartz (1984).
43. See Cecchetti et al. (2000) for this view.
44. Bernanke (2002b).
45. Bernanke (2002b).
46. For more on the debate on macroprudential policy and central banking, see Galati and Moessner (2010).
47. The FDR-Eccles exchange is cited in Eccles (1951, 386). For the proposed consolidation in 1965, see Scott (1977, 12–13). For the Clinton-era consolidation, see Hutnyan (1994). For the George W. Bush administration's proposal, see U.S. Department of Treasury (2008). Volcker's discussion is in Tracy (2015). For a partial academic volunteer to answer Volcker's call for defending the current system, see Romano (2010).
48. Although Dodd-Frank multiplied the number and complexity of agencies in banking, there was some consolidation: the act eliminated the Office of Thrift

Supervision, the regulatory agency in charge of regulating "thrifts" like Washington Mutual. 12 U.S. Code § 5413.

49. For the quote, see Green (2012, 57). A seminal paper on monetary policy and financial stability is Goodhart and Schoenmaker (1995). For a more recent discussion, see Garicano and Lastra (2010).

50. For an example of those who make this argument, see Representative Scott Garrett, quoted in Appelbaum (2015).

CHAPTER 8. THE PRESIDENT AND THE FEDERAL RESERVE: THE LIMITS OF LAW AND THE POWER OF RELATIONSHIPS

1. Weaver (1986, 371).
2. For more on the vast literature linking economic performance and elections, see Blomberg and Hess (2000); Bagehot from the epigraph.
3. As quoted in Willis (1923). For "bureau," see Hackley (1972, 71–72).
4. Bremner (2004, 1, 2, 90, 116, 117, 151, 160, 180); Silber (2012, 191–95, 266–67); Greenspan (2007, 142, 146, 153, 293, 478, 479).
5. Chang (2003, 4). For more on this important literature, see Havrilesky (1992).
6. 12 U.S.C. § 242.
7. Vermeule explores these and related arguments. His conclusion is that "formal independence" is unnecessary at the Fed, because its chair is widely perceived to be independent without reference to the Federal Reserve Act. Because of that silence, "its independence is protected by a network of statutory provisions and hoary conventions" (Vermeule 2013, 1176). In reaching this conclusion, Vermeule considers the structurally similar situation of the chair of the Consumer Product Safety Commission, whose five members enjoy statutory removability protection, but whose chair does not. In that case, the Office of Legal Counsel concluded that the president could remove the chair at will, but that the chair would continue to serve as a commissioner even if removed. See Vermeule (2013).

Vermeule isn't convinced this works as a matter of law and notes that the Supreme Court, in *Free Enterprise Fund*, "accepted a joint stipulation of the parties to that effect, despite the rule that parties may not stipulate to the law." Vermeule (2013, 1166–67). I'm not convinced. Such assumptions come close to a logical fallacy. A cruder version of this argument goes like this. Three premises: The formal definition of agency independence means that an agency is independent only if the agency head is protected against arbitrary firing. Everyone understands the Fed to be an independent agency. The Federal Reserve Act is silent as to the removability of the chair of the Federal Reserve. Therefore, there is widespread acceptance among the engaged public and members of Congress that the president is restricted from firing at will the Fed chair.

Both the premises and conclusion are flawed. The more accurate statement is that the concept of "independence" without further specification is incoherent, and that even when further specified, there is more to legal independence than removability protection. This reconciliation is one of the main contributions of this book: there is both more and less to the law of Fed independence than meets the eye.

8. 295 U.S. 602, 629–30 (1935).

9. For more on McCabe's resignation, see Bremner (2004, 81).

10. For Truman's quote on White and the surrounding events, see Steil (2013, 324). For the "bled" quote, see Kane (1974, 743).

11. On William Miller, see Kettl (1986, 169–71), Greider (1987, 154–60), Meltzer (2010b, 922–47). On Goldberg, Fortas, and Johnson, see Dallek (2005, 291). On Helms and Nixon, see Weiner (2007, 323). "The man was a shit," Helms said of Nixon, as he recalled the experience.

12. This is, of course, my argument of what courts should do, not my sense of what they would actually do. If a president sent an FDR-like letter to a Fed chair terminating her employment, and the chair then sued for reinstatement, it is an open question whether the court would follow its stipulation of protection in *Free Enterprise Fund* or its much older precedents that cut the other way. *Parsons v. United States*, 167 U.S. 324, 343 (1897). *Shurtleff v. United States*, 189 U.S. 311, 318 (1903). See Vermeule (2013, 1168–73).

13. See *Current FAQs*, "What does it mean that the Federal Reserve is 'independent within the government'?"—available at http://www.federalreserve.gov /faqs/about_12799.htm.

14. 12 U.S.C. § 242. For the idea of a staggered term, see Bressman and Thompson (2010, 607–8). For the "prevent day-to-day," see Pozo (2002, 90). See also Barkow (2010, 24); M. Bernstein (1989, 148 n. 182).

15. See Membership of the Board of Governors of the Federal Reserve System, 1914–present, available at http://www.federalreserve.gov/bios/boardmember ship.htm. As this source also indicates, George W. Mitchell served from 1961 through 1976. Edward W. Kelley Jr. served between 1987 and 2001; J. L. Robertson served from 1952 to 1973. Note, too, that M. S. Szymczak served from 1933 to 1961, the longest serving member of the board. His appointment is not included in this analysis, because he was appointed to the Federal Reserve Board, not the 1935 Board of Governors. He was thus not subject to precisely the same appointment procedure.

16. 12 U.S.C. § 242.

17. This does not mean that the Fed will always get the president's first choice for those slots. President Obama nominated Peter Diamond for an open spot on the board, but Diamond was deemed unqualified by Republicans opposed to the nomination. Diamond won the Nobel Prize while his nomination was pending. See Diamond (2011).

18. See Levinson (2004) for more on empire building.

19. See Bremner (2004, 196–205).

20. See Silber (2012, 229–34). For more on the Iran-Contra scandal and the way it weakened the Reagan presidency, see Patterson (2007, 207–13).

21. See Greenspan (2007, 51–53); Woodward (2000); Suskind (2011).

22. See Carpenter (2001); Carpenter (2010). Arthur Burns was the exception that

proved the rule: According to Meltzer, "Burns tried hard to get reappointed. He wanted to be reappointed by a Democrat, perhaps to remove the charge that he had used monetary policy to reelect President Nixon. When Hubert Humphrey, a friend of Vice President Walter Mondale's, made a very critical speech about Burns's policy, he recognized that he would be replaced." Meltzer (2010b, 923). Burn's experience proves the rule because he had almost no support from any significant quarter.

23. This was not true at all of Eccles's relationship to other members of the Roosevelt inner circle, including and especially Secretary of the Treasury Henry Morgenthau. Brinkley (1995, 80–82). Eccles (1951, 401).
24. Nixon (1962, 309–10).
25. Burns (2010, 32–49).
26. Patman (1975, 183).
27. Ehrlichman (1982, 248–49).
28. Burns (2010, 39–40).
29. Woolley (1986, 110–13). Some Senate Democrats even thought Burns might have been involved in assisting the Watergate burglars, although there was never direct evidence of these rumors. See Meltzer (2010b, 837–38).
30. As cited in Kane (1974, 750).
31. Woodward (2000, 126).
32. Greenspan (2007, 143).
33. Clinton (1993). See Greenspan (2007, 144) for his take.
34. Greenspan (2007, 159).
35. R. Rubin (2003, 193).
36. R. Rubin (2003, 194).
37. Ramo (1999).
38. Ramo (1999).

CHAPTER 9. CONGRESS AND THE FED: THE CURIOUS CASE OF THE FED'S BUDGETARY AUTONOMY

1. Bernanke (2013).
2. Shull (2005).
3. Binder and Spindel (2013a). Also, appointments are not exclusively within the purview of presidential influence. The Senate can and has exercised enormous influence on the appointments process. See Chang (2003).
4. Kettl (1986, 141).
5. Bremner (2004, 190). For a sympathetic treatment of Patman, see Young (2000). As Young argues, although Patman was resolutely opposed to the Fed in many respects, his political worldview was much broader than that. The Fed does not figure prominently into Young's treatment.
6. Caro (1982, 76); Bremner (2004, 191).
7. For the quote from LBJ, see Bremner (2004, 191). Patman was finally successful at securing a one-time audit of the Fed by the GAO in 1978. Meltzer (2010b).

Meltzer had personal experience with these hearings and didn't think members of the House Banking Committee—including Patman—thought the proposals were headed anywhere. As Meltzer recounts it,

> Karl Brunner and I served as adjunct staff of the committee. The reports that we prepared (1964) were part of the hearings, but Congressman Patman's legislative proposals came from other sources. Based on my conversations with him I do not believe he expected these proposals to be enacted. He liked the exchanges with Martin and others and believed that these exchanges were an important part of congressional oversight. The Federal Reserve had to treat the proposals as serious recommendations though they disliked them. Members of the committee had a similar interpretation. Some members of the Banking Committee also held the view that Chairman Patman did not expect the proposals to become law.

See Meltzer (2010a, 403).

8. For example, Meltzer (2010b, 1224) credits Martin's failure as one of insufficient distance between him and the Johnson administration.
9. Bremner (2004, 200–203). Romer and Romer (2003); Meltzer (2010b).
10. Kettl (1986, 141); Young (2000, 65).
11. Auerbach (2008). Gonzalez also proposed televising these meetings live; Greenspan (2007, 151). For more on this remarkable period of forced Fed transparency, see Lindsey (2003). Lindsey's history was written, according to a disclaimer on its cover, as a "strictly confidential" inside document. Fortunately, the Fed released it in 2009.
12. Milton Friedman and Anna Schwartz attribute their monetary history as contributing to the decision to issue the transcripts. See Friedman and Schwartz (1993).
13. Auerbach (2008, 88–90). For the most important of these lawsuits, which the Fed won, see *FOMC v. Merrill*, 443 U.S. 340 (1979). For an excellent overview of the case throughout its litigation, see Goodfriend (1985).
14. Auerbach (2008, chapter 7).
15. Greenspan (2007, 150–53); Auerbach, a former Gonzalez staffer, has written extensively about the Greenspan-Gonzalez feud. See Auerbach (2008).
16. For more on Norman's mystique, see Einzig (1932, 23–40, 100–110). For a compelling account of Norman's approach to central banking during the interwar years, see Ahamed (2009).
17. While spending bills initiate with the Congress, the president also plays a significant role in shaping the federal budget. For more, see Huq (2013, 29); C. Berry et al. (2010).
18. "What does it mean that the Federal Reserve is 'independent within the government'?" available at http://www.federalreserve.gov/faqs/about_12799.htm.
19. For a thorough albeit dated overview of these various types of funding structures, see Leader (1976). For a more recent discussion of funding sources for various agencies, see Barkow (2010).
20. These outlays are not truly mandatory, as Congress, of course, retains the ability to repeal them. "Mandatory spending" refers to whether they must be reinitiated each year, as is the case with the rest of the federal budget.
21. Board of Governors of the Federal Reserve System (2013, 1) (available at

http://www.federalreserve.gov/publications/budget-review/files/2013
-budget-review.pdf). The Fed also receives income for "priced services" provided to private banks, which include the cost of transporting and printing
new currency, check clearing, and other services related to currency distribution and the general payment system. Some scholars—Barkow (2010), for
example—have supposed that the Fed funds itself through assessments on
private banks. While it is true that the Fed collects money from member
banks for "charged services," such assessments cover just 25 percent of its
expenses. The rest, as stated, comes from the proceeds from its open market
operations.

22. See Statement Regarding Transactions in Agency Mortgage-Backed Securities
and Treasury Securities, September 13, 2012 (available at http://www.new
yorkfed.org/markets/opolicy/operating_policy_120913.html). See Board of
Governors (2005). Chair Bernanke has contested a "money-printing" characterization of the Fed's monetary authority. See *60 Minutes* Interview Transcript, December 6, 2010 ("One myth that's out there is that what we're
doing is printing money. We're not printing money. The amount of currency
in circulation is not changing. The money supply is not changing in any significant way."). This is a factually accurate but conceptually misleading point
aimed at controlling a debate not directly relevant to our discussion. Bernanke is of course correct that the Fed's monetary policy framework is based
on extensions of bank reserves, not the increase of paper currency (unlike,
say, the Reichsbank's stunning printing bonanza during the hyperinflation of
the 1920s in Weimar Germany), see Ahamed (2009, 20–25). Technically, then,
the Fed isn't printing money at all, but filling the banking system with additional reserves, in return for which it receives income-generating bonds. The
inflationary effects of these policies are hotly disputed, but that the Fed has
the ability to create money with which it buys interest-bearing bonds is not a
contested point. It can "print" the money it uses to implement its monetary
policy decisions, and use the proceeds of those decisions to fund its budget.

23. 12 U.S.C. § 243. See Congressional Budget Office (2010, 3), which noted that
the Fed is not subject to the appropriations process and that it is able to operate independently from government influence.

24. Meltzer (2003, 75–82). This open market autonomy led to some interesting
natural experiments: for example, the state of Mississippi was divided between different reserve bank districts, one serviced by the Atlanta Fed, the
other by the St. Louis Fed. During the banking crisis of 1930, the St. Louis
Fed practiced the real bills doctrine, which prevented it from lending against
anything but bills of trade; the Atlanta Fed practiced a more Bagehotian form
of central banking. Richardson and Troost exploited that fact to show that
the banks in the Atlanta district survived at a higher rate than those in the St.
Louis district. Richardson and Troost (2006).

25. Banking Act of 1935, Pub. L. No. 74-305, 49 Stat. 684. An exception is the
way in which the government treated the funds that came into the Reserve
System, whether via assessment on member banks or from open market operations. In 1923, the comptroller general of the United States determined,

separate from a franchise tax, that the "funds collected by the Board by assessments on the Reserve Banks were public funds" subject to various restrictions and impositions. In 1933, however, Congress amended the statute to liberate the government claim on those funds completely. See Hackley (1972, 7–8).

26. For more on the gold standard, see Eichengreen (1992). For a popular account, see P. Bernstein (2008). Bernanke's book on the Fed, written while he was chair (a first in Fed history, so far as I'm aware), engages directly with the question of the Fed and the gold standard. Bernanke (2012, 9–14). For Bagehot and the "caste-iron system," see Bagehot (1873/1999, 25).

27. For more on the failure of the post–World War I gold standard restoration, see Ahamed (2009).

28. Mints (1945) coined the term and provides an excellent overview of the doctrine.

29. Grossman (2010, 37).

30. Meltzer (2003, 24).

31. Grossman (2010, 37). See also West (1977).

32. For a more detailed overview of usury in world history, including in its theological context, see Geisst (2013).

33. Mints (1945). For more on the real bills doctrine in the pre-Fed era, see West (1977, 155–57, 201–3).

34. For more on Laughlin's contribution, see Mehrling (2002) and Rotemberg (2014).

35. Friedman and Schwartz (1963, 194); Kettl (1986, 23); Richardson and Troost (2006).

36. C. Glass (1914, 563).

37. Quoted in Kettl (1986, 22).

38. Clifford (1965, 25). Interestingly, while scholars have long commented on the Fed's budgetary independence, every legal scholar to have engaged this question has been unaware of the lack of statutory authorization. Some scholars understandably suppose that the board is funded by assessments on member banks, since the statute appears to be written that way. See Barkow (2010, 44); Leader (1976); Ramirez (2000, 503). Others correctly note that the Fed is funded by assessments on the *Federal Reserve* Banks, rather than the member banks but do not note the role played by proceeds from open market operations. See, for example, Bressman and Thompson (2010). Still others correctly note that the board uses the proceeds from open market operations but then cite the provision that authorizes assessments on the Reserve Banks. Dombalagian (2010, 795 n. 88); Lazarus (2009).

A more recent article argues that "independent agencies such as the Federal Reserve . . . still 'cannot afford to flout the views of the President,' who continues to exercise substantial control as a consequence of his effective power of the purse," without reference to the Fed's unique budgetary independence. Huq (2013, 29). A partial exception to these characterizations is a passing reference in E. Rubin (2012), which acknowledges that the Fed's self-funding arose "without prior planning," but the point there seems to be that budgetary planning is part of the motivation of the monetary policy function.

39. See Binder (2013).
40. Meltzer (2010b, 891).
41. Meltzer (2010a, x). See Irwin (2013a, 208, 273), who describes far-flung meetings of the world's central bankers and finance ministers, explaining that the "Fed chair usually flies commercial; if he were to routinely catch a ride on the treasury secretary's Air Force jet, it could be seen as compromising the central bank's independence." The Fed's scandal-free history has long been a point of pride for Fed insiders. As Clifford (1965, 386) noted, "[o]ne of the glories of the Federal Reserve banks, according to Allan Sproul, as all the investigations there was no established evidence of scandals, influence peddling, or figures given in receipt in connection with the operations of the reserve banks."

CHAPTER 10. CLUB FED: THE COMMUNITIES OF THE FEDERAL RESERVE

1. See Woolley (1986, 88–107).
2. McClosky (1964, 362). For an excellent overview of different conceptions of ideology, see Gerring (1997).
3. There is another connection between central banks and private market participants that is more abstract, but also very important, and that is the fact that the Fed effectuates its monetary policies *through* the markets and relies on markets to determine the efficacy of its policies. That efficacy is communicated through price signals updated by nanoseconds. As Alan Blinder has noted, the question of "independence" from markets is not about whether working through markets is a bad idea—it's clearly necessary. The problem is when central bankers become "so deeply respectful of markets" that a new danger emerges: "that monetary policymakers might be tempted to 'follow the markets' slavishly, essentially delivering the monetary policy that the markets expect or demand." Blinder elaborates:

> Central bankers are only human; they want to earn high marks—from whomever is handing out the grades. While the only verdict that really matters is the verdict of history, it takes an amazingly strong constitution to wait that long. In stark contrast, the markets provide a kind of giant biofeedback machine that monitors and publicly evaluates the central bank's performance in real time. (Blinder [2004, 60])

The problem with this kind of performance for the markets is that playing to the markets makes the central banks facilitators of swings in asset price, not called for in their role as wise, patient managers of monetary risk with long time horizons. The need for insulating monetary policy from politicians makes good enough sense. Blinder's point is that insulation from market signals is a concern that requires more attention. See Blinder (2004, 66).
4. This differentiated attention to New York is an old one. Carter Glass, after

all, loved the Federal Reserve System generally but often had little patience for the Federal Reserve Bank of New York. Perino (2010, 82–84) gives an example of this from the beginning of the Great Depression.

5. Suasion as a tool of monetary policy has a long history. See Meltzer (2003, 92–100, 131–39). For a theory of moral suasion as an instrument of economic policy, see Romans (1966). As applied specifically to one of the cases below, see Furfine (2006). The regulatory suasion I'm describing here is different in two respects: it is specifically regulatory, as opposed to monetary, and it is used in place of other regulatory alternatives.

6. Lowenstein (2000) provides the definitive account, and the source for the story ahead unless otherwise noted.

7. A "short" is Wall Street lingo for a specific kind of transaction. To short an asset, a trader needs to find someone on the market who owns the asset, borrow it at a fee, sell it to someone else, and wait. If the price of the asset drops, the trader buys it back, gives it back to the person he borrowed it from in the first place, and pockets the difference. For a short to work you have to find willing counterparties across the board, and the drop in the asset price has to be bigger than the fee the trader paid the person from whom he borrowed the asset in the first place.

8. See Zweig (2011) for the problem with citing Keynes for this famous proposition.

9. Lowenstein (2000).

10. Lowenstein (2000, 186, 195).

11. Lowenstein (2000, 178).

12. I discussed some of these problems in Conti-Brown (2010). For data on 2007 derivatives markets, see Bank of International Settlements (2007). For the Greenspan and spaghetti quotes, see Geithner (2014, 102–3).

13. Geithner (2014, 103).

14. Geithner (2014, 99).

15. Carpenter and Moss (2013, 13).

16. Zingales (2013). For more, see Kwak (2013) on "cultural capture," especially for his theory of cultural capture as consisting of regulators' perception that they and regulated entities share common identities, statuses, and social relationships. See Buiter (2008) for the related concept of "cognitive capture."

17. For the difficulties in measuring capture, see Carpenter (2013, 3–4) and Engstrom (2013). For the quotes, Geithner (2014, 167). For empirical confirmation of overlapping social networks, see Acemoglu et al. (2013), which measures the value to firms affiliated, through the New York Fed and through common nonprofit board memberships, with New York Fed president and treasury secretary designee Tim Geithner.

18. Eavis (2014).

19. Geithner (2014, 88, 91).

20. For Mullins, see Lowenstein (2000, 36–37). For Bernanke and Citadel, see Sorkin and Stevenson (2015). For Kwak's response, see Kwak (2015).

21. For more on the revolving door between industry and the Fed, see Johnson

and Kwak (2010). For a skeptical view of revolving door criticisms, see Zaring (2013).

22. Greenspan seems to have anticipated this result after the LTCM transactions. As Lowenstein reports, "Alan Greenspan freely admitted that by orchestrating a rescue of [LTCM], the Fed had encouraged future risk takers and perhaps increased the odds of a future disaster. 'To be sure, some moral hazard, however slight, may have been created by the Federal Reserve's involvement,' the Fed chief declared. However, he judged that such negatives were outweighed by the risk of 'serious distortions to market prices had [LTCM] been pushed into bankruptcy.'" Lowenstein (2000, 229–30).

23. Truman (2014, 1); Ahamed (2009).

24. Federal Open Market Committee (2008) (September 16 and October 28). For an overview of the Fed's swap agreements, see H. James (2014) and Baker (2013).

25. Irwin (2013).

26. For an excellent introduction to this issue, see Admati and Hellwig (2013).

27. See Goodhart (2011) for more on the Basel Committee's history as a regulatory body.

28. For more on why capital adequacy occurs in the way it does on the international stage, see Brummer (2011). While the BIS and the BCBS are closely related, they are legally distinct entities.

29. See LeBor (2013) for a journalistic, somewhat conspiratorial account of the Basel Accords. Toniolo and Clement (2005) and Goodhart (2011) provide the academic accounts of different features of the Basel system.

30. See Mehrling (2002) for more on the debates among economists at the origins of the Fed.

31. Friedman and Schwartz (1963). See Silber (2012, 148) for Friedman at the New York Fed in 1957 preaching "the gospel truth."

32. Quoted in Silber (2012, 148–49).

33. Hall (1993, 277). In the second quote, Hall is quoting Heclo (1974, 312).

34. For more on the importance of ideology in financial regulation, see Kwak (2013). Levitin (2014) also discusses the problem of ideology and identification with outside financial interests on Fed policy makers.

CHAPTER 11. PROPOSALS

1. Will (2013); Hubbard (2013).

2. Bar-Gill and Warren (2008). This was, in fact, only the version with footnotes, as David Skeel has called it. Skeel (2010, 106). Warren had written a more accessible version of the general idea for the journal *Democracy* called "Unsafe at Any Rate," a play on Ralph Nader's famous expose of the auto industry *Unsafe at Any Speed*. Warren (2007).

3. On the Obama administration's ambivalence over Warren and her proposals, see Suskind (2011, 77–81); Skeel (2010, 99–115). For Summers's quote, see Geithner (2014, 404).

4. Zywicki (2013). Ironically, some of the very features that made Republicans angriest were in fact Republican ideas. Kaiser (2013). The constitutional issue was resolved (against the president) in *National Labor Relations Board v. Noel Canning*, 134 S. Ct. 2550 (2014). On filibuster reform, see Peters (2013).

5. Merkley (2010).

6. Meyer (2004, 14–15).

7. And, perhaps, because he was more politically palatable than some of the names Clinton had previously floated. See Chang (2003, 3–4). On the CRA, compare Calomiris and Haber (2014, 206–8, 217–20) with Barr (2005).

8. This is not to say that every feature of the CFPB's institutional design is required to make this kind of public accountability possible. For example, the CFPB is funded with a portion of the Fed's own autonomous budget, from the same proceeds of open market operations the Fed uses to fund itself. Except the CFPB's funding is guaranteed, by statute, to come from the Fed at a fixed rate of the Fed's expenses, not earnings. I'm less convinced of the need to give the CFPB as much budgetary autonomy as the Federal Reserve, largely because the Ulysses/punch-bowl theory of independence has no bearing on the CFPB's activities. The other main controversy, that the bureau is led by a single director as opposed to a committee, is also irrelevant. The point is only that the bureau's existence as something other than a division led by a Fed governor hired for expertise in macroeconomic forecasting allows for more effective engagement than was possible under the previous regime. See 12 U.S.C. § 5497 for the full description of the CFPB's funding formula. See Levitin (2013) for a thorough overview of the CFPB, its institutional structure, and some of the controversies surrounding its establishment.

9. 12 U.S.C. § 242.

10. For Diamond's take on his rejection, see Diamond (2011).

11. I first made these arguments about Diamond and board vacancies in Conti-Brown (2014c).

12. *Edmond v. United States*, 520 U.S. 651, 659 (1997) (citing in part *Buckley v. Valeo*, 424 U.S. 1, 125 [1976]).

13. Blinder (1997).

14. As quoted in Cassidy (1996, 42)

15. Truman (2014).

16. Daniel Tarullo is the career lawyer; Jerome Powell graduated from law school in 1979 but switched to investment banking in 1985 (followed by service in the George H. W. Bush administration and work as a partner in the private equity firm the Carlyle Group).

17. Kahan and Rock (2009).

18. See, for example, *Intercollegiate Broadcasting System, Inc. v. Copyright Royalty Board*, (684 F.3d 1332, 1334, D.C. Cir., 2012), which found a similar constitutional defect and followed the *Free Enterprise Fund* court in judicially reconstructing the relevant statute.

19. For an explanation of filibuster reform, see Peters (2013).

20. For more on the politics of the Reserve Bank Organizing Committee (the

body that selected the sites for the Reserve Banks), see Binder and Spindel (2013b).

21. For more on Reed's proposals, see McGrane (2014).

22. The Federal Reserve Act does give the Board of Governors approval over the appointment of the Reserve Banks. While there are anecdotal reports about the frequency with which the board exercises this veto, this still needs to be confirmed systematically. "The president shall be the chief executive officer of the bank and shall be appointed by the Class B and Class C directors of the bank, with the approval of the Board of Governors of the Federal Reserve System, for a term of 5 years" (12 U.S.C. § 341). On geographic distribution of the original Federal Reserve System, see Binder and Spindel (2013b).

23. For more on Fischer's students and performance as Bank of Israel governor, see Coy (2013).

24. For controversy surrounding the Fischer appointment, due to his previous work at Citigroup, see Warren (2014).

25. For more on the mix of banking and politics, see Calomiris and Haber (2014), Hoffmann (2001). For a detailed study of the Rothschilds' navigation of various political thickets, see Ferguson (1998, 1999).

26. Fox (2015).

27. See Censky (2012) on Bernanke's fight against auditing the Fed. See Wessel (2015) for an overview of "audit the Fed" and its difficulties.

28. For scandal at the GSA, see Rein and Davidson (2012). For an example of a serious treatment of the Fed's balance sheet, see Reis (2013). For Senator Paul's discussion, see Weigel (2015).

29. Taylor (1993). For a discussion of how Taylor's and Friedman's rules interact, see Nelson (2008).

30. For Taylor's defense of these proposals, see Taylor (2009).

31. See Blinder (2015). On Korean policy rules, see Seong Ho (2014).

32. See DeLong (2008)

CONCLUSION: THE FREEMASONS AND THE FEDERAL RESERVE

1. Goodhart (1995, ix).

ACKNOWLEDGMENTS

1. Bagehot (1873/1999, xi).

BIBLIOGRAPHY

Acemoglu, Daron, Simon Johnson, Amir Kermani, James Kwak, and Todd Mitton. 2013. *The Value of Connections in Turbulent Times: Evidence from the United States*. Working Paper. National Bureau of Economic Research, December. http://www.nber.org/papers/w19701.

Acharya, Viral. 2015. "Financial Stability in the Broader Mandate for Central Banks: A Political Economy Perspective." *Brookings Institution*. Accessed April 21. http://www.brookings.edu/research/papers/2015/04/14-financial-stability-mandate-central-banks.

Admati, Anat R., Peter Conti-Brown, and Paul C. Pfleiderer. 2012. "Liability Holding Companies." *UCLA Law Review* 59: 852–913.

Admati, Anat, and Martin Hellwig. 2013. *The Bankers' New Clothes: What's Wrong with Banking and What to Do about It*. Princeton, N.J.: Princeton University Press.

Ahamed, Liaquat. 2009. *Lords of Finance: The Bankers Who Broke the World*. New York: Penguin Books.

Alesina, Alberto, and Lawrence H. Summers. 1993. "Central Bank Independence and Macroeconomic Performance: Some Comparative Evidence." *Journal of Money, Credit and Banking* 25, no. 2 (May 1): 151–62.

Alvarez, Scott G. 2010. *Interview of Scott Alvarez and Kiernan Fallon*. Board of Governors of the U.S. Federal Reserve System.

———. 2012. *Examining the Settlement Practices of US Financial Regulators, Hearing Before the Committee on Financial Services, U. S House of Representatives*. 112th Cong., March 17. http://financialservices.house.gov/uploadedfiles/112-128.pdf.

American Bankers Association. 2014. "ABA Statement on Fed Gov. Tarullo's Fiduciary Duty Remarks." American Bankers Association, June 9. http://www.aba.com/Press/Pages/060914StatementonTarulloFiduciaryDutyRemarks.aspx.

Andrews, Edmund L. 2007. "Fed Shrugged as Subprime Crisis Spread." *New York Times*, December 18, sec. Business. http://www.nytimes.com/2007/12/18/business/18subprime.html.

———. 2008a. "Greenspan Concedes Error on Regulation." *New York Times*, October 24. http://www.nytimes.com/2008/10/24/business/economy/24panel.html.

———. 2008b. "A New Role for the Fed: Investor of Last Resort." *New York Times*, September 18, sec. Business. http://www.nytimes.com/2008/09/18/bus iness/18fed.html.

———. 2009. "Forget Aloof, Bernanke Goes Barnstorming." *New York Times*, July 27, sec. Business. http://www.nytimes.com/2009/07/27/business/27ber nanke.html.

Appelbaum, Binyamin. 2015. "In Republican Attacks on the Fed, Experts See a Shift." *New York Times*, April 7. http://www.nytimes.com/2015/04/08/business /economy/in-republican-attacks-on-the-fed-experts-see-a-shift.html.

Asness, Cliff, Michael J. Boskin, Richard X. Bove, Charles W. Calomiris, Jim Chanos, John F. Cogan, Niall Ferguson, et al. 2010. "Open Letter to Ben Bernanke," November 15. http://blogs.wsj.com/economics/2010/11/15/open-letter -to-ben-bernanke/.

Auerbach, Robert D. 2008. *Deception and Abuse at the Fed: Henry B. Gonzalez Battles Alan Greenspan's Bank*. Austin: University of Texas Press.

Axilrod, Stephen H. 2013. *The Federal Reserve: What Everyone Needs to Know*. Oxford: Oxford University Press.

Bade, Robin, and Michael Parkin. 1982. "Central Bank Laws and Monetary Policy." Unpublished Manuscript, University of Western Ontario, 1982.

Bagehot, Walter. 1867. *The English Constitution*. London: Chapman and Hall.

———. 1873/1999. *Lombard Street: A Description of the Money Market*. New York: Wiley.

Baker, Colleen. 2012. "The Federal Reserve as Last Resort." *University of Michigan Journal of Law Reform* 46, no. 1: 69–133.

———. 2013. "The Federal Reserve's Use of International Swap Lines." *Arizona Law Review* 55, no. 3: 603–54.

Bank of International Settlements. 2007. *International Banking and Financial Market Developments*. Basel, Switzerland, December.

———. 2013. *Basel III: The Liquidity Coverage Ratio and Liquidity Risk Monitoring Tools*. Basel, Switzerland, January.

Bar-Gill, Oren, and Elizabeth Warren. 2008. "Making Credit Safer." *University of Pennsylvania Law Review* 157: 1–101.

Barkow, Rachel E. 2010. "Insulating Agencies: Avoiding Capture through Institutional Design." *Texas Law Review* 89: 15–79.

Barnett, Kent H. 2015. "Codifying Chevmore." *NYU Law Review* 90: 1–70.

Barr, Michael S. 2005. "Credit Where It Counts: The Community Reinvestment Act and Its Critics." *NYU Law Review* 80: 513–652.

Barro, Robert J., and David B. Gordon. 1983. *Rules, Discretion and Reputation in a Model of Monetary Policy*. NBER Working Paper. National Bureau of Economic Research. https://ideas.repec.org/p/nbr/nberwo/1079.html.

Beim, David. 2009. "Report on Systemic Risk and Bank Supervision." Federal Reserve Bank of New York, September 10. http://www.propublica.org/docu ments/item/1303305-2009-08-18-frbny-report-on-systemic-risk-and.html.

Berk, Jonathan. 2011. "Bank Reform Needs Unlimited Liability for Owners." *Bloomberg Business*, December 15. http://www.bloomberg.com/news/articles

/2011-12-16/proper-bank-reform-needs-owners-to-be-liable-commentary-by
-jonathan-berk.

Berg, A. Scott. 2013. *Wilson*. New York: Berkley Trade.

Bernanke, Ben S. 1999. "Japanese Monetary Policy: A Case of Self-Induced Paralysis?" Presented at the American Social Science Association meetings, Boston, Mass., January 9.

———. 2000. *Essays on the Great Depression*. Princeton, N.J.: Princeton University Press.

———. 2002a. "Asset-Price 'Bubbles' and Monetary Policy." Speech presented at the New York Chapter of the National Association for Business Economics, New York, October 15.

———. 2002b. "Deflation: Making Sure 'It' Doesn't Happen Here." Speech presented at the National Economists Club, Washington, D.C., November 21.

———. 2008. "Liquidity Provision by the Federal Reserve." Speech presented at the Federal Reserve Bank of Atlanta Financial Markets Conference, Sea Island, Ga., May 13. http://www.federalreserve.gov/newsevents/speech/bernanke2008 0513.htm.

———. 2012. *The Federal Reserve and the Financial Crisis*. Princeton, N.J.: Princeton University Press.

———. 2013a. "Press Conference." Presented at the Board of Governors of the Federal Reserve System, Washington, D.C., December 18. https://mninews .marketnews.com/content/bernanke-qa-transcript-important-respect-congress -role.

———. 2013b. *The Federal Reserve and the Financial Crisis*. Princeton, N.J.: Princeton University Press.

Bernanke, Ben S., and Vincent R. Reinhart. 2004. "Conducting Monetary Policy at Very Low Short-Term Interest Rates." *American Economic Review* 94, no. 2: 85–90. doi:10.1257/0002828041302118.

Bernanke, Ben S., Vincent R. Reinhart, and Brian P. Sack. 2004. *Monetary Policy Alternatives at the Zero Bound: An Empirical Assessment*. Finance and Economics Discussion Series. Board of Governors of the Federal Reserve System (U.S.). https://ideas.repec.org/p/fip/fedgfe/2004-48.html.

Bernhard, William T. 2002. *Banking on Reform: Political Parties and Central Bank Independence in the Industrial Democracies*. Ann Arbor: University of Michigan Press.

Bernstein, Jake. 2013a. "New Allegations from Fired Examiner Describe Chaotic Workplace at New York Fed." *ProPublica*, December 6, 1:09 p.m. Accessed October 11, 2014. http://www.propublica.org/article/new-allegations-from -fired-examiner-describe-chaotic-workplace-at-ny-fed.

———. 2013b. "NY Fed Fired Examiner Who Took on Goldman." *ProPublica*, October 10, 2:44 p.m. Accessed October 11, 2014. http://www.propublica.org /article/ny-fed-fired-examiner-who-took-on-goldman.

———. 2013c. "So Who Is Carmen Segarra? A Fed Whistleblower Q&A." *ProPublica*, October 28, 2:29 p.m. Accessed October 11, 2014. http://www.pro publica.org/article/so-who-is-carmen-segarra-a-fed-whistleblower-qa.

————. 2014. "Inside the New York Fed: Secret Recordings and a Culture Clash." *ProPublica*, September 26, 5:00 a.m. Accessed October 11, 2014. http://www .propublica.org/article/carmen-segarras-secret-recordings-from-inside-new -york-fed.

Bernstein, Mark F. 1989. "The Federal Open Market Committee and the Sharing of Governmental Power with Private Citizens." *Virginia Law Review* 75: 111–53.

Bernstein, Peter L. 2008. *The Power of Gold: The History of an Obsession*. New York: John Wiley and Sons.

Berry, Christopher R., Barry C. Burden, and William G. Howell. 2010. "The President and the Distribution of Federal Spending." *American Political Science Review* 104: 783–99.

Berry, John M. 1996. "At the Fed, a Power Struggle over Information." *Washington Post*, July 8, A1.

Bilbiie, Florin O., and Roland Straub. 2013. "Asset Market Participation, Monetary Policy Rules, and the Great Inflation." *Review of Economics and Statistics* 95, no. 2: 377–92.

Binder, Sarah. 2013. "Would Congress Care If the Federal Reserve Lost Money? A Lesson from History." *Monkey Cage*. Accessed April 21, 2015. http://the monkeycage.org/2013/02/24/would-congress-care-if-the-federal-reserve-lost -money-a-lesson-from-history/.

Binder, Sarah, and Mark Spindel. 2013a. "Congress and the Federal Reserve: Independence and Accountability." *Manuscript*, December, 1–31.

————. 2013b. "Monetary Politics: Origins of the Federal Reserve." *Studies in American Political Development* 27, no. 1 (April): 1–13. doi:10.1017/S0898 588X12000120.

Blair, Tony. 2010. *A Journey: My Political Life*. New York: Knopf.

Blinder, Alan S. 1997. "Is Government Too Political?" *Foreign Affairs*, December. http://www.foreignaffairs.com/articles/53584/alan-s-blinder/is-govern ment-too-political.

————. 2004. *The Quiet Revolution*. New Haven, Conn.: Yale University Press.

————. 2010. "Quantitative Easing: Entrance and Exit Strategies." *Federal Reserve Bank of St. Louis Review*. 92, no. 6 (November/December). http:// research.stlouisfed.org/publications/review/article/8508.

————. 2012. "Global Policy Perspectives: Central Bank Independence and Credibility during and after the Crisis." In *Federal Reserve Bank of Kansas City Symposium*. Jackson Hole, Wyo., 483–91.

————. 2013. *After the Music Stopped: The Financial Crisis, the Response, and the Work Ahead*. New York: Penguin.

————. 2015. "Beware of Woolly-Minded Attacks on the Fed." *Wall Street Journal*, January 27, sec. Opinion. http://www.wsj.com/articles/alan-s-blinder-beware-of -woolly-minded-attacks-on-the-fed-1422401124.

Blinder, Alan S., and Ricardo Reis. 2005. "Understanding the Greenspan Standard." *Proceedings—Economic Policy Symposium—Jackson Hole*, August, 11–96.

Blinder, Alan S., and Jeremy B. Rudd. 2013. "The Supply-Shock Explanation of the Great Stagflation Revisited." In *The Great Inflation: The Rebirth of Modern Central Banking*, edited by Athanasios Orphanides and Michael D. Bordo, 119–81. Chicago: University of Chicago Press.

Blomberg, S. Brock, and Gregory D. Hess. 2000. Is the Political Business Cycle for Real? Working Paper. Federal Reserve Bank of Cleveland. https://ideas.repec.org/p/fip/fedcwp/0016.html.

Blustein, Paul. 2001. *The Chastening: Inside the Crisis That Rocked the Global Financial System and Humbled the IMF*. New York: PublicAffairs.

Board of Governors of the Federal Reserve System.1942. *Twenty Eighth Annual Report of the Board of Governors of the Federal Reserve System Covering Operations for the Year 1941*. Washington, D.C.

———. 1952. *Thirty-Eighth Annual Report of the Board of Governors of the Federal Reserve System Covering Operations for the Year 1951*. Washington, D.C.

———. 2005. *The Federal Reserve System: Purposes and Functions*. Washington, D.C.

Bodenhorn, Howard. 2000. *A History of Banking in Antebellum America: Financial Markets and Economic Development in an Era of Nation-Building*. Cambridge: Cambridge University Press.

———. 2002. *State Banking in Early America: A New Economic History*. Oxford: Oxford University Press, USA.

Bolles, Albert Sidney. 1883. *The Financial History of the United States: From 1789 to 1860*. New York: D. Appleton.

Bordo, Michael D. 1989. "The Lender of Last Resort: Some Historical Insights." Working Paper. National Bureau of Economic Research, June. http://www.nber.org/papers/w3011.

Bordo, Michael D., and Athanasios Orphanides, eds. 2013. *The Great Inflation: The Rebirth of Modern Central Banking*. Chicago: University of Chicago Press.

Boughton, James M. 2012. *Tearing Down the Walls: The International Monetary Fund 1990–1999*. Washington, D.C.: International Monetary Fund.

Bradley, Richard. 2014. "Is the Rolling Stone Story True?" *Shots in the Dark*, November 24. http://www.richardbradley.net/shotsinthedark/2014/11/24/is-the-rolling-stone-story-true/.

Brands, H. W. 2007. *The Money Men: Capitalism, Democracy, and the Hundred Years' War over the American Dollar*. New York: W. W. Norton.

———. 2008. *Traitor to His Class: The Privileged Life and Radical Presidency of Franklin Delano Roosevelt*. New York: Doubleday.

Brandeis, Louis D. 1913. *Other People's Money and How the Bankers Used It*. New York: Frederick A. Stokes Company

Bremner, Robert P. 2004. *Chairman of the Fed: William McChesney Martin Jr. and the Creation of the Modern American Financial System*. New Haven: Yale University Press.

Brennan, Thomas J., and Andrew W. Lo. 2014. "Dynamic Loss Probabilities and Implications for Financial Regulation." *Yale Journal on Regulation* 31: 667–94.

Bressman, Lisa Schultz, and Robert B. Thompson. 2010. "The Future of Agency Independence." *Vanderbilt Law Review* 63: 599–672.

Brinkley, Alan. 1995. *The End of Reform: New Deal Liberalism in Recession and War*. New York: Knopf.

Broz, J. Lawrence. 1997. *The International Origins of the Federal Reserve System*. Ithaca, N.Y.: Cornell University Press.

Brummer, Chris. 2011. *Soft Law and the Global Financial System*. Cambridge: Cambridge University Press.

Bruner, Robert F., and Sean D. Carr. 2009. *The Panic of 1907: Lessons Learned from the Market's Perfect Storm*. Hoboken, N.J.: Wiley.

Bryan, William Jennings. "Cross of Gold." 1896. http://historymatters.gmu.edu /d/5354/.

Buiter, Willem H. 2008. "Central Banks and Financial Crises." In *Federal Reserve Bank of Kansas City Symposium*. Jackson Hole, Wyo., 495–633.

Burns, Arthur. 2010. *Inside the Nixon Administration: The Secret Diary of Arthur Burns, 1969–1974*, edited by Robert H. Ferrell. Lawrence: University Press of Kansas.

Calomiris, Charles W., and Stephen H. Haber. 2014. *Fragile by Design: The Political Origins of Banking Crises and Scarce Credit*. Princeton, N.J.: Princeton University Press.

Cannadine, David. 2006. *Mellon: An American Life*. New York: Knopf.

Canova, Timothy A. 2011a. "Black Swans and Black Elephants in Plain Sight: An Empirical Review of Central Bank Independence." *Chapman Law Review* 14: 237–310.

———. 2011b. "Central Bank Independence as Agency Capture: A Review of the Empirical Literature." *Banking and Financial Services Policy Report* 30, no. 11 (November): 11–25.

Caro, Robert A. 1982. *The Path to Power: The Years of Lyndon Johnson*. New York: Vintage.

———. 2013. *The Passage of Power: The Years of Lyndon Johnson*. New York: Vintage.

Carpenter, Daniel P. 2001. *The Forging of Bureaucratic Autonomy: Reputations, Networks, and Policy Innovation in Executive Agencies, 1862–1928*. Princeton, N.J.: Princeton University Press.

———. 2010. *Reputation and Power: Organizational Image and Pharmaceutical Regulation at the FDA*. Princeton, N.J.: Princeton University Press.

———. 2013. "Detecting and Measuring Capture." In *Preventing Regulatory Capture: Special Interest Influence and How to Limit It*, edited by Daniel P. Carpenter and David A. Moss, 57–69. New York: Cambridge University Press.

Carpenter, Daniel P., and David A. Moss. 2013. "Introduction." In *Preventing Regulatory Capture: Special Interest Influence and How To Limit It*, edited by Daniel P. Carpenter and David A. Moss. 1–23. New York: Cambridge University Press.

Carroll, Joseph. 2006. "Greenspan Gets High Marks from the Public." *Gallup: Business*, January 30. http://www.gallup.com/poll/21160/greenspan-gets-high -marks-from-public.aspx.

Carter, James Earl. 1979. Address to the American Public. July 15, Washington, D.C. http://millercenter.org/president/speeches/speech-3402.

Cassidy, John. 1996. "Fleeing the Fed." *New Yorker*, February 19, 38–46.

Cecchetti, Stephen G., Hans Genberg, John Lipsky, and Sushil Wadhwani. 2000. *Asset Prices and Central Bank Policy*. Geneva Report on the World Economy, May 30.

Censky, Annalyn. 2012. "Audit the Fed? Bernanke Fights Back against Ron Paul." *CNNMoney*. Accessed April 21, 2015. http://money.cnn.com/2012/07/18/news/economy/fed-bernanke-ron-paul/index.htm.

Chait, Jonathan, and Stephen Glass. 1998. "Praised Be Greenspan: The Strange Rituals of Federal Reserve Fanatics." *New Republic* 218, no. 13 (March 30): 19–25.

Chandler, Lester Vernon. 1958. *Benjamin Strong, Central Banker*. Washington, D.C.: Brookings Institution.

Chang, Kelly H. 2003. *Appointing Central Bankers: The Politics of Monetary Policy in the United States and the European Monetary Union*. Cambridge: Cambridge University Press.

Chapman, John M., Ray B. Westerfield, Gilbert E. Jackson, and Maurice Megrah. 1942. *Branch Banking: Its Historical and Theoretical Position in America and Abroad*. New York: Harper and Brothers.

Chernow, Ron. 1990. *The House of Morgan: An American Banking Dynasty and the Rise of Modern Finance*. New York: Atlantic Monthly Press.

Chodorow-Reich, Gabriel. 2014. "Effects of Unconventional Monetary Policy on Financial Institutions." *Brookings Institution*. Accessed April 21, 2015. http://www.brookings.edu/about/projects/bpea/papers/2014/unconventional-monetary-policy-financial-institutions.

Choi, Stephen J., G. Mitu Gulati, and Eric A. Posner. 2007. *Professionals or Politicians: The Uncertain Empirical Case for an Elected Rather Than Appointed Judiciary*. SSRN Scholarly Paper. Rochester, N.Y.: Social Science Research Network, August 1. http://papers.ssrn.com/abstract=1008989.

Clark, William Roberts. 2002. "Partisan and Electoral Motivations and the Choice of Monetary Institutions under Fully Mobile Capital." *International Organization* 56, no. 4 (October 1): 725–49.

Clifford, A. Jerome. 1965. *The Independence of the Federal Reserve System*. Philadelphia: University of Pennsylvania Press.

Clinton, William Jefferson. 1993. Address before a Joint Session of Congress on Administration Goals. February 17. Washington, D.C. http://www.presidency.ucsb.edu/ws/?pid=47232.

Cochrane, John H. 2014. "Monetary Policy with Interest on Reserves." *Journal of Economic Dynamics and Control* 49 (December): 74–108.

Cohan, William D. 2014. "Why the Fed Will Always Wimp Out on Goldman." *politico Magazine*. Accessed October 11, 2014. http://www.politico.com/magazine/story/2014/09/why-the-fed-will-always-wimp-out-on-goldman-111356.html.

Congressional Budget Office. 2010. *The Budgetary Impact and Subsidy Costs of the Federal Reserve's Actions during the Financial Crisis*, May.

Conti-Brown, Peter. 2010. "A Proposed Fat-Tail Risk Metric: Disclosures, Derivatives, and the Measurement of Financial Risk." *Washington University Law Review* 87: 1461–74.

———. 2011a. "Elective Shareholder Liability." *Stanford Law Review* 64: 409–67.

———. 2011b. "We Have Winners!—and a Paean to Law Librarians." *Conglomerate*, May 26. http://www.theconglomerate.org/2011/05/we-have-winners-and-a-paen-to-law-librarians.html.

———. 2013. "Is the Federal Reserve Constitutional?" *Library of Law and Liberty*, September 1. http://www.libertylawsite.org/liberty-forum/is-the-federal-reserve-constitutional/.

———. 2014a. "Bagehot's Other Dicta: Clear Writing and Central Bank Transparency." *Notice and Comment: Yale Journal on Regulation*, October 20. http://www.yalejreg.com/blog/bagehot-s-other-dicta-clear-writing-and-central-bank-transparency-part-2-of-2-by-peter-conti-brown.

———. 2014b. "Basel III, Municipal Finance, and Administrative Arguments Good and Bad." *Notice and Comment: Yale Journal on Regulation*, September 15. http://www.yalejreg.com/blog/basel-iii-municipal-finance-and-administrative-arguments-good-and-bad.

———. 2014c. "The Constitutional Crisis at the Fed." *politico Magazine*, April 13. http://www.politico.com/magazine/story/2014/04/federal-reserve-constitutional-crisis-105663.html.

———. 2014d. "The Mythology of Walter Bagehot." *Notice and Comment: Yale Journal on Regulation*, October 15. http://www.yalejreg.com/blog/the-mythology-of-walter-bagehot-part-i-of-ii-by-peter-conti-brown.

———. 2015a. "The Institutions of Federal Reserve Independence." *Yale Journal on Regulation* 32, no. X: 000–000.

———. 2015b. "The Twelve Federal Reserve Banks: Accountability and Governance in the 21st Century." Working Paper of the Hutchins Center for Fiscal and Monetary Policy. Brookings Institution, March.

Conti-Brown, Peter, and Simon Johnson. 2013. "Governing the Federal Reserve System after the Dodd-Frank Act." *Peterson Institute for International Economics Policy Brief* 13-25(October): 1–10.

Cook, Nancy. 2013. "The Fed's Last Troublemaker." *National Law Journal*, October 31. http://www.nationaljournal.com/magazine/the-fed-s-last-troublemaker-20131031.

Cooper, John Milton. 1983. *The Warrior and the Priest: Woodrow Wilson and Theodore Roosevelt*. Cambridge, Mass.: Harvard University Press.

Coy, Peter. 2013. "How Stanley Fischer Became a Central-Banking Legend." *BloombergView*, December 11. http://www.bloomberg.com/bw/articles/2013-12-11/how-stanley-fischer-became-a-central-banking-legend-before-joining-the-fed.

Cukierman, Alex. 1992. *Central Bank Strategy, Credibility, and Independence: Theory and Evidence*. Cambridge, Mass.: MIT Press.

Dallek, Robert. 2005. *Lyndon B. Johnson: Portrait of a President*. Oxford: Oxford University Press.

Datla, Kirti, and Richard L. Revesz. 2013. "Deconstructing Independent Agencies (and Executive Agencies)." *Cornell Law Review* 98, no. 4: 769.

DeLong, J. Bradford. 2008. "Republic of the Central Banker." *American Prospect,* October 23. https://prospect.org/article/republic-central-banker.

Diamond, Peter A. 2011. "When a Nobel Prize Isn't Enough." *New York Times,* June 5, sec. Opinion. http://www.nytimes.com/2011/06/06/opinion/06diamond.html.

Dombalagian, Onnig H. 2010. "Requiem for the Bulge Bracket: Revisiting Investment Bank Regulation." *Indiana Law Journal* 85: 777.

Dworkin, Ronald. 2010. "The Temptation of Elena Kagan." *New York Review of Books,* August 19. http://www.nybooks.com/articles/archives/2010/aug/19/temptation-elena-kagan/.

Eavis, Peter. 2014. "New York Fed Chief Expresses Concern on New Leverage Rule." *DealBook.* Accessed April 19, 2015. http://dealbook.nytimes.com/2014/03/20/dudley-expresses-concern-on-leverage-rule/.

Eccles, Marriner S. 1951. *Beckoning Frontiers: Public and Personal Recollections.* New York: Alfred A. Knopf.

Eccles, Marriner S., and Lauchlin Currie. 1934/2004. "Desirable Changes in the Administration of the Federal Reserve System." *Journal of Economic Studies* 31: 267.

Eggertsson, Gauti B., and Michael Woodford. 2003. "The Zero Bound on Interest Rates and Optimal Monetary Policy." *Brookings Institution.* Accessed April 21, 2015. http://www.brookings.edu/about/projects/bpea/papers/2003/zero-bound-interest-rates-monetary-policy-eggertsson.

Ehrlichman, John. 1982. *Witness to Power: The Nixon Years.* New York: Simon and Schuster.

Eichengreen, Barry. 1992. *Golden Fetters: The Gold Standard and the Great Depression, 1919–1939.* New York: Oxford University Press.

———. 2015. *Hall of Mirrors: The Great Depression, the Great Recession, and the Uses—and Misuses—of History.* New York: Oxford University Press.

Eijffinger, S.-C.-W., and J. de Haan. 1996. "The Political Economy of Central-Bank Independence." Special Papers in International Economics, no. 19, International Finance Section, Department of Economics Princeton University, Princeton, New Jersey.

Einzig, Paul. 1932. *Montagu Norman: A Study in Financial Statesmanship.* London: Kegan Paul, Trench, Trubner.

Eisenhower, Dwight. 1953. "Annual Message to the Congress on the State of the Union," February 2. http://www.eisenhower.archives.gov/all_about_ike/speeches/1953_state_of_the_union.pdf.

———. 1956. "The President's News Conference," April 25. http://www.presidency.ucsb.edu/ws/index.php?pid=10787.

Eisinger, Jesse. 2013. "The Power behind the Throne at the Federal Reserve." *New York Times DealBook,* July 31. http://dealbook.nytimes.com/2013/07/31/the-power-behind-the-throne-at-the-federal-reserve/.

Elster, Jon. 1977. "Ulysses and the Sirens: A Theory of Imperfect Rationality." Social Science Information 16, no. 5: 469–526.

———. 2000. *Ulysses Unbound: Studies in Rationality, Precommitment, and Constraints.* Cambridge: Cambridge University Press.

Engel, Kathleen C., and Patricia McCoy. 2011. *The Subprime Virus: Reckless Credit, Regulatory Failure, and Next Steps.* Oxford: Oxford University Press.

Engstrom, David Freeman. 2013. "Corralling Capture." *Harvard Journal of Law and Public Policy* 36: 31–39.

Faust, Jon. 1996. "Whom Can We Trust to Run the Fed? Theoretical Support for the Founders' Views." *Journal of Monetary Economics* 37, no. 2 (April): 267–83.

Fay, Stephen. 1988. *Portrait of an Old Lady: Turmoil at the Bank of England.* Harmondsworth, Middlesex, England: Viking Adult.

Federal Open Market Committee. 2008. *Transcript of the Federal Open Market Committee.* Washington, D.C.

———. 2013. *Transcript of the Federal Open Market Committee.* Washington, D.C.

Federal Reserve Bank of New York. 2014. "Statement Regarding New York Fed Supervision," September 26. http://www.newyorkfed.org/newsevents/statements/2014/0926_2014.html.

Ferejohn, John, and Charles Shipan. 1990. "Congressional Influence on Bureaucracy." *Journal of Law, Economics, and Organization* 6 (January 1): 1–20.

Ferguson, Niall. 1998. *The House of Rothschild.* Vol. 1, *Money's Prophets: 1798–1848.* New York: Penguin Books.

———. 1999. *The House of Rothschild.* Vol. 2, *The World's Banker: 1849–1999.* New York: Penguin Books.

Fernández-Albertos, José. 2015. "The Politics of Central Bank Independence." *Annual Review of Political Science* 18, no. 1. doi:10.1146/annurev-polisci-071112-221121.

Financial Crisis Inquiry Commission. 2011. *The Financial Crisis Inquiry Report, Authorized Edition: Final Report of the National Commission on the Causes of the Financial and Economic Crisis in the United States.* New York: PublicAffairs.

Financial Times. 2000. " 'Greenspan Put' May Be Encouraging Complacency." *Financial Times,* December 8, 1.

Fischer, Stanley. 1995. "Central-Bank Independence Revisited." *American Economic Review* 85, no. 2 (May 1): 201–6.

Fisher, Richard. 2015. "Suggestions after a Decade at the Fed (with Reference to Paul Volcker, Roosa Boys, Hogwarts, the Death Star, Ebenezer Scrooge, Mae West, Herb Kelleher, Worms and Camels, Peter Weir, Charles Kindleberger, Pope Francis and Secretariat)." Speech presented at the Economic Club of New York, New York, February 11.

Flaherty, Michael. 2014. "Federal Reserve Chair Janet Yellen Makes Less Than 113 Other Staffers at the Fed," October 17. http://www.huffingtonpost.com/2014/10/17/federal-reserve-pay-janet-yellen_n_6001202.html.

Fletcher, William A. 1988. "The Structure of Standing." *Yale Law Journal* 98: 221–91.

Fligstein, Neil, Jonah Stuart Brundage, and Michael Schultz. 2014. "Why the

Federal Reserve Failed to See the Financial Crisis of 2008: The Role of 'Macroeconomics' as a Sense Making and Cultural Frame." *Institute for Research on Labor and Employment*, Working Paper 111–14 (September).

Fox, Justin. 2014. "How Economics PhDs Took Over the Federal Reserve." *Harvard Business Review*, February 3. https://hbr.org/2014/02/how-economics-phds-took-over-the-federal-reserve/.

———. 2015. "The Fed Is Weird. Get Over It." *BloombergView*, March 3. http://www.bloombergview.com/articles/2015-03-03/federal-reserve-is-strange-creature-and-we-should-get-used-to-it.

Freeman, Jody, and Jim Rossi. 2012. "Agency Coordination in Shared Regulatory Space." *Harvard Law Review* 125: 1133.

Friedberg, Barry J., and Abram S. Gordon. 1988. "Judicial Review of the Federal Banking Regulatory Agencies." *Annual Review of Banking Law* 7: 365.

Frieden, Jeffry A. 2014. *Currency Politics: The Political Economy of Exchange Rate Policy*. Princeton, N.J.: Princeton University Press.

Friedman, Milton. 1962. "Should There Be an Independent Monetary Authority?" In *In Search of a Monetary Constitution*, edited by Leland B. Yeager, 219–43. Cambridge, Mass.: Harvard University Press.

———. 1969. *The Optimum Quantity of Money*. New Brunswick, N.J.: Aldine Transaction.

———. 1973. *Money and Economic Development: The Horowitz Lectures of 1972*. New York: Praeger.

Friedman, Milton, and Anna Jacobson Schwartz. 1963. *A Monetary History of the United States, 1867–1960*. Princeton, N.J.: Princeton University Press.

———. 1993. "A Tale of Fed Transcripts." *Wall Street Journal*, December 20, A12.

Fry, Maxwell. 2000. "Key Issues in the Choice of Monetary Policy Framework." In *Monetary Policy Frameworks in a Global Context*, edited by L. Mahadeva and G. Sterne. 1–15. London: Routledge.

Furfine, Craig. 2006. "The Costs and Benefits of Moral Suasion: Evidence from the Rescue of Long-Term Capital Management." *Journal of Business* 79, no. 2 (March 1): 593–622. doi:10.1086/499132.

Gaddis, John Lewis. 2011. *George F. Kennan: An American Life*. New York: Penguin.

Galati, Gabriele, and Richhilde Moessner. 2010. "Macroprudential Policy: A Literature Review." *DNB Working Paper* 267.

Galbraith, John Kenneth. 1965. Statement, Hearings before the Joint Economic Committee on the Recent Federal Reserve Action and Economic Policy Coordination, 89th Congress, 1st sess.

———. 2009. *The Great Crash 1929*. Boston: Mariner Books.

Garicano, Luis, and Rosa M. Lastra. 2010. "Towards a New Architecture for Financial Stability: Seven Principles." Journal of International Economic Law 13, no. 3: 597–621.

Geisst, Charles R. 2012. *Wall Street: A History*. Updated ed. Oxford: Oxford University Press.

———. 2013. *Beggar Thy Neighbor: A History of Usury and Debt*. Philadelphia: University of Pennsylvania Press.

Geithner, Timothy F. 2014. *Stress Test: Reflections on Financial Crises*. New York: Crown.

Gerding, Erik F. 2013. *Law, Bubbles, and Financial Regulation*. Abingdon, Oxon: Routledge.

Gerring, John. 1997. "Ideology: A Definitional Analysis." *Political Research Quarterly* 50, no. 4 (December 1): 957–94. doi:10.2307/448995.

Gersen, Jacob. 2010. "Designing Agencies: Public Choice and Public Law." In *Research Handbook in Public Choice and Public Law*, edited by Anne Joseph O'Connell and Daniel A. Farber. Cheltenham: Edward Elgar.

Glass, Carter. 1914. Speech in the House of Representatives. *Congressional Record* 51, no. 17 (December 22): 563.

———. 1927. *An Adventure in Constructive Finance*. New York: Doubleday.

Glass, Stephen. 1997. "Peddling Poppy." *New Republic*, June 9, 20.

———. 1998a. "Washington Scene: Hack Heaven." *New Republic*, May 18, 11.

———. 1998b. "Washington Scene: Monica Sells." *New Republic*, April 13, 11.

Glennon, Michael J. 2014. *National Security and Double Government*. New York: Oxford University Press.

Gluck, Abbe R. 2014. "What 30 Years of Chevron Teach Us about the Rest of Statutory Interpretation." *Fordham Law Review* 83: 607–32.

Goodfriend, Marvin. 1985. *Monetary Mystique : Secrecy and Central Banking*. Working Paper 85-07. Federal Reserve Bank of Richmond. 1–47. https://ideas .repec.org/p/fip/fedrwp/85-07.html.

Goodhart, Charles. 1969. *The New York Money Market and the Finance of Trade, 1900–1913*. Cambridge, Mass.: Harvard University Press.

———. 1988. *The Evolution of Central Banks*. Cambridge, Mass.: MIT Press.

———. 1995. *The Central Bank and the Financial System*. Cambridge, Mass.: MIT Press.

———. 2011. *The Basel Committee on Banking Supervision: A History of the Early Years 1974–1997*. Cambridge: Cambridge University Press.

Goodhart, Charles, and Ellen Meade. 2003. "Central Banks and Supreme Courts," London School of Economics, Centre for Economic Performance, working paper, http://ccp.lse.ac.uk/seminarpapers/16-10-03-GOO.pdf.

Goodhart, Charles, and Dirk Schoenmaker. 1995. "Should the Functions of Monetary Policy and Banking Supervision Be Separated?" *Oxford Economic Papers* 47, no. 4: 539–60.

Goodman, John B. 1991. "The Politics of Central Bank Independence." *Comparative Politics* 23, no. 3 (April 1): 329–49. doi:10.2307/422090.

Goodwin, Doris Kearns. 2014. *The Bully Pulpit: Theodore Roosevelt, William Howard Taft, and the Golden Age of Journalism*. New York: Simon and Schuster.

Gormley, Ken. 2010. *The Death of American Virtue: Clinton vs. Starr*. New York: Crown.

Gorton, Gary B. 2010. *Slapped by the Invisible Hand: The Panic of 2007*. Oxford: Oxford University Press.

Green, D. 2012. "The Relationship between Micro-Macro-Prudential Supervision and Central Banking." In *Financial Regulation and Supervision: A Post-Crisis Analysis*, edited by Guido Ferrarini, Klaus Hopt, Eddy Wymeersch, and Guido Ferrarini. Oxford: Oxford University Press.

Greenspan, Alan. 1993. *Statement before Joint Economic Committee*. Washington, D.C.

———. 2007. *The Age of Turbulence: Adventures in a New World*. New York: Penguin.

Greider, William. 1987. *Secrets of the Temple: How the Federal Reserve Runs the Country*. New York: Simon and Schuster.

Griffin, G. Edward. 2010. *The Creature from Jekyll Island: A Second Look at the Federal Reserve*. 5th ed. Westlake Village, Calif.: American Media.

Grilli, Vittorio, Donato Masciandaro, Guido Tabellini, Edmond Malinvaud, and Marco Pagano. 1991. "Political and Monetary Institutions and Public Financial Policies in the Industrial Countries." *Economic Policy* 6, no. 13 (October 1): 342–92. doi:10.2307/1344630.

Grim, Ryan. 2009. "Priceless: How the Federal Reserve Bought the Economics Profession." *Huffington Post*, October 23. http://www.huffingtonpost.com /2009/09/07/priceless-how-the-federal_n_278805.html.

Gross, Leo, and Daniel Tarullo. 1985. "Book Review, Managing Trade Relations in the 1980s: Issues Involved in the GATT Ministerial Meeting of 1982." *American Journal of International Law* 79: 1089–91.

Grossman, Richard S. 2010. *Unsettled Account: The Evolution of Banking in the Industrialized World since 1800*. Princeton, N.J.: Princeton University Press.

Grove, David L. 1952. *Central Bank Independence and the Government-Bank Relationship*. Washington, D.C.: U.S. Board of Governors of the Federal Reserve System, April 2.

Hackley, Howard. 1972. "The Status of the Federal Reserve System in the Federal Government." Board of Governors of the Federal Reserve System, January, manuscript on file with the author.

Hall, Peter A. 1993. "Policy Paradigms, Social Learning, and the State: The Case of Economic Policymaking in Britain." *Comparative Politics* 25, no. 3 (April): 275–96.

Hammond, Bray. 1957. *Banks and Politics in America from the Revolution to the Civil War*. Princeton, N.J.: Princeton University Press.

———. 1970. *Sovereignty and an Empty Purse: Banks and Politics in the Civil War*. Princeton, N.J.: Princeton University Press.

Harris, Seymour. 1965. Statement, Hearings before the Joint Economic Committee on the Recent Federal Reserve Action and Economic Policy Coordination, 89th Congress, 1st sess., pt. 1.

Havrilesky, Thomas. 1992. *The Pressures on American Monetary Policy*. Boston: Springer.

Heclo, Hugh. 1974. *Modern Social Politics in Britain and Sweden: From Relief to Income Maintenance*. New Haven, Conn.: Yale University Press.

Henderson, M. Todd, and Frederick Tung. 2011. "Pay for Regulator Performance." *Southern California Law Review* 85: 1003–68.

Henry, O. 2014. *Roads of Destiny*. London: King Press.

Hetzel, Robert L., and Ralph Leach. 2001. "The Treasury-Fed Accord: A New Narrative Account." *Federal Reserve Bank of Richmond Economic Quarterly* 87, no. 1: 33–55.

Hickman, Kristin E. 2014. "The Three Phases of Mead." *Fordham Law Review* 83: 527–54.

Hilsenrath, Jon. 2015. "Washington Strips New York Fed's Power." *Wall Street Journal*, March 5, sec. Economy. http://www.wsj.com/articles/washington-strips -new-york-feds-power-1425526210.

Hilsenrath, Jon, and Damian Paletta. 2009. "Fed's Tarullo Shakes Up Bank Rules." *Wall Street Journal*, October 27, sec. U.S. http://online.wsj.com/news/articles /SB125650760801506825?mg=reno64-wsj&url=http%3A%2F%2Fonline.wsj .com%2Farticle%2FSB125650760801506825.html#mod=todays_us_money _and_investing.

Hockett, Robert, and Saule Omarova. 2014. " 'Private' Means to 'Public' Ends: Governments as Market Actors." *Theoretical Inquiries in Law* 15: 53–76.

Hoffmann, Susan. 2001. *Politics and Banking: Ideas, Public Policy, and the Creation of Financial Institutions*. Baltimore: Johns Hopkins University Press.

Hofstadter, Richard. 1960. *The Age of Reform*. New York: Vintage.

Holmes, Douglas R. 2013. *Economy of Words: Communicative Imperatives in Central Banks*. Chicago: University of Chicago Press.

Hoover, Herbert. 1952. *The Memoirs of Herbert Hoover: The Great Depression, 1929–1942*. New York: Macmillan.

Howe, Daniel Walker. 2007. *What Hath God Wrought: The Transformation of America, 1815–1848*. New York: Oxford University Press.

Hubbard, R. Glenn. 2013. "How to Pick a Fed Chairman." *National Review*, September 12. http://www.nationalreview.com/article/358303/how-pick-fed -chairman-r-glenn-hubbard.

Huber, John D., and Charles R. Shipan. 2002. *Deliberate Discretion? The Institutional Foundations of Bureaucratic Autonomy*. Cambridge: Cambridge University Press.

Huq, Aziz Z. 2013. "Removal as a Political Question." *Stanford Law Review* 65: 1–76.

Hurst, James Willard. 2001. *A Legal History of Money in the United States, 1774–1970*. Lincoln, Neb.: Beard Books.

Hutnyan, Joseph D. 1994. "Fed, Industry Lobbying Halts Administration's Restructuring Proposal." *Banking Policy Report* 13, no. 6 (March 21): 4–5.

Hyman, Sidney. 1976. *Marriner S. Eccles: Private Entrepreneur and Public Servant*. Stanford, Calif.: Graduate School of Business, Stanford University.

Ip, Greg. 2006. "Paul Krugman: Gone but Not Forgotten." *Wall Street Journal*, August 28. http://blogs.wsj.com/washwire/2006/08/28/gone-but-not-forgotten/.

Irwin, Neil. 2013a. *The Alchemists: Three Central Bankers and a World on Fire*. New York: Penguin.

———. 2013b. "Why We Shouldn't Think of Central Bankers as Hawks and Doves." *Washington Post Wonkblog*, July 30. http://www.washingtonpost.com

/blogs/wonkblog/wp/2013/07/30/why-we-shouldnt-think-of-central-bankers
-as-hawks-and-doves/.

Jacobs, Meg. 2007. *Pocketbook Politics: Economic Citizenship in Twentieth-
Century America*. Princeton, N.J.: Princeton University Press.

James, Harold. 2012. *Making the European Monetary Union*. Cambridge, Mass.:
Harvard University Press.

———. 2014. "The Secret History of the Financial Crisis." *Project Syndicate*,
March 7. http://www.project-syndicate.org/commentary/harold-james-examines
-the-real-story-behind-the-international-response-to-the-near-meltdown-in
-2008.

James, John A. 1978. *Money and Capital Markets in Postbellum America*.
Princeton, N.J.: Princeton University Press.

John, Richard R. 1998. *Spreading the News: The American Postal System from
Franklin to Morse*. Cambridge, Mass.: Harvard University Press.

Johnson, Simon, and James Kwak. 2010. *13 Bankers: The Wall Street Takeover
and the Next Financial Meltdown*. New York: Pantheon.

———. 2012. *White House Burning: The Founding Fathers, Our National Debt,
and Why It Matters to You*. New York: Pantheon.

Jones, Jeffery M., and Lydia Saad. 2013. "Americans Sour on IRS, Rate CDC and
FBI Most Positively." *Gallup: Politics*, May 23. http://www.gallup.com/poll
/162764/americans-views-irs-sharply-negative-2009.aspx.

Judge, Kathryn. 2014. "Three Discount Windows." *Cornell Law Review* 99: 795–
855.

Kahan, Marcel, and Edward Rock. 2009. "How to Prevent Hard Cases from
Making Bad Law: Bear Stearns, Delaware and the Strategic Use of Comity."
Emory Law Journal 58: 713–59.

Kaiser, Robert G. 2013. *Act of Congress: How America's Essential Institution
Works, and How It Doesn't*. New York: Vintage.

Kane, Edward J. 1974. "The Re-politicization of the Fed." *Journal of Financial
and Quantitative Analysis* 9, no. 5 (November 1): 743–52. doi:10.2307/2329662.

Karabell, Zachary. 2014. "The Fed Is Not as Powerful as We Think." *Slate*, August 25. http://www.slate.com/articles/business/the_edgy_optimist/2014/08
/janet_yellen_jackson_hole_speech_let_s_stop_deifying_the_fed.html.

Katznelson, Ira. 2013. *Fear Itself: The New Deal and the Origins of Our Time*.
New York: W. W. Norton.

Kemmerer, E. W. 1922. "The Purposes of the Federal Reserve Act as Shown by Its
Explicit Provisions." *Annals of the American Academy of Political and Social
Science* 99 (January 1): 62–69.

Kennedy, David M. 2001. *Freedom from Fear: The American People in Depression and War, 1929–1945*. Oxford: Oxford University Press.

Kettl, Donald F. 1986. *Leadership at the Fed*. New Haven, Conn.: Yale University
Press.

Keynes, John Maynard. 1936. *The General Theory of Employment, Interest and
Money*. London: Palgrave Macmillan.

King, Larry, and Larry Greenfield. 1998. "Gennifer Flowers Reacts to Clinton's
Videotaped Testimony." *CNN Larry King Live*, September 24.

Kingson, Jennifer A. 1987. "Harvard Tenure Battle Puts 'Critical Legal Studies' on Trial." *New York Times*, August 30, sec. Week in Review. http://www.nytimes .com/1987/08/30/weekinreview/harvard-tenure-battle-puts-critical-legal-studies -on-trial.html.

Kirshner, Jonathan. 2007. *Appeasing Bankers: Financial Caution on the Road to War*. Princeton, N.J.: Princeton University Press.

Kocherlakota, Narayana. 2014. "Economics at the Federal Reserve Banks." Speech presented at the American Economic Association Annual Meeting, Philadelphia, January 4.

Kolko, Gabriel. 1963. *The Triumph of Conservatism*. New York: Free Press.

Krishnamurthy, Arvind, and Annette Vissing-Jorgensen. 2011. *The Effects of Quantitative Easing on Interest Rates: Channels and Implications for Policy*. Working Paper. National Bureau of Economic Research, October. http://www .nber.org/papers/w17555.

Kroft, Steve. 2007. "60 Minutes: The Private Clarence Thomas," October 12. http://www.cbsnews.com/videos/the-private-clarence-thomas/.

Krugman, Paul 1998. "It's Baaack: Japan's Slump and the Return of the Liquidity Trap." *Brookings Paper on Economic Activity* 2. Accessed April 21, 2015. http://www.brookings.edu/about/projects/bpea/papers/1998/japans-slump -liquidity-trap-krugman.

———. 2009. The Return of Depression Economics and the Crisis of 2008. New York: W. W. Norton.

Kwak, James 2013. "Cultural Capture and the Financial Crisis." In *Preventing Regulatory Capture: Special Interest Influence and How To Limit It*, edited by Daniel P. Carpenter and David A. Moss. New York: Cambridge University Press.

———. 2015. "Say It Ain't So, Ben—Bull Market." *Medium*. Accessed April 21, 2015. https://medium.com/bull-market/say-it-ain-t-so-ben-72d55d00cef7.

Kydland, Finn E., and Edward C. Prescott. 1977. "Rules Rather Than Discretion: The Inconsistency of Optimal Plans." *Journal of Political Economy* 85, no. 3 (June 1): 473–91.

Laidler, David. 1999. *Fabricating the Keynesian Revolution: Studies of the Interwar Literature on Money, the Cycle, and Unemployment*. Cambridge: Cambridge University Press.

Lastra, Rosa Maria. 1996. *Central Banking and Banking Regulation*. London: London School of Economics and Political Science.

———. 2006. *Legal Foundations of International Monetary Stability*. Oxford: Oxford University Press.

———. 2015. *International Financial and Monetary Law*. Oxford: Oxford University Press.

Lazarus, Richard J. 2009. "Super Wicked Problems and Climate Change: Restraining the Present to Liberate the Future." *Cornell Law Review* 94: 1153–231.

Leader, Laurie. 1976. "The Federal Bank Commission Act: A Proposal to Consolidate the Federal Banking Agencies." *Cleveland State Law Review* 25: 475–513.

LeBor, Adam. 2013. *Tower of Basel: The Shadowy History of the Secret Bank That Runs the World*. New York: PublicAffairs.

Lee, Carol E. 2013. "White House Calls Yellen a Consensus-Builder." *Wall Street Journal*, October 9. http://blogs.wsj.com/washwire/2013/10/09/white-house -calls-yellen-a-consensus-builder/.

Lemann, Nicholas. 2014. "The Hand on the Lever." *New Yorker*, July 21. http:// www.newyorker.com/magazine/2014/07/21/the-hand-on-the-lever.

Levinson, Daryl J. 2004. "Empire-Building Government in Constitutional Law." *Harvard Law Review* 118: 915–972

Levitin, Adam J. 2013. "The Consumer Financial Protection Bureau: An Introduction." *Review of Banking and Financial Law* 32: 321–69.

———. 2014. "The Politics of Financial Regulation and the Regulation of Financial Politics." *Harvard Law Review* 127: 1991–2067.

———. 2015. "Safe Banking." *University of Chicago Law Review* 86, no. 1: 000–000.

Lindsey, David E. 2003. *A Modern History of FOMC Communication*. Washington, D.C.: Board of Governors of the Federal Reserve System. http://www .federalreserve.gov/foia/files/20030624.History.FOMC.Communications.pub lic.pdf.

Livingston, James. 1989. *Origins of the Federal Reserve System: Money, Class, and Corporate Capitalism, 1890–1913*. Ithaca, N.Y.: Cornell University Press.

Logevall, Fredrik. 2001. *Choosing War: The Lost Chance for Peace and the Escalation of War in Vietnam*. Berkeley: University of California Press.

Lohmann, Susanne. 1992. "Optimal Commitment in Monetary Policy: Credibility versus Flexibility." *American Economic Review* 82, no. 1 (March 1): 273–86.

———. 2006. "The Non-politics of Monetary Policy." In *The Oxford Handbook of Political Economy*, edited by Barry R. Weingast and Donald Wittman, 523–44. Oxford: Oxford University Press.

Lowenstein, Roger. 2000. *When Genius Failed: The Rise and Fall of Long-Term Capital Management*. New York: Random House.

Magill, Elizabeth, and Adrian Vermeule. 2011. "Allocating Power within Agencies." *Yale Law Journal* 120: 1032–83.

Magliocca, Gerard N. 2012. "The Constitution Can Do No Wrong." *University of Illinois Law Review* 2012: 723–35.

Mahoney, James, and Kathleen Thelen, eds. 2009. *Explaining Institutional Change: Ambiguity, Agency, and Power*. Cambridge: Cambridge University Press.

Malekan, Omid. 2010. *Quantitative Easing Explained*. https://www.youtube .com/watch?v=PTUY16CkS-k.

Mankiw, N. Gregory. 2014. *Principles of Economics*. 7th ed. Stamford, Conn.: Cengage Learning.

Martin, William McChesney. 1955a. "Address before the New York Group of the Investment Bankers Association of America," October 19. http://www.federal reservehistory.org/Media/Material/People/113-140.

———. 1955b. Hearing before a Subcommittee of the Committee on Banking and Currency, United States Senate, 84th Congress, 1st sess. (July).

Maya, Feministing. 2014. "Sotomayor Gives Sesame Street Some Career Advice." Accessed November 1. http://www.salon.com/2012/11/12/sotomayor_gives _semsame_street_some_career_advice/.

McAdoo, William Gibbs. 1931. Crowded Years: The Reminiscences of William G. McAdoo. New York: Houghton Mifflin.

McClosky, Herbert. 1964. "Consensus and Ideology in American Politics." American Political Science Review 58, no. 2 (June 1): 361–82. doi:10.2307/1952868.

McCollom, James P. 1987. The Continental Affair: The Rise and Fall of the Continental Illinois Bank. New York: Dodd, Mead.

McCubbins, Matthew D., Roger G. Noll, and Barry R. Weingast. 1987. "Administrative Procedures as Instruments of Political Control." Journal of Law, Economics, and Organization 3: 243–77.

———. 1989. "Structure and Process, Politics and Policy: Administrative Arrangements and the Political Control of Agencies." Virginia Law Review 75: 431–82.

McCubbins, Mathew D., and Thomas Schwartz. 1984. "Congressional Oversight Overlooked: Police Patrols versus Fire Alarms." American Journal of Political Science 28, no. 1 (February 1): 165–79. doi:10.2307/2110792.

McGowan, Carl. 1981. "Congressmen in Court: The New Plaintiffs." Georgia Law Review 15: 241–70.

McGrane, Victoria. 2014. "Lawmaker Seeks More Oversight of New York Fed President." Wall Street Journal, November 18, sec. U.S. http://www.wsj.com /articles/lawmaker-seeks-more-oversight-of-new-york-fed-president-14163 52549.

———. 2014. "N.Y. Fed President Dudley: I'm More of a Fire Warden, Not a Cop on the Beat." Wall Street Journal, November 21. http://blogs.wsj.com/econo mics/2014/11/21/n-y-fed-president-dudley-im-more-of-a-fire-warden-not-a -cop-on-the-beat/.

McLean, Bethany, and Peter Elkind. 2003. Smartest Guys in the Room: The Amazing Rise and Scandalous Fall of Enron. New York: Portfolio Hardcover.

Mehrling, Perry. 2002. "Retrospectives: Economists and the Fed; Beginnings." Journal of Economic Perspectives 16, no. 4: 207–18. doi:10.1257/08953300 2320951046.

———. 2010. The New Lombard Street. Princeton N.J.: Princeton University Press.

Meltzer, Allan H. 2003. A History of the Federal Reserve. Vol. 1, 1913–1951. Chicago: University of Chicago Press.

———. 2009. "Inflation Nation." New York Times, May 4, sec. Opinion. http:// www.nytimes.com/2009/05/04/opinion/04meltzer.html.

———. 2010a. A History of the Federal Reserve. Vol. 2, bk. 1, 1951–1969. 1st ed. Chicago: University of Chicago Press.

———. 2010b. A History of the Federal Reserve, Vol. 2, bk. 2, 1970–1986. Chicago: University of Chicago Press.

———. 2013. "Quantitative Quicksand." Project Syndicate, June 6. http://www

.project-syndicate.org/commentary/why-quantitative-easing-has-failed-to-boost -us-investment-and-jobs-by-allan-h--meltzer.

Merkley, Jeff. 2010. "Statement on Proposal to House Consumer Financial Protection Agency within the Federal Reserve," March 2. http://www.merkley.senate .gov/news/press-releases/merkley-statement-on-proposal-to-house-consumer -financial-protection-agency-within-the-federal-reserve.

Meyer, Laurence H. 2004. *A Term at the Fed: An Insider's View*. New York: HarperBusiness.

Mian, Atif, and Amir Sufi. 2014. *House of Debt: How They (and You) Caused the Great Recession, and How We Can Prevent It from Happening Again*. Chicago: University of Chicago Press.

Milkis, Sidney M. 2009. *Theodore Roosevelt, the Progressive Party, and the Transformation of American Democracy*. Lawrence: University Press of Kansas.

Miller, Marcus, Paul Weller, and Lei Zhang. 2002. "Moral Hazard and the US Stock Market: Analysing the 'Greenspan Put.'" *Economic Journal* 112, no. 478 (March 1): C171–86.

Mints, L. W. 1945. *A History of Banking Theory in Great Britain and the United States*. Chicago: University of Chicago Press.

Moe, Terry M. 1989. "The Politics of Bureaucratic Structure." In *Can the Government Govern?*, edited by John E. Chubb and Paul E. Peterson, 267–329. Washington, D.C.: Brookings Institution Press.

Moe, Thorvald Grung. 2013. *Marriner S. Eccles and the 1951 Treasury–Federal Reserve Accord: Lessons for Central Bank Independence*. SSRN Scholarly Paper. Rochester, N.Y.: Social Science Research Network, January 18. http:// papers.ssrn.com/abstract=2202815.

Morgan, J. Pierpont. 1912. Testimony before the Bank and Currency Committee of the House of Representatives. December 18 and 19. Washington, D.C.

Morgenson, Gretchen, and Joshua Rosner. 2011. *Reckless Endangerment: How Outsized Ambition, Greed, and Corruption Led to Economic Armageddon*. New York: Times Books.

Morning Edition. 2014. "Former Fed Bank Examiner Says Secret Tapes Show Fed Leniency." *NPR.org*. Accessed April 20, 2015. http://www.npr.org/2014 /09/26/351520037/former-fed-bank-examiner-says-secret-tapes-show-fed -leniency.

Mui, Ylan Q. 2014. "Three Lessons the World Can Teach the Federal Reserve." *Washington Post*, June 18. http://www.washingtonpost.com/blogs/wonkblog/wp /2014/06/18/three-lessons-the-world-can-teach-the-federal-reserve/.

Neal, Larry. 2011. "A Reading List for Economic Historians on the Great Recession of 2007–2009: Its Causes and Consequences." *Journal of Economic History* 71, no. 4 (December 1): 1099–106.

Nelson, Caleb. 2000. "Preemption." *Virginia Law Review* 86: 225–305.

Nelson, Edward. 2008. "Friedman and Taylor on Monetary Policy Rules: A Comparison." *Federal Reserve Bank of St. Louis Review* 90, no. 2 (April): 95–116.

Nixon, Richard. 1962. *Six Crises*. New York: Doubleday.

Nou, Jennifer. 2013. "Agency Self-Insulation under Presidential Review." *Harvard Law Review* 126: 1755–837.

O'Connell, Anne Joseph. 2009. "Vacant Offices: Delays in Staffing Top Agency Positions." *Southern California Law Review* 82: 913–99.

Office of President-Elect Barack Obama. 2008. "Press Release: President-Elect Obama Announces Choices for SEC, CFTC and Federal Reserve Board," December 18. http://www.presidency.ucsb.edu/ws/?pid=85085.

Omarova, Saule T. 2009. "The Quiet Metamorphosis: How Derivatives Changed the 'Business of Banking.'" *University of Miami Law Review* 63: 1041–109.

———. 2011. "From Gramm-Leach-Bliley to Dodd-Frank: The Unfulfilled Promise of Section 23A of the Federal Reserve Act." *North Carolina Law Review* 89: 1683–776.

———. 2013. "The Merchants of Wall Street: Banking, Commerce, and Commodities." *Minnesota Law Review* 98: 265–355.

Omarova, Saule T., and Margaret E. Tahyar. 2011. "That Which We Call a Bank: Revisiting the History of Bank Holding Company Regulation in the United States." *Review of Banking and Financial Law* 31: 113–98.

Orphanides, Athanasios, and John C. Williams. 2013. "Monetary Policy Mistakes and the Evolution of Inflation Expectations." In *The Great Inflation: The Rebirth of Modern Central Banking*, edited by Athanasios Orphanides and Michael D. Bordo, 255–300. Chicago: University of Chicago Press.

Parkin, Michael. 2012. "Central Bank Laws and Monetary Policy Outcomes: A Three Decade Perspective." Conference presentation, Central Bank Independence: Reality or Myth? San Diego, Calif., December. https://ideas.repec.org/p/uwo/epuwoc/20131.html.

Partnoy, Frank, and Jesse Eisinger. 2013. "What's Inside America's Banks?" *Atlantic*, February. http://www.theatlantic.com/magazine/archive/2013/01/whats-inside-americas-banks/309196/.

Patman, Wright. 1966. "Floor Speech—US House of Representatives." *Congressional Record*, July 11, 15031.

———. 1975. "What's Wrong with the Federal Reserve and What to Do about It." *American Bar Association Journal* 61, no. 2 (February): 179–84.

Patterson, James T. 1967. *Congressional Conservatism and the New Deal: The Growth of the Conservative Coalition in Congress, 1933–1939*. Lexington: University of Kentucky Press.

———. 1997. *Grand Expectations: The United States, 1945–1974*. New York: Oxford University Press.

———. 2007. *Restless Giant: The United States from Watergate to Bush v. Gore*. New York: Oxford University Press.

Paulson, Henry M. 2010. *On the Brink: Inside the Race to Stop the Collapse of the Global Financial System*. New York: Business Plus.

Penenberg, Adam. 1998. "Lies, Damn Lies, and Fiction." *Forbes*, May 11. http://www.forbes.com/1998/05/11/otw3.html.

Perino, Michael. 2010. *The Hellhound of Wall Street: How Ferdinand Pecora's Investigation of the Great Crash Forever Changed American Finance*. New York: Penguin Books.

Peters, Jeremy W. 2013. "In Landmark Vote, Senate Limits Use of the Filibuster." *New York Times*, November 21. http://www.nytimes.com/2013/11/22/us /politics/reid-sets-in-motion-steps-to-limit-use-of-filibuster.html.

Pethokoukis, James. 2014. "Why Is Janet Yellen So Concerned and Disturbed about Income Inequality?" *American Enterprise Institute*, February 11. https:// www.aei.org/publication/why-is-janet-yellen-so-concerned-and-disturbed -about-income-inequality/.

Plotz, David. 2003. "Steve and Me." *Slate*, September 30. http://www.slate.com /articles/news_and_politics/life_and_art/2003/09/steve_and_me.html.

Posen, Adam. 1993. "Why Central Bank Independence Does Not Cause Low Inflation: There Is No Institutional Fix for Politics." In *Finance and the International Economy*, edited by Richard O'Brien, 41–54. Oxford: Oxford University Press.

———. 1998. "Central Bank Independence and Disinflationary Credibility: A Missing Link?" *Oxford Economic Papers* 50, no. 3 (July 1): 335–59.

Posner, Eric A. 2014. *How Do Bank Regulators Determine Capital Adequacy Requirements?* SSRN Scholarly Paper. Rochester, N.Y.: Social Science Research Network, September 9. http://papers.ssrn.com/abstract=2493968.

Posner, Richard A. 2010. *How Judges Think*. Cambridge, Mass.: Harvard University Press.

Pozo, Jorge J. 2002. "Bank Holiday: The Constitutionality of President Mahuad's Freezing of Accounts and the Closing of Ecuador's Banks." *New York International Law Review* 15: 61–97.

Protess, Ben, and Jessica Silver-Greenberg. 2014. "Bank of Tokyo Fined for 'Misleading' New York Regulator on Iran." *DealBook*. Accessed April 21, 2015. http://dealbook.nytimes.com/2014/11/18/lawsky-fines-bank-of-tokyo-mitsu bishi-ufj-another-315-million/.

Rahman, K. Sabeel. 2012. "Democracy and Productivity: The Glass-Steagall Act and the Shifting Discourse of Financial Regulation." *Journal of Policy History* 24, no. 4: 612–43.

Rakove, Jack N. 1996. *Original Meanings: Politics and Ideas in the Making of the Constitution*. New York: Knopf.

Ramirez, Steven A. 2000. "Depoliticizing Financial Regulation." *William and Mary Law Review* 41: 503–93.

Ramo, Joshua C. 1999. "The Three Marketeers." *Time*, February 15. http://content .time.com/time/world/article/0,8599,2054093,00.html.

Rao, Neomi. 2011. "Public Choice and International Law Compliance: The Executive Is a They, Not an It." *Minnesota Law Review* 96: 194–277.

———. 2014. "Removal: Necessary and Sufficient for Presidential Control." *Alabama Law Review* 65: 12–76.

Redish, Martin H., and Sopan Joshi. 2014. "Litigating Article III Standing: A Proposed Solution to the Serious (but Unrecognized) Separation-of-Powers Problem." *University of Pennsylvania Law Review* 162, no. 6: 1373–417.

Rein, Lisa, and Joe Davidson. 2012. "GSA Chief Resigns amid Reports of Excessive Spending." *Washington Post*, April 2. http://www.washingtonpost.com

/politics/gsa-chief-resigns-amid-reports-of-excessive-spending/2012/04/02
/gIQABLNNrS_story.html.

Reis, Ricardo. 2013. "The Mystique Surrounding the Central Bank's Balance Sheet, Applied to the European Crisis." Working Paper 18730. National Bureau of Economic Research, January.

Richardson, Gary, and William Troost. 2006. *Monetary Intervention Mitigated Banking Panics during the Great Depression: Quasi-experimental Evidence from the Federal Reserve District Border in Mississippi, 1929 to 1933.* Working Paper. National Bureau of Economic Research, October. http://www.nber.org/papers/w12591.

Rodgers, Daniel T. 2011. *Age of Fracture.* Cambridge, Mass.: Harvard University Press.

Rodrigues, Usha. 2008. "The Fetishization of Independence." *Journal of Corporation Law* 33: 447–95.

Rogoff, Kenneth. 1985. "The Optimal Degree of Commitment to an Intermediate Monetary Target." *Quarterly Journal of Economics* 100, no. 4: 1169–89.

Romano, Roberta. 2010. *Against Financial Regulation Harmonization: A Comment.* SSRN Scholarly Paper. Rochester, N.Y.: Social Science Research Network, November 20. http://papers.ssrn.com/abstract=1697348.

Romans, J. T. 1966. "Moral Suasion as an Instrument of Economic Policy." *American Economic Review* 56, no. 5 (December 1): 1220–26.

Romer, Christina D., and David H. Romer. 2003. "Choosing the Federal Reserve Chair: Lessons from History." *Journal of Economic Perspectives* 18, no. 1: 129–62.

Rotemberg, Julio J. 2014. "The Federal Reserve's Abandonment of Its 1923 Principles." Working Paper. National Bureau of Economic Research, September. http://www.nber.org/papers/w20507.

Rubin, Edward. 2012. "Hyperdepoliticization." *Wake Forest Law Review* 47: 631.

Rubin, Robert. 2003. *In an Uncertain World: Tough Choices from Wall Street to Washington.* New York: Random House Trade Paperbacks.

Rubin, Seymour J., ed. 1984. *Managing Trade Relations in the 1980s: Issues Involved in the GATT Ministerial Meeting 1982.* Totowa, N.J.: Rowman and Littlefield.

Samuelson, Robert J. 2008. *The Great Inflation and Its Aftermath: The Past and Future of American Affluence.* New York: Random House Trade Paperbacks.

Sanders, Elizabeth. 1999. *Roots of Reform: Farmers, Workers, and the American State, 1877–1917.* Chicago: University of Chicago Press.

Satterlee, Herbert Livingston. 1939. *J. Pierpont Morgan: An Intimate Portrait.* New York: Macmillan.

Schlesinger, Arthur Meier. 1960. *The Politics of Upheaval.* Boston: Houghton Mifflin.

Schonhardt-Bailey, Cheryl. 2013. *Deliberating American Monetary Policy: A Textual Analysis.* Cambridge, Mass.: MIT Press.

Schwarcz, Daniel, and Steven L. Schwarcz. 2014. "Regulating Systemic Risk in Insurance." *University of Chicago Law Review* 81: 1569–640.

Schweitzer, Mary M. 1989. "State-Issued Currency and the Ratification of the U.S. Constitution." *Journal of Economic History* 49, no. 2 (June 1): 311–22.

Scism, Leslie. 2014. "Trial in $40 Billion Lawsuit against AIG Bailout Begins." *Wall Street Journal*, September 29, sec. Markets. http://www.wsj.com/articles/trial-in-40-billion-lawsuit-against-aig-bailout-begins-1412015133.

Scott, Kenneth E. 1977. "The Dual Banking System: A Model of Competition in Regulation." *Stanford Law Review* 30: 1–50.

Seong Ho, Jun. 2014. "Monetary Authority Independence and Stability in Medieval Korea: The Koryŏ Monetary System through Four Centuries of East Asian Transformations, 918–1392." *Financial History Review* 21, no. 3 (December): 259–80. doi:10.1017/S0968565014000213.

Shafer, Jack. 1998. "Glass Houses." *Slate*, May 15. http://www.slate.com/articles/news_and_politics/flame_posies/1998/05/glass_houses.html.

Shane, Peter M. 2014. "Chevron Deference, the Rule of Law, and Presidential Influence in the Administrative State." *Fordham Law Review* 83: 679.

Shepsle, Kenneth A. 1992. "Congress Is a 'They,' Not an 'It': Legislative Intent as Oxymoron." *International Review of Law and Economics* 12, no. 2 (June): 239–56. doi:10.1016/0144-8188(92)90043-Q.

Shill, Greg. 2015. "Does the Fed Have Legal Authority to Buy Equities." *Confessions of a Supply-Side Liberal*, March 19. http://blog.supplysideliberal.com/post/114021461013/greg-shill-does-the-fed-have-the-legal-authority.

Shlaes, Amity. 2008. *The Forgotten Man: A New History of the Great Depression*. New York: Harper Perennial.

Shugerman, Jed Handelsman. 2012. *The People's Courts: Pursuing Judicial Independence in America*. Cambridge, Mass.: Harvard University Press.

Shull, Bernard. 2005. *The Fourth Branch: The Federal Reserve's Unlikely Rise to Power and Influence*. Westport, Conn.: Praeger.

Silber, William L. 2012. *Volcker: The Triumph of Persistence*. New York: Bloomsbury.

Skeel, David A. 2010. *The New Financial Deal: Understanding the Dodd-Frank Act and Its (Unintended) Consequences*. Hoboken, N.J.: Wiley.

Skidelsky, Robert. 2003. *John Maynard Keynes: 1883–1946: Economist, Philosopher, Statesman*. New York: Penguin Books.

Skocpol, Theda, and Vanessa Williamson. 2012. *The Tea Party and the Remaking of Republican Conservatism*. Oxford: Oxford University Press.

Smith, Rogers M. 1999. *Civic Ideals: Conflicting Visions of Citizenship in U.S. History*. New Haven, Conn.: Yale University Press.

Smith, Vera C. 1936. *The Rationale of Central Banking and the Free Banking Alternative*. Rpt. 1990, Washington, D.C.: Liberty Fund.

Sorkin, Andrew Ross. 2009. *Too Big to Fail: The Inside Story of How Wall Street and Washington Fought to Save the Financial System—and Themselves*. New York: Viking.

Sorkin, Andrew Ross, and Alexandra Stevenson. 2015. "Ben Bernanke Will Work with Citadel, a Hedge Fund, as an Adviser." *New York Times*, April 16. http://www.nytimes.com/2015/04/16/business/ben-bernanke-will-work-with-citadel-a-hedge-fund-as-an-adviser.html.

Steil, Benn. 2013. *The Battle of Bretton Woods: John Maynard Keynes, Harry Dexter White, and the Making of a New World Order.* Princeton, N.J.: Princeton University Press.

Suskind, Ron. 2011. *Confidence Men: Wall Street, Washington, and the Education of a President.* New York: Harper.

Tabellini, Guido. 2005. "Finn Kydland and Edward Prescott's Contribution to the Theory of Macroeconomic Policy." *Scandinavian Journal of Economics* 107, no. 2 (June 1): 203–16.

Tarullo, Daniel. 1986a. "Foreword: The Structure of US-Japan Trade Relations." *Harvard International Law Journal* 27: 343–60.

———. 1986b. "Law and Politics in Twentieth Century Tariff History." *UCLA Law Review* 34: 285–370.

———. 1987. "Beyond Normalcy in the Regulation of International Trade." *Harvard Law Review* 100: 546–628.

———. 2008. *Banking on Basel: The Future of International Financial Regulation.* Washington, D.C.: Brookings Institution Press.

———. 2012. "Regulation of Foreign Banking Organizations." Speech, Yale School of Management Leaders Forum, New Haven, Conn., November 28.

———. 2013. "Letter from Governor Daniel K. Tarullo to Senator Elizabeth Warren," June. http://graphics.thomsonreuters.com/13/06/Tarullo%20Resp%20to%20Warren.pdf

———. 2014. "Corporate Governance and Prudential Regulation." Speech, Association of American Law Schools 2014 Midyear Meeting, Washington, D.C., June 9.

Taylor, John B. 1993. "Discretion versus Policy Rules in Practice." *Carnegie-Rochester Conference Series on Public Policy* 39: 195–14.

———. 2009. *Getting Off Track: How Government Actions and Interventions Caused, Prolonged, and Worsened the Financial Crisis.* Stanford, Calif.: Hoover Institution Press.

Temin, Peter. 1969. *The Jacksonian Economy.* New York: W. W. Norton.

Thornton, Henry. 1802. *An Enquiry into the Nature and Effects of the Paper Credit of Great Britain.* London: Hatchard.

Thornton, Daniel L., and David C. Wheelock. 2014. "Making Sense of Dissents: A History of FOMC Dissents." *Federal Reserve Bank of St. Louis Review* 96, no. 3 (September 15). http://research.stlouisfed.org/publications/review/article/10205.

Timberlake, Richard. 2012. "From Constitutional to Fiat Currency: The US Experience." *Cato Journal* 32 (Spring/Summer): 349–62.

Tobin, James. 1965. Letter to the editor, *New York Times*, December 15, 1965, 46.

Toniolo, Gianni, and Piet Clement. 2005. *Central Bank Cooperation at the Bank for International Settlements, 1930–1973.* Cambridge: Cambridge University Press.

Torres, Craig, and Cheyenne Hopkins. 2012a. "Daniel Tarullo, a Fed Regulator Who Actually Regulates." *BusinessWeek: Global Economics*, March 22. http://www.businessweek.com/articles/2012-03-22/daniel-tarullo-a-fed-regulator-who

-actually-regulates?chan=global_economics+politics_%26_policy+markets
_%26_finance+channel_news+-+global+economics.

———. 2012b. "Fed's Stress-Test Champion Reshapes Regulation of Biggest Banks." *Bloomberg*, March 15. http://www.bloomberg.com/news/2012-03-15 /tarullo-s-revolution-reprograms-fed-s-regulation-of-u-s-banks.html.

Tracy, Ryan. 2015. "Volcker Outlines Plan for Overhauling Financial Regulation." *Wall Street Journal*, March 20. http://blogs.wsj.com/moneybeat/2015/03 /20/volcker-outlines-plan-for-overhauling-financial-regulation/.

Tracy, Ryan, and Victoria McGrane. 2014. "Fed to Banks: Shape Up or Risk Breakup." *Wall Street Journal*, October 20, sec. Markets. http://online.wsj.com /articles/fed-to-banks-shape-up-or-risk-breakup-1413847436.

Treaster, Joseph B. 2005. *Paul Volcker: The Making of a Financial Legend*. Hoboken, N.J.: Wiley.

Truman, Edwin M. 2014. "The Federal Reserve Engages the World (1970–2000): An Insider's Narrative of the Transition to Managed Floating and Financial Turbulence." *Peterson Institute for International Economics Policy Brief* 14, no. 5 (August): 1–54.

Tucker, Paul. 2014. *The Lender of Last Resort and Modern Central Banking: Principles and Reconstruction*. SSRN Scholarly Paper. Rochester, N.Y.: Social Science Research Network, September 1. http://papers.ssrn.com/abstract =2504686.

U.S. Department of Treasury. 2008. *The Department of Treasury Blueprint for a Modernized Financial Regulatory Structure*, March. http://www.treasury.gov /press-center/press-releases/Documents/Blueprint.pdf.

Vanatta, Sean. 2012. "History Suggests Operation Twist Should Get More Airtime." *BloombergView*, December 12. http://www.bloombergview.com/articles /2012-12-12/history-suggests-operation-twist-should-get-more-airtime.

Vermeule, Adrian. 2005. "The Judiciary Is a They Not an It: Interpretive Theory of the Fallacy of Division." *Journal of Contemporary Legal Issues* 14: 549–84.

———. 2013. "Conventions of Agency Independence." *Columbia Law Review* 113: 1163–238.

Volcker, Paul A. 2008. Remarks at a Luncheon of the Economic Club of New York, New York, April 8, http://blogs.denverpost.com/lewis/files/2008/04 /volckernyeconclubspeech04-08-2008.pdf.

Walker, Christopher J. 2014. "Chevron Inside the Regulatory State: An Empirical Assessment." *Fordham Law Review* 83: 703–29.

Wallach, Philip A. 2014. "Competing Institutional Perspectives in the Life of Glass-Steagall." *Studies in American Political Development* 28, no. 1 (April): 26–48. doi:10.1017/S0898588X13000175.

———. 2015. *To the Edge: Legality, Legitimacy, and the Responses to the 2008 Financial Crisis*. Washington, D.C.: Brookings Institution Press.

Wallison, Peter J. 2015. *Hidden in Plain Sight: What Really Caused the World's Worst Financial Crisis and Why It Could Happen Again*. New York: Encounter Books.

Warburg, Paul Moritz. 1930. *The Federal Reserve System: Its Origin and Growth*. New York: Macmillan.

Warren, Elizabeth. 2007. "Unsafe at Any Rate." *Democracy Journal*, Summer. http://www.democracyjournal.org/5/6528.php.

———. 2014. "The Citigroup Clique." *politico Magazine*, April 29. http://www.politico.com/magazine/story/2014/04/the-citigroup-clique-106125.html.

Weaver, R. Kent. 1986. "The Politics of Blame Avoidance." *Journal of Public Policy* 6, no. 4 (October): 371–98. doi:10.1017/S0143814X00004219.

Weigel, David. 2015. "Rand Paul Rallies Iowans to Audit the Federal Reserve." *Bloomberg*, February 6. http://www.bloomberg.com/politics/articles/2015-02-07/rand-paul-rallies-iowans-to-audit-the-federal-reserve.

Weiner, Tim. 2007. *Legacy of Ashes: The History of the CIA*. New York: Doubleday.

Wessel, David. 2009. *In Fed We Trust: Ben Bernanke's War on the Great Panic*. New York: Crown Business.

———. 2013. *Red Ink: Inside the High-Stakes Politics of the Federal Budget*. New York: Crown Business.

———. 2015. "Q and A: Explaining 'Audit the Fed.' " *Wall Street Journal*. February 17. http://blogs.wsj.com/economics/2015/02/17/qa-explaining-audit-the-fed/.

West, Robert Craig. 1977. *Banking Reform and the Federal Reserve, 1863–1923*. Ithaca, N.Y.: Cornell University Press.

White, Eugene Nelson. 1983. *The Regulation and Reform of the American Banking System, 1900–1929*. Princeton, N.J.: Princeton University Press.

Wicker, Elmus. 1996. *The Banking Panics of the Great Depression*. Cambridge: Cambridge University Press.

———. 2000. *Banking Panics of the Gilded Age*. Cambridge: Cambridge University Press.

Wiebe, Robert H. 1962. *Businessmen and Reform: A Study of the Progressive Movement*. Cambridge, Mass.: Harvard University Press.

———. 1966. *The Search for Order, 1877–1920*. New York: Hill and Wang.

Wilentz, Sean. 2005. *The Rise of American Democracy: Jefferson to Lincoln*. New York: W. W. Norton.

Will, George F. 2013. "The Fed Has Become a Creature of Politics." *Washington Post*, September 27. http://www.washingtonpost.com/opinions/george-will-the-fed-has-become-a-creature-of-politics/2013/09/27/69741ff4-2793-11e3-b75d-5b7f66349852_story.html.

Willis, Henry Parker. 1923. *The Federal Reserve System*. New York: Ronald.

Wilmarth, Arthur. 2004. "The OCC's Preemption Rules Exceed the Agency's Authority and Present a Serious Threat to the Dual Banking System and Consumer Protection." *Annual Review of Banking and Financial Law* 23: 225–364.

Wilmarth, Arthur E. 2014. "Citigroup: A Case Study in Managerial and Regulatory Failures." *Indiana Law Review* 47: 69–137.

Wilson, Woodrow. 1885/2006. *Congressional Government: A Study in American Politics*. Mineola, N.Y.: Dover.

Woodford, Michael. 2007. "The Case for Forecast Targeting as a Monetary Policy Strategy." *Journal of Economic Perspectives* 21, no. 4: 3–24. doi:10.1257/jep.21.4.3.

Woodward, Bob. 2000. *Maestro: Greenspan's Fed and the American Boom.* New York: Simon and Schuster.

Woolley, John T. 1986. *Monetary Politics: The Federal Reserve and the Politics of Monetary Policy.* Cambridge: Cambridge University Press.

Yellen, Janet L. 2014. "Perspectives on Inequality and Opportunity from the Survey on Consumer Finances." Presented at the Conference on Economic Opportunity and Inequality, Federal Reserve Bank of Boston, October 17.

Young, Nancy Beck. 2000. *Wright Patman: Populism, Liberalism, and the American Dream.* Dallas: Southern Methodist University Press.

Zaring, David T. 2013. "Against Being against the Revolving Door." *Illinois Law Review*, no. 2: 507–50.

Zeleny, Jeff and Jackie Calmes. 2011. "Perry Links Federal Reserve Policies and Treason." New York Times, August 16, http://www.nytimes.com/2011/08/17/us/politics/17perry.html?_r=0.

Zelizer, Julian E. 2015. *The Fierce Urgency of Now: Lyndon Johnson, Congress, and the Battle for the Great Society.* New York: Penguin.

Zingales, Luigi. 2013. "Preventing Economists' Capture." In *Preventing Regulatory Capture: Special Interest Influence and How to Limit It*, edited by Daniel P. Carpenter and David A. Moss. 124–51. New York: Cambridge University Press.

Zweig, Jason. 2011. "Keynes: He Didn't Say Half of What He Said. Or Did He?" *Wall Street Journal*, February 11. http://blogs.wsj.com/marketbeat/2011/02/11/keynes-he-didnt-say-half-of-what-he-said-or-did-he/.

Zywicki, Todd J. 2013. "The Consumer Financial Protection Bureau: Savior or Menace?" *George Mason Law Review* 81: 856–928.

INDEX

The names of people may refer to the individual or the administration or both. Page numbers in bold type are figures or tables.

Freemasons, 268, 270
Frieden, Jeffry, 146
Friedman, Milton, 136, 192, 213; on inflation, 55; on Miller, 52; monetarism and,
233–35
funding in government: annual appropriations process and, 206; the Fed, autonomy of, 10, 208–10, 215–16; mandates
and, 206; self-funding and, 206–7

Galbraith, John Kenneth, 135–36
Geithner, Timothy, 76, 88, 89, 90, 95, 119;
Bernanke and, 156; CFPB and, 243; de-
rivative trades and, 224, 225; on the
Doomsday Book, 97; financial crisis of
2008 and, 156–57, 227; 13(3) and, 96;
Troubled Asset Relief Program (TARP)
and, 156
general counsel of the Fed, 86, 93, 97–98;
lack of reviewability and, 101–2; presi-
dential appointment and, 248, 253;
value judgments and, 253–54. See also
Alvarez, Scott G.
*General Theory of Employment, Interest,
and Money* (Keynes), 26–27, 140
Gensler, Gary, 77
Glass, Carter, 20–22, 39, 43, 281n9; on the
Fed and the president, 180; New Deal
and, 30
Glass, Stephen, 58–59
Glass-Steagall Act of 1933, 25, 30, 160; demise of, 98–100. See also financial crisis
of 2008; Glass, Carter
Goldberg, Arthur, 184
Goldman Sachs, 165–67
gold standard, 209–10
Gonzalez, Henry, 203; Gonzalez Hearings
and, 205, 217
Goodhart, Charles, 31, 270
governance, xi–xiii, 3–5, 7–11, 13–14, 18–
19, 28, 82, 119–20, 241, 298n18; governors, terms of, 186; Great Depression
and, 24, 154; ideologies and, 93–97; instrument independence and, 137–38;
law vs. governance and, 5–6, 82; lawyers and, 93–97 (*see also* Alvarez, Scott
G.); legal division of, 93–97; open market autonomy and, 306n24; organizational complexity of, x; power of, x;

"priced services" and, 305n21; private
bankers and, 229; removal and, 290n5;
staff and, 84–97; structure and, 9–10;
supervision of banks and, 164, 168–69;
tenure and, 185–87
government agencies, independent vs. executive, 111–12
"government-sponsored bank," 280n2
Gramlich, Ned, 228
Great Depression, 24–26; Federal Reserve
Bank of New York and, 309n4; gold
standard and, 210; international coordination and, 230; Section 13(3) and,
94. See also New Deal; Roosevelt,
Franklin D.
Great Inflation, 54
Greenspan, Alan, x, 42, 58–67, 195–97;
Clinton and, 190; "Collective" and, 63–
64; on derivative trading, 224; financial
crisis of 2008 and, 63, 66–68; "Greenspan Put" and, 61–63, 67, 170; on
hedge funds, 224; leadership of, 62–63;
maximal flexibility and, 61; popular
faith in, 58–60; Rand, Ayn and, 63–64,
289n47; Reagan and, 190; reappointment of, 190; regulation and, 64;
Ulysses/punch-bowl view and, 68
Greider, William, 53, 287n27

Hackley, Howard, 284n35
Hall, Peter, 235
Hammond, Bray, 146
Harris, Seymour, 135–36
Hayes, Alfred, 46
hedged arbitrage, 221–22
Helms, Richard, 184
Henry, O., 164–65
Hofstadter, Richard, 25
Hoover, Herbert, 24
Hubbard, R. Glenn, 240
Humphrey, William, 110–11
Humphrey's Executor v. United States,
110–11, 114
Hutchinson, Kay, 124

ideology, policy makers and, 93–97, 240;
capture and, 226; central bankers and,
10–11, 148, 300n24; definition of, 219;
policy-making space and, 219, 230;